FROM PROSPERITY TO DECLINE
EIGHTEENTH CENTURY BENGAL

For

Sweta

FROM PROSPERITY TO DECLINE
EIGHTEENTH CENTURY BENGAL

Sushil Chaudhury

MANOHAR
1995

ISBN 81-7304-105-9

First Published 1995

© Sushil Chaudhury

Published by
Ajay Kumar Jain
Manohar Publishers & Distributors
2/6, Ansari Road, Daryaganj
New Delhi - 110002

Lasertypeset by
A J Software Publishing Co. Pvt. Ltd.
305, Durga Chambers,
1333, D.B. Gupta Road,
Karol Bagh, New Delhi - 110005

Printed at
Rajkamal Electric Press
G.T. Karnal Road
Delhi

CONTENTS

Contents   vii

LIST OF TABLES

LIST OF FIGURES

ABBREVIATIONS

Records

BPC	Bengal Public Consultations
Beng. Letters Recd.	Bengal Letters Received
C & B Abstr.	Coast and Bay Abstracts
DB	Despatch Books
HB	Hughli to Batavia
Fact. Records	Factory Records
HR	Hoge Regering van Batavia
Home Misc.	Home Miscellaneous Series
Orme Mss.	Orme Manuscripts
Mss. Eur.	Manuscript European
OC	Original Correspondence
VOC	Verenigde Oostindische Compagnie
NAI	National Archieves of India
f.2vo	means folio 2 verso

Journals

BPP	*Bengal Past and Present*
CHJ	*Calcutta Historical Journal*
IESHR	*Indian Economic and Social History Review*
IHR	*Indian Historical Review*
JAS	*Journal of Asian Studies*
JESHO	*Journal of the Economic and Social History of the Orient*
MAS	*Modern Asian Studies*

ACKNOWLEDGMENTS

While collecting material and writing the book in the last decade and a half, I have received generous help, assistance and cooperation from many individuals and institutions to all of whom I am deeply grateful. The book would not have been completed without the encouragement and generosity of Maurice Aymard to whom my indebtedness is more than I can express through my gratitude. D.H.A. Kolff and his wife, Annemarie, extended me warm hospitality at their home during my several visits when I did not have much resources to work in the Algemeen Rijksarchief, The Hague. I am most grateful to them. A special word of thanks to K.N. Chaudhuri who has provided me with some of the detailed quantitative data which he had collected from the English Company's archives. The maps were prepared in the Cartographic Section, Centre of Advanced Study in History, AMU for which I am most thankful to Irfan Habib and his son, Faiz. I am also indebted to friends and colleagues who took the time to read through drafts of all or parts of the manuscript and who made valuable comments and suggestions. These include Maurice Aymard, Gautam Bhadra, Wayne te Brake, Basudeb Chattopadhyay, Benoy Bhusan Chaudhuri, D.H.A. Kolff, Michel Morineau and Immanuel Wallerstein. My thanks also go to the many colleagues with whom I have privately exchanged views on various themes of this book, and from whom I have profited much. In particular I would mention Muzaffar Alam, S. Arasaratnam, C.A. Bayly, Richard Barnett, Paul Butel, J.R. Bruijn, Satish Chandra, K.N. Chaudhuri, Ashin Das Gupta, Richard Eaton, F.S. Gaastra, Irfan Habib, Philippe Haudrerés, Eugene Irshick, Keram Kevonian, Denys Lombard, P.J. Marshall, Shireen Moosvi, Frank Perlin, Om Prakash, Tapan Raychaudhuri,

Dietmar Rothermund, H. van Santen, Sanjay Subrahmanyam, Agnes Vercamann and André Wink.

The research in the various archives and the writing of the book have been possible through awards and grants from several institutions. I am thankful to the Commonwealth Commission in the U.K. for awarding me a Commonwealth Staff Academic Fellowship for 1978-79 which enabled me to work in the British archives. Subsequent grants and assistance from the British Council, Indian Council of Historical Research, Indian Council of Social Science Research, University of Leiden and Maison des Sciences de l'Homme, Paris, helped me in pursuing my research in India and abroad. My special thanks to the Royal Netherlands Academy which invited me to spend a year (1990-91) as a Fellow-in-Residence at the Netherlands Institute of Advanced Study where I completed the first draft of the book. I am grateful to D.J. van de Kaa who extended every possible assistance during my stay at the NIAS. It was at the NIAS that Eves de Roo introduced me to Lotus 1-2-3 programme with which I have been able to process and analyze the enormous amount of quantitative data I have collected over the years. He also helped me in drawing the figures in Harvard graphics. I am extremely thankful to him. I also learnt about computer programmes from my son Shiladitya who helped me in various stages of my work.

Several of the themes of this book, at various stages of its evolution, were presented in lectures/seminars I have given at different universities and institutions. These include Asiatic Society of Bangladesh, Dhaka; University of British Columbia, Vancouver; University of California, Berkeley; Centre d'Etudes de l'Inde et de l'Asie du Sud, Paris; Columbia University; Heidelberg University; University of Leiden; Oxford University; School of Oriental and African Studies, London; University of Virginia, Charlottesville; University of Washington, Seattle. I wish to express my gratitude to all the learned colleagues who attended these lectures and generously offered comments and suggestions.

The main bulk of the manuscript was typed in the computer by Pilar van Breda-Bergueño and Anne Simpson at the NIAS with great patience and competence. I am thankful to both of them. My thanks are also due to my colleague Arun Bandopadhyay, my wife Mahasweta and my daughter Parama who helped me in correcting the page-proofs. I am grateful to Ramesh Jain of Manohar for the interest and care taken in the publication of the book. Indranath Majumdar has kindly provided me with the illustration for the cover. My wife has borne with my work on this book for many years with great patience and understanding. I gratefully dedicate it to her.

Dietmar Rothermund, H. van Santen, Sanjay Subrahmanyam, Agnes Vercamann and André Wink.

The research in the various archives and the writing of the book have been possible through awards and grants from several institutions. I am thankful to the Commonwealth Commission in the U.K. for awarding me a Commonwealth Staff Academic Fellowship for 1978-79 which enabled me to work in the British archives. Subsequent grants and assistance from the British Council, Indian Council of Historical Research, Indian Council of Social Science Research, University of Leiden and Maison des Sciences de l'Homme, Paris, helped me in pursuing my research in India and abroad. My special thanks to the Royal Netherlands Academy which invited me to spend a year (1990-91) as a Fellow-in-Residence at the Netherlands Institute of Advanced Study where I completed the first draft of the book. I am grateful to D.J. van de Kaa who extended every possible assistance during my stay at the NIAS. It was at the NIAS that Eves de Roo introduced me to Lotus 1-2-3 programme with which I have been able to process and analyze the enormous amount of quantitative data I have collected over the years. He also helped me in drawing the figures in Harvard graphics. I am extremely thankful to him. I also learnt about computer programmes from my son Shiladitya who helped me in various stages of my work.

Several of the themes of this book, at various stages of its evolution, were presented in lectures/seminars I have given at different universities and institutions. These include Asiatic Society of Bangladesh, Dhaka; University of British Columbia, Vancouver; University of California, Berkeley; Centre d'Etudes de l'Inde et de l'Asie du Sud, Paris; Columbia University; Heidelberg University; University of Leiden; Oxford University; School of Oriental and African Studies, London; University of Virginia, Charlottesville; University of Washington, Seattle. I wish to express my gratitude to all the learned colleagues who attended these lectures and generously offered comments and suggestions.

The main bulk of the manuscript was typed in the computer by Pilar van Breda-Bergueño and Anne Simpson at the NIAS with great patience and competence. I am thankful to both of them. My thanks are also due to my colleague Arun Bandopadhyay, my wife Mahasweta and my daughter Parama who helped me in correcting the page-proofs. I am grateful to Ramesh Jain of Manohar for the interest and care taken in the publication of the book. Indranath Majumdar has kindly provided me with the illustration for the cover. My wife has borne with my work on this book for many years with great patience and understanding. I gratefully dedicate it to her.

1

INTRODUCTION

Bengal was the first Indian province to succumb to foreign
domination, and as such a study of its pre-colonial history,
especially its trade, industries and economy becomes pertinent.
This will give us an indication of what the state of things was
before the British conquest of Bengal following the battle of
Plassey in 1757 and, how and to what extent they changed during
the colonial period. Though the impact of colonial rule on the
traditional economy of Bengal has been discussed at length in
numerous studies[1], the precise situation before the colonial
period has not been studied in much detail so far. The present
study attempts an in-depth analysis of this aspect of Bengal's
history. It will be argued in this volume that Bengal's prosperity[2]
before the British conquest can not be in doubt at all, and that
the decline in the traditional trade and industry can be discerned
only in the second half of the eighteenth century. In order to
emphasize the first aspect which is little known, we have
concentrated mainly on an analysis of the period up to 1757,
pointing out at the same time clear indications of the decline that
set in in the later period. Thus eighteenth century Bengal

---

[1]For some of the recent studies, see N.K.Sinha, *Economic History of
Bengal*, 3 vols.; D.B.Mitra, *Cotton Weavers of Bengal;* Hameeda Hossain,
Company Weavers of Bengal; T. Raychaudhuri, 'The mid-Eighteenth
Century Background' and S. Bhttacharya 'Regional Economy (1757-
1857): Eastern India' in *Cambridge Economic History of India,* vol. II.

[2]The word 'prosperity' is used here in the sense indicating a
thriving state of affairs, especially in trade and industry, in contradis-
tinction to the decline which was clearly manifest in the second half of
the eighteenth century and culminated in the early nineteenth.

provides a classic model of how a country slipped down from a certain level of prosperity under indigenous rule to that of unmistakable decline under an alien domination. Geographically the Mughal *suba* of Bengal comprised the present-day states of West Bengal, Bihar and Orissa, together with modern Bangladesh.

For about two centuries, Bengal was one of the most prosperous *subas* of the Mughal empire. From around the mid-seventeenth century, if not earlier, it had also become one of the most important centres of international trade. Its fertile land along with rich and varied agricultural output, the high level of skill of its innumerable weavers and artisans, and its excellent and highly developed financial and communication network made it the most valuable prop of the erstwhile Mughal empire. Almost throughout the first half of the eighteenth century, it sent large revenue remittances either in cash or by bills of exchange to the imperial court in Delhi. Its ability to generate huge surpluses which could be easily converted into cash made it a lucrative prize in the eyes of the Europeans. So it is little wonder that Bengal would become a target of the European territorial ambitions. By the end of the seventeenth century, it became the most important partner in the Asiatic trade of the major European East India Companies. It had such a favourable balance of trade for which the exporters had to bring in bullion or cash that it had acquired the bad reputation of being the sink where everything disappeared without the least prospect of return.[3] In this connnection it is important to note that it was not only the Europeans who had to import silver but the Asians too had to bring in cash or bullion to pay for their purchases. There is little doubt that Bengal was highly self-sufficient and as such, the market for any import commodity, other than silver, was severely restricted. The only commodity imported was salt and to some extent, cotton and a few non-precious metals and luxury items,—the total value of which was quite negligible compared to that of its exports.

By the mid-eighteenth century, the Europeans trading in Bengal became fully aware of the rich potential of the province and began to harbour dreams of conquering it. There is ample evidence to show that many of the Europeans in the early 1750s

[3]Alexander Dow, *Hindostan*, vol. III, p. lxii.

were freely writing about or discussing the possibility of conquering Bengal.[4] So it was neither by chance nor by accident that the British conquered Bengal in 1757. And Plassey indeed laid the foundation of the British empire in India. Bengal was the springboard from which the British expanded their territorial acquisition and subsequently built up the empire which gradually engulfed most parts of India and ultimately many other parts of Asia as well. In the process, the once-prosperous province in the first half of the eighteenth century was gradually reduced to abject poverty. Under colonial rule, it was transformed from the world's major centre of artisanal production to a mere producer of agricultural raw materials. For a proper understanding of the magnitude of the change and the relative position of the province before and after the British conquest, it is imperative to take up a detailed study of Bengal's trade, industries, markets and merchants in the pre-Plassey period. That is the aim of this volume. There can be little doubt that the traditional industries, especially the textiles and silk industries, were virtually ruined by the early nineteenth century under the aegis of colonial rule. But these were the industries which once fed the increasing demand of the world market in the first half of the eighteenth century. As such, we have tried to analyze the traditional structure and organization of these industries in detail (chapters 6, 8 and 9) which will help us explain how Bengal could meet the huge demand of the Europeans and Asians even without any significant change in the techniques of production.

The present study takes up for analysis several broad issues connected with the history of the period and the region. In most works on India in general and Bengal in particular, the role of the European trade has been over-emphasized.[5] In the process, the export trade from Bengal by the Asian merchants was almost ignored. There is no denying the fact that the increasing European trade with the consequent influx of bullion during the period under review was quite significant. But it has been shown

[4]Brijen K. Gupta, *Sirajuddaullah*, pp. 35-37.
[5]S. Bhattacharya, *East India Company* (1954); S. Chaudhuri, *Trade and Commercial Organizataion* (1975); K.N. Chaudhuri, *Trading World* (1978); Om Prakash, *Dutch Company* (1985); S. Arasaratnam, *Merchants, Companies and Commerce* (1986).

here that even in the mid-eighteenth century, the export by Asian merchants from Bengal, especially of the two most valuable commodities namely, textiles and silk, was much higher than that of the Europeans. This only indicates that the overland trade from Bengal to other parts of India and possibly even to West and Central Asia was not absolutely ruined even following the decline of the three great empires—Mughal, Safavid and Ottoman. It is significant that even in the 1770s when the trade of the Asian merchants from Bengal was almost totally suppressed by the British, some amount of silk was still being exported by the former to Lahore and Multan which were the traditional nodal points in the caravan trade to the Middle East. Extensive searches in the European and Asian archives would possibly yield more detailed information about the overland and caravan trade in Asia in the first half of the eighteenth century.

The noted Dutch historian J.C.van Leur characterized Asian trade as the sum total of the peddling trade and trade mainly in luxury goods.[6] The thesis of the peddling trade has been reinforced in recent years by another reputed scholar while yet another authority has diluted the thesis to such an extent that he thinks that even the great Surat merchant, Mulla Abdul Gaffur, was a mere peddler.[7] The latter, however, shows conclusively that the Asian trade consisted mainly of non-luxury goods.[8] In Bengal's case it can be demonstrated that most of the textile exports to Asia comprised cheap and ordinary calicoes, not highly expensive muslins or fine calicoes.[9] As far as the peddling trade is concerned, it has been shown here (chapter 5) that the merchant princes of Bengal namely, the famous banking house of Jagat Seths, the Calcutta merchant Umichand and the Armenian Khwaja Wazid can hardly be considered as peddlers. In the scale of their operations and their business empires, they can well be regarded as equivalents of the Medicis, Fuggers or

[6]J.C. van Leur, *Indonesian Trade and Society*, pp. 132-33, 197-201, 219-20.

[7]Niels Steensgaard, *Asian Trade Revolution*, pp. 22-59; Ashin Das Gupta, *Indian Merchants*, pp. 11-13.

[8]Ashin Das Gupta, 'The Maritime Merchant, 1500-1800', *Proceedings of the Indian History Congress*, Presidential Address, 35th Session, pp. 99-111.

[9]See chapter 7.

Tripps.

The activities of the Bengal merchants, however, confirm the other thesis of van Leur that the Asian merchants were closely connected with the ruling elite.[10] The rise to power and eminence of the merchant princes in Bengal throughout the first half of the eighteenth century was mainly due to the favour of the Bengal nawabs. It has been shown in this study (chapter 5) how the main prop of these merchant princes, the *darbar* backing, was so very crucial for their survival that when it was withdrawn in the post-Plassey period, all of them crashed headlong, sooner or later. This finding is entirely different from that of two other recent studies on Gujarat and Surat which depicted the merchants as completely divorced from the administration. The merchants were shown by them as fending for themselves without any support from the ruling elite.[11] In Bengal, however, the close connection between the merchants and the state is amply demonstrated in this volume.

Another important issue which the present study addresses is the conquest of Bengal. So far, most of the historians have tried to explain the conquest, more or less, in the same vein. Even the latest studies emphasize that Bengal's internal crisis, both political and economic, 'inevitably brought in the British'. It has also been pointed out that there was no 'calculated plotting' on the part of the British and that they had no role at all in the origin and/or the development of the Plassey conspiracy which brought about the downfall of the last independent nawab of Bengal. The suggestion that they offer is that the European trade with the consequent influx of bullion in its train resulted in an interlocking of interests of the Bengal ruling elite (represented by military aristocrats, merchant-bankers and landholders) and the Europeans. So the 'expulsion' of the British from Calcutta in 1756 could not be borne by the indigenous ruling elite, and hence the Plassey revolution of 1757 which heralded the British domination of Bengal.[12] The political crisis theory is sought to be proved by

[10] J.C. van Leur, *Indonesian Trade and Society*, p. 204.

[11] M.N. Pearson, *Merchants and Rulers*; Ashin Das Gupta, *Indian Merchants*.

[12] P.J. Marshall, *Bengal*, 56, 63, 65, 67, 77, 91; C.A. Bayly, *Indian Society*, 49-50; Rajat Kanta Ray, 'Colonial Penetration and Initial Resistance', *IHR*, vol. XII, nos. 1-2, 1986, pp. 4, 6, 7, 14.

demonstrating the alienation of the dominant ruling class by the nawab which brought to an end the unity of the 'new class alliance' that underpinned the nawabi regime in the first half of the eighteenth century. Added to this, it has been stated, was the deteriorating economic condition in Bengal in the period prior to the British conquest.[13] And so far, most historians have shown that there was a 'marked and sustained' increase in the prices of commodities in Bengal, especially in the 1740s and 1750s.[14]

But we have tried to establish here that the British conquest was hardly unintentional or accidental. The main argument that has been developed (chapter 11) is that the private trade interest of the Company servants was the motivating force behind the conquest. The British private trade was facing a crisis in the late 1740s and the early 1750s because of the substantial increase in French private trade. So the destruction of the French (which would also prevent the possibility of a Franco-Bengali alliance against the British) on the one hand and the deposition of the nawab (who was raising the uncomfortable questions regarding illegal private trade and misuse of *dastaks*) on the other became the objective of the Company servants' sub-imperialism. The thesis of the intertwining of the interests of the Bengali elite and the Europeans has been discounted on the ground that the main source of the accumulation of wealth of the merchant princes who were the Indian ring leaders of the revolution was not their connection with the European trade. While discussing the political structure (chapter 2), it has been shown that the new class alliance was based on vested interests of the persons involved and had no institutional basis; as such, it was bound to be short-lived. Further it has been demonstrated in chapter 10 that there was hardly any increase in the prices of commodities which can be described as 'marked and sustained'.

The activities of the European companies in Bengal, as analyzed in chapter 3, will show that there was no remarkable decline in the European exports from Bengal even in the 1750s. It is true that the export of the English Company in the early

---

[13]P.J. Marshall, *Bengal*, p. 91.
[14]Brijen K. Gupta, *Sirajuddaullah*, p. 33; K.N. Chaudhuri, *Trading World*, pp. 99-108, 159, 311-12; P.J. Marshall, *East Indian Fortunes*, p. 35; *Bengal*, pp. 71, 73, 91, 142-43, 163-64, 170.

fifties declined to some extent from the levels of the 1730s and the 1740s. But that does not necessarily mean that it was because of the economic crisis in Bengal following the Maratha invasions. It has been shown that the impact of the Maratha incursions has been over-emphasized so far. The Maratha raids, no doubt, had disrupted the economy to some extent but this was mainly localized and only a temporary phenomenon. This is confirmed by the fact that neither the total volume nor the total value of either the European or the Asian export from Bengal declined to any remarkable extent in the late 1740s or the early 1750s. No doubt that the English trade declined in the early 1750s but this was balanced, so far as the total export trade from Bengal was concerned, by the increase in the Dutch export.

As textiles formed the major component of exports of the European companies from Bengal, a detailed analysis of the volume and value of the English and Dutch export of textiles has been made in chapter 7 A close scrutiny of the change in the composition of the different categories of textiles in the English and Dutch exports yields interesting results. This helps refute the argument that the price of textiles increased sharply in the 1740s and the 1750s.[15] Similarly, an analysis of the export of silk by the English and the Dutch has been made in chapter 8; and it has been demonstrated that the silk export by the Asian merchants even in the mid-eighteenth century was much larger than that of the Europeans. It is quite significant that the value of the Asian silk export (at its peak) alone was almost equal to that of the total exports (including textiles and raw silk) of the two major European companies—the English and the Dutch—in the early 50s of the eighteenth century.

It has been argued by some historians that by the 1720s or the 1740s, a major part of the province's economy had passed into the European/British hands.[16] This is far from correct. We shall see in the course of our analysis that though the Europeans were quite important in the Bengal economy in the pre-Plassey period, the Asians were far more significant in the commercial

[15]Brijen K. Gupta, *Sirajuddaullah*, p. 33; K.N. Chaudhuri, *Trading World*, pp. 99-108; P.J. Marshall, *East Indian Fortunes*, p. 35; *Bengal*, pp. 73, 142-43, 163-64, 170.

[16]S. Bhattacharyya, *East India Company*, p. 17. Marshall, *Bengal*, p. 80.

economy of Bengal throughout the first half of the eighteenth century. The European companies faced many a problem in procuring their investments in Bengal which has been discussed in chapter 4. It has been shown that the Europeans, confronted with a chronic shortage of liquid capital, borrowed extensively in the local credit market. The difficulties they had to face in converting their bullion and specie into local currency are analyzed in detail as also how far, if at all, they could make any change in the traditional system of commercial organization.

In the work that follows, chapter 2 sets out the eighteenth-century political and economic background, and chapter 3 traces the activities of the European companies in Bengal. Chapters 4 and 5 analyze the Companies' commercial organization in the region vis-à-vis the merchant community of Bengal while chapters 6, 7, and 8 deal with the structure and organization of the textile and silk industries and trade. Chapter 9 examines the role of other minor commodities in the Asian and European trade, and chapter 10 analyzes the important question of the eighteenth-century price trends. Finally, chapter 11 reexamines the British conquest of Bengal, and chapter 12 summarizes the conclusions that could be arrived at on the basis of this analysis.

The main arguments put forward in the present volume are as follows. First, despite a general breakdown of law and order in most parts of the erstwhile Mughal Empire in the early eighteenth century, Bengal was an exception which prospered under the nawabi regime. As a matter of fact, Bengal in the first half of the eighteenth century witnessed a strong and stable government which fostered trade and industry. The British conquest followed not due to any political or economic crisis in Bengal, but because of the sub-imperialism of the Company servants who, in their frantic efforts to revive their dwindling private trade fortunes in the face of severe competition from Asian and French private trade, had to take recourse to conquest.

Secondly, this work argues that there was no sign of any economic decline in the first half of the eighteenth century. Even in the mid-eighteenth century, there was hardly any economic 'crisis'. Trade and industry flourished. There was no 'sharp and marked' increase in the prices of commodities. Nor was there any perceptible decline in the volume and value of European exports from Bengal in the 1750s from the level of the 1730s and the early

1740s which was the peak period of European trade in Bengal. The Asian merchants also were exporting a substantial amount of Bengal textiles and silk in the mid-eighteenth century. And it was the Asians, not the Europeans, who were the major importers of bullion into Bengal even during the period prior to Plassey.

Thirdly, it has been argued here that it was only in the second half of the eighteenth century—following the British conquest—that Bengal gradually slipped into the grip of an economic decline. During this period, there was a sea-change in the condition of the artisans who were the 'hinge' of Bengal economy. The weavers, spinners, silk-winders, and others who could manufacture their goods freely and without oppression or restriction in general were reduced to the position of virtual slavery under Company rule in the second half of the eighteenth century. The Asian merchants who were so very active in the export trade were now systematically eliminated from Bengal's commercial world by the British. As a result, both trade and industry languished. In short, the prosperity which Bengal enjoyed under nawabi rule in the first half of the eighteenth century came to an end gradually after Plassey. With the Company and its servants at the helm of affairs, the economic decline set in, and Bengal's traditional trade and industries were ultimately ruined. All this resulted in untold misery—a fact that became more than evident in the early nineteenth century.

2

POLITICAL AND INSTITUTIONAL SETTING

The first half of the eighteenth century witnessed the general disintegration and virtual collapse of the Mughal empire. After the death of Aurangzeb in 1707, disruptive and centrifugal forces were let loose in most parts of the empire. Though the signs of decay and dissolution were apparent during the last years of Aurangzeb, they manifested themselves in no uncertain terms after his demise. Chaos and anarchy reigned supreme in many parts of India. But Bengal was a happy exception to the general picture of political decay and economic decadence. Throughout the first half of the eighteenth century, political and economic affairs in Bengal were conducted with vigour and efficiency. Thus even during the period of administrative and political disintegration in general, the provincial administrative system in Bengal appears to have grown stronger. It has been pointed out in a recent study that 'an elite ruling group which was representative of the political realities of the day coalesced and maintained rather high standards of administrative efficiency'.[1]

2.1 ADMINISTRATIVE AND POLITICAL STRUCTURE

The provincial administration in Bengal in the seventeenth century was organized on the standard Mughal model. The upper levels of the administration were filled by mansabdars who were appointed by the Mughal government at the centre. They

[1] P.B. Calkins, 'The Formation of a Regionally Oriented Ruling Group in Bengal, 1700-1740', *JAS*, vol.XXIX, no.4, 1970, p.799.

were transferred from one province to another at frequent intervals, with the idea that they could be prevented from developing vested interests in a particular area. The government at the centre retained strong control over the provincial administration by frequent transfers of the top officials and by maintaining a system of checks and balances within the province. The administration of the province was divided into two distinct parts—executive and revenue—which were independent of each other. The former was the responsibility of the *nawab-nazim*, also called subadar, and the latter was under the *diwan*. Both the officers were appointed by imperial order and were guided in the affairs of administration by rules and regulations laid down in *dastur-al-amal* or code of procedures issued by the emperor's orders.[2]

But this system of diarchy and, checks and balances broke down early in the eighteenth century because of two major developments in the history of the province. The first was the appointment of Murshid Quli Khan as *diwan* of Bengal in 1700. An efficient administrator, he was sent to Bengal by Aurangzeb for reorganizing the province's revenue administration and thus be able to send regular and satisfactory remittances to the emperor. Aurangzeb was in dire need of funds from Bengal for his disastrous Deccan campaign, as most of the other sources had already dried up. Murshid Quli performed his job well, and in the very first year, after proper assessment and collection, sent a revenue of 10 million rupees (which was further raised in subsequent years) to the central treasury. The old and exhausted emperor was so pleased with the regular remittances by Murshid Ouli that he left him free to do whatever he wanted in the province. In the process, Murshid Quli consolidated his position in Bengal and transferred the seat of the *diwani* from Dhaka to Maksudabad (which was renamed by him as Murshidabad) in 1704, even ignoring the subadar Prince Azim-us-Shan, the grandson of Aurangzeb.[3] The course of the *diwan's* ascendency to power and prestige was complete when the office of the subadar was conferred on him around 1717, thus both the offices being merged in the same person for the first time in Bengal. As

[2] *Riyaz*, p.248
[3] Ibid.,

such, in the early eighteenth century, the administrative structure
of Bengal changed radically from what it was in the seventeenth
century. This was a complete break from the Mughal tradition.

The second development, which ended the system of checks
and balances, was the cessation from around 1713[4] of the regular
practice of deputing officials from the centre to Bengal. These
officers sent by the central gevernment at Delhi, along with the
subadar and the *diwan*, stood as a hinge, as the representatives
of the imperial authority, between the central government and
the local elements. But with the stoppage of the flow of
bureaucrats from north India, the organic link which had so long
tied Bengal with the centre came to an end. From now onward,
neither Murshid Quli nor his successors had to receive administrative personnel sent by the imperial authority. This was a
natural consequence of the chaos and disorder that engulfed the
empire. In the process, the nizamat in Bengal became more
powerful. The Bengal nawabs were left free to recruit men of
their choice to run the administration from the insulated Mughal
officals, their own relatives and the local people. Thus, though
Bengal still remained nominally a *suba* of the Mughal empire,
everyone even in the upper level of administration owed his
allegiance only to the nazim (governor) and had no connection
with the imperial government at the centre. This led to the
strengthening of the hands of the nazim and in consequence, to
the establishment of a new nizamat based on local forces.

The administrative structure in Bengal was somewhat different from that of other provinces because most of the land in
Bengal was controlled at the local level by indigenous landholders
called zamindars. As collectors of revenue and keepers of peace,
these zamindars played a very important role. The provincial
government indirectly controlled the lesser landholders and
peasants by controlling the zamindars. There were several levels
of intermediary landholders between the zamindars and the
cultivators. In most cases, the revenue collected from the peasants
reached the zamindars through these intermediaries. In the
seventeenth century, it seems, most of the zamindars were
relatively small,[5] and as such it was not very difficult for the

[4] J.N. Sarkar (ed.), *History of Bengal*, vol.II, p.410.
[5] James Grant, 'Finances of Bengal' in W.K. Firminger (ed.), *Fifth Report*, vol. II, pp. 176-91.

Mughals to control them. But Murshid Quli's revenue reforms in the early eighteenth century led to the creation of big zamindaries which changed the power structure in the province as we shall see shortly.

The appointment of Murshid Quli as the *diwan* of Bengal heralded a new era in the history of Bengal. Not only did it witness the setting up of a new pattern of provincial administration, but it convulsed the entire Bengal polity as well. Murshid Quli, a man of proven ability, was sent to the province with specific instructions to try to increase the revenue. The decision was taken in view of the fact that Bengal was underassessed for a long time and the increased income was being appropriated by the mansabdars and zamindars.[6] But the process of increasing revenue collection led to significant changes in the landholding and political structure of Bengal resulting as they did in the 'formation of a new, regional group'. These changes can be described in the following manner : emergence of big zamindaries with a consequent decline in the total number of zamindaries, the increasing importance of larger zamindaries in the political system of the province and the enhancement in the power of the moneylender and banking class.[7]

With the weakening of the central authority in Delhi in the first half of the eighteenth century, the administrative system in Bengal was adapted successfully to account for the changing power relationships. As has been pointed out in a recent study, the shift in the focus of political power from the centre to the province was accompanied by a similar shift in the balance of power within the province.[8] The Mughal mansabdars who were the dominant ruling group earlier became less powerful in the changed circumstances because they could no longer get any support or assistance from the centre. Hence they compromised to share power with local elements. The various socio-economic groups which so far remained subdued now got an opportunity to assert themselves. One of these groups, especially the bigger and stronger zamindars who emerged as a result of Murshid Quli's revenue reorganization, became much more powerful in

[6] *Risala*, f.8b; also quoted in Calkins, 'Ruling Group', p.801.
[7] Ibid., p.800.
[8] Ibid.

the new set-up. As the demand for revenue increased, it also signalled the increase in the power of the zamindars. In fact, the history of the large zamindaries shows that Murshid Quli made it a policy to increase the power of the loyal and big zamindars. They also became partners in the new ruling group. Similarly, the merchant-bankers who began to play a significant role in the administrative and revenue reforms of Murshid Quli were drawn into the new ruling councils. Thus a new power-bloc was created in Bengal in the first half of the eighteenth century.

But it would not be correct to assume the new ruling alliance as a bureaucratic superstructure or a solid bloc. It was a group of different people with divergent interests who came close to rally round the nazim to enhance their own interests. In the particular setting of Bengal politics, their policy was directed towards strengthening the hands of the nawab on the one hand and furthering their personal interests on the other. The nazim (or nawab) on his part needed the help of the insulated Mughal mansabdars, the landed magnates and the merchant-bankers for running the administrative machinery and for generating economic resources. Murshid Quli found a group of people from various sections looking upon him at the head of the administration as their sole benefactor. He and his successors utilized the services of this group to fill up the vacuum created in the special circumstances of the early eighteenth century. A pyramid-type structure was evolved in Bengal in which the nawab was seated at the top, and the members of the ruling alliance deriving their power from him.

As a matter of fact, there was no conscious attempt on the part of the nizamat to share power with the various groups so as to forge a 'partnership'. The emergence of the big zamindars was the result of Murshid Quli's prime concern—revenue reforms. The merchant-banking class came into prominence because of the administrative reorganization and the fostering of trade and commerce. The Mughal mansabdars were rendered less powerful as a consequence of the decline of the central authority. The relationship between the nizamat and these segmented groups was more of a personal character. It had no institutional basis.[9] It was an arrangement in which new vistas of

[9] M. Mazibor Rahman, 'Nizamat in Bengal', unpublished M. Phil. thesis, JNU, 1988.

glory were open to efficient and successful adventurers by meeting the state demand. At the same time the state became assured of the help and support of those who received the benefit of it. The most striking example of the personalized character of the alliance was the house of Jagat Seths. Starting as a mere usurer, the house, by developing a personal relationship with the nizamat, became the 'direct beneficiary' and built up the richest banking house in Bengal.

Since the relationship in the new alliance was based on personal vested interests, the prime concern of the various groups was to protect and promote their own interests, even if that meant change in alignments. This is well illustrated throughout the first half of the eighteenth century. After Murshid Quli's death, in deference to his wishes his grandson Sarfaraj Khan became the nawab. But when Sarfaraj's father, Shujauddin, then deputy governor of Orissa, wanted the *masnad* for himself, the former gave in at the pleading of Murshid Quli's wife,[10] and there was no scope for any intervention by the new ruling groups. Even the great banker, Jagat Seth, was not very sure in the beginning, as reported by the English factors, of his position in the changed circumstances.[11] That the new alliance was purely based on personal relationships is demonstrated by the fact that the two adventurer brothers, Haji Ahmed and Alivardi Khan, who were to play a crucial role in Bengal politics later on, were appointed to high posts by Shujauddin as they were his personal friends.[12] None of them belonged to the important mansabdar or zamindar group when they were inducted into the administrative machinery.

Again, the new alliance was not a monolith. It showed definite cracks under stress. When Sarfaraj became nawab after Shujauddin's death, he wanted to give promotion and *mansabs* to his father's old officers. But the triumvirate of Haji Ahmed, Alam Chand (*diwan*) and Jagat Seth, whom he allowed to continue to act as councillors according to his father's last instructions, opposed the move. Thus a rift was created in the court. It was the personal intrigues of the triumvirate which brought about the revolution of 1740 in favour of Alivardi Khan. The personal ambition and conspiracy of a few persons only resulted in the

---

[10] *Riyaz*, p. 288.
[11] BPC, vol. 6, f.490, 14 Aug. 1727.
[12] *Riyaz*, pp. 294-95.

deposition of nawab Sarfaraj Khan; it was not so much due to the latter's inefficiency and corruption, nor was it the result of the new ruling group's concerted effort. The author of *Riyaz* writes: 'This Revolution in the Government threw the City (Murshidabad—the capital) as well as the Army and the people of Bengal, into a general and deep convulsion.'[13] Even in the battle of Giria where Sarfaraj died fighting, quite a sizeable group of important mansabdars and zamindars like Ghaus Khan, Mir Sharafuddin, Mir Muhammed Bakir Khan, Bijay Singh, Raja Ghandarab Singh etc. fought on the side of Sarfaraj while another group joined Alivardi's army, thus clearly indicating the division in the mansabdar-zamindar alliance on personal and other considerations.[14] That personal ambition was the driving force with little regard for the cohesion in the alliance is clearly reflected in Mir Jafar's [Alivardi's commander-in-chief] conspiracy to assassinate nawab Alivardi Khan in 1747.[15]

2.2 BENGAL UNDER THE NAWABS, 1700-1757

Murshid Quli came to Bengal in 1700 and from then on till his death in 1727 (with the exception of two years when he was away from Bengal during 1708-09), he remained the most important administrator in Bengal. He was the *diwan* of the province and around 1717 he became the subadar as well. From the very beginning his aim was to increase the collection of revenue. With this end in view, he tightened the control over revenue administration so that some of the surplus which was appropriated by the zamindars and other small landholders could now be taken by the government. He proceeded toward his goal of increasing revenue collection by three principal measures. First, he transferred the *jagir* lands of the mansabdars from the fertile province of Bengal to the less productive region of Orissa, thus making it possible for the crown to resume the old *jagir* lands. The second measure of Murshid Quli was to insist that zamindars pay their rent in full. If they failed due to whatever reason, they were punished with imprisonment and sometimes even physically tortured. Thirdly, he sent sagacious and efficient officers to each

---

[13] Ibid., p.320.
[14] Ibid., pp. 311, 314-15, 319-20.
[15] K.K. Datta, *Alivardi*, p. 81.

and every revenue-paying unit to make an accurate assessment of revenue. With their help, he prepared a perfect revenue roll and collected information about the productivity of the soil and the capacity of the cultivators to pay.[16] Though the survey does not seem to be as thorough as Salimullah, the near-contemporary Persian chronicler, would have us believe, there is little doubt that Murshid Quli was able to collect and prepare a more accurate revenue roll, partly by actual survey and partly with the help of old records.

As a result of Murshid Quli's enhancement of revenue collection, the zamindars were now required to pay the enhanced rate of revenue or lose their zamindary to the government or a moneylender. If the government seized the zamindary of a defaulting zamindar, it was generally given to another zamindar who was regarded as capable of meeting the government's demand.[17] As a consequence of this policy, the weaker and less efficient zamindars were mostly weeded out. Murshid Quli's policy of encouraging large zamindaries and the support given by him for their consolidation resulted in the emergence of quite a few big zamindaries. The most obvious example of such a zamindary was that of Rajshahi. Other zamindaries too, like those of Burdwan, Nadia, Dinajpur, etc. consolidated their position during Murshid Ouli's reign.[18] When Murshid Quli died in 1727, fifteen large zamindaries accounted for about half of the revenue of the province.[19]

A by-product of Murshid Ouli's revenue policy was the emergence of a moneylending and banking class which played an increasingly important role in Bengal. A group of *mahajans* or small moneylenders began to lend money to the zamindars (who were required to pay revenue in time) with the expectation that the latter would fail to repay the money so that the former could

[16] *Riyaz*, 248-49, 255-56; Salimullah, *Tarikh-i-Bangala,* pp. 32-33, 43-45.

[17] *Risala*, ff. 7a-9b; also quoted in Calkins, p.803.

[18] For an account of the growth of these zamindaries, see, N.K. Sinha, *Economic History of Bengal*, vol. II, pp. 119-22.

[19] The details of these zamindaries and their revenue assessments are given in James Grant, 'Finances of Bengal', in W.K. Firminger (ed.), *Fifth Report*, vol. II, pp. 194-98.

get hold of the zamindary.[20] The most conspicuous example of
the power and influence which the banking class acquired was
the house of Jagat Seths. But it should be emphasized that the
house owed its emergence as the most powerful economic force
in Bengal only to the personal patronage of Murshid Quli. A
great source of profit of the house was the interest on the loan
that it advanced to the zamindars.[21] By 1730 the house became
the government treasurer. The Jagat Seths also stood security for
the defaulting zamindars.

Murshid Quli was shrewd enough to realize that in view of
the intermittent revolutions in Delhi and the consequent weakening of the central authority, he could have a free hand in
Bengal affairs so long as he sent the revenue regularly. He did
keep the imperial government in good humour by regular
remittances of revenue while consolidating his position by
gaining the loyalty of the officials, zamindars and merchant-
bankers. He also won the loyalty of the officials by appointing his
own relatives and favourites in high offices, and removing those
mansabdars who were potentially hostile to him.[22] The big
zamindars were loyal to him because he encouraged their growth
and actively helped the process. The banking and financial
interests, too, were patronized by the nazim whose revenue policy
was a source of profit to them.

Murshid Quli did not only reorganize the revenue administration but also introduced certain measures for the improvement of general administration. Salimullah gives some idea of the
measures he took to provide security against highway robbery.
The robbers and thieves were meted out harsh punishment. In
order to secure peace, Murshid Quli established *thanas* or police
stations in different parts of the country.[23] Salimullah also
records how the nawab tried to maintain the standard price of
grain, thus alleviating the distress of the poor. Murshid Quli
always provided against famine and severely prohibited monopolies of grain.[24] But the most important contribution of Murshid
Quli was that he provided Bengal with peace and stability at a time

[20] *Risala*, ff, 7a-7b; also quoted in Calkins, p.804.
[21] See chapter 5.
[22] Salimullah, *Tarikh-i-Bangala*, pp.42-43.
[23] Ibid., p.108.
[24] Ibid., p. 112.

when there was so much chaos and confusion in the imperial capital and in many parts of the Mughal empire. The author of another near-contemporary chronicle, *Riyaz*, wrote: 'The Khan, [Murshid Quli] having introduced order in the financial condition of the Mahals of Bengal, devoted his attention to the improvement of other administrative and internal affairs. His administration was so vigorous and successful that there was no foreign incursion nor internal disturbance, and consequently the military expenditure was nearly abolished.'[25] In short, Murshid Quli laid the foundation of a strong and stable government in Bengal in the early eighteenth century.

Shujauddin Khan succeeded Murshid Quli as the nazim of Bengal. Though perhaps an able administrator, he lacked the exceptional ability and the great prestige of his father-in-law. He sent the provincial revenue to the tune of 13 million rupees regularly to the imperial court, and thus was left to rule his province the way he liked.[26] Soon after his accesssion, he appointed an advisory council, the famous triumvirate, consisting of Haji Ahmed, *diwan* Alamchand and the banker, Jagat Seth. This, as a matter of fact, became virtually responsible for the administration of the province.[27] But it is not correct to assume that the government in the 1730s looked more like 'government by cooperation', indicating the rising power of the zamindar-mansabdars and bankers because of the creation of the council.[28] Both Haji Ahmed and Alivardi who had earlier no link with Bengal had been appointed to high posts by Shujauddin just after his accession, and none of them really belonged to the important mansabdar-zamindar group. As Shujauddin was pleasure-loving and had already become old, he wanted to be relieved of the drudgery of the day to day administration, and hence appointed the council to look after the business of government.[29] However, according to the Persian chroniclers, Shujauddin's reign (1727-

---

[25] *Riyaz*, p.257.

[26] Ibid., p.289. Murshid Quli remitted regularly an annual revenue of Rupees 10.3 million, *Riyaz*, p.259. But Salimullah (pp.63-64) states that the amount was Rs13 million.

[27] *Riyaz*, 291-92; Saluimullah, *Tarikh-i-Bangala*, p.133; *Sier*, vol.I, pp.279, 281; J.N. Sarkar (ed.), *History of Bengal*, vol.II, pp. 423,425.

[28] Calkins, 'Ruling Group', p. 805.

[29] *Riyaz*, p.292-93.

1739) was generally marked by peace and prosperity. The author of *Riyaz* stated: 'Constantly animated by a scrupulous regard for justice, and always inspired by fear of God, he uprooted from his realm the foundations of oppression and tyranny.'[30] Gholam Hossein Khan asserted that Bengal under Shujauddin 'came to enjoy so much prosperity, as to exhibit everywhere an air of plenty and happiness'.[31] John Shore, too, wrote in 1789 that Shujauddin's reign was 'moderate, firm and vigilant, and seems the only part of the whole period (from Murshid Quli to Mir Qasim), with an exception of the last years of Alivardi Khan, in which the conduct of the government was in any respect calculated for the improvement of the country'.[32]

Shujauddin was succeeded by his son Sarfaraj but soon Alivardi defeated him to become the new nawab. Alivardi's reign (1740-56) has been depicted in glorious terms by the Persian chroniclers. Gholam Hossein Khan went so far as to assert that it was marked by all round prosperity and that the nawab was so careful to promote the comfort and welfare of his subjects, especially of the cultivators, that they felt completely secure under him.[33] But the first several years of Alivardi's administration witnessed a period of storm and stress mainly because of the recurring Maratha invasions (1742-51) and Afghan insurrection—a period during which he had little time to devote to the welfare of his subjects. After he bought peace from the Marathas in May/June 1751 agreeing to pay them Rs 1.2 million a year, Alivardi did not fail to realize that measures of reconstruction were needed to heal the wounds of long-continued warfare. So he applied himself 'with judgment and alacrity to the repose and security of his subjects, and never afterwards deviated in the smallest degree from those principles'.[34] He soon devoted his attention toward rebuilding and restoring many towns and villages which had been desolated by the Marathas. A wise and benevolent ruler that he was, he then tried to secure the uplift

[30] Ibid., pp. 290-91.

[31] *Sier*, vol.I, p.280.

[32] Minute of Sir John Shore, W.K. Firminger (ed.), *Fifth Report*, vol.II, p.9.

[33] *Sier*, quoted in K.K. Datta, *Alivardi*, p.140.

[34] *Calendar of Persian Correspondence*, vol. II, pp.191, 197, quoted in K.K. Datta, *Alivardi*, p.140.

of the villages and the improvement of agriculture. That Alivardi was able to heal the impact of the Maratha invasions and introduce a period of peace and prosperity is evident from Karam Ali's description how the capital city, Murshidabad, extended and flourished during the last years of the nawab.[35] The next nawab, Sirajuddaullah, reigned for only sixteen months and his fall after the battle of Plassey in 1757 ended the independent nizamat of Bengal, ushering in the beginning of the British domination of the province.

A rather disquieting feature of the history of Bengal in the first half of the eighteenth century was the collection of *abwabs* or additional imposts besides the land revenue. The land revenue was collected under two heads: *tumar jumma* or the standard assessments and *abwabs* or special imposts. The standard assessment in 1728 remained the same as in Murshid Quli's time i.e. Rs 14,245,561.[36] But to this an additional impost of Rs 1,914,095 was realized by Shujauddin through the imposition of *abwabs* in imitation of an old practice followed particularly by Murshid Quli Khan.[37] The *abwabs* were levied in general on the zamindars in proportion to the assessment of each of them but they were authorized to collect it from the *ryots* or cultivators. Alivardi raised an additional amount of Rs 2,225,554 through *abwabs*. Though it is difficult to measure the impact of the imposition of *abwabs* on Bengal economy, the assertion that the levying of the imposts led to the decline in production and rise in prices, and finally to the impoverishment of the Bengal economy is hardly tenable.[38] John Shore observed that these impositions might not have been then felt to be burdensome, and 'it may be that, due to the growth of commerce and increased imports of specie, the resources of the country were at that period adequate to the measure of exactions'.[39] However, the redeeming feature during this period was that the collectors of revenue were authorized by

---

[35] *Muzaffarnama*, quoted in K.K. Datta, *Alivardi*, p.140.

[36] Minute of John Shore, in Firminger (ed.), *Fifth Report*, vol.II, p.7.

[37] Ibid., vol.II, pp.209-12. Murshid Quli's *abwab* did not amount to more than Rs. 2,58,857, Sinha, *Economic History of Bengal*, vol.II, p.5.

[38] Brijen K. Gupta, *Sirajuddaullah*, p.33. On the question of rise in prices, see, chapter 10 of this volume.

[39] Minute of John Shore, in Firminger (ed.), *Fifth Report*, vol.II, pp. 11-12.

Murshid Quli to give agricultural loans (*taqavi*) to poorer
cultivators for purchasing necessary materials and seed grains -
a practice which, it seems, was followed by both Shujauddin and
Alivardi Khan.[40]

2.3 ECONOMIC ENVIRONMENT

During the reign of Murshid Quli Khan and his successors, as we
have analyzed earlier, the Mughal *suba* of Bengal witnessed
peaceful transition to a stable political order and the foundation
of a strong nizamat. As a result, new outlets were found in
increasing economic activity, in production and maximization of
revenue, in the development of trade and commerce, and in the
expansion of markets. The rich prospects of trade in Bengal, and
the comparative peace and stability in the region in the first half
of the eighteenth century attracted to the province many traders
from different parts of India and Asia as also from Europe.
Grose who visited Bengal in 1756-57 wrote that the 'foreign and
domestic trade of Bengal are very considerable; as may appear
from the great number of Persians, Abyssinians, Arabs, Chinese,
Gujarats, Malabarians, Turks, Moors, Jews, Georgians, Armenians and merchants from all parts of Asia who resort there'.[41]
Such assertions are to be found in abundance in contemporary
sources.[42]

Indeed, the wealth of Bengal in the seventeenth and early
half of the eighteenth century was legendary, and the cheapness
of wares there was attested to by most foreign travellers and
chroniclers of the period. The author of *Riyaz* described Bengal
as *Jinnat-ul-bilad* or 'Paradise of Provinces' while Aurangzeb was
said to have styled Bengal 'the Paradise of Nations'.[43] No official
Mughal *farman*, *parwana* or other document ever mentioned
Bengal without adding 'Paradise of India'—an epithet, according
to Jean Law, the chief of the French factory at Kasimbazar in the
fifties of the eighteenth century, given to it *par excellence*.[44] The

---

[40] Abdul Karim, *Murshid Quli*, p.90; Salimullah, *Tarikh-i-Bangala*,
p.45; J.N. Sarkar (ed.), *History of Bengal*, vol.II, p.412.

[41] Grose, *East Indies*, vol.II, p.234.

[42] S.C. Hill, *Bengal in 1756-57*, vol.III, p.390; Orme, *Military
Transactions*, vol.II p.4.

[43] *Riyaz*, p.4.

French traveller Bernier wrote in the 1660s that 'the rich exuberance of the country... has given rise to a proverb... that the Kingdom of Bengal has a hundred gates open for entrance, but not one for departure'.[45] Undoubtedly, the natural products of Bengal were various and abundant. Like the rest of India, Bengal had a predominantly agricultural economy, but had attained a high degree of commercialization within the broad framework of the agrarian economy, and also had trade connections with various parts of Asia and Europe.

Regarding the manufactures of Bengal, Bernier wrote that 'there is in Bengale such a quality of cotton and silks, that the Kingdom may be called the common storehouse for these two kinds of merchandise, not of Hindoustan or of the Empire of the Great Mogul only, but of all the neighbouring Kingdoms, and even Europe'.[46] In craftsmanship, too, Bengal enjoyed an enviable position. As Pyrard de Laval observed: 'The inhabitants, both men and women, are wonderously adroit in all such manufactures such as of cotton, cloth and silks and in needlework such as embroideries which are worked so skillfully down to the smallest stitches that nothing prettier is to be seen anywhere.'[47] As a result, in the pre-colonial period, 'the balance of trade was against all nations in favour of Bengal; and it was the sink where gold and silver disappeared without the least prospect of return'.[48]

At least up to the early 1730s, Hughli was still the dominant port of Bengal, its commercial capital, though the rise of Calcutta gradually reduced the importance of Hughli from around the mid-1730s. From its emergence as the royal port in 1632, after the decline of Satgaon, Hughli witnessed a boom period throughout the seventeenth and the early eighteenth century.[49] Until the time of Murshid Quli, the *faujdars* of Hughli were appointed directly by the Mughal emperor, and had little connection with

[44] Hill, *Bengal in 1756-57*, vol.III, p.160.
[45] Bernier, *Travels*, p.440.
[46] Ibid., p.439.
[47] Pyrard de Laval, *Voyages*, vol.I, p.329.
[48] Dow, *Hindostan*, vol. I, p.ciii.
[49] For the decline of Satgaon and emergence of Hughli as the royal port, see S. Chaudhury, 'Rise and Decline of Hughli', *BPP*, Jan.-June 1967, pp. 33-67.

the subadar of Bengal. It was Murshid Quli who brought the
office of the *faujdar* of Hughli under his jurisdiction, as an
appendage to the nizamat and *diwani* of Bengal.[50] The author of
Riyaz asserted that Murshid Quli maintained 'peaceful and
liberal' relations with all the merchants from various parts of the
world at Hughli and 'did not even levy one dam[51] oppressively
or against the established usage'. As a result, he added, the port
of Hughli, 'became more populous' during Murshid Quli's
time.[52] Salimullah wrote: 'The encouragement which was given
to trade by Jaffer Khan [Murshid Quli], who directed that
nothing but the established rate of duties should be exacted, soon
made the port of Hooghly a place of great importance. Many
wealthy merchants, who resided there, had ships of their own
which they traded to Arabia, Persia and other countries.'[53]

As a matter of fact, Hughli became a Shia colony before the
full growth of Murshidabad in the first half of the eighteenth
century when, because of the Shia dynasty in Bengal, many
Persian immigrants came to the region. Even later, the cosmo-
politan port was preferred to the political capital at Murshidabad
by the Persian fortune hunters who had no employment or family
ties in Mushidabad.[54] But gradually Hughli lost its importance to
Calcutta. The main reason for the decline of Hughli appears to
be the shrinking of the intra-Asian trade of the Asian merchants
of Hughli in the face of the severe competition of the European
private trade conducted mainly from Calcutta. The eighteenth
century Persian chroniclers, however, attributed the decline of
Hughli to the increasing 'oppressions and extortions of the
faujdars' and the rise of Calcutta to the 'liberty and protection
afforded by the English, and the lightness of the duties levied
there'.[55] The assertion, mainly on the basis of shipping lists in the
Dutch records, that Calcutta became much more important than
Hughli after about 1715 is quite doubtful.[56] The value of the

---

[50] *Riyaz*, pp. 30, 262-63.
[51] *dam* was the lowest denomination of Mughal coin.
[52] *Riyaz*, p.30.
[53] Salimullah, *Tarikh-i-Bangala*, p.81.
[54] J.N. Sarkar (ed.), *History of Bengal*, vol.II, p.419.
[55] *Riyaz*, p.30; Salimullah, p.136.

trade which passed through Hughli in 1728 can be guessed from the fact that the 'Syer Bakshbandar' (export and import duties on foreign merchandise) in that year yielded Rs 221,975 at the rate of 2.5 per cent on the value of goods.[57] In other words, according to this account, the annual value of trade of Hughli was around Rs 8.9 million. Even if we assume, in order to eliminate the chance of any possible overestimation, that the usual rate of custom duties was 3.5 per cent (not 2.5 per cent as stated in the said estimate) then also the annual value of trade at Hughli would have been around Rs 6.3 million. If this was so, there can be little doubt that Hughli was still far ahead of Calcutta and only lost its premier position probably from the mid-1730s.

Be that as it may, the Asian merchants in Bengal had a long established tradition of both maritime and overland trade which they kept alive for most part of the early eighteenth century. Besides, the European companies, too, derived a lucrative trade in Bengal during this period. Thus trading activities in Bengal were brisk in the first half of the eighteenth century. Provisions in Bengal were cheap, much cheaper than in other parts of India. Even the Court of Directors in London wrote in 1735 that 'Bengal is not only the cheapest part of India to live in, but perhaps the most plentiful country in the whole of the world'.[58] Again the Court added next year that 'provisions of all kind are at such low rates in Bengal and... perhaps it is one of the most plentiful parts of the globe'.[59] Labour was not only abundant but cheap too. Moreover, the region enjoyed political and administrative stability which fostered the growth of trade and commerce. Its economy was self-sufficient and the market for import commodities was strictly limited. The export goods had to be paid for by importation of bullion and specie—the only items for which there was an ever increasing demand in Bengal. It is against this backdrop that we shall examine the various aspects of Bengal's

[56] P.J. Marshall, *Bengal*, p.65; *East Indian Fortunes*, chapter 3.

[57] O'Mally and M.M. Chakraborty, *Hugli District Gazetteer*, p.47; J.C. Sinha, *Economic Annals*, p.7. However the 'Syer Bakshbandar' in the *Fifth Report* is given as Rs. 297, 941, W.K. Firminger (ed.) *Fifth Report*, vol. II, p.199.

[58] DB, vol.106, f.413, para. 41, 31 Jan. 1735.

[59] Ibid., vol.106, f.610, para. 79, 23 Jan. 1736.

trade and economy in the first half of the eighteenth century, and
see to what extent they changed, if at all, in the second half of
the century, especially following the British conquest of Bengal.

3

EUROPEAN COMPANIES IN BENGAL *SUBA*, 1720-57

The major European companies, the Dutch and the English, which played a significant role in the export trade from Bengal in the first half of the eighteenth century, began their trade almost at the same time in the middle of the seveneenth century. The discovery of the Cape route threw open direct maritime trade between Europe and Asia, and the Portuguese set the example of extensive and direct spice trade from Asia to Europe, especially in the late sixteenth century. It was the vast market in Europe and the high profit from the spice trade that prompted the establishment of the English East India Company in 1600 and the United Dutch East India Company (Verenigde Oostindische Compagnie, in short VOC) in 1602. The French East India Company was founded later and it began its operations in Bengal in the 1680s. It was only in the early eighteenth century that the Ostend and the Danish Companies began their trade in Bengal on a rather modest scale. Throughout the first half of the eighteenth century, it was the English and the Dutch Companies which were most active in the export trade from Bengal. Indeed, their trade overshadowed other European companies through- out the period under review, except the French, who under the energetic management of governor Dupleix, pursued the Bengal trade with some vigour in the 1730s.

3.1 CHIEF PARTNER OF COMPANIES' ASIATIC TRADE

In the beginning both the Dutch and the English were interested only in procuring spices in the East Indies, the so-called spice islands, mainly in the Indonesian archipelago. With silver obtained from the 'new world', the Companies went to these islands to buy spices. But to their utter astonishment, they found that in these places it was not silver but cheap Indian coarse calicoes which were in great demand. So they turned their attention to India for cheap, coarse piece-goods so that they could buy spices in the Indonesian archipelago in exchange for Indian cloth. But as yet, trade with Bengal was not their objective. They preferred the Coromandel Coast for procuring the Indian textiles for exchange in the spice islands. However, when the Coromandel trade became uncertain and expensive because of wars, famines and political instability in the region, the Companies turned their attention to Bengal. They realized that trade in Bengal had certain advantages. Bengal was not only the largest producer of cheap cotton piece-goods, but also of high quality and inexpensive raw silk which was in great demand in Europe, gradually replacing Persian and Italian silk. A third lucrative item of trade for the Companies was saltpetre, an essential ingredient of gunpowder which was in high demand in Europe because of chronic wars, and which could also be profitably used for ballast for Europe-bound ships.[1]

So it was on these considerations that both the Dutch and the English Companies established their factories or trading posts in Bengal in the early 1650s, incidentally both in Hughli, which was the premier port of Bengal in the seventeenth century. But it was not until the mid-70s that the Bengal trade assumed any significant importance in the Asiatic trade of either Company. From about the 1670s, there was a sudden expansion in the European export of Bengal raw silk, which received a further boost in the eighties because of the high demand for the commodity in Europe. However, it was the big boom in the export of Bengal textiles from around the early 1680s that revolutionized the pattern of the Asiatic trade of the European companies. From then onward, Bengal became the most dominant partner of the European trade from Asia which was mostly carried on by the two major Companies, the Dutch and the English East India Companies. Thus, from about the early 1680s till the middle of

---

[1] For details, S. Chaudhuri, *Trade and Commercial Organization*, pp. 11-16.

the eighteenth century, these two Companies among the Euro-
peans played the most important role in Bengal's martime and
international trade. But after the British victory at the battle of
Plassey in 1757, it was a different story because the English
Company along with its servants, by virtue of its total control over
Bengal polity and economy, became intent on wiping out all other
European and Asian rivals from any worthwhile trade in Bengal.[2]

It is thus interesting to note that the Asiatic trade of the
European companies which began as a bilateral trade between
Europe and the spice islands changed its character completely in
the course of time. From the original bilateral trade, it changed
to triangular trade—between Europe, India (for cheap cotton
piece-goods) and the spice islands (where the Indian textiles were
exchanged for spices to be exported to Europe). Finally, it
became bilateral again, mainly between Europe and Bengal, with
the marked difference from about the 1680s that Bengal
emerged as the chief partner of the Asiatic trade of the European
companies. By the beginning of the eighteenth century, Bengal
supplied about 40 per cent of the average annual value of Asian
commodites the Dutch Company sent to Holland. And more than
50 per cent of the total value in textiles the Dutch exported from
Asia was in the form of Bengal textiles. Thus in the early
eighteenth century, Bengal became the most important theatre
of the Dutch Company's activity not only in India but in the whole
of Asia. Similar was the case with the English Company. The
Bengal trade was often described by the English factors as the
'best flower of the Company's garden' or 'the choicest jewel'. An
English factor wrote towards the close of the seventeenth century
that 'Bengal is the most considerable to the English nation of all
their settlements in India'. That the Dutch and the English were
the major partners in Bengal's maritime trade in the first half of
the eighteenth century is also borne out by the fact that
Alexander Hume, the chief of the Ostend Company in Bengal,
wrote in 1730 that 'the English and Dutch ... are the greatest
traders in this country'.[4]

[2] Kristof Glamann, *Dutch Asiatic Trade*, p. 144.

[3] Om Prakash, *Dutch Company*, p. 8.

[4] Alexander Hume's 'Memoir', Stadsarchief Antwerp, General
Indische Compagnie, 5769.

A very significant feature of Bengal-Europe trade was that the Companies had to import into Bengal mostly precious metals for purchasing the export commodities. This was, of course, true about the Asian merchants too who exported goods from Bengal. Though the Companies also brought some other items, mainly broadcloth, their volume or value was extremely limited. The amount of treasure imported by the Companies can be gauged from the fact that the proportion of precious metals to the total value imported by the Dutch in the second half of the seventeenth and first two decades of the eighteenth century works out to be 87.5 per cent.[5] The pattern was not very different in the case of the English Company. While the average proportion of treasure in the total English imports to the East Indies as a whole came to about 75 per cent,[6] this proportion in Bengal varied between 90 to 94 per cent in the first two decades of the eighteenth century.[7] It does not seem that the position changed to any significant extent for the rest of the period under review. The main reason for this was that the market for imported goods in Bengal was strictly limited.

The suggestion that this was because of the rigidity of consumer taste or the hoarding habit of the people in the East is hardly tenable. The alternative explanation given in a recent study that it was because of 'the inability of Europe to supply western products at prices that would generate a large enough demand for them' seems to be too simplistic.[8] The European products that were sent to Bengal comprised mainly broadcloth and woollens. Even if these were offered for sale at a throw-away price, there would have been hardly any big market for them, given the hot climate in most parts of India. The main reason why there was such a small and restricted market for imported goods was that Bengal was extremely self-sufficient and hardly needed anything which the western countries could provide even at a very competitive price. However, the influx of bullion stopped almost completely after the British conquest of Bengal in 1757

---

[5] Om Prakash, *Dutch Company*, pp. 65-68.

[6] Calculated from K.N. Chaudhuri, *Trading World*, p. 512 by Om Prakash, p. 12.

[7] S. Chaudhuri, *Trade and Commercial Organization*, p. 208.

[8] Om Prakash, *Dutch Company*, p. 12.

when the English Company's investments were financed by resources of Bengal. Most of the other European companies' investments shrank gradually and whatever was left was mostly financed by private British individuals' money for which they received bills of exchange in Europe. It should be noted here that the Europeans were not the only importers of bullion, and for that matter, not the largest at that.[9] The Asian merchants whose exports from Bengal were much greater than that of the Europeans too had to bring in silver or cash to Bengal to pay for their purchases. In this connection, Dupleix's notion that the Bengal nawab was so heavily dependent upon European trade for silver that the Europeans could impose any terms on him by blockading his ports[10] seems to be an empty boast, as was his conviction expressed in a letter to Bussy in 1751 that Bengal could easily be conquered just by 'sending four to five hundred people ... and a few artillery'.[11]

3.2 ENGLISH EAST INDIA COMPANY

The most significant development in the English East India Company's trade in the early eighteenth century was the grant of an imperial *farman* from the Mughal emperor Farrukhsiyar in 1717 for duty-free trade in lieu of an annual payment of Rs 3,000. The English were anxious for a long time to secure a consolidated *farman* enjoining free trade in the country. The Surman embassy which was sent from Fort William (Calcutta) to the Mughal emperor was successful in obtaining the much-desired *farman*.[12] The *farman* has been regarded as the 'Magna Carta of the English trade in Bengal' and 'a real diplomatic

---

[9] See chapters 7 and 8.

[10] I. Ray, 'Some Aspects of French Presence in Bengal, 1731-40', *CHJ*, vol. I, 1976, p. 110. P.J. Marshall cites this as an example of the important role played by the Europeans as suppliers of silver, *Bengal*, p. 65.

[11] Dupleix's letter to Bussy, 16 July 1751, quoted in Brijen K. Gupta, *Sirajuddaullah*, p. 36.

[12] For Surman embassy, see Home Misc., vols. 69-71; Fact. Records, Misc., vols. 19, 20. For the provisions of the *farman* and *hasb-ul-hukm*, see S. Bhattacharyya, *East India Company*, pp. 28-29; A. Karim, *Murshid Quli*, pp. 166-68.

success of the English'.[13] In view of the fact that great importance
has been attached to the *farman* and its working became a bone
of contention between the Company and the Bengal administration, it is imperative to make a close and critical analysis of the
main provisions of the *farman*, and see what the privileges
granted by it meant or implied in real and concrete terms.

There is no denying that the *farman*, at least on paper,
removed various obstacles to English trade—raised often by local
authorities on the ground that there was no valid *farman* for the
alleged privileges claimed by the Company. The most significant
gain for the English Company was the grant of freedom of trade,
sanctioned by an imperial *farman* on payment of Rs 3,000 a year.
No imperial *farman* had so far given the English any such
freedom, though they enjoyed the privilege of duty-free trade by
virtue of *nishans* and *parwanas* from local rulers, procured
through bribes and presents. The effect of this provision in the
farman was to establish the English Company as one of the most
privileged groups of merchants in Bengal. The *farman* was rather
vague as to what kind of trade was exempted from customs
duties. But the context and spirit of the *farman* hardly leave any
doubt that the exemption was only for the Company's export and
import trade, and definitely not for either inland trade or private
trade of the Company servants. The simple fact was that the
embassy to the emperor was officially sent by the English Council
at Fort William, obviously to obtain the privileges for the
Company which was engaged in export and import trade in
Bengal. Hence, the concessions made to the Company, despite
the fact that they were not specifically mentioned as such in the
farman, could hardly be meant to include inland trade or private
trade of the Company servants. The Bengal nawabs clarified this
stand time and again but the servants of the Company insisted
on their own interpretation of the *farman* to include inland trade
and private trade, resulting in tension between them.

The *farman* does not entail any provision for the use of the
mint and *dastaks* (permit which exempts customs duties), but the
husb-ul-hukm (document issued by imperial command) enjoined
upon the provincial officers to allow the Company to coin money

[13] S. Bhattacharyya, *East India Company*, p. 29; C.R. Wilson, *Early Annals*, vol. II, pt.I, p. XLVI.

at the Murshidabad mint for three days in the week 'according to former custom' provided that 'it does not go against the King's interest'. But it did not specify whether the use of the mint was to be allowed duty-free as demanded by the Company. However, the qualifying phrase ('if it does not go against the King's interest') seems to have left the final say in the hands of the provincial authorities. And if the 'former custom' is taken into consideration, it should be noted that the English Company had never enjoyed the privilege of duty-free minting in Bengal. As for the *dastaks,* the wording in the *husb-ul-hukm* that 'A list taken from under the seal of the chief of the factory and that, according to it you give sunnuds [permission] under your own seal' made the Company's *dastak* ineffective unless it was accorded by the provincial officers. Much of the bitterness between the Company and the Bengal nawabs in the first half of the eighteenth century, as we shall see shortly, centred round mainly the questions of the free use of the mint, the abuse of *dastaks* and inland and private trade of the Company servants in Bengal.

During Murshid Quli's reign, the combine of the nawab and the Jagat Seth stood as a stumbling block to the free use of the mint by the English. As a matter of fact, the house of Jagat Seth virtually monopolized the mint business throughout the first half of the eighteenth century. But it was the abuse of *dastaks* which was most resented by the nawabs, beginning with Murshid Quli. That the allegation of misuse of *dastaks* was quite justified was even acknowledged by the English Council at Fort William. It wrote to London in May 1726 that both the governments of Murshidabad and Hughli had complained on several occasions of the 'great abuse made of our Dustucks which abuse we apprehend may at one time or other be of singular prejudice to our Honble Masters affairs and the Trade of Bengal in general'. It added further that the abuse of *dastaks* was a 'pernicious evil' and 'we are senceble [sensible] great abuses have been made by disposing of part of the goods brought out of the country by virtue of our Dustucks'.[14]

Similarly, the inland trade of the Company servants which was not permitted by the *farman* was another irritant to the administration in Bengal. The Kasimbazar Council wrote to

[14] BPC, vol.6, f.215vo, 23 May 1726; Home Misc., vol.68, ff.70-71, 23 May 1726.

Calcutta on 20 March 1727 advising that 'the Nabob has been very incensed against us, on account of complaints made about our dealing in rice and grain'. It reported that the nawab told them if they did not 'apply remedies to these abuses for the future', he should himself take stern measures. It also noted that it was public talk at Murshidabad that more than 200,000 maunds of rice were sent down to Calcutta in that year by the *gomastas* (agents) of the Company servants.[15] The usual method resorted to by the nawabs to chastise the English was to put a stop on latter's trade in some factories or *aurungs* (manufacturing centres) while the English generally took recourse to blockading of the river Hughli to put pressure on the nawab. The blockading of the Hughli was generally very effective because it meant the stoppage of the trade of the Muslim and Armenian merchants who were involved extensively in maritime trade. Thus both in 1723 and 1727, when the English blockaded the Hughli, the 'nakhudas' (captains) of the 'Moors' ships' and Armenian merchants put pressure on the nawab to settle matters with the English.[16]

The first issue which embittered the relations between the next nawab Shujauddin and the English, and brings out clearly the ramification of the question of English privileges in Bengal, was the problem of inland trade in salt, though the English regarded Shujauddin before his accession as 'friendly' towards them.[17] The Kasimbazar Council reported in September 1727 that a complaint had been made at the *darbar* alleging that the English carried salt in the Patna fleet which was sent there to bring saltpetre to Calcutta and that 'the farmers of that Branch of Revenues reckon themselves considerable sufferers'. The boats were seized by the government officials and a huge quantity of salt found therein was unloaded at Bhagalpur.[18] When the Council made a representation for release of the salt, the government absolutely refused and told that 'no disinterested

---

[15] BPC, vol. 6, f. 399vo, 20 March 1727.

[16] Ibid., vol. 5, f. 388, 28 Nov. 1723; f. 393vo, 12 Dec. 1723; vol. 6, f. 389vo, 27 Feb. 1727.

[17] DB, vol. 104, f.427, para. 32, 21 Feb. 1729.

[18] BPC, vol. 6, f. 500, 18 Sept. 1727. The quantity of salt was reported to have been 100,000 maunds, BPC, vol. 6, f. 562, 4 March 1728.

person can think the Phirmaund privileges us to trade in anything customs free but what we Import and Export, which they think ought to satisfy us, being what no other European Nations or the Mahometans themselves are favoured with'. The government further alleged that the English trade 'is much encreased of late, that we deal in many more commodities than we used to do insomuch that the Foreign trade of the Natives is very much decayed and that if they do not put an effective stop to our encroachments on the Inland Trade we shall undersell all others, engross the whole trade of the province and thereby deprive vast numbers of the Natives of the means of a livelihood'.[19]

The Kasimbazar Council informed Calcutta that the matter could only be settled by presenting a sum of Rs 10,000 to the nawab. The position of the government was made absolutely clear—'as they do not deny us [English] the privilege of trading custom free in all such goods as we bring in or carry out of the kingdom, so they can't injure the natives as to suffer us to encroach in their trade by dealing Inland in such merchandise as is produced in the country'.[20] The Calcutta Council did not only regard the amount too high, but more significantly believed that the English 'acquiescence in this affair would be of the worst consequence, and become a precedent for them to lay hold on every trifle occasion'.[21] The stand taken by the Bengal administration, though justified, alarmed the English who were most reluctant to give up their inland and private trade, however illegal these might have been. The Calcutta Council noted that 'were we to confine our trade to Nothing else but what we import and export, the Honble Company's servants (as well as the Company whose revenues would be vastly lessened thereby) would be great sufferers by having one of the most beneficial branches of their trade lost'. It maintained that it was not the salt which was 'a very inconsiderable part but besides every other branch of the inland trade is struck at'. The Council regarded this to be 'so growing an abuse from the Government to us'.[22] If this was the attitude

---

[19] BPC, vol. 6, f.510vo, 9 Oct. 1727.
[20] Ibid., vol. 6, f. 577, 18 March 1728.
[21] Ibid.
[22] Ibid., vol. 6, f. 577vo, 18 March 1728.

of the Company servants, it is no wonder that they were primarily responsible for the outbreak of hostilities between the Company and the Bengal nawab, Sirajuddaullah, in 1756-57. At the same time, it is against this backdrop that the nawabs occasionally extorted some money from the Europeans, and hence it would be wrong to assume that they treated the latter as milch cows.

Nawab Shujauddin told the English that he was 'greatly surprised' to find that they entertained such 'unreasonable thought' that the *farman* gave them 'an unbounded privilege to trade in anything they had a mind to' and added that as 'he could not deny the privilege allowed us (which was only to trade custom free in what we export and import) so he would not suffer us to extend it farther'. He also added that by doing so he would not only be a 'detriment to the king's revenues, but a hardship on the natives, who have only the Inland Trade to get their livelihood by'.[23] But the Calcutta Council was in no mood to comply with the proposal of Kasimbazar to settle matters by paying a sum to the nawab. It held that compliance therewith would only be a 'sure and certain inducement' to the government to make further extravagant demand in future, and hence resolved that it was 'absolutely necessary to make a stand against the daily growing abuses of this new viceroy'. And therefore it decided to blockade the Hughli.[24] However, through the mediation of *diwan* Alamchand and banker Fatechand, the matter was settled after a payment to the nawab and his officers. John Stackhouse, the chief of the Kasimbazar factory, gave an undertaking that the English would not involve themselves in any way in inland trade or abuse the *dastaks*.[25]

But the Calcutta Council did not approve of the undertaking and held that Stackhouse had acted 'unwarrantedly in giving the obligation by which the king's farman and husb-ul-hukm were annulled'. On the other hand, the Kasimbazar Council maintained that it was absolutely necessary for securing the Company's investments and 'the obligation might be repudiated, if necessary, at a more convenient and opportune time'.[26] The Bengal nawab was quite concerned at the growing influence of the

---

[23] Ibid., vol. 6, f. 582, 1 April 1728.
[24] Ibid., vol. 6, ff. 586-86vo, 15 April 1728.
[25] Ibid., vol. 8, f. 497, 11 Nov. 1731.
[26] Ibid., vol. 8, ff.501vo-502vo, 22 Nov. 1731.

English and in a letter to the imperial court at Delhi thus expressed his anxiety: 'Their investments of late have been immoderate and they both import and export other merchants' goods in their own names.... They now begin to farm severall Towns, which it is feared, may in time become strongholds and consequently a difficult matter for the government to remove them.'[27] Even the high officials of the state became worried at the invasion by the Company servants of inland trade and the extent of their private trade. One of them, Mir Habib, expressed his concern in a letter to the Dhaka factory:[28]

> ...do you imagine the whole trade of the country is to be carried on by you, much to the prejudice of the King and his subjects or can you believe the merchants of the country could see their own proper trade swallowed up by you Foreigners, without regret and they are starving. It is true the King's Phirmaund gives the English Company liberty to trade in Commoditys to and from Europe custom free, Instead of which you carry on a Private Trade far exceeding the Company's under their cover....

The Court of Directors in London, too, was well aware of the abuses perpetrated by the Company servants in Bengal and that the clash between the Company and the government was mainly because of these abuses and involvement in inland trade, contrary to the provisions of the *farman*. It wrote to Calcutta in 1732 that all the 'troubles' in Bengal appeared to have been 'owing to our servants, who by an extravagant unheard of trade, covering the Black Merchants' goods under their Dustucks and other bad practices, have saddled us with the payment of a very great sum...not only so, but have endangered our Phirmaund Privileges, and where all this will end God only knows'.[29] In another general letter, it was stated categorically that the 'late troubles' arose from a clandestine trade carried on by 'our servants' and 'by a gross abuse of Dustucks'.[30] A few years later, the Court

---

[27] Ibid., vol. 9, ff. 343vo-344, 18 June 1733.
[28] Ibid., vol. 9, f.357vo, 8 July 1733.
[29] DB, vol. 105, f. 544, para. 33, 10 Nov. 1732.
[30] Ibid., vol. 105, f. 624, para. 7, 8 Dec. 1732.

became convinced that 'our servants have given him [nawab] some real cause for being thus troublesome'.[31]

The relation between the Company and the nawab deteriorated further during Alivardi's reign. Jean Law wrote about Alivardi that he 'understood perfectly well the interests of his government, favoured the poor merchants, and administered justice when complaints succeeded reaching him'.[32] But hard pressed by the Maratha invasions, Alivardi tried to raise contributions from various people — the zamindars, bankers, merchants and also the Europeans — for recruiting and maintaining an army.[33] It was two years after the advent of the Marathas that he demanded contributions from the Europeans in 1744. His justification was that he had provided security to the European trade for the last five years, because of which they reaped great profit, and now that the country faced danger from the Marathas, the Europeans should pay as did the others in the state.[34] But this was resented by the Europeans, especially the English. When the English sought Jagat Seth Fatechand's advice on the matter, he cleverly told them: 'At present there is no government; they fear neither God nor the king but seemed determined to force money from everybody. I have suffered greatly by them.'[35] But it would be wrong to conclude from this, as has been done in a recent study, that everyone was 'harried ruthlessly'.[36] Fatechand's answer was rather the usual diplomatic way of telling the English that they had to pay the nawab. He used to take recourse to such tactics on many occasions. As for example, when the *batta* on Madras rupees was raised at the instance of Fatechand in 1736 as evident from Kasimbazar Council's letter which mentioned him as 'the chief promoter of this order', he told the English, when they represented to him, that 'it affected himself as much as anybody' and that he 'had

[31] Ibid., vol. 107, f. 69, para 21, 3 Nov. 1736.

[32] S.C. Hill, *Bengal in 1756-57*, vol. III, p. 160.

[33] Fact.Records, Kasimbazar, vol. 6, Consult. 29 Aug. 1743; BPC, vol. 17, f. 747vo, 18 Nov. 1745.

[34] BPC, vol. 17, f. 152, 12 July 1744; Fact. Records, Kasimbazar, vol. 6, Consult. 7 July 1744; C. & B. Abstr., vol. 5, f. 16, para 24, 3 Aug. 1744.

[35] BPC, vol. 17, f. 155, 13 July 1744.

[36] P.J. Marshall, *Bengal*, p. 71. Marshall cited Jagat Seth's answer from J.H. Little.

made several attempts to get the order revoked but in vain'.[37] He actually told the Kasimbazar Council later about the nawab's demand from the English that 'all the people who have hitherto carried on their business scott free, should assist him [nawab] in this emergency by paying their share'.[38] No doubt, there had been some cases of extortions, but the stories of large scale robbing and torture of merchants seem to be an exaggeration. The English, however, had to pay Rs 350,000 to the nawab.

But the relation between the Company and the nawab did not improve. Two Armenian ships on their way to Bengal from Basra and Jedda were captured by the English fleet in 1748. When the Hughli merchants reported the matter, the nawab told the English that he had warned earlier both the English and the French not to molest ships of other nations bound for Bengal. To that the English had paid no regard and as such, he was resolved to 'do justice to those who had suffered by such usage'.[39] He ordered guards to be placed on all the English Company's *dadni* merchants' *gomastas* at the *aurungs*. The Calcutta Council, in retaliation, issued an order that no Armenian ships would be allowed to pass the fort [Fort William]. The embargo on the Armenian ships did not have the desired effect.[40] In a strong letter to Barwell, the President of Fort William Council, the nawab wrote: 'As you were not permitted to be in this country to commit piracies... deliver up all the Merchants goods and effects to them... otherwise you may be assured of due chastisement in such a manner as you least expect.'[41] The matter was ultimately settled through the mediation of the Jagat Seths. The English paid Rs 120,000 to the nawab, out of which Rs 20,000 was given to satisfy the Armenians.[42]

The final rupture in the relations occurred during the next

[37] BPC, vol. 12, f. 135vo, 16 April 1737.
[38] Fact. Records, Kasimbazar, vol. 6, Consult. 7 Aug. 1744.
[39] BPC, vol. 22, f. 49vo, 19 Dec. 1748.
[40] Ibid., vol. 22, f.64vo, 31 Dec. 1748; f. 105, 23 Jan. 1749.
[41] Ibid., vol. 22, f. 96, 9 Jan.1749.
[42] Fact. Records, Kasimbazar, vol. 8, Consults. 9, 26 Sept., 16 Oct. 1749; BPC, vol. 22, f.200vo, 4 May 1749.

nawab Sirajuddaullah's time.[43] The young nawab had three
specific grievances against the British — the strong fortification
built by the Company at Fort William, the abuse of *dastaks* and
shelter given to his offending subjects. He made his intentions
clear in a letter to the Armenian merchant prince, Khwaja Wazid,
whom he sent several times to the English as his emissary for an
amicable settlement of the dispute. He wrote: '...if the English are
contented to remain in my country they must submit to have their
forts raized, their ditch filled up, and trade upon the same terms
they did in time of Nawab Jaffier Khan [Murshid Quli]; otherwise
I will expel them out of the provinces of which I am the Subah
[nawab].' In a second letter to Khwaja Wazid, the nawab further
clarified his stand: 'if they [the English] will promise to remove
the foregoing complaints of their conduct...I will pardon their
fault and permit their residence here....'[44] But that was not be.
It is not a fact that Sirajuddaullah attacked the British for money.
He asked for money only when he was on his way to Calcutta after
the capitulation of Kasimbazar factory. If he really wanted
money, he could have plundered Kasimbazar, but he did not. As
the anonymous author of an English manuscript pointed out, 'it
was not money that the Subadar required'.[45] Regarding the
money paid by the Dutch and the French to the nawab, it should
be noted that Sirajuddaullah asked for the customary presents
from them only on his way back to Murshidabad after the fall of
Calcutta. This sort of customary gift after a victory was exacted
by all Bengal nawabs.[46] As I have tried to argue elsewhere,[47] the
British in Bengal were not ready to give up their illegal private
and inland trade, and the great privilege of the *dastaks*, and hence
the Plassey revolution of 1757 which ushered in the beginning

[43] For a detailed account, see my article, 'Sirajuddaullah, English
Company and the Plassey Conspiracy — A Reappraisal', *IHR*, vol. XIII,
nos. 1-2, pp. 111-134.

[44] Sirajuddaullah to Wazid, 28 May 1756, Hill, *Bengal in 1756-57*, vol.
I, pp. 3,4.

[45] Mss. Eur. D. 283, f. 27.

[46] That the nawab was after money is implied even in the latest study,
P.J. Marshall, *Bengal*, p. 76. I have discussed the issue in detail in my
article 'Sirajuddaullah', *IHR*, pp. 116-117.

[47] See chapter 11 and my article on 'Sirajuddaullah' in *IHR*.

of the foundation of the British empire in India.

So far as the actual export of the Dutch and the English Companies in the first two decades of the eighteenth century is concerned, the Dutch were much ahead of the English, even excluding their trade within Asia. But in the second decade it was almost a near thing, though the Dutch export including the intra-Asian trade was still higher than that of the English. This will be apparent from the following table (Table 3.1).

TABLE 3.1
Value of English and Dutch Exports from Bengal
1701-1720

Years	Average Annual English Exports to Europe	Average Annual Dutch Exports to Europe	Average Annual Dutch Exports (to Europe and Asia)
	(in Florins)	(in Florins)	(in Florins)
1701-1710	1,382,595	2,315,384	3,274,369
1710-1720	2,666,764	2,650,607	3,616,242

[Source & note: English exports calculated from K.N. Chaudhuri, *Trading World*, p. 509 with one-year lag. Dutch exports computed from Om Prakash, *Dutch Company*, p. 70. £=12 Florins, 1 Rupee=1.5 Florin.]

The English Company's export to Europe reached its zenith in the first quinquennial period of the 1740s. As a matter of fact, the English export from Bengal increased substantially from the early 1730s. Though there was a slight decline in the average annual value of the English exports in the first quinquennial period of the 1750s, it can be asserted that the average annual value of the English exports did not show any marked decline over the period from 1730-1755, which is evident from Table 3.2. It is important to note that the slight decrease in the average annual value of the English exports in the first half of the 1750s was compensated by the increase in the value of the Dutch exports during this period. So there is no reason to believe that the decline in the English exports was due to any economic 'crisis' in Bengal.

TABLE 3.2
Quinquennial Total and Average Annual Value
of English Exports, 1730-1755

Years	Total (£)	Average (£)	Average (Florins)
1730/31-1734/35	2,117,689	423,538	5,082,453
1740/41-1744/45	2,401,785	480,357	5,764,284
1750/51-1754/55	2,033,244	406.649	4,879,785

[Source & note: Computed from K.N. Chaudhuri, *Trading World*, pp. 509-10, with one-year lag.]

3.3 DUTCH EXPORTS TO EUROPE AND ASIA

Though the Dutch export in the 1720s declined to some extent, it picked up from the early 1730s. As a matter of fact, the value of the Dutch export shows a steady increase throughout the period from the early 1730s to the middle of the 1750s. The growth of the Dutch export was more remarkable in the early 1750s when the value of the English export declined though not considerably. It is interesting to note that the Dutch who were much behind the English in the early 1730s almost equalled the English exports in the early 1750s. Of course, the Dutch export included export to different parts of Asia as well. The table below will bear the point out (Table 3.3).

TABLE 3.3

Quinquennial Total and Average Annual Value of English and Dutch Exports, 1730-1755
[in Florins]

Years	English	Dutch	
	Average Annual Value of Exports to Europe	Average Annual Value of Exports to Europe	Average Annual Value of Total Exports (Europe and Asia)
1730/31-1734/35	5,082,453	2,020,460	3,489,567
1740/41-1744/45	5,764,284	2,390,558	3,475,770
1750/51-1754/55	4,879,785	3,417,306	4,480,104

[Source & note: Dutch exports compiled and computed from export invoices in VOC records. The figures for English exports calculated with one-year lag from K.N. Chaudhuri, *Trading World*, pp. 509-10. The rate of conversion used is £ 1 = *f* 12]

In this connection, it is significant that though the Dutch export from Bengal to different parts of Asia was so much an important part of their trade in the late seventeenth and early decades of the eighteenth century, shows a steady decline in the period 1730-1755. On the contrary, the value of the export to Europe was steadily increasing in the years from 1730 to 1745 and was marked by a substantial increase in the early 1750s. This is clear from the table below (3.4).

In the first quinquennial periods of the decades from 1730 to 1755, the value of the Dutch exports to Batavia showed a steady increase, though as we mentioned earlier, the Dutch intra-Asiatic trade declined as a whole. The percentage share of the average annual value of the Dutch export from Bengal to Batavia in the total value of Dutch exports from the province to different parts of Asia was 64.83 in the early 1730s, increasing to 77.02 in the first half of the 1740s and to 89.92 in the 1750s. But the export

TABLE 3.4

Quinquennial Total, Average Annual Value and Percentage Composition of
Dutch Exports to Europe and Asia, 1730-55

[in Florins]

Years	Total (Europe)	Average (Europe)	Europe Percentage	Total (Europe & Asia)	Average (Europe & Asia)	Asia Percentage
1730/31-34/35	10,103,300	2,020,460	58%	17,447,838	3,489,567	42%
1740/41-44/45	11,952,792	2,390,558	69%	17,378,849	3,475,770	31%
1750/51-54/55	17,086,532	3,417,306	76%	22,400,521	4,480,104	24%

[Source: Compiled and computed from export invoices in VOC records]

to two other important Dutch markets for Bengal goods namely, Japan and Persia, showed a gradual decline in general during this period, though the export to Persia in the early 1740s was an exception. The Dutch export to other centres in Asia was almost negligible in the period from 1730-1755. The table below (3.5) will illustrate our point.

TABLE 3.5

Percentage Share in Total Value of the Dutch Exports
from Bengal to other Asian Markets
1730-1755

Places	1730-35	1740-45	1750-55
Batavia	64.83	77.02	89.92
Japan	25.39	11.64	5.26
Persia	4.44	6.20	3.64
Others	5.34	5.14	1.18
	100	100	100

[Source: Compiled and computed from export invoices in VOC records. Persia includes Basra, Gombroon and Mocha. 'Others' include Ceylon, Cochin, Coromandel, Malacca, Malabar, Siam, Macassar, etc.]

Thus, a few interesting features of the export trade by the English and the Dutch Companies from Bengal emerge from the above analysis. The Dutch had a definite lead over the English in the first decade of the eighteenth century while it was almost equal in the second. From around the early 1720s, the Dutch fell behind the English but were picking up from the 1730s. The average annual value of the exports by the English reached the high mark in the first quinquennial period of the 1740s but it declined marginally in the first five years of the 1750s. On the other hand, the value of the Dutch exports, including exports to

Asia, nearly equalled that of the English in the early 1750s. And considering the total value of exports by the two Companies, there was hardly any decline from 1730 to 1755. The decline in the value of the English exports in the early 1750s was made up for, as far as Bengal's export trade was concerned, by the increase in that of the Dutch during these years. So far as the Dutch intra-Asiatic trade was concerned, there was a gradual decline throughout the period, though the percentage share of Batavia in the total value increased steadily. This was mainly because of the steady growth of the opium export to Batavia.[48]

Figure 3.1
Value of English and Dutch Exports 1730-1755

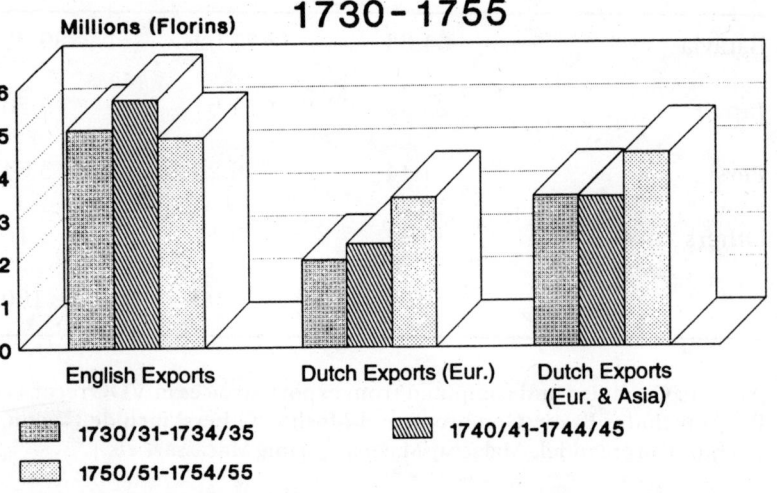

[Source : Table 3.3]

4

PRE-MODERN SOUTH ASIAN COMMERCIAL ORGANIZATION AND COMPANIES

It has been established, thanks to the researches of several historians of trade in the last few decades, that the European companies trading in South Asia in the seventeenth and eighteenth centuries had to adjust themselves to the prevalent commercial system and tradition in the given areas of their trade. Seldom were the cases when the Companies could effect notable changes in the traditional system of commerce in the South Asian countries they traded with. Of course, in all fairness, it should be admitted that the activities of these Companies resulted in certain innovations as also modifications in the existing system which were in a way novel in the commercial order of the time, though these were probably not very significant in the overall structure of the pre-modern South Asian commercial system.

We shall examine here the investment pattern of the European companies—mainly the English and the Dutch East India companies which were the major foreign trading concerns in Bengal in the first half of the eighteenth century, and see how the Companies tried to achieve the twin goals of investment and procurement within the broad framework of the traditional commercial system. A few questions crop up in this connection. Did the Companies have to change the small details within the broad structure of the traditional system? What were the problems that they had to face in their investments? How did they try to solve them and what was the extent of success? In the course of the discussion we shall try to answer these questions as far as

possible, given the limitations of the source material. Though the
illustrations will be taken mainly from the activities of the English
East India Company, and supplemented by those of the Dutch
Company, the broad conclusions will be applicable to all the
European companies trading in Bengal. With minor changes in
detail and allowance for local variations, they will also be valid in
general for all the European companies trading in different parts
of South Asia during the period under review.

4.1 INVESTMENT PATTERN

The successful investments[1] of the European companies in
Bengal depended not primarily on the economic laws of supply
and demand. The Companies had to face many a problem in
securing their investments which were peculiar to the Indian
situation. Their servants in India were not familiar with the
market mechanism of the country, and most often ignorant of
the local language. Under the circumstances, they had to depend
on a group of merchant-middlemen, generally under a chief
merchant, often called broker by the Companies, in every major
trading centre. Thus the Companies appointed local brokers in
most of their factories and depended solely on them for the
provision of their investments. The brokers helped the Companies in making contracts with local merchants—most often
recommended by the brokers themselves—for provision of
goods for the return voyage of the ships. These merchants,
however, were required to be paid advance or *dadni* by the
Companies on the amount contracted for. The *dadni* merchants
in their turn gave advances to weavers, artisans and other
primary producers through their *gomastas* or agents scattered
through various production centres or *aurungs* to ensure the
supply of goods at the proper time and according to specified
standards. The Companies, however, also purchased goods with
'ready money' at the shipping season but this invariably entailed
paying a much higher price than at the normal time. Naturally
they preferred, in order to minimise the cost price of commodities bought for export, the investment by *dadni* or an advance

---

[1] The term 'investment' is used here in the same sense as that in
which the Companies used to denote their purchases in India.

payment system.

The Institution of Broker

The practice of employing a broker became an integral part of the Companies' machinery for providing investments in Bengal. The custom of engaging a broker who was intimately connected with the investments of the Europeans in India was reported as being common by travellers like Fryer and Ovington during the last quarter of the seventeenth century.[2] In Calcutta, Kasimbazar, Dhaka and other factories in Bengal, the English Company contracted for investments with the *dadni* merchants through the brokers who also helped in the pricing and sorting of commodities brought in by those merchants. As the Company's investment in Calcutta was quite considerable, the office of the broker there became important and influential. The office of the broker was equally important in Surat where one had to buy the office by offering a considerable sum but it was not the case in Calcutta.[3] It is important to note that these brokers, though employees of the European companies, were themselves merchants of repute and substantial credit, and often conducted their own business quite independent of the Companies through their host of relatives and *gomastas*. As such, whenever these brokers were dismissed from the Companies' service, it did not absolutely ruin them as would be evident from the various evidence to be found in the Company records.

Calcutta Brokers

The two families which provided most of the brokers to the English Company in Calcutta and Kasimbazar were the Setts and Katmas respectively. As the investments in Calcutta largely

---

[2] S. Chaudhuri, *Trade and Commercial Organization in Bengal*, p. 144; John Fryer, *A New Account*, p. 217; J. Ovington, *Voyage to Surat*, p. 401.

[3] It was reported that Vithaldas Parekh paid Rs 100,000 to become the broker of the Company at Surat. Another broker, Rustomjee Maneckjee, paid Rs 20,000 as the customary present to the English Company, *vide* OC, 7222, para 48, vol. 58, 14 Sept. 1700. The Bengal factors reported in 1703 that 'it was never the custom here in Bengal for brokers to buy their places', OC, 8110, vol. 65, 25 Jan. 1703.

consisted of silk and cotton piece-goods produced by the Bengali
weavers, none could better play the role of a broker than the Setts
who themselves belonged to the weaving caste. They, together
with the Basaks of the same caste, were the most powerful groups,
both economically and socially, of their community in Calcutta.
Being firmly established in the site of Calcutta for generations
before the arrival of the English, and already having acquired
great fortune through trade with the Europeans, not only did the
Setts and Basaks command the respect of the weavers' community, but also as their virtual leaders they could alone persuade
them to work for the Company under their guidance. As the
majority of the *dadni* merchants of Calcutta belonged to their
community, they could also exercise direct control over them as
they wished. It was, therefore, not for nothing that the Setts filled
the most important post of the Company's broker in the first half
of the eighteenth century almost by hereditary succession.[4]

Towards the close of the seventeenth century, Jayakrishna
was the broker to the Company in Calcutta on a salary of Rs 1,000
per annum but was dismissed from service in 1699 for accepting
dosturee or brokerage from the *dadni* merchants.[5] Janardan Sett
who was described by the Calcutta Council 'as the person best
qualified for a broker' was appointed to the post on condition
that he would be allowed 3/4 per cent brokerage on the value of
total investment in Calcutta, in lieu of a regular salary.[6] Though
a broker to the Company, Janardan was also an eminent
merchant who supplied part of the Company's investment
throughout the tenure of his office till he died in February 1712.[7]
The Court of Directors in London looked down upon Janardan
as a villain who, as it alleged, through his malpractices cheated
the Company, monopolized all the trade and thus amassed a vast
fortune for himself.[8] In January 1714 it wrote to the Calcutta
Council: 'No wonder that the late broker Janardan declared
himself worth several lack [lakh] of Rupees who but a few years

[4] For a detailed study of the Setts of Calcutta, see Benoy Ghose,
'Some Old Family Founders in the 18th Century Calcutta', *BPP*, vol. 79,
pp. 42-55.

[5] Fact. Records, Calcutta, vol. 2, pt.I, f. 133.

[6] Ibid., vol. 3, pt. II, f. 90.

[7] BPC, vol. 2, f. 189vo.

[8] For details of the Court's allegations against Janardan Sett, see S.
Chaudhuri, *Trade and Commercial Organization*, p. 145.

ago was Mr. Beard's servant and not worth one hundred rupees'.[9]

After Janardan's death, his brother Baranasi Sett was appointed the Company's broker.[10] But the Directors regarded him too as the chief source of all the mischief leading to bad quality and high price of the English investments in Bengal. By now, it seems, the broker's power was immense, and the Court was not prepared to tolerate such a position. The Directors ordered in 1716 that the broker's power and the 'Confederacy of the present merchants' set up by him with his 'Relatives and Creatures' must be broken. They wrote indignantly to Calcutta: 'The exorbitant power of your broker is what we will never again bear with nor with those who are his advocates and support nor will we suffer any broker to rival much less to overstep our President.'[11] Again they complained, not without some justification, that Baranasi was not only a broker but 'by himself and creatures' supplied most of the goods provided for the Company.[12] When Robert Hedges succeeded Russell as President of the Bengal Council, he wrote frequently to the Court of Directors about the misdeeds of the broker and tried to curtail his power. He reported to the Directors that the previous President had set a bad example of depending wholly on Baranasi Sett and he was so indifferent to investment that Baranasi and his family provided two-thirds of the investments, and influenced the sorting and pricing also. Till this was 'cured', held Hedges, there was no possibility of getting goods at cheaper rates. 'Benarse Seat rules as much abroad as in the Warehouse, Revenues rose or fell as he pleased, the Collectors being his Creatures.'[13] Such was the power of the Setts as brokers. Hedges was not entirely in favour of removing Baranasi Sett but wanted only to 'hinder his power which prejudices the Company's Affairs', because 'it cannot be the Company's interest that the Chief Merchant should be Broker for, if so, goods will come dear'.[14] The Court of Directors,

[9] DB, vol. 98, f. 106, 13 Jan. 1714.

[10] BPC, vol. 2, f. 189vo; C&B. Abstr. vol. 1, f. 342.

[11] DB, vol. 99, f. 189, 15 Feb. 1716.

[12] Ibid., vol. 98, f. 462, 12 Jan. 1715.

[13] Quoted in Benoy Ghose, 'Some Old Family Founders', BPP, vol. 79, p. 47.

[14] C & B. Abstr., vol. 1, f. 472.

however, was adamant and following its order, Baranasi was replaced in April 1715 by Ramkrishna Khan, a merchant of repute and influence in Calcutta.[15]

Both the Court of Directors and the Calcutta Council seemed gratified with Ramkrishna's appointment which resulted in better and cheaper investments for the Company. But the Directors cautioned the Calcutta Council in the following words: 'It will be incumbant on all of you to prevent this Broker getting the ascendant the last had. Encourage and support him in his place while he diligently performs his Duty but don't let him overstep you or be in effect Your Master.'[16] Ramkrishna, however, could not enjoy the coveted post for long and died in November 1716 when Harinath was made broker on the recommendation of Robert Hedges.[17] In the beginning, this Harinath appeared to be 'able, diligent and faithful' from the goods he provided. Despite this, the Council observed that 'if he should prove unfaithful will turn him out with disgrace and suffer no broker to have too great authority'.[18] But Harinath was primarily a servant of Hedges, and the Council soon found him to be 'unskilled in goodness or value of muslins and of mean capacity and no repute'.[19] The Council wrote home that 'we wonder Mr. Hedges should put him in when he would not trust him in his own Affairs but Barnarse Seat'.[20] In April 1719, the Calcutta Council declared in a long minute that Harinath was altogether unsuitable for his job, and as it was looking for 'an honest experienc't man to direct the merchants in making the species of cloth', it thought the only competent person in Calcutta for the office of the broker was the much maligned Baranasi Sett.[21] Thus Baranasi was reappointed broker in 1719.

The reasons for reinstating Baranasi, as the Council put it, were that he 'is perfectly capacitated for business and as honest

[15] BPC, vol. 30, ff. 26vo, 31vo; C & B. Abstr., vol. 2, f. 28.

[16] DB, vol. 99, ff. 76-77, 18 Jan. 1717.

[17] C & B. Abstr., vol. 2, f. 175, para. 57, 6 Dec. 1718.

[18] Ibid., vol. 2, f. 79, para. 42, 27 Nov. 1716.

[19] Ibid., vol. 2, f. 175, para. 58, 6 Dec. 1718.

[20] Ibid., vol. 2, f. 276, para. 72, 28 Dec. 1720.

[21] BPC, vol. 4, ff. 46-46vo, C & B. Abstr., vol. 2, f. 175, para. 59, 6 Dec. 1718.

as of his cast[e]'.[22] The Council wrote home: 'The large and early investment will show his capacity, the goods are generally better made and cheaper than for sometime past.'[23] That Baranasi Sett was a capable man and quite successful as a broker is evident from the Council's letter of 31 January 1722: '... none but he could have influenced the merchants and secured the last and this year's Investment on credit, he being bound with each merchant for what they borrowed of the shroffs, this shows his zeal for the Company's Interest.'[24] The Court of Directors, too, wrote to Calcutta Council appreciating the services rendered by Baranasi.[25]

It is evident from the records of the Company that the Setts were the only persons in Calcutta in the first half of the eighteenth century who, as the social and economic leaders of the weaving community, could serve the interest of the Company best. The case of Baranasi Sett proves beyond doubt that there was none else in Calcutta in his time who could secure the Company's investments on better terms. Despite many a pious resolution by the Company, the power of the Setts could hardly be curbed, and as brokers they continued to exercise absolute control over the Company's investments.

Baranasi died in October 1724 and was succeeded by his brother Bishnudas Sett.[26] Justifying his appointment, the Council wrote to the Directors that he appeared:

'the properest person on many Accounts, and principally in regard to his Credit in the Country which is apparent from the recommendation of all the Government of Hugly in his favour and his being a very Substantial Man, which will

---

[22] C & B. Abstr., vol. 2, ff. 236-37, para. 82, 29 Nov. 1719; f. 320, para. 60, 31 Jan. 1722.

[23] Ibid., vol. 2, f. 237, para. 83, 29 Nov. 1719.

[24] Ibid., vol. 2, f. 320, para. 60, 31 Jan. 1722.

[25] DB, vol. 101, f. 463, para. 36, 14 Feb. 1723.

[26] C & B. Abstr., vol. 2, f. 437, para. 53, 9 Jan. 1725. On 6 December 1718 the Bengal Council referred to Bishnudas as a weak brother of the family, the most unqualified, C & B. Abstr., vol. 2, f. 172, para. 35. But Benoy Ghose holds that Bishnudas was the son of Janardan and nephew of Baranasi Sett, Benoy Ghose, 'Some Old Family Founders', BPP, vol. 79, p.49.

enable him upon an emergency to assist our Hon'ble Masters
Affairs as Barnassoeseat did three years ago'.

As regards his capacity for the post, the Council pointed out that
it thought him as good as any of the rest and the trust Baranasi
Sett reposed in him by leaving him 'the sole Direction of his
affairs', showed the good opinion he had both of Bishnudas'
integrity and capacity.[27]

Notwithstanding this confidence in the new broker, and his
being presented with a 'seerpaw' and a horse as ordered by the
Court, his conduct was called into question as early as January
1728.[28] It was alleged that he, together with Umichand, a *dadni*
merchant, had engrossed most of the investments, especially of
the finer sorts, to the exclusion of most other merchants. On 21
July 1731, the Calcutta Council noted that the broker in collusion
with Umichand had monopolized under fictitious names 'much
the largest part of the Company's investment' and corrupted
most, if not all, black servants in the 'cottah'.[29] Two members of
the Council, Wastell and Bourchier, wanted the immediate
dismissal of Bishnudas. But the Council, led by President Deane,
gave the following reasons for not turning out the broker 'at this
season of the year':[30]

It is incontestable that the Merchants, who contract for
investment, borrow large sums of money to carry it on before
money is advanced, that many goods are purchased and that
the Broker must be engaged on that account for relations and
friends in a large sum of money and security for all the
Merchants in general, wherefore his being displaced will
immediately bring his creditors upon him and make advantages to themselves (at the several aurungs) by his disgrace.

It was further argued by the Council that only recently the
discredit of the Company's broker at Kasimbazar resulted in 'our
credit almost gone with the shroffs and entirely ruined with

---

[27] BPC, vol. 5, f. 568, 9 Nov. 1724.
[28] C & B. Abstr., vol. 2, f. 586, para. 54, 28 Jan. 1728.
[29] BPC, vol. 8, f. 419, 21 July 1731.
[30] BPC, vol. 8, ff. 434, 434vo, Annex. to Consult. 9 Aug. 1731.

Futtichund who was the only person that could assist us in any pressing occasion'.[31] This throws interesting light on the ramifications of the *dadni* system as also the delicately balanced credit mechanism on which the system was primarily based.

It is interesting to note that two members of the Calcutta Council, Humphreys Cole and Edward Carteret, submitted the results of their 'enquiry into the state of the Broker's affairs',[32] wherein they came to the conclusion that 'the charges against the broker were unfairly represented and insufficiently proved'. They had shown in their report that the names of the merchants in the *dadni* list were not fictitious, only sometimes the contract in the name of one particular merchant was fulfilled by another, sometimes a part of it and at other times the whole amount. Thus the contract in the name of Kunjabehari Sett 'who broke two years ago' was performed by Jagannath Sett and Gangacharan Basak. Similarly, the contract in the name of Santosh Ghose who became insolvent was carried out by Krishna Chandra Khan and Balaram Pramanick. There was practically nothing unusual in this sort of commercial practice which seems to have been quite in vogue during the period under review. We learn from the same report that Gangacharan Basak provided all the *soosies* contracted by Umichand while the latter supplied *Burron khasas* contracted by the former. As to the main leaders of the move to remove the broker, namely Samsundar Sett, Jagannath Sett and Paramananda Basak who complained that they had not received the sums allotted as *dadni* to them, the report retorted that it was because the money was given at their instance to several of their dependents, which the Broker was ready to prove, and that this had been the case for several years. Regarding the fact that the entire investment of Malda was given to Umichand and his brother Kissenchand, the report affirmed that they were the fittest men the broker knew for the procurement of those goods, and it was given to them as others were reluctant to contract for Malda goods.

However, in deference to the wishes of the Court of Directors, the Calcutta Council ultimately decided to remove Bishnudas Sett from the office of broker in March 1732, and

Samsundar Sett, the son of the former broker, Baranasi Sett, was appointed in preference to Jadu Sett because the latter's 'great age and Infirmity of body will oblige him to leave a great share of the management to his son, who none of us think fit in anything of that consequence'.[33] It is interesting to note that the office of the broker passed on from one member of the Sett family to another without hindrance. This only means that for the Company there was no option except seeking the assistance of the Sett family in procuring its investments in Bengal. Meanwhile the Court of Directors thus remonstrated to the Calcutta Council:[34]

> '... it appears that the greatest part of our Investment was provided by the relations and Freinds of the late Broker, you must be guarded against this practice, which is naturally attended with bad consequences on a supposition that you are guided by his Judgement in the sorting or pricing of our goods, and otherwise we don't see any use he is of, indeed it is alleged he is security for the money advanced to the merchants, but that amounts to a very great sum ... it would be much better to pay every individual merchant yourselves than to entrust a middle person.

The Directors were apprehensive that the broker and the servants of the Company bought goods on their own accounts and sold them to the Company at an advanced price which, if it had been the case, 'easily accounts for the high prices given for silk, gurrahs and other goods' provided both at Calcutta and Kasimbazar. So they laid down a standing rule that none of the covenant servants or brokers should be directly or indirectly concerned in the goods supplied to the Company. If anyone was found doing so, he would be dismissed from service. The

[33] Ibid., vol. 9, ff. 9-9vo, 13 March 1732; C & B. Abstr., vol. 3, f. 233, para. 4, 26 June 1732. Benoy Ghose holds that Samsundar was Bishnudas' eldest son but a Fort William General (C & B. Abstr. vol. 2, para. 82, 29 Nov. 1719) mentions categorically that Samsundar was Baranasi's son.

[34] DB, vol. 106, f. 182, para. 38, 29 Jan. 1734.

Directors also suggested the abolition of the post of broker.[35] The Calcutta Council stressed in its reply that it would guard against all the evils connected with investment as pointed out by the Court but 'as to having no broker cannot think it for the Company's Interest, it being certainly necessary to have some-body of Wealth and Reputation in that Capacity'.[36]

But the Court of Directors was hardly convinced and was now determined to abolish the post of broker. It is worth quoting at length from the letter it wrote to Calcutta touching upon the evils which grew out of the office of broker, and the reasons it gave for abolishing the post.[37]

> And whereas by means of our Brokers, several of our servants have been enabled to get credit amongst the shroffs and merchants to our great prejudice and loss, and we have good reason to believe that in all our factorys many other evils have been brought upon us in the course of Investments by their Influence. Therefore we do absolutely abolish the Said office of Broker, not only at Calcutta but also in our subordinate factorys, requiring you and all our Servants, to make our future contracts without the intervention of such a person, who by his influence and interest may not only abuse us in our Dadney, as has been formerly done, but also greatly prejudice us, by admitting or debarring merchants to or from transacting with us, who are not suited to his interest.

This raised considerable alarm both in Calcutta and Kasimbazar.

The Kasimbazar Council became very much concerned and wrote to Calcutta about the serious consequences the abolition of the broker's office would have in the procurement of investment as also the void it would create in the Company's relations with the government at a time when it was expecting a 'revolution' in the government. It pointed out further that the continuation of a broker was absolutely necessary for the safety of the Company's estate, and 'the security of their money and effects'.[38] The

[35] Ibid., vol. 106, f. 183, para. 41, 29 Jan. 1734.
[36] C & B. Abstr., vol. 4, ff. 66-67, para. 52, 24 Jan. 1735.
[37] DB, vol. 107, ff. 414-15, para. 17, 19, 21, 2 Feb. 1738.
[38] BPC, vol. 13, f. 429vo, 20 Dec. 1738; f. 456vo, 17 Jan. 1739.

Calcutta Council deliberated on the issue and came to the
conclusion that 'we cannot abolish that office here no more than
at Kasimbazar without running a great risk of the Company's
estate' and in view of the 'ill consequences that may attend our
contracting with private merchants without some such person
being security for the Dadney advanced them'.[39] So Samsundar
Sett was allowed to continue in the office of broker for the time
being and confirmed on 15 February 1739.[40] The Dhaka letter
to Calcutta pointing out the consequences of abolishing the
broker's post is revealing. The factors at Dhaka wrote that it 'will
be Irritating the great men at Dacca by whose intercession this
post [of broker] was given him [Manikchand] by which their
business may be prejudiced if not entirely stopped'.[41]

Meanwhile, the question whether the broker should be
retained or not was debated by the Calcutta Council, and in
January 1739 it wrote to the Court listing up the reasons in favour
of retaining the broker's office.[42] These reasons were: first, the
principal 'end' in employing a broker was to secure the *dadni*
advanced to the merchants and if the post was abolished, there
would be no security for the money advanced as the broker only
was responsible for the amount advanced. Secondly, the broker
only knew the real circumstances of the merchants and thus could
advise the Council as to who were the merchants to be trusted
with money. Thirdly, if the post was abolished, many parties
would arise among the merchants who could be suppressed 'by
a Man of Fortune and Figure being at the Head'. Fourthly,
'though some few merchants have indisputable fortunes yet
giving the investment to so few will be very prejudicial by their
advancing the prices more than a greater number can, who are
a check upon one another' and hence the neccesity for a large
number of *dadni* merchants over whom the broker should rule.

The Court of Directors, however, was insistent on abolishing
the office of the broker. In its general letter of 21 March 1740,
it wrote that the *dadni* charged to the Company's accounts as paid
to the merchants was not duly received by them and 'the Broker

[39] Ibid., vol. 13, f. 434, 23 Dec. 1738.

[40] For the Council's reasons for confirming Samsundar Sett, see C
& B. Abstr., vol. 4, f. 308, para. 99, 24 Dec. 1739.

[41] BPC, vol. 13, f. 324vo, 14 Aug. 1738.

[42] C & B. Abstr., vol. 4, ff. 285-86, para. 108-9, 29 Jan. 1739.

was doubtless Privy thereto'. It further alleged that the money was diverted to provide goods for the 'enormous' private trade of the Company's servants. 'And a Broker', the letter pointed out, 'is the Middle Person who cloaks all such collusions and malpractices, beside the Dustore of One Rupee nine annas percent, or whatever is allowed to the broker by the Merchants is a tax upon us, and our investment comes out so much dearer to us'.[43] Hence it enjoined upon the Calcutta Council that its earlier order directing to abolish the broker's post be absolutely complied with at Calcutta, Kasimbazar and other subordinate factories. It further directed the Council to procure the goods on the best and cheapest terms by contracting with the most reputable merchants.[44] The Calcutta Council at last decided on 3 January 1741 that the office of the broker would be abolished after that year's investment was completed and that it would henceforth contract for goods with the 'most substantial merchants'.[45] In July that year it informed the Court that it had finally decided to do away with the broker's office.[46] In December the Council called the merchants and informed them that the office of the broker was abolished, and to secure the Company from bad debts proposed that they should become 'jointly and separately bound one for the other for all sums advanced on Dadney', which the merchants refused. They presented three lists of merchants who proposed to be bound 'one for the other', with Samsundar Sett for the first list, Bishnudas Sett and Umichand the second, and Ramkrishna Sett for the third, 'who are esteemed men of fortune and credit which was agreed to'.[47]

Captain Fenwick who claimed to have been in the East India Company's service for thirty years emphasized in 1747-48 the necessity of employing a broker as 'the best times [regarding investments] have been under the management of the broker'. In advocating the re-appointment of the broker, he stated the important functions of the broker as follows:[48]

[43] DB, vol. 108, f. 155, para. 95, 21 March 1740.

[44] Ibid., vol. 108, f. 155, para. 96-97, 21 March 1740.

[45] C & B. Abstr., vol. 4, f. 348, para. 160, 3 Jan. 1741.

[46] Ibid., vol. 4, f. 372, para. 4, 26 July 1741.

[47] Ibid., vol. 4, f. 379, para. 98, 11 Dec. 1741.

[48] Orme Mss., India VI, f. 1513, Letter of Captain Fenwick on Company's affairs in Bengal.

I shall state the duty of a broker against the maxim of having none; as he ought to be an excellent merchant himself to know every merchant's Capacity, Integrity and Circumstances he introduces to the Council to be employed; for it is not sufficient that he is answerable for the contracts, as to the sums, but that such people do conduct their affairs, that the Company be not disappointed of any part of their Investments. He ought to be so good a judge of cloth, even to know at first sight in what part of the country every sortment is fabricated.

Interestingly enough, a few years later the Court of Directors revoked its earlier decision and asked the Calcutta Council to revive the office of broker. It wrote to Calcutta in January 1753: 'We have taken great pains to enquire into the utility of the office of a Broker at Calcutta and ... it appears to us that the reviving that office upon the old footing will be of great service to the Company, as it will be the best means of carrying on our investment with regard to the quantity, quality and price.'[49] And it empowered the Calcutta Council to appoint such a person as broker who 'from his circumstances, capacity and reputation may be the best able to serve us'. But by the time the suggestion reached Calcutta, the Company's pattern of investment had been changed from the *dadni* to *gomasta* system.[50] The Calcutta Council wrote back that 'such an office can be of no manner of use in the present model of conducting the business'.[51] Even as late as 1755, the Directors asked the Calcutta Council to revive the office of broker[52] but the *gomasta* system for the procurement of investment had by then been firmly established, and there was absolutely no scope for a broker in the new system of investment.

Kasimbazar Brokers

The Company's broker in Kasimbazar from about the second decade of the eighteenth century was a merchant named Kantu.

[49] DB, vol. 111, f. 537, para. 38, 24 Jan. 1753.

[50] For this change over and motives behind it, see chapter 5.

[51] C & B. Abstr., vol. 5, f. 428, para. 62, 3 Sept. 1753; Beng. Letters Recd., vol. 22, ff. 428-29; *FWIHC*, vol. 1, p. 692.

[52] DB, vol. 112, f. 214, para. 48, 23 Jan. 1755.

He claimed to have served seven chiefs at Kasimbazar but was brought to discredit in 1730 following his insolvency which resulted, as he alleged, from the extortions and undue privileges wrested from him by Stackhouse, the then chief of the Company at Kasimbazar. He was indebted to Fatechand Seth, the famous banker, to the tune of Rs 215,000 which he borrowed for the transactions of the Company's business. The Company seized Kantu's 'effects' but Fatechand insisted that Kantu be reinstated in the office of broker and that he be paid the sum owed to him by Kantu. The affair dragged on for some time and ultimately the Company paid Fatechand a part of his due but dismissed Kantu.[53] Fatechand knew well the importance of the position of a broker of the Company and objected to Kantu being called a 'Dellol'.[54] It appears from the proceedings of the Kasimbazar factory that Kantu was not only a broker to the Company but a substantial merchant on his own account, often freighting goods on European ships. In 1730 the proceeds of his *dosooties* sent to Manila amounted to Rs 4,053 which was appropriated by the Company following his dismissal.[55] He had connections with Calcutta investment too as we find that Baranasi Sett was his 'bondsman'.[56] As the Company's broker, the *dasturi* or commission on investment that he earned amounted to Rs 12,000 (at the rate of Re 1.9 ans. per cent) but the Calcutta Council observed that 'as he is to be esteem'd at the Durbar and the Country round as our Broker, he is obliged to live up to that character and the numerous family depending upon him will make that amount barely sufficient to defray his expenses'.[57]

The Kasimbazar Council dismissed Kantu in June 1730 and tried to appoint either Burro Datta or Hathu (Huttoo) Katma, the two substantial merchants of Kasimbazar but both refused on the plea that the season had far advanced for investment and that it would be impossible to make the investment unless the Company's dispute with Fatechand was resolved.[58] In October the Council

[53] For Kantu's affair, see BPC, vol. 8, ff. 203-3vo, 219, 226vo, 234-34vo, 236vo, 237, 248-48vo, 249-49vo, 256, 257-60.

[54] BPC, vol. 8, f. 257, 10 July 1730.

[55] Ibid., vol. 8, f.249vo, 22 June 1730.

[56] Ibid., vol. 8, f. 203, 28 April 1730.

[57] Ibid., vol. 8, f. 249-49vo, 22 June 1730.

[58] Ibid., vol. 8, f. 248vo, 22 June 1730.

sent for Burro Datta and apprised him of his being appointed
broker but was surprised to find that he declined accepting the
post directly, desiring time to consult his brother who was at
Hughli.[59] However, it ultimately appointed Hathu Katma, 'a man
of unquestionable credit and the properest person for that post'
as broker. He was also reported to be 'a man of considerable
estate' and his father, Nidhi Katma, offered to be his security.[60]
He enjoyed the position for some time but was dismissed in early
1737 following a complaint from Calcutta that he took four annas
per seer for Mr. Barker, the chief at Kasimbazar, on the silk
provided by the merchants, and the Calcutta Council ordered his
immediate removal and the appointment of a new broker.
Accordingly, Bally [Balai or Balaram] Katma was appointed
broker because of his 'great experience' in the Company's affairs
and the 'great wealth that is in his family'. His security bond was
signed by Benode Katma.[61] Balai Katma continued in the post
until 1741 when the office was altogether abolished in all the
factories in Bengal.

The Kasimbazar Council was very much concerned at the
abolition of the broker's office and wrote to Calcutta: '... consider
how impracticable it is for us to come at the knowledge of the
worth of any of the merchants here when there is no broker
whose interest it is to tell us the truth and such an one has many
ways to learn more exactly who are fit to be trusted than we can
possibly so....'[62] Even some time after the abolition of the broker's
post, the Kasimbazar Council wrote to the Court in 1748
underlining the bad effects of it:[63]

> ... the abolishing of the office of broker has been by
> experience found highly detrimental to your Honour's
> affairs, especially in contract for the investment, the mer-

---

[59] Ibid., vol. 8, f. 298, 5 Oct. 1730.

[60] Ibid., vol. 8, f.321, 7 Dec. 1730.

[61] Fact. Records, Kasimbazar, vol. 5, Consult. 5 Feb; 21 Feb; 19
March 1737; C & B. Abstr., vol. 4, f. 210, para. 4, 15 Feb. 1737; BPC,
vol. 12, f. 162, 16 April 1737.

[62] Fact. Records, Kasimbazar, vol. 6, Consult. 16 Sept. 1742.

[63] Beng. Letters. Recd., vol. 21, ff. 283-84, 10 Jan. 1748; BPC, vol.
19, f. 239, 15 May 1747; FWIHC, vol. 1, p. 232.

chants being come to such a pitch as to fix what prices they pleased on their goods, which evil they conceived could be cured by no other method than by a ruler over them, of Wealth and Credit of their own cast[e].

There can be hardly any doubt that the Indian brokers of the European companies played a crucial role in securing their investments and as such performed a significant function in the commercial life of Bengal in the first half of the eighteenth century. He was the essential link between the indigenous commercial agencies and the centralised investment organization of the European companies. Hume, the chief of the Ostend Company in Bengal, wrote in 1730:[64]

> The English and Dutch, who are the greatest Traders in this Country, do their business wholly by their Brokers who are their principal merchants. Notwithstanding they have numbers of Rich men Established in their bounds, who need no Security but they find their business the best regulated by having their Merchants act in Concert, by means of their Broker, everyone taking upon him according to his force, they know one another better than they can be known by Europeans.

But the broker notwithstanding, as Hume pointed out, the *dadni* merchants had to make the contracts in their own names, and the Company was at liberty to reject or receive the merchants known to be of credit and substance though not recommended by the broker. Hume elaborated further the advantages of the system: 'By which you secure yourselves from having a Cabal being formed among your Merchants, to prejudice you in the price of your goods.'[65]

The brokers also played a vital role in the relation between the European companies and the local administration. They often acted as mediators between the two parties and helped diffuse a crisis. The post of the broker was so important and

[64] Hume's 'Memorie', Stadsarchief Antwerp, General Indische Compagnie, 5769.
[65] Ibid.

significant that even the ruling elite took active interest in the appointment of a broker. The Companies, too, on their part always tried to appoint someone who had influence with the local administration or at the *darbar*. The point is clearly borne out by the fact that when Sabra, the Company's broker at Dhaka, died, the Council there reported that 'great solicitations have been made to us by the Dellols and Persons of the Greatest Importance' to appoint his nephew, Manikchand, as the broker. The Dhaka Council 'not being able to find out a more proper person having great Interest at the Durbar, worth some money and much esteem'd in the place' agreed on 27 January 1738 to appoint Manikchand as the broker at Dhaka.[66]

The above analysis of the activities of the brokers and their relation with the English Company brings to relief certain interesting aspects of the role played by them in the commercial sector of Bengal's economy. They were essentially middlemen who organized the procurement of the Company's investments, and though they were the Company's employees and as such subordinate to it, yet in no way subservient. They were not only mere brokers of the Company—that being only one facet of their activities—but merchants of repute and substantial credit, carrying on their own trade independent of the Company. This is well illustrated by the career of Baranasi Sett, Bishnudas Sett, Samsundar Sett, etc. The dismissal of Baranasi from the office of broker hardly affected his position as an independent merchant, and he carried on his trade quite independently and the Company was ultimately forced to re-employ him in the exalted office. Bishnudas' dismissal, too, had little effect on his own independent business, and later the Company accepted him as a 'substantial merchant' to be security for a group of merchants after the abolition of the broker's post. Samsundar, too, was regarded as a 'man of fortune and credit' by the Company even after he ceased to be a broker, and accepted him as security for another group of merchants. These brokers had, more often than not, a strong link with the ruling elite which sometimes even intervened in or tried to influence the appointment of a broker, as we have seen in the case of Bishnudas Sett in Calcutta and Manikchand in Dhaka. There can be hardly any doubt that men

[66] Fact. Records, Dacca, vol. 2, Consult. 27 Jan. 1738.

like Baranasi Sett, the English Company's broker at Calcutta, Indranarain Chaudhuri, the French Company's broker at Chandernagore and Harikrishna Roy, the Dutch Company's broker at Chinsurah, were men of considerable wealth and social eminence in Bengal in the first half of the eighteenth century.

4.2 PROBLEMS IN INVESTMENTS AND MEASURES ADOPTED

The European companies had to face many a problem in securing their investments in Bengal. One of the major problems throughout the period under review was a chronic shortage of working capital. The problem of inadequate funds for investments was accentuated by the poor demand for the European companies' imports into Bengal. Though the quantity of merchandise imported by the Companies was not generally large, the market for even this small amount was strictly limited. The only items for which there was a steady demand in Bengal were bullion and specie. But as their supply was seasonal and limited, the Companies had to explore additional means of financing their investments in Bengal. Moreover, the Companies had to confront some peculiar problems in Bengal in converting the bullion and specie into local currency. Another difficulty that the Companies had to face was to provide funds for investment in the proper season which generally started after the shipping season was over. As the price of most of the commodities went up considerably (sometimes even by 40 to 50 per cent)[67] during the time of shipping, the Companies had to start contracting for goods just after the departure of Europe-bound ships, that is, generally from February or March, and hence they always needed a stock to be left for such investments in India after paying for the previous year's supplies. Here we shall try to examine the various problems that the Companies had to encounter in securing their investments and the measures adopted to solve them.

[67] DB, 28 Jan. 1659, vol. 84, f. 411. The shipping season in Bengal was generally from September to February.

Chronic Shortage of Capital

The main problem which plagued the English Company as well
as the Dutch and the French was the chronic shortage of liquid
capital to secure the investments almost throughout the period.
After the ships from Europe had left by February or March at
the latest, and when it was the best time for giving out *dadni* for
next year's investment, the Companies were left with little money.
The problem was aggravated by the fact that often the Companies failed to pay the arrears due to the merchants for the
previous year's investment. Almost every year at this time, with
the departure of Europe-ships and the time for investment
approaching, the merchants would clamour on the one hand for
payment of their arrears for the previous year and an advance
for the next year's investment on the other. The Council of the
different European factories were often in a helpless position.
The Calcutta Council of the English Company noted in 1720 that
their merchants were 'very uneasy and daily complaining for
want of usual advancement on Dadney besides their last year's
arrears due to them'.[68] The situation was sometimes exasperating
as is apparent from the Fort William Consultations of 29 May
1721:[69]

> There being due ...[a large amount] to our merchants on
> balance of the past year's account and we having no money
> to clear off those balances or advance them on this year's
> contract ... they are very clamorous for either money or bills
> at Interest to be given them alleging they cannot perform the
> new contract without being forced to borrow all the money
> they can get at Interest to send to the aurungs.

The problem continued to plague the Company. Even as late as
8 August of the same year (1721), the Council noted in
desperation: 'We as yet having no news of any ship from England
Our Merchants are very clamorous for the Dadney to be
advanced them on the goods contracted for this year, and insist

---

[68] BPC, vol. 4, f. 274, 18 Aug. 1720.
[69] Ibid., vol. 4, ff. 404vo-405, 29 May 1721.

upon giving them Bills of Debt for that and the Balance of their last year's account.'[70]

Local Credit Market

Naturally, the Companies had no other way of solving the problem of shortage of working capital but by borrowing from the local credit market. Luckily for the Companies, the credit market in Bengal was highly organized and efficiently managed. There was indeed a remarkable growth of the financial machinery for credit and exchange, and the specialized activities of a large class of merchants, especially the *shroffs*, undoubtedly point towards the fact that merchant capital and commercial organization were highly developed in early eighteenth century Bengal. So the European companies tried to solve the problem of acute shortage of working capital by borrowing heavily from the local money market. Though there is no systematic account of the amount borrowed yearly in different factories, quite a few references here and there in the Company records give an indication of the sum borrowed at different times in different factories.

Towards the beginning of the eighteenth century, the English Company's debts to merchants in Calcutta and Kasimbazar at certain specific dates amounted to around Rs 0.7 million and Rs 0.25 million respectively.[71] In 1720/21 the Company's debt in Bengal amounted to Rs 2.4 million while the amount of debt turned out to be Rs 5.5 million in 1747/48, exclusive of interest.[72] The Dutch Company also borrowed from the local capital market. Its debt to the Kasimbazar merchants (with interest) in September 1724 amounted to around Rs 1.5 million.[73] Even at the risk of a little digression, it is worthwhile to have a close look at

[70] Ibid., vol. 4, f. 432, 8 Aug. 1721.

[71] S. Chaudhuri, *Trade and Commercial Organization*, p. 114. For the Company's borrowings and debts in Calcutta and Kasimbazar in the first two decades of the 18th century, see Ibid., pp. 114-116.

[72] DB, vol. 101, f. 372, para. 32, 21 Dec. 1722; C & B. Abstr., vol. 5, f. 117, para. 261, 10 Jan. 1748.

[73] VOC, 2030, ff. 156-158, 16 March 1725; all fractions are rounded off to the nearest figures.

the names of the merchants to whom the Dutch Company was indebted. It is a pity that the list which could have thrown significant light on the social composition of the merchants and the regions they came from gives only the first names of most of the merchants, leaving us in the dark about their last names. Yet the list provides us with certain interesting clues. Though names are often mentioned such as Ramnath, Jadu, Kunja, Kartick, Paran, etc. (typical Bengali names), luckily enough the Katmas are mentioned with their full names.[74] The list mentions names like Lahorimal, Onupchand, Teakchand, Bhirguram, etc. who probably came from other parts of India (both Western and Northern India). But the most interesting part is that we find Punjabi merchants with the surname of Kapur (Caporeij in Dutch, Coppree in English records) whom we meet for the first time in the records.

Among the main creditors of the Dutch Company, the house of Jagat Seth is unfailingly there even in that early period. In two separate entries on 1 September 1724, the credit of the house to the Company totalled Rs 0.26 million.[75] The Katmas did not lag far behind. According to the list, wherein there are as many as 8 Katmas, the Company owed them Rs 206,794.[76]

Coming back to the story of the borrowings by the European companies, we find the Ostend and the French also borrowed freely from the local capital market. The Ostend Company was lent money by the local *shroffs* and merchants. Alexander Hume reported in 1730 that among other merchants, Nainsook Babu, a near relation of Jagat Seth Fatechand, had lent large sums of money to the Company.[77] Similarly, the French too relied heavily on the local money market for securing their investment. Fatechand was indispensable to them as their most important

[74] One wonders why—was it because the Katmas were the most influential merchants and trading family, specialized in money lending and trade in silk and silk piece-goods?

[75] VOC, 2030, ff. 156-57, HB 16 March 1725. The house used to lend money in the name of Jagat Seth but sometimes also in the name of and referred to as Manickchand and Anandchand, or simply Anandchand. Also see chapter 5.

[76] VOC, 2030, ff. 156-57, HB 16 March 1725.

[77] Hume's 'Memorie'.

money lender. Though Dupleix described Fatechand as the 'greatest of Jews' and 'our chopping-block', he had to seek often loans of one to three hundred thousand rupees from him. He had to borrow money also from the rich and powerful family of merchants and money-lenders of Kasimbazar—the Katmas.[78] Of course, the most substantial lender to the European companies was the house of Jagat Seth. Even in the early years between 1718 and 1730, the English Company borrowed from the Jagat Seths at Murshidabad on an average more than 0.4 million rupees a year.[79] In the three years between 1755 and 1757, the Dutch debt to the house of Jagat Seth amounted to Rs 2.4 million.[80] In 1757 alone the Dutch borrowed 0.4 million rupees from the Seths and the French debt at the time of the fall of Chandernagore in March 1757 amounted to one and a half million rupees.[81] Captain Fenwick estimated the French debt in 1747-48 to be 'upward of 17 lakhs' (1.7 million) while Watts wrote to Clive on 18 February 1757 that the French owed some 1.3 million rupees to the Seths.[82]

Though the English Company borrowed money locally in all the factories in Bengal, Kasimbazar was one of the main centres where it procured money freely for investments. The reason was two-fold: first, a lot of the Company's investment was made here; secondly, because of the presence of a large number of big merchants and *shroffs* from various parts of India in Kasimbazar which was the most important trade mart in Bengal in the first half of the eighteenth century, money was easily available. The Council at Kasimbazar often borrowed quite a large amount of money for securing the investments at the proper season. Thus we find in March 1728 that it borrowed Rs 0.4 million for giving advances for investments.[83] But the Court was not very happy with this large amount of borrowing at a high rate of interest. It

[78] Indrani Ray, 'Some Aspects of French Presence in Bengal, 1731-40', *CHJ*, vol. 1, No. 1, July 1976, p. 99-101.

[79] J.H. Little, *Jagat Seth*, p. X (Introduction by N.K. Sinha); see also Kantu Papers, BPC, vol. 8, f. 256, Annex. to Consult, 29 June 1730.

[80] Computed from VOC, vol. 2874.

[81] J. H. Little, *Jagat Seth*, p. XI, Introduction by N.K. Sinha.

[82] Orme Mss., India VI, f. 1525; Watt's letter to Clive, 18 Feb. 1757, quoted in S.C. Hill, *Bengal in 1756-57*, vol. II, p. 229.

[83] BPC, vol. 6, f. 564vo, 12 March 1728.

wrote to Calcutta with great concern that 'upwards of 4,000 £ sterling was paid for interest' at Kasimbazar during the year May 1730 to April 1731, besides Rs 643,832 'running at the extravagant rate of twelve percent per annum from that time' and that the Kasimbazar factors had borrowed another Rs 257,180 afterwards. It asked the Calcutta Council that the high rate of interest (at 12 per cent) which was 'canker to the Company's estate' should be rooted out.[84]

But despite all the reprimands from the Directors, the different factories in Bengal borrowed heavily from the local credit market almost throughout the period under study. Even as late as 1745, the Company's debt at Calcutta amounted to Rs 0.9 million whereas in Kasimbazar and Dhaka it was computed at 1 million rupees.[85] The English debt at Dhaka in 1749 amounted to Rs 755,400. Of this amount as big a sum as Rs 584,000 was due to the house of Jagat Seth and the rest to several other *shroffs*.[86] In Calcutta in the course of a single day in 1743 the English Company borrowed a sum of Rs 825,000 from the *dadni* merchants.[87] And just a week later, the Company borrowed from the Jagat Seths a sum of Rs 326,750 for paying advances for its investments.[88]

In this connection, it should be emphasized that the mainstay of the capital market in Bengal in the first half of the eighteenth century was the famous banking house of the Jagat Seth. The house itself had grown gradually into a great financial institution during the period under review.[89] It came to the rescue of the European companies which, as we have seen earlier, suffered from a chronic shortage of working capital. So they borrowed heavily and freely from the house. The extent of the reliance on this banking house by the English Company will be evident from

[84] DB, vol. 105, ff. 688-89, para. 100, 6 Feb. 1733; C & B. Abstr., vol. 3, para. 86, f. 345, 2 Dec. 1733.

[85] C & B. Abstr., vol. 5, f. 59, para. 18, 11 Aug. 1745.

[86] Fact. Records, Dacca, Consult. 8 Sept. 1749.

[87] BPC, vol. 16, f. 177, 6 June 1743.

[88] Ibid., vol. 16, ff. 184vo, 203vo, 13 June 1743.

[89] For a detailed study of the rise and growth of the banking house of the Jagat Seths and the role of these Seths in the economic and political life of Bengal, see chapter 5.

the fact that even in the subordinate factory at Dhaka where the investment was quite small compared to that in Calcutta and Kasimbazar, it borrowed a sum of Rs 470,000 in the period between 3 December 1744 and 20 October 1745.[90] In Kasimbazar the Company owed the Seths an amount of Rs 836,037 in 1746 and Rs 630,213 including interest in 1748.[91] Even in 1751 the English debt to the banking house in Kasimbazar amounted to Rs 562,820.[92] In Calcutta on one single occasion in 1742 the Calcutta Council borrowed Rs 0.2 million from the Jagat Seths.[93] The Company preferred to borrow from Jagat Seth Fatechand 'as he might prove serviceable at the Durbar'.[94]

The Jagat Seths lent money to the Europeans at the rate of 12 per cent per annum which was the prevalent rate at the time. But consequent to a request from the English Company to reduce the rate of interest to 9 per cent, the banking house lowered the rate accordingly in 1740.[95] Following this the interest rate charged by other shroffs and bankers was also reduced to 9 per cent.[96] But still the Company preferred to borrow from the Seths. The Kasimbazar Council noted in 1741: 'Futtychund having favoured us in lowering the Interest and as we are apprehensive he may be displeased, should we take up money of other people and so raise the interest again on us, agreed that we give him preference'.[97]

Generally, the practice was to borrow money from merchants and shroffs in large amounts either at Calcutta or Kasimbazar, and then to send the money to the subordinate factories in cash or by bills of exchange.[98] As the biggest creditor of the Company was the house of Jagat Seth which had its kuthis[99] in all the trade marts of Bengal (and also in most trade centres all over India), the

[90] Fact. Records, Dacca, vol. 2, Consult. 30 July 1746.
[91] Fact. Records, Kasimbazar, vol. 7, Consults. 15 April 1746; 22 Aug. 1748.
[92] Fact. Records, Kasimbazar, vol. 10, Consult. 11 Nov. 1751.
[93] BPC, vol. 15, f. 84vo, 29 March 1742.
[94] C & B. Abstr., vol. 3, f. 345, para. 86, 26 Dec. 1733.
[95] BPC, vol. 14, ff. 317, 317vo, 11 Dec. 1740; f. 337, 26 Dec. 1740.
[96] Ibid., vol. 14, f. 338, 26 Dec. 1740.
[97] Fact. Records, Kasimbazar, vol. 6, Consult. 5 Feb. 1741.
[98] See chapter 5.
[99] Agency house, subordinate office.

Company borrowed from the house in all the subordinate factories. But as mentioned earlier, the Company also freely borrowed from other *shroffs* and merchants. It is interesting to find that in Calcutta many of the merchants from whom the Company quite often borrowed money were themselves *dadni* merchants of the Company.

It is significant to note that not only did the merchants, bankers and *shroffs* lend money to the European companies, but often members of the ruling elite too invested money with these Companies. The most conspicuous case of such money lending by the ruling class, as could be found in the records, is that of Kissendeb Poddar who was the *diwan* of Hakim Beg, the *pachotra daroga*,[100] and an important member of the administration.[101] This Kissendeb was reported to have had great influence on the nawab and Hakim Beg, and a 'person of very great interest and authority in the government'.[102] He lent the English Company in Kasimbazar an amount of Rs 335,000 on different dates between 2 January 1750 and 16 August 1753.[103] It appears that most of the money that Kissendeb lent the Company belonged to his master Hakim Beg. Perhaps that is why after Kissendeb's death, Hakim Beg demanded from the Company in Kasimbazar the repayment of an interest note due to Kissendeb for Rs 100,000 [principal] and the Kasimbazar Council paid the amount with interest to Hakim Beg on 31 May 1754.[104]

[100] *Daroga* of the customs houses. Jan Karseboom, the chief of the Dutch Company in Bengal, described Hakim Beg in 1755 as 'Daroga van de Pansjoutra of tholplaatsen' (Daroga of Pachotra or Tollplaces [custom houses]), and 'een grote favoriet van den Nawab' (a great favourite of the Nawab), VOC, 2862, ff. 125vo, 127vo.

[101] He emerged as the key figure in the nawab's relations with the English Company when Alivardi gave him the charge of the nawab's relations with the Europeans in Bengal in 1750. BPC, vol. 23, f. 306vo, 25 Aug. 1750.

[102] Fact. Records, Kasimbazar, vol. 10, 10 Oct. 1751; vol. 11, 2 Dec. 1751.

[103] Computed from Fact. Records, Kasimbazar, vols. 9, 10, 12.

[104] Fact. Records, Kasimbazar, vol. 12, Consults. 4 May 1753; 31 May 1754.

Problems in Borrowing

There is little doubt that the capital market in Bengal eased to a great extent the European companies' problem of chronic shortage of working capital for investments. But it was not all smooth sailing for the Companies as they had to face various problems in borrowing from the.local money market.

Short term Loans

One of the main difficulties in borrowing from Bengal's credit market was that as a general rule money was lent only on a short term basis throughout the period under review, and there was no tradition of long term loan. As a result, the *shroffs* and merchants, including the banking house of Jagat Seth, demanded money as soon as the ships from Europe arrived with their supply of treasure. It was as impossible for the Companies to repay so many creditors as it was to pay the merchants' arrears. Even the Jagat Seths often threatened the Companies with stoppage of their business if their money was not repaid at the usual time. The English factory at Dhaka reported in November 1749 that Jagat Seth Mahtab Rai's *gomasta* 'absolutely insisted on the payment of the sum due to his master threatening in rough terms that in case of non-payment he would immediately put a stop to our Business'.[105] In Kasimbazar in 1749, it was with great difficulty that the Company could borrow from the Seths Rs 120,000 which it agreed to pay the nawab in connection with the dispute of the Armenian ships.[106] The Kasimbazar Council wrote to Calcutta that the Seth's *gomasta* Ruidas 'complained heavily of our not having paid them anything this season of the large debt the Company owed them at that factory notwithstanding so much treasure had been imported by several ships lately arrived'.[107] The Seths were often importunate in recovering their money and insisted on the loan being repaid with the arrival of the ships— something which put the Company into great inconvenience.

[105] Fact. Records, Dacca, vol. 3, 9 Nov. 1749; BPC, vol. 22, f. 420, 15 Nov. 1749.

[106] See chapters 3 and 5.

[107] BPC, vol. 22, ff. 338-338vo, 20 Oct. 1749.

The Kasimbazar letter of 25 August 1750 illustrates the point clearly.[108]

> ...the Seats on the arrival of the treasure sent to demand it and gave them to understand and they expected the whole of their debt at that factory should be paid off out of the money which might arrive by this year's shipping and instead of being able to raise a further credit with them it was with the utmost difficulty they could obtain their consent to apply any part of what was lately sent them to the use of the investment ....

The desperate situation that sometimes the factors were confronted with is amply clear from the Dhaka letter wherein the factors reported in 1751 that the *gomasta* of the Seths insisted that the 'whole of the Debt to be immediately paid him' and they requested the Kasimbazar Council to prevail on Seth Mahtab Rai not to insist on the payment of any of the money that it might send them 'as it would stop their business and render it unpracticable for them to purchase any Ready money goods'.[109] A close study of the Company records reveals that in Bengal during this period money was lent only for short term, generally for a few months and the interest was calculated at a monthly rate, and the loan not carried generally beyond a year.

Occasional Scarcity

The Companies' problem was aggravated by the fact that there was occasional scarcity in the credit market resulting from various factors, the most important of which was the reluctance of the money-merchants and *shroffs* to show up money for fear of exactions by the government. Though this was true in general for the whole period under review, it became more acute in the wake of the Maratha invasions of Bengal in the 1740s and the early 1750s. Even the great banking house of the Jagat Seth was not free from the fear psychosis. Of course, one should remember

[108] Ibid., vol. 23, f. 303vo, 25 Aug. 1750.
[109] Beng. Letters Recd., vol. 22, f. 117; NAI, Home Misc., vol. 16, p. 189, para. 83, Letters to Court, Feb. 1751; C & B. Abstr., vol. 5, f. 275.

that the nawab, Alivardi Khan, harassed by the Maratha incursions, was badly in need of money to raise and maintain a large army, and tried to get it from whatever source he could. So, though very good friends of the nawab, the Seths were quite scared of Alivardi's extortions. This is evident from the Kasimbazar letter of 1746: ' ... they have not a prospect of borrowing more ... for the scarcity of money is so great that it has been with some difficulty Futtichand's house has been able to pay for the bullion sold them....'[110] The Kasimbazar Council further added that ' it appears to us that if they [the Seths] have money, they don't care to produce it for fear of the Government'. If this was the position of the Seths who were the closest ally of the nawab and who wielded so much power in the political and economic life of Bengal during this period, one can well imagine the inclinations of other *shroffs* and money merchants.

An important factor behind the occasional scarcity of money in Bengal's capital market was the fact that the availability of money depended to a large extent on the rate of exchange with Agra. If the latter rate was high, money would become scarce in Bengal, the reason being that the *shroffs* and money merchants would then employ their money in the exchange to Agra, which was more profitable than lending even at 12 per cent. This was the general pattern of the money market in Bengal throughout the second half of the seventeenth century and the early decades of the eighteenth. Our point is well borne out by the letter of the Kasimbazar Council which noted in 1700: 'We cannot get any money at interest here being very little ready money in the country and the exchange current from hence to Delhi and Agra is but 6 percent and the shroffs make use of what ready money they have that way.'[111] From about the third decade, however, one does not find reference in the records to money being employed in the exchange to Agra. Probably by this time the banking house of the Jagat Seth had already extended its sway in the money and exchange marts of Northern India which perhaps resulted in a stability in the market, and the wide fluctuation in the exchange rate was controlled.

[110] Fact. Records, Kasimbazar, vol. 7, Consult. 22 June 1746; BPC, vol. 18, f. 265vo, 30 June 1746.
[111] Fact. Records, Calcutta, vol. 10, pt. II, f.92.

High Rate of Interest

The high rate of interest, which was the prevailing rate in Bengal till 1740, was quite a deterrent to the Companies' borrowing in the local money market. The Home authorities always discouraged taking money at 12 per cent which they considered 'exorbitant' and hence 'rank poison' to their commerce. They often advised the different factories to 'desist' from running into debt, 'the interest of which eats deep and insensibly'.[112] But as we have noted, the servants of the Companies in Bengal could hardly avoid borrowing money and accepted the high interest rate as a necessary evil.

Though the house of Jagat Seth and consequently other *shroffs* reduced the rate of interest to 9 percent in 1740, it was often difficult for the English Company to borrow money at that rate, especially in the subordinate factories. Taking advantage of the helpless condition of the Company, the merchants and *shroffs* occasionally tried to impose a higher rate of interest. The Dhaka factors wrote in August 1746 that 'as we find it will be impossible for us to raise any more money here under the rate of 12 percent per annum Interest', they desired the Calcutta Council's permission to borrow money at that rate of interest.[113] The latter wrote back immediately that it 'positively ordered that on no acocunt they give more than 9 percent for money at interest for it would be of utmost ill consequence to our Honble Masters should they give a higher premium to any one person and we doubt not that who have money to spare will let them have it at the same rate as we get everywhere else'.[114] But the Dhaka factors replied on 16 September 1746 that they saw no possibility of borrowing money at 9 percent 'having already tried all the shroffs in the place who insist on 12 percent'.[115] Even as late as 12 October they wrote to Calcutta that 'they are sorry to inform us that all their endeavours to obtain money from the shroffs of that place at the rate of 9 percent per annum have been fruitless'.[116]

---

[112] DB, vol. 95, f. 519, 18 Jan. 1705.

[113] Fact. Records, Dacca, vol. 2, Consult. 19 August 1746.

[114] BPC, vol. 18, f. 354vo, 5 Sept. 1746.

[115] Fact. Records, Dacca, vol. 2, Consult. 16 Sept. 1746.

[116] BPC, vol. 18, f. 391vo, 12 Oct. 1746.

The Calcutta Council believed that the situation in Dhaka would improve with the arrival of the ships from Europe with treasure. So when three ships from Europe arrived in October, it wrote to Dhaka that 'we hope the arrival of these ships will give them credit to Borrow money at the usual rate'.[117] But the Dhaka factors reported in November that they 'can get no credit there'.[118] There was no improvement in the situation even in 1747 when the factors from Dhaka reported that they could borrow no money there under 12 per cent interest rate.[119] On the contrary, the situation deteriorated as no ships from Europe arrived even by November. The Dhaka factory wrote that 'no one being willing to lend them a single rupee their credit being quite gone, none of the Company's ships arriving with any treasure'.[120] However, with the arrival of five ships from Europe with treasure, the Calcutta Council hoped 'it will raise their credit to enable them to go on with the Investment'.[121] But that was not to be. The Dhaka factory reported in January 1748 that without a supply of money either from Calcutta or Kasimbazar 'it will be impossible to send down any Goods this season as they could get no money there'.[122]

4.3 DIFFICULTIES IN MINTING AND SELLING BULLION

Minting

The problem would have been much less severe for the Companies if they could coin freely the treasure which was imported to Bengal to pay for the export commodities. But despite their best efforts almost throughout the period, the Companies failed to obtain free minting privileges in Bengal. The main obstacle to such a privilege to the Companies was the house of Jagat Seth which, it appears, from the early third decade of

[117] Ibid., vol. 18, f. 408, 16 Oct. 1746.
[118] Ibid., vol. 18, f. 434, 11 Nov. 1746.
[119] Ibid., vol. 20, f. 76vo, 31 July 1747.
[120] Ibid., vol. 20, f. 235vo, 24 Nov. 1747.
[121] Ibid., vol. 20, f. 283vo, 28 Dec. 1747.
[122] NAI, Home Misc., vol. 13, f. 85, para. 70, Letter to Court, 10 Jan. 1748; Beng. Letters Recd., vol. 21, f. 237; *FWIHC*, vol. 1, pp. 203-4.

the eighteenth century monopolized the business of the mint.
The English factors at Dhaka reported as early as January 1722
that they tried to obtain the use of the mint but 'Futtichund
Shroff who it is said Trades for the Nabob hindered, fear it will
never be granted, the Nabob gets so much by it'.[123] Nonetheless,
the Court of Directors urged the Calcutta Council to try to secure
the privilege of minting coins and wrote in one of its letters:[124]

> We hope our now constituted President and Council will give
> us a convincing specimen of their ability and zeal for our
> Service among other things in obtaining the grant of
> Coynage We have so often and with such earnestness prest
> you to endeavour and shew'd you the loss we suffered and
> wherein in the sale of Silver and by the batta on our Madras
> rupees we can't add thereto.

But all the efforts on the part of the Company came to nothing.
Alexander Hume wrote in 1730 that he did not earnestly try for
the minting privilege 'lest the Company lost a good friend in
Fatechand who has the Tansal [Taksal - mint] wholly in his
hands'.[125]

The Company's servants in Bengal, however, did not desist
from trying to secure coining privileges at the Murshidabad mint.
But they were at the same time conscious of the reality of the
situation. Thus the Calcutta Council 'forbid' Patna in 1741 from
applying to the *darbar* at Delhi for the 'liberty of the mint' as this
would be of no use so long as Fatechand Seth was alive and 'in
these unsettled times'.[126] Next year, the Kasimbazar Council
suggested that in view of the government's great need for money
to ward off the Marathas, 'possibly a sum properly applied might
even procure the liberty of the mint'.[127] But after serious
consideration it gave up the idea because such a step might
'exasperate Futtichand so far as to make him impede the

[123] C & B Abstr., vol. 2, f. 321, para. 77, 31 Jan. 1722.
[124] DB, vol. 101, f. 162, para. 56, 16 Feb. 1722.
[125] Hume's Memoire.
[126] C & B Abstr., vol. 4, f. 336, para. 124, 3 June 1741.
[127] BPC, vol. 15, f. 334vo, 19 Oct. 1742.

Company's business'.[128] Even as late as 1753 William Watts wrote from Kasimbazar that the establishment of a mint at Calcutta 'could not be effected with the Nabob as it would be overset by Jagatseat ... as he is a great gainer by being the sole purchaser of all Bullion imported'.[129] Though the Company secured the privilege of establishing a mint in Calcutta by the Treaty of Alinagar (February 1756), and established its protectorate over Bengal following the battle of Plassey (June 1757), the Seths still remained the main obstacle to the Company's minting of coins. The Bengal General Letter to the Court of Directors pointed out in December 1759 that as the coining of *siccas* in Calcutta interfered so much with the interest of the Seths that 'they will not fail of throwing every obstacle in our way to deprecate the value of our money in the country, notwithstanding its weight and standard is in every respect as good as the *siccas* of Murshidabad so that a loss of Batta will always arise on our money, let our influence at the Durbar be ever so great'.[130] Of course, soon the story was very different—the Seths approaching their doom fast, and the English having the stranglehold over the political and economic life of Bengal.

Selling Bullion

The European companies would have been in a much better position than they actually were, had it been possible for them to sell the imported treasure in the open market or pay for their investments in bullion. But as a result of the virtual monopoly of the mint business by the house of Jagat Seth, they were forced to sell their treasure imported to Bengal, both bullion and specie, to the banking house. The *dadni* merchants, too, were in general reluctant to accept bullion for their supplies, and only occasion-

---

[128] C & B. Abstr., vol. 4, f. 430, para. 8, 30 Jan. 1743; BPC, vol. 16, f. 92, 29 March 1743.

[129] Ibid., vol. 5, f. 399, 12 Feb. 1753; Beng. Letters Recd., vol. 22, ff. 384-85, 8 Feb. 1753.

[130] NAI, Public Letters to Court , s. no. 6, f. 25, para. 60, Bengal General Letter to the Court of Directors, 29 Dec. 1759.

ally and very rarely agreed to be paid in bullion.[131] In 1746 the
English Company offered bullion to the merchants in payment
of what was 'due to them on account the investment' but they
refused it alleging that nothing but 'Rupees would pass at the
aurungs [and] that they could no ways turn the Bullion into
Rupees but by selling it to Juggutseat's House who they were well
assured would not buy it of them'.[132] Obviously, the Companies
had little choice but to sell the bullion to the Jagat Seths and they
had to accept whatever price the house offered.

Though according to an estimate of Hedges (the then
President in Bengal) and Feake in 1718, 240 *sicca* weight of
English standard silver produced nearest to $218 \, ^3/_4$ *sicca* rupees,
and the *shroffs* and merchants received *sicca* Rs 210 : 7 : 9 for 240
sicca weight of silver after paying 5 per cent custom duties, the
house of Jagat Seth generally paid Rs 203 for 240 sicca weight.[133]
On a visit to the Kasimbazar factory in September 1743,
Fatechand Seth informed the English that the Nawab had tried
the French silver in his own presence and adjusted the value at
205 *siccas* for 240 *sicca* weight, and that if he found the English
silver of the same fineness, he would allow the same rate to them.
The Calcutta Council advised Kasimbazar to agree to the rate and
to dispose of the bullion 'lying dead' (125 chests) there which
would help them to pay the debts and lessen the 'heavy load of
interest'.[134]

Fatechand made a trial of the English silver at the mint in
November 1743 and submitted the valuation made at the mint
as also the rates at which he would take it.[135]

---

[131] C & B. Abstr., vol. 5, f. 69, para. 14, 4 Feb. 1746; f. 80, para.
66, 30 Nov. 1746; BPC, vol. 24, f. 49, 31 Jan. 1751. Occasionally,
however, Umichand and some of the substantial *dadni* merchants were
paid in bullion as is evident from the records of the Company.

[132] Beng. Letters Recd., vol. 21, ff. 49-50, para. 66, 30 Nov. 1746.

[133] C & B. Abstr., vol. 2, f. 175, para. 62, 6 Dec. 1718; vol. 4, f. 454,
para. 46, 13 Feb. 1744.

[134] BPC, vol. 16, ff. 272vo-273vo, 19 Sept. 1743.

[135] Ibid., vol. 16, f. 332vo, 9 Nov. 1743.

Estimates	Value in the Mint	Fatechand's rate
Pillar Dollars @	206 siccas per 240 @ sicca weight	204 siccas per 240 sicca weight
Mexico Dollar @	205 siccas per 240 @ sicca weight	203 siccas per 240 sicca weight
French Crowns @	207 siccas per 240 @ sicca weight	205 siccas per 240 sicca weight
Duccatoons	2 : 7 : 3 siccas each	2 : 6 : 9 siccas each

As the English silver consisted mainly of Mexico dollars, this rate was lower than what Fatechand said he would take at. While the Kasimbazar Council made representation to him, he shrewdly replied that he had not then tried the silver and that he would expect some profit over the value of the mint for his troubles which he thought 'little enough in the price he proposed to give'.[136] The Calcutta Council advised Kasimbazar that if representation to Fatechand proved 'ineffectual', then they should let him have the silver but at the same time 'to acquaint him that we cannot think of importing any more silver if this is to be made a precedent of'.[137] Fatechand knew well that the Company was bound to import treasure in order to pay for its investments in Bengal, and hence was least concerned with the English representation. The French and the Dutch, too, were in the same difficulty. The Kasimbazar Consultation of 18 November 1743 noted: 'The French are in the same dilemma as us having their bullion in the Factory without being able to come to terms with him [Jagat Seth Fatechand] nor have the Dutch coined a Rupee having had a dispute with the Government which is not yet adjusted.'[138]

The Court of Directors, knowing little as it did about Bengal's money market, thought of some alternative measures of freeing from the clutches of Fatechand Seth. It instructed the Calcutta Council in 1745 in the following manner:[139]

[136] Ibid., vol. 16, ff. 332vo-333, 9 Nov. 1743.
[137] Ibid., vol. 16, f. 333, 9 Nov. 1743.
[138] Fact. Records, Kasimbazar, vol. 6, Consult. 18 Nov. 1743.

> By delivering our silver to the merchants at the current value
> as part of their dadney, it may prevent Fatehchund's
> lowering it according to his will and pleasure, on his shuffling
> in such an unheard of manner. Some of the other great
> shroffs should have been tryed, whereas offers being made
> to him only, flung the Power wholly into his hands off getting
> it at his own price.

But as we have seen earlier, the *dadni* merchants were almost
'averse' to take bullion in lieu of their supplies and no other *shroff*
would even dare buy bullion from the Company.

The death of Fatechand in 1744, the Court earnestly hoped,
would change the situation for the better and it expected that the
Company's bullion would now yield a higher price through
Bengal Council's 'prudent management of his young successors
in the Business'.[140] But unfortunately for the Directors, that was
not to be, as will be seen shortly. Fatechand's successors, Jagat
Seth Mahtab Rai and Maharaja Swaroopchand actually tried to
reduce the rate that was allowed by their grandfather. In June
1745 the Company requested the Seths to buy the bullion
imported recently which they 'agreed to take at the prices paid
for the last provided we will send it up there [Kasimbazar] for
they will receive it nowhere else'. When the Kasimbazar Council
proposed to them 'to raise the price to what Futtichund formerly
paid' for the Company's silver, they absolutely refused to
advance anything on the last price alleging that it was not owing
to them but due to the government that the price was lowered.[141]
Again in June 1746, the English wanted to sell their silver but
Swaroopchand offered no more than the 'last price given namely
203 sicca rupees for 240 sicca weight'.[142] In October of the same
year the Seths agreed to take English bullion but refused to give
'more than last year'. The Calcutta Council assessed the situation

---

[139] DB., vol. 108, f. 288, para. 15, 7 Feb. 1745.
[140] Ibid., vol. 109, f. 463, para. 19, 7 May, 6 & 12 June 1746.
[141] BPC, vol. 17, f. 604, 13 June 1745.
[142] Ibid., vol. 18, ff. 265vo-266, 30 June 1746.

well and wrote to Kasimbazar: 'We cannot pretend to dispute the price of bullion with Futtichund's house at this time and that we agree to let them have it at the price of last year.'[143]

Soon the Jagat Seths raised another difficulty for the Company in the sale of its imported treasure. The Kasimbazar Council reported to Calcutta in November 1746 that Seth Mahtab Rai had started an objection to Kasimbazar price of silver at the rate of 203 *siccas* for 240 *sicca* weight, stating that as he received the bullion in Calcutta he was expected to pay no more for it than what it was sold for there. If the Company wanted the Kasimbazar price, he was to be allowed the charges of sending the silver from Calcutta to Kasimbazar.[144] The Calcutta Council advised Kasimbazar to acquaint him that his *gomasta* demanded earlier the charges of carrying the silver to Kasimbazar but later on relinquished the demand. At the same time it urged Kasimbazar Council 'in case he persists in requiring it of them, they must agree to it rather than alter the price of the bullion'.[145]

Next year the Seths refused to pay more than Rs 201 *siccas* for 240 *sicca* weight 'alleging by way of excuse to the imposition that the profit thereon is not near so great as formerly occasioned by Rupees being made of finer silver than usual'.[146] The Calcutta Council wrote in utter desperation that 'we must submit thereto as we had it not in our power to resist their imposition, there being no other purchasers'.[147] The Seths demanded a deduction of one per cent in the price of silver that they bought from the English in view of the charges and risk involved in bringing the silver from Calcutta to Kasimbazar. The Calcutta Council strongly objected to this and asked Kasimbazar Council not to give in to the Seths' demand.[148] But the Company could not hold against the Seths for long and agreed in October 1750 to allow the Seths 'to deduct half percent in consideration of the risque

---

[143] Ibid., vol. 18, ff. 394, 398, 14 & 15 Oct. 1746.

[144] Ibid., vol. 18, f. 431, 8 Nov. 1746.

[145] Ibid., vol. 18, f. 431vo, 8 Nov. 1746.

[146] Ibid., vol. 19, f. 292vo, 23 June 1747; Beng. Letters Recd., vol. 21, f. 285, 10 Jan. 1748; *FWIHC*, vol. 1, p. 233.

[147] Beng. Letters Recd., vol. 21, ff. 289-90, para. 195, 10 Jan. 1748; BPC, vol. 20, f. 187vo, 9 Oct. 1747; *FWIHC*, vol. 1, p. 236.

[148] BPC, vol. 21, ff. 198vo-200vo, 22 Sept. 1748.

and charges up'.[149]

The situation was not entirely different for the Dutch. There is no doubt that in principle the Mughal mints in Bengal were open to all and everyone could coin money by paying the usual seigniorage. But in actual practice, minting was almost an exclusive privilege of the house of Jagat Seth which through its great influence at Murshidabad *darbar* could easily retain it. The Dutch, however, coined money at the mint from time to time but often had to face insurmountable difficulties in doing so. As a result, they too had to sell their bullion quite often to the Jagat Seths. The simplest way to manipulate things for the Seths was to see that the minting for the Dutch or other Europeans was delayed, something that could be easily done by giving the hint to the mint master. Neither the Dutch nor any other European company could afford the long delay in minting money because of the urgent need for liquid capital for procuring investments or paying arrears to the *dadni* merchants. The Dutch Director Sichtermann noted in his 'Memorie' in 1744 the inordinate delay the Company had to face in minting and suggested that selling silver could have been a solution had the price in the market been not so low at the time.[150] Even as late as 1755, Taillefert wrote of 'unheard of delays' in the mint, which he suspected was partly because of the intrigues of the house of Jagat Seth.[151] So the Dutch also were often forced to sell silver to the Seths as we find that even in 1755 the Dutch sold silver to the Jagat Seths' *gomasta*, Baijnath, at Hughli.[152]

Madras and Arcot Rupees

The English Company's problem was accentuated by the fact that the Madras and Arcot rupees which it coined in the mints in the South and which it imported to Bengal were current only at a *batta* or discount which again was manipulated by the house of Jagat

---

[149] Ibid., vol. 23, f. 356vo, 20 Oct. 1750; C&B. Abstr., vol. 5, f. 278, paras. 126, 127, 4 Feb. 1751; *FWIHC*, vol. 1, pp. 482-83.

[150] Sichtermann's 'Memorie', VOC, 2629, ff. 920, 926-28, 14 March 1744.

[151] Taillefert's 'Memorie', VOC, 2849, ff. 214-15, 27 Oct. 1755.

[152] VOC, 2862, ff. 855-56, HB, 14 March 1755.

Seth to its advantage. One of the reasons why the Company wanted the minting privilege for coining *sicca* rupees was that 'at most aurungs Madras rupees go for no more than Current whereas siccas at 3, 4 or 5 percent more, the merchants at Fort William take them at 10 percent'.[153] The Kasimbazar Council reported in 1731 that at the 'instigation' of Fatechand, a representation was made to the nawab (though not true at all) that the English brought only Madras and Arcot rupees, and no bullion that season, whereupon the nawab had forbidden the currency of those rupees, and ordered that they should be received only as bullion. Fatechand was the first to obey the order by putting fifty thousand rupees into the mint to be melted down. But the other *shroffs* were 'very clamorous upon the occasion, as they are likely to be great sufferers by it'.[154]

The *batta* or discount on Madras and Arcot rupees rose or fell according to the manipulation of the Jagat Seths. The house could influence the nawab to issue orders relating to the *batta* on Madras and Arcot rupees in its favour. This is quite clear from the Bengal General Letter of 24 January 1737: 'Futtichund has this year again influenced the Nabob to lessen the value of Madras and Arcot Rupees and procured orders that 107 $^3/_4$ of either should pass for no more than 100 siccas ... they used to pass 103 $^1/_2$ Madras for 100 siccas.'[155] Again in 1738 the nawab issued an order 'forbidding Arcot rupees to go current' and asking all persons who had any in their possession to bring them to Fatechand's house to be changed into *siccas* 'which he had settled at Twelve and half per cent Batta on Arcot Rupees'.[156] Similarly, the Seths obtained an order in 1750 from the nawab which 'forbids all persons beside themselves from purchasing any silver or taking any Arcot rupees'.[157] The Company was helpless in the face of these impositions and could hardly do anything but to submit with a grudge. Even as late as 1752 the *diwan* Roy

---

[153] C&B. Abstr., vol. 2, f. 175, para. 61, 6 Dec. 1718.

[154] BPC, vol. 8, ff. 451vo-452, 13 Sept. 1731; C&B. Abstr., vol. 3, f. 172, para. 2, 5 Jan. 1732.

[155] C&B. Abstr., vol. 4, f. 198, para. 60, 29 Jan. 1737.

[156] Fact. Records, Kasimbazar, vol. 2, Consult. 20 March 1738; BPC, vol. 13, f. 216, 3 April 1738.

[157] BPC, vol. 23, f. 28, 11 Jan. 1750.

Kiritchand ordered that all money whether bullion or rupees
must be sent to the mint at Murshidabad to be coined into *siccas*
or dispose off to the house of Jagat Seth, and that the Company
should not pay any money to its merchants except in new *siccas*
as 'no others are to pass current in the country'. The Company
found that on disposing of the Arcot rupees to Jagat Seth's house
'they will allow us only 87: 11: 3 *sicca* rupees for 100 Arcot rupees
and ninety two siccas for one hundred Bombay Rupees, by which
a difference arises on the Arcot Rupees of about 14 percent and
on Bombay 9 percent which is $7 \frac{1}{2}$ percent more than the Batta
was on Arcot Rupees in the year 1750'.[158]

The *dadni* merchants, too, were often reluctant to take
Madras or Arcot rupees in payment for their supplies because of
the fact that they suffered loss in exchanging those rupees for
siccas, thus adding to the Company's difficulties. In 1738 the
Kasimbazar Council acquainted the merchants that it expected
that they would take Madras rupees in part of *dadni* at the usual
batta but they represented that they would be great sufferers by
it as the government would oblige them to pay a duty of $2 \frac{1}{2}$ per
cent and that they would be at a further loss in 'putting them off'.
The Council knew well that the only remedy was to seek help of
the Jagat Seths in the matter. So it asked the broker to 'solicit his
[Fatechand's] interest for the currency of them [Madras rupees]
again'. Fatechand Seth was shrewd enough to tell the English
broker that 'the French had been the sole occasion of our
complaint by agreeing to pay a custom on Madras and Arcot
rupees and that it was not in his power to be of any service to us,
he himself not being exempted from this custom'. But it was
ultimately he who came to the rescue of the Company and told
the broker that he was willing to take $106 \frac{1}{4}$ Madras rupees for
100 *siccas* which was half per cent more than 'we could put them
off for anywhere else'.[159] Throughout the period, however, the
Company tried to coerce the merchants to take part of their *dadni*
in Madras and Arcot rupees. The Kasimbazar Council reported
in 1752 that it had paid their merchants with Madras rupees at
106 rupees per 100 *siccas* which was 'the lowest batta they could

[158] Fact. Records, Kasimbazar, vol. 11, 31 Jan. 1752; C&B. Abstr.,
vol. 5, f. 357, para. 79, 18 Sept. 1752.
[159] BPC, vol. 13, ff. 183-83vo, 2 March 1738.

take them at, and at which rate there is a less loss arising to the Company than on any other sort'.[160]

4.4 MEASURES ADOPTED TO RAISE ADDITIONAL FUNDS

Intra-Asiatic and Freight Trade

Though the local credit market eased to a great extent the Companies' problem of shortage of working capital, they often tried to augment their resources by engaging in intra-Asiatic and freight trade as also borrowing from the servants of the European companies including their own. The intra-Asiatic trade and freight voyages not only provided additional sources of funds for investments but also saved the English Company the demurrage for its ships lying idle in Bengal. The Dutch and the French, too, did the same. As a matter of fact, one of the main props of the Dutch Company in the second half of the seventeenth century was its intra-Asiatic trade.[161] Though this declined gradually in the first half of the eighteenth century, still it was quite significant in the overall picture of the Dutch Asiatic trade.[162] The ships which failed to sail for Europe in the proper season were obliged to stay on, thus incurring heavy demurrage. Under the circumstances, the Companies asked their servants to put in their best efforts to employ these ships in intra-Asiatic commerce and freight trade. These commercial ventures certainly helped the Companies to some extent to solve the problem of shortage of liquid capital, though in the absence of adequate data it is not possible to make any accurate estimate of the proceeds from such ventures. Only occasional references to the earnings of some of the ships are to be found in the records.

In the first two decades of the eighteenth century, the intra-Asiatic trade of the English was mostly in the Bengal-Surat-Persia sector. This trend continued for the rest of our period

[160] C & B. Abstr., vol. 5, f. 356; BPC, vol. 25, f. 162, 8 June 1752; *FWIHC*, vol. I, f. 6.

[161] For Dutch Company's intra-Asian trade in the second half of the 17th century, see, Om Prakash, *Dutch Company*.

[162] See chapters 3 and 7.

though the trade to Surat declined quite a bit from about the early thirties. The Indian and Armenian merchants at Hughli and Calcutta often freighted European ships for particular voyage to Surat or Persia either jointly or on their separate account, especially in the first two decades of the eighteenth century.[163] A few illustrations of the intra-Asiatic and freight voyages will give an indication of the earnings from such endeavours. It was reported in January 1728 that the ship *Hertford* 'being ordered a country voyage' sailed for Surat 'with a tolerable good freight'.[164] In the preceding year ship *Sarum*'s earnings on a voyage to Surat produced only Rs 18,550, 'Surat almost being ruined by country Government'.[165] Consequent to the prospects of a poor freight, the ship *Compton* was let out in October 1728 for a freight voyage to Jedda for a sum of Rs 20,000 which was proportionate to the sum for which *Walpole* was let out the previous year.[166] The Calcutta Council reported in 1737 that the earning of *Halifax*'s voyage to Surat was Rs 48,304.[167] In November 1754 the Company let out ship *St. George* to Captain Rannie for Rs 40,000.[168]

But even in intra-Asiatic trade and freight voyages the Company had to face various difficulties. The English Company had to compete with other European companies and Muslim shipowners. As other European companies, mainly the Dutch and the French, were also engaged in intra-Asiatic trade, the English Company had to face their rivalry. In freight trade, the main competitors were the French and the Muslims. The Calcutta Council reported in 1727 that two Muslim ships arrived from Surat and the supercargoes told the merchants at Murshidabad that their ships were safer than those of the English who were then at war with Angria. They further informed the merchants that they would carry goods 'at half freight and no expence in

---

[163] For English Company's intra-Asiatic trade, and freight voyages by Indian and Armenian merchants in the early 18th century, see S. Chaudhuri, *Trade and Commercial Organization*, pp. 124-25.

[164] C&B. Abstr., vol. 2, f. 583, para. 18, 28 Jan. 1728.

[165] DB, vol. 104, ff. 420-21, para. 6, 21 Feb. 1729; C&B. Abstr., vol. 2, f. 583, para 19, 28 Jan. 1728.

[166] BPC, vol. 6, f. 656, 7 Oct. 1728.

[167] C&B. Abstr., vol. 4, f. 233, 30 Nov. 1737.

[168] BPC, vol. 27, f. 334, 7 Nov. 1754.

boat hire'. And they secured most of the freight goods.[169] Next year, the Council wrote that the Muslim ships 'have run away with the major parts of the freights at Rs 4 and 4 $\frac{1}{2}$ per maund'. It further added that 'were the English to lower theirs to 4 Rupees per maund the Moors would still sink under even to 1 Rupee per maund because [they] can afford to take less'.[170] In July that year the Council noted that the ship *Compton* could be set up for a freight voyage to Surat but 'cannot expect many freight Bales because the French and Moors take in Bales at $\frac{1}{2}$ freight'.[171] In 1729 a French Captain came to Bengal in a large Muslim ship with a French pass and 'has got the major part of the freight by agreeing for it at Surat at an under rate'[172] The Court of Directors too pointed out the lowering of earnings from freight trade, especially to Surat, because of the 'badness of Trade, and the low freights which the Moors ships carrying goods for who sailing at much less charge than our shipping can afford to do'.[173]

Borrowing from Europeans

The English Company also borrowed from local Europeans, including servants of various European companies, free merchants and ships' captains. These short-term borrowings which were really bridging finance did to some extent ease the Company's problem of cash shortage for investments in the proper season. In the early decades of the eighteenth century, the Company's servants deposited money with the Company against bills of exchange on the Court of Directors to be paid in England. As for example, Abraham Adams, the accountant at Calcutta, deposited Rs 27,728 at Calcutta against a bill of exchange on the Court prior to his departure for England in 1716.[174] Even the Presidents of the Fort William Council remitted money to England by this method. Thus we find Robert Hedges, the President in Bengal, transferred Rs 40,045 by means of a bill on

---

[169] C&B. Abstr., vol. 2, ff. 524-25, para. 15, 28 Jan. 1727.

[170] Ibid., vol. 2, ff. 583, para. 18, 28 Jan. 1728.

[171] Ibid., vol . 3, f. 26, para. 18, 31 July 1728.

[172] Ibid., vol. 3, f. 30, para. 16, 2 Feb. 1729.

[173] DB, vol. 104, ff. 420-21, para. 6, 21 Feb. 1729.

[174] BPC, vol. 3, f. 117.

the Court in 1717.[175] Samuel Feake, the next President, received
a bill on the Court for his deposits amounting to Rs 10,000 in
1718.[176] In the same year Henry Frankland who was the export
warehousekeeper paid a sum of Rs 88,000 into the Company's
treasury in Calcutta for which he received a bill of exchange on
the Court for £ 11,000.[177] As a matter of fact, the Company
borrowed money locally from the Europeans in Bengal almost
throughout the period under review, though it is difficult to
compute the amount borrowed yearly. However, an idea of the
amount borrowed from the Europeans could be given for some
years. In the period of one year from June 1746 to May 1747,
the English Company borrowed from the Europeans Rs 475,640
while next year, from June 1747 to May 1748, the amount
borrowed was Rs 510,967.[178]

To sum up, it can be said with little doubt that the European
companies were able to solve, though with some difficulty, the
problems facing them in securing their investments in Bengal.
This will be evident from the increasing volume of the European
trade during the period under review. The Companies tried to
solve their main problem in procuring investments — the acute
shortage of working capital — by recourse to borrowing from
local credit market which was highly efficient and well organized,
and this local money market was the main source of their
borrowings. They also borrowed from local Europeans including
their servants and free merchants, and tried to augment their
finances by earnings from intra-Asiatic trade and freight voyages. The main obstacles in borrowing from local capital market
were the tradition of short-term loan extending not beyond a few
months generally, the occasional scarcity of money in the market
and the high rate of interest. The Companies could hardly
modify this traditional system. The interest rate was, however,
lowered but that was surely granted as a grace rather than
anything else by the house of Jagat Seth. They faced various

[175] Ibid., vol. 3, f. 460.
[176] Ibid., vol. 4, f. 1vo.
[177] Ibid., vol. 4, f. 3.
[178] Computed from relevant volumes of BPC.

problems in converting the bullion and failed to procure any minting privilege. They could neither sell the imported bullion and specie in the open market, nor could they freely impose the Madras and Arcot rupees on the merchants and markets. In all these they were hindered and harassed by the Jagat Seths who were the most powerful economic force in Bengal under the patronage of the nawabs.

Thus the Companies could do little to change even the small detail in the traditional commercial organization. One of the new elements that they could introduce in the traditional system was perhaps the office of broker or chief merchant. Though the brokers were not unknown in the traditional organization of commerce, the role played by the brokers of the European Companies in the commercial and social life was something new in the traditional system. The brokers of these Companies were altogether a new institution in the commercial life of the country, quite different from the traditional Indian broker in their functions and importance. The other new elements introduced by the Europeans were mainly in the field of organizations of trade and procurement system. For the first time in Bengal, the English Company organized the saltpetre merchants into a joint stock.[179] Another new element introduced by the Europeans was that the price of the goods to be supplied according to specifications was fixed at the time of the contract—something not usually done earlier. It is also interesting to note that a study of the European investments gives us an insight, however inadequate, into the working of the complex structure of traditional commercial organization, credit machinery and capital market, and the mercantile class in the pre-colonial period.

[179] See chapter 9.

5

MERCHANTS, COMPANIES AND RULERS

An analysis of the trading activities of Asian merchants, and the nature and character of their commercial organization vis-à-vis the European companies is necessary for an understanding of the position of these merchants in the socio-political milieu of Bengal in the first half of the eighteenth century. The Asian merchants engaged in Bengal trade had certain distinct features. They often acted as brokers, agents or merchants to the European companies, supplying their investments or buying their imports. At the same time they traded with their own capital, quite independently of the European companies. They also acted simultaneously as *shroffs* or money changers and bankers, received and arranged remittances by means of bills of exchange or letters of credit on their various agents in different trade marts of Bengal, as also in other parts of India.

The term Asian merchant has been used here in preference to Bengal merchants in view of the fact that merchants from various parts of Asia including the Arabs, Turks, Persians, Mughals and Armenians as also from different parts of India traded in Bengal in first half of the eighteenth century. From a close and critical analysis of the trading activities of the Asian merchants, we would attempt to make a few generalizations and inferences as to whether the sum total of the activities of the Asian merchants can be described merely as *peddling trade*, how far the Asian merchant was an *independent entity* without a close link with the political and ruling elite, whether the change in the English Company's investment pattern from *dadni* to *gomasta* system was due to the decline of the merchants in Bengal, and whether these merchants were *subservient* to the European companies.

5.1 ASIAN MERCHANTS AND COMPANIES

It is almost common knowledge that the European companies in Bengal as elsewhere in India except Madras procured their investments through the *dadni* system, which rested on a contractual agreement between the merchants and the Company. The former undertook to supply the Company a specific quantity of export commodities by a certain date and organized their purchase and transport from the production centres. The Company in return paid them a certain proportion of the total value of the goods in advance known as *dadni*, the rest being paid on delivery. The risk of default by weavers, artisans or other producers were underwritten by the merchants. At each principal factory the Companies employed a number of Asian merchants whose financial standing and integrity were assured in the local market. An indigenous merchant middleman, often called broker by the European companies, was appointed in each factory, and he was responsible for money advanced to the *dadni* merchants as also for the timely supply of the export commodities.

The amount of *dadni* or advance given to the merchants against the contract for goods was a bone of contention between the merchants on the one hand and the English Company on the other throughout the period. In the first two decades of the eighteenth century the merchants received from the Company generally between 70 to 75 per cent of the total cost of the investments. It appears that the full amount of the *dadni* was not paid all at once but in instalments. Again, sometimes only a part of the *dadni* was paid in cash, the rest by bills of debt. In 1718 the Calcutta Council reduced the *dadni* to 60 per cent of the total cost of investment. It was again reduced to 50 per cent in 1722 of which 20 per cent was paid in cash and the rest by bills of debt.[1] Other European companies—the Dutch, the French and the

[1] C & B. Abstr., vol. 2, f.319, para. 55, 31 Jan. 1722.

Ostend Company—too paid *dadni* or advance to secure their investments.[2]

The English Company, however, could not stick to the principle of 50 per cent advance against contracts for goods in the face of protest and insistence from the *dadni* merchants. In the forties the *dadni* was again raised to 70 per cent on the whole quantity of goods contracted for, obviously under pressure from the merchants.[3] In 1749 the Company came to a new understanding with the merchants who agreed to provide one-third of the investment for ready money and two-thirds on *dadni*, but the amount of *dadni* was raised to 85 per cent.[4] The Company was always apprehensive of the *dadni* merchants and tried its best to foil any combination of them which would be detrimental to its interests. The merchants too on their part tried to evade the impositions of the Company and make as much profit as possible on the procurement of investments. In order to guard against any monopoly by the merchants' group, the Calcutta Council took rather an unusual measure in 1733 and wrote to the Court of Directors[5]:

> Finding it necessary to employ some of the poor merchants to prevent a combination of the Rich, they thought it for the Company's advantage to employ them accordingly as it prevents their going to the Dutch and French who give them great encouragement, but at the same time give the preference to the substantial ones, keeping both as independent of the broker as possible.

The Kasimbazar merchants seem to have enjoyed more independence vis-à-vis the European companies than their counterparts in Calcutta. Often they formed rings of their own fraternity and foiled the Company's attempt to coerce them. In 1741 the

[2] For Ostend Company, see 'Memorie' of Alexander Hume, 1730, Stadsarchief Antwerp, Generaal Indische Compagnie, 5769. I am indebted to Professor K.N. Chaudhuri for letting me have a photocopy of this document.

[3] BPC, vol. 17, f. 72vo, 30 April 1744.

[4] C & B. Abstr., vol. 5, f. 193, 13 Jan. 1750; *FWIHC*, vol.I, p.248.

[5] C & B. Abstr., vol. 3, f. 264, para. 124, 16 Jan. 1733.

merchants refused to pay the penalty for deficiency in the previous year's contract, stating emphatically that 'they never had paid any penalty nor would not now'. The Kasimbazar Council reported to Calcutta in utter frustration: 'Having taken into consideration the refusal of the merchants we are of opinion that should they remain obstinate in their refusal to comply that it is not in our power to force them....'[6]

The merchants in Kasimbazar further refused to give any security for the *dadni* advanced to them. The Council's letter to Calcutta of 26 February 1742 brings to bold relief the independence of the mercantile class in Kasimbazar:[7]

> ...as to giving security as demanded of them [the merchants] is what they would not do on any account that some of them did business for Guzzeraters, Multaners, Armenians and other merchants and for greater amounts than with us and yet no such thing was ever demanded of them...besides there were none among them but what were esteemed men of credit and many of them substantial men .... In short that none of them would submit to the reproaches/as they call it/ of giving security....

Ultimately the Council 'finding no hope of gaining their point of getting them to give security', thought it better to contract with the merchants for raw silk at the earliest.[8]

Despite the virtuous recommendation of the Court of Directors that 'all manner of Combinations among the merchants must be prevented',[9] the Kasimbazar Council had often to face such 'rings' of merchants which it failed to break on most occasions. It was noted in the Consultation of 23 April 1743 that when the merchants were asked to pay the previous year's balances, eight prominent merchants told the Council 'that they had entered into a contract not to depart from their demands on the Company...and that whoever of them makes up his acocunt with the Company shall forfeit 10,000 Rupees and pay the others'

[6] Fact. Records, Kasimbazar, vol. 6, 25 Dec. 1741.
[7] Ibid., vol. 6, 26 Feb. 1742.
[8] Ibid.
[9] DB, vol. 108, f. 623, para. 45, 4 Feb. 1743.

Ballances and this contract they have lodged in the hands of Sautoo Cotma'.[10] Finding the merchants 'so obstinate', the Council decided to contract with other merchants.

The Kasimbazar merchants were very sensitive about giving security for the *dadni* advanced by the Company and tried to hold their ground against the Company as long as possible. The Council at Kasimbazar reported on 27 January 1744 that the merchants alleged that as several of them did business on a large scale with traders from various parts of India and Asia, 'having it known they had given security would destroy all such trade because those other merchants they did business with would look on it that they were not responsible without it'. The merchants stood firm in their resolution not to give security and told the Council that 'they would not do business on such terms for even a report that security was demanded of them would hurt their credit abroad'[11] However the Kasimbazar Council finally succeeded in bringing the silk merchants 'to be joined in security, three or four of them together for the Dadney they advance them'.[12]

But the Company had only a limited success since it failed to get any security whatsoever from some prominent merchants dealing in silk piece-goods, and who, it seems, were ready to forgo the Company's contract rather than give security. The Calcutta Council noted in 1744:[13]

...it is impossible to get the quantity of silk piece-goods ordered, without employing many other merchants residing at Muxidabad and Sidabad and other places some of whom being wealthy in good credit will not be persuaded to give any security, particuarly Ram Singh, Gosseram and Ramnaut Echenaut, without whose assistance they [Kasimbazar Council] fear they shall fall very short in the article of Taffaties which the above-mentioned chiefly deal in and provide the

10 Fact. Records, Kasimbazar, vol. 6, 23 April 1743.
11 Ibid., vol. 6, 27 Jan., 1744.
12 BPC, vol. 17, f. 27vo, 25 Feb. 1744.
13 Ibid., f. 66, 23 April 1744; Fact. Records, Kasimbazar, vol. 6, 19 April 1744.

very best and which the other merchants do not care to
meddle with as they are liable to occasion bad debts among
the weavers...they absolutely refused to give [security] as they
are very substantial people, and they apprehend no risque of
any money entrusted with them, and in case they throw them
out of Dadney, the Dutch and the French will gladly employ
them....

Needless to say the Calcutta Council gave its consent to Kasimbazar
to contract with these merchants despite their refusal to render
any security for the *dadni* advanced.

Turning to Calcutta we find that after the abolition of the
broker's office in 1741, the merchants there contracted with the
Company giving proper securities for the *dadni* advanced. But
they were not very happy with the system and in a joint petition
in 1744 informed the Council that they 'cannot agree to this
method again when we contract for next year's investment'.[14] The
Council informed the merchants on 8 March 1745 that it would
not make any change in the system. On 14 March the Council
asked the merchants to divide themselves into three sets or
groups as usual but the latter absolutely refused to do so and
insisted on dividing into six or seven sets for the security of the
Company's *dadni*—something that was ultimately accepted by the
Council.[15]

The Setts and the Basaks were the most important merchant
families of Calcutta who provided the lion's share of the
Company's investments. In fact throughout the period of our
study many members of the Sett family traditionally held the post
of broker and the great commercial influence of this family
reduced the Company's textile merchants in Calcutta to a 'closed
corporation'. Even the Court of Directors in London was aware
of the importance of and services rendered by the Sett family,
and wrote to Calcutta appreciating the Setts' assistance in the
Company's business.[16] But the Setts were shrewd merchants, not

[14] Ibid., vol. 17, f.119, Annex. to Consult., 28 May 1744.
[15] Ibid., f.482vo, 8 March 1745; f. 488vo, 14 March 1745; C&B.
Abstr. vol.5, f. 57, para. 4 & 5, 11 Aug. 1745.
[16] Ibid., vol. 19, f. 147vo, 16 March 1747.

to be satisfied only with sweet words, and ready to bargain hard with the Company whenever the occasion arose. Indeed they were the leaders of the Calcutta merchants who came to serious disagreement with the Company regarding the investment and *dadni* in 1747. Consequent to the disturbed political situation in Bengal which the Maratha incursions resulted in, the Court of Directors asked the Calcutta Council in 1746 to reduce and, if possible, to dispense with the *dadni* payments altogether and to provide investment with 'ready money' goods.[17] The Calcutta Council placed the proposal before the merchants on 19 March 1747 and the latter refused 'in a body' to agree to it, submitting detailed arguments for not discontinuing the *dadni*.[18]

The Kasimbazar merchants too refused to accept the new proposals for investments of the Company. The Council at Kasimbazar reported to Calcutta: '...to both of which propositions they are extremely averse that they think it impossible for them ever to bring them to agree thereto'.[19] Meanwhile the tussle and bargaining went on between the merchants and the Council in Calcutta. As for the final answer the merchants, obviously led by the Setts, told the Council on 25 May 1747 that they could contract 'on no other terms' than the following: that they would provide one-fourth of the investments for ready money and the remaining three-fourths on *dadni* of which 85 per cent to be advanced 'as last year'. Finding the merchants 'obstinate', the Council decided to try to enter into contract with some other merchants on better terms.[20] Accordingly the Company made a contract with sixteen merchants of whom seven were new (including two Dutch *dadni* merchants, Otteram and Gosseram Occoor, and a few Kasimbazar merchants led by the Katmas) for about one-third of the Company's investment amounting to about 0.8 million rupees.[21] The Setts and other merchants gave

---

[17] DB, vol. 109, f. 465, para. 33-39, 6-12 June 1746.

[18] For the merchants' arguments, see BPC, vol. 19, ff.151vo-152; C&B. Abstr., vol. 5, para. 32, f. 108; Beng. Letters Recd., vol. 21, ff. 213-14, para. 32; *FWIHC*, vol. 1, pp. 190-91.

[19] BPC, vol. 19, ff. 209vo, 210, 22 April 1747.

[20] Ibid., f. 255-55vo, 25 May 1747; f. 257, 28 May 1747; Beng. Letters Recd., vol. 21, ff. 216, 218; *FWIHC*, pp. 92-93.

[21] BPC, vol. 19, f. 280, 13 June 1747; C&B. Abstr., vol. 5, f. 109, para. 39, 13 June 1747; Beng. Letters Recd., vol. 21, ff. 220-21; *FWIHC*, vol. 1, p. 194.

a new proposal that they would undertake the remaining two-thirds of the investment on condition that 50 per cent of the *dadni* would be paid within August and the rest, 35 per cent, on delivery of goods, 'but if there are new men introduced into the Dadney they will do no business at all'.[22] The Calcutta Council noted in utter exasperation: 'As the Seths [Setts] and other merchants obstinately refuse to contract with us unless upon their own terms and impertinently refuse to let us employ any other merchants agreed that we look out for such as will contract'.[23]

The commercial organization of the Calcutta merchants was caste-based. When asked to contract for investment for 1748, the Calcutta Council noted the reaction of the Setts thus:[24]

> The Seats being all present...inform us that last year they dissented to the employing of Tillickchund, Gosseram Occoor and Otteram they being of a different cast[e] and consequently they could not do any business with them upon which account they refused the Dadney and the same objection to make they propose taking their shares of the Dadney if we should think proper to consent thereto.

The majority of the Council was in favour of employing the Setts and the contract was made accordingly.

But all was not well with the Company's investment policy and its relations with the merchants gradually deteriorated to such an extent that it reached a point of no return. The Maratha invasions and the Nawab's desperate need for resources to meet the challenge resulted in a serious, though temporary, dislocation of the country's economy, and it seems the *dadni* merchants were not in a position now to accept contract from the Company until and unless they were commensurate with the rapidly declining profit and the growing hazards of conducting the business in textiles. The first serious disagreement arose in 1751 when the merchants refused to sign the accounts as prepared by the Council wherein the merchants were charged penalty for

[22] Ibid., vol. 19, f. 286, 16 June 1747.

[23] Ibid., vol. 19, f. 289vo, 18 June 1747.

[24] Ibid., vol. 21, f. 69, 18 May 1748; C&B. Abstr., vol. 5, para. 33, pp. 134-35; *FWIHC*, vol. 1, p. 298.

deficiency in delivery of goods.[25] Though the Setts too refused
'in a body' to sign the account, the lead this time was given by
the Basaks. Sobharam Basak, the leading member of the Basak
family, refused to sign the account, pointing out much to the
chagrin of the Calcutta Council, that 'he esteemed his contract
of no validity and paid no regard to it'. The Council retaliated
with the only measure it could take and reported: '...Sooberam
bysaack persisting in obstinate refusal and it appearing to us most
probably from this and some other circumstances that he had
been greatly instrumental in working up several of the other
merchants to the same refusal... dismissed him from Dadney and
forbid him coming to the factory'.[26] Ramkrishna Sett also refused
to sign the contract and he too was dismissed from the Company's
dadni contract and forbidden entry to the factory. But he was soon
readmitted into the Company's service at the request of his
nephew Laksmi Chandra Sett, and so was Sobharam Basak.[27]

There was a big deficiency in the investments again in 1752.
When the Council wanted an explanation from the merchants,
they replied that the shortfall in supply was 'owing to our cutting
them in the prices, the dearness of cloth at the aurungs and our
sorting their goods by old musters whereby they suffered a
considerable loss'.[28] As a result when the Company asked the
merchants to sign their accounts, the latter objected to the
manner in which the account was drawn. They informed the
Council clearly and firmly that they would not undertake any
business for 1753.[29] The Calcutta Council, anxious as it was to
contract for the investments for 1753, asked the merchants for
their terms. The merchants were reluctant to enter into any
contract as they had 'suffered these three years past by the
Company's business'. They made it amply clear that they would

[25] For merchants' reasons for refusing to pay penalty, see C&B.
Abstr., vol. 5, f. 303, para. 123, 20 Aug. 1751; *FWIHC*, vol. 1, p. 523.
[26] BPC, vol. 24, ff. 133, 134 vo, 17 & 20 May 1751; C&B. Abstr.,
vol. 5, ff. 303-304, para. 126, 20 Aug. 1751; *FWIHC*, vol. 1, pp. 523-24.
[27] BPC, vol. 24, ff. 136, 137 vo, 23 & 27 May 1751; C&B. Abstr.,
vol. 5, f. 304, para. 130, 128, 20 Aug. 1751; *FWIHC*, vol. 1, p. 524.
[28] C&B. Abstr., vol. 5, f. 354, para. 42, 18 Sept. 1752; *FWIHC*, vol.
1, p. 594.
[29] BPC, vol. 26, ff. 66vo-67, 1 March 1753; C&B. Abstr., vol. 5, f.
401, para. 32; *FWIHC*, vol. 1, pp. 680-81.

not on any account undertake the investment on the same terms
as they did the previous year. But as they 'served the Company
almost from their infancy and lived under the English protection,
they would do their utmost to forward their business', and only
as such were willing to contract on their own terms and no
others.[30] The Council regarded these terms as 'extremely
unreasonable' and asked the merchants if they would not recede
from what they had proposed. The reply came from Ramkrishna
Sett, obviously the leader of the *dadni* merchants, that he would
contract only on the terms the merchants had offered, otherwise
'he absolutely refused to undertake any part of the investment
himself'.[31]

The Council acted swiftly and perhaps in utter desperation.
It noted:[32]

> Esteeming this preemptory behaviour of Ramkissen Seat's to
> be extremely insolent and meriting our Resentment and as
> an example made of so considerable a person may have a
> good effect upon the rest of the merchants and reduce them
> to offer us better terms, Ramkissenseat was told we had no
> further business for him as a Dadney merchant and ordered
> to withdraw.

But this was hardly of any avail as the subsequent events would
prove. Five days later, the merchants were called again by the
Council and acquainted of the Court of Directors' orders
regarding investment.[33] The merchants flatly refused contracting on these terms. They were in an advantageous position in the
bargain inasmuch as the time factor was in their favour. It was
the beginning of June and the Council must come to an
agreement if it wanted to secure full investment for the year. So
the Council was almost solicitious and asked the merchants if they

[30] For the merchants' terms, see BPC, vol. 26, ff. 157vo-158, 31 May
1753.

[31] Ibid., f. 158, 31 May 1753; C&B. Abstr., vol. 5, f. 425; Beng.
Letters Recd., vol. 22, para. 30-31, ff. 416-17; *FWIHC*, vol. 1, pp. 680-
81, 3 Sept, 1753.

[32] BPC, vol. 26, f. 158, 31 May 1753; C & B. Abstr., vol. 5, f. 425;
Beng. Letters Recd., vol. 22, f. 417, para. 31; *FWIHC*, vol. 1, p. 681.

[33] For these orders, see BPC, vol. 26, f. 161, 4 June 1753.

could offer any other terms 'more reasonable' and particularly if they would undertake the investment at an advance of *dadni* of less than 85 per cent. The merchants answered in the negative. The Council had now no other alternative but to arrange for investment by some other means. The merchants were called again and told 'they were no more Hon'ble Company's Dadney merchants'. Thus ended the *dadni* system of investment which had its life of about a hundred years and was replaced by the *gomasta* system under which the *gomastas* (paid agents or servants) procured the export commodities from different *aurungs* or manufacturing centres.[34]

It has been suggested in a recent study that the change over from the *dadni* to the *gomasta* system for the procurement of the English Company's investments was due to the decline of the Bengal merchants. The scholar relies for his conclusion heavily on the report of Charles Manningham and William Frankland (1753), the two export warehouse keepers in Calcutta, and finds corroborative evidence in the 'memorie' of the Dutch Director Jan Kerseboom. And he concludes: '... the textile trade of Bengal and the merchants connected with it were already approaching the end of the road. That end came in 1753.'[35] But a careful and critical reading of the two documents mentioned by the reputed scholar hardly justifies the conclusion that there was an absolute decline of the merchants in Bengal necessitating the change over from the *dadni* to *gomasta* system. It is true that in his 'memorie', written in 1755, Kerseboom referred to four Santipur merchants who, as reported by a servant of the Raja of Nadia in whose territory lay Santipur, were ruined men and no money-lenders or bankers [*wisselaars of banquiers*] were willing to stand security for them. The excuse given by these *shroffs* was that the trade had become extremely hazardous and dangerous too.[36] As such the Dutch Company decided to procure their investment through

[34] Ibid., f. 161vo, 4 June 1753; C&B. Abstr., vol. 5, ff 425-26; Beng. Letters Recd., vol 22, ff. 417-19, para. 32-35; *FWIHC*, pp. 682-83, para. 33-35, 3 Sept. 1753.

[35] K.N. Chaudhuri, *Trading World*, pp. 311-12.

[36] Dutch Director Jan Kerseboom's 'Memorie', VOC, 2849, ff. 93vo-94vo, 14 Feb. 1755.

gomastas who would buy cloth at the *aurungs*.[37]

What actually happened was that the financial position of the four Santipur merchants namely, Kinkar Chaudhury, 'Jeggoebun' Khan, Gokul Chand Khan and 'Bakeban Gopie' Khan was in doubt and that alarmed their creditors, with the latter demanding their money back. The merchants were thus forced to pay 'full or partial of their debts'. This made the Dutch Company suspicious of the 'solvency' of these merchants and their two associates, Radhamohan Chaudhury and Radha Kanta Khan.[38] As the time was not too congenial for normal trade and commerce in the face of the Maratha invasions and the consequent exactions on the merchants by the administration to raise funds for maintining an army, the Dutch wanted to play it safe and not advance money to the merchants about whose pecuniary circumstances there was doubt. But what is significant in this context is that Kerseboom never mentioned the 'insolvency' or ever expressed any doubt about the credit-worthiness of the merchants in general, and his observation was confined only to these few merchants in Santipur and not to the substantial number of merchants in prominent trade centres like Hughli, Kasimbazar, Dhaka, Calcutta or Patna. Moreover, his particular reference that the Dutch Company had decided to employ several *gomastas* 'in this village' [in dit dorp] only indicates the Dutch tried the experiment first in Santipur and later extended it to other places in view of the prevalent uncertainty. Again, it is extremely important to remember that the Dutch tried the experiment for three years (from 1747 to 1749) only and then reverted to the old system of contracting with the merchants from 1750 while the English Company changed over from the *dadni* to *gomasta* system in 1753. Had there been really any decline of the Bengal merchants, which was the alleged reason for changing over to the *gomasta* system by the English, how was it that the Dutch returned to the *dadni* system in 1750? This would only indicate that there was hardly any precipitate decline of the merchants in Bengal even in the 1750s and that it was certainly not the sole reason for the English change over in 1753. There

---

[37] Ibid., f.95vo, 14 Feb. 1755.
[38] Ibid., f. 94vo.

was some other motive for the English, which we shall try to explain later.

However, the Dutch Director Jan Huijghens, during whose time the Company made the experiment with *gomastas* and finally reverted to the *dadni* system, wrote in his 'memorie' that the Company's investment in textiles suffered because of the 'total ruin of the principal merchants and bankers [totale ruine van diverse der principalste koop[lieden] ende banquerouten]. As such, the Company tried to procure coarse textiles through *gomastas* in 1747 and the system was extended to fine textiles in 1748. But he made it absolutely clear that the Dutch wanted to continue the new system only 'until they found some merchants with sufficient capital [ten minsten tot dat er sufficante koopl[ieden] gevonden werden].[39] So it is evident from the above that only some of the Dutch Company's merchants' credit was in doubt and not that of the mercantile class in Bengal as a whole. And the very fact that the Dutch went back to the old *dadni* system after only three years is a clear negation of the suggestion that there was any precipitate decline of the merchants in Bengal.

In this context, one has to take into account that because of the 'troubled times', the merchants and bankers in general were extremely reluctant to show up their wealth and pretended that their financial position was precarious. This is well illustrated by the fact that even the most eminent and fabulously rich banking house of the Jagat Seths would not care, as reported by the English Council at Kasimbazar in 1746, 'to produce cash for fear of government ... even though they have money'.[40] The Companies, no doubt, occasionally referred to insolvency of some of the merchants in different parts of Bengal from time to time but never really indicated a general decline of the banking-mercantile class in the first half of the eighteenth century. The Dutch Director Sadelijn referred in his 'memorie' in 1732 to a 'row of bankruptcies' of the Company's merchants but added significantly that their place was taken up by other merchants. It is interesting that he mentioned about a conflict between the

[39] 'Memorie' of Jan Huijghens, VOC, 2763, ff. 450-51, 20 March 1750.

[40] Fact. Records, Kasimbazar, vol. 7, 22 June 1746; BPC, vol. 18, f.265vo, 30 June 1746.

Company and four important textile merchants who refused to contract with the Dutch and moved over to French Chandernagore.[41] One can well suspect that such defiance of the Companies by the merchants might often have led the former to talk about the insolvency of the latter in order to cover up their failure to curb the merchants. Hence, the alleged bankruptcy of the four Santipur merchants has to be viewed with some caution.

The Dutch Company, however, had considerable difficulty in finding a sufficient number of capable *gomastas* and in maintaining uniformity of standards of goods supplied. This experiment which the Company tried out from 1747 to 1749 did not work satisfactorily and hence from 1750 the Dutch entrusted the merchants again, both 'rich and poor', divided into five groups [vief ploegen], with contracts for fine goods.[42] Besides, to make Kerseboom's reference to the decline of four Santipur merchants a general issue and to conclude from that a general decline of the Bengal merchants are hardly logical. However, it should be borne in mind that in the late forties and early fifties the merchants were passing through a critical period as a consequence of the disruption, though temporary, in the economy following the Maratha invasions and the exactions of the state but these did not seem to have seriously impaired either their credit or their ability to carry on business, whether for the Europeans or other Asian merchants.

So far as the report of Mannigham and Frankland is concerned, only an uncritical reading of it would give the impression that a change over from the *dadni* to the *gomasta* system was essential because the *dadni* merchants were no longer capable of fulfilling the contracts and that their credit was very much in doubt. A careful study of the document will reveal that the change was necessary because the merchants were reluctant to contract with the Company except absolutely on their own terms, and the Company had no other alternative but to switch over to the *gomasta* system, and the decline in the position of Bengal merchants was not really the deciding factor. It was the

---

[41] 'Memorie' of Sadelijn, VOC, 2196, ff. 422-23, 15 Jan. 1732. The four merchants were Jiban Chaudhury, Gokul Mukund [Khan?], Jangemaat[?] Khan and Radhakrishna Chaudhury.

[42] Kerseboom's 'Memorie', VOC, 2849, f. 95vo, 14 Feb. 1755.

independence, the uncompromising attitude and the strong
determination not to recede from their terms that sealed the fate
of the *dadni* system. As the report notes:[43]

> We are by necessity obliged to have recourse to the present
> method [*gomasta* system], as the only one left, for whilst our
> merchants' proposals are so very contrary to the Interests
> and Commands of our Hon'ble Employers they render it
> impossible for us to consent thereto ... by their proposals they
> seem to think we are absolutely in their hands and must
> submit to their demands however extravagant, on a suppo-
> sition that it is not in our power to procure an investment
> without them.

The report, however, tried to make out a case that 'the original
intent and design of conducting the Investments by means of
Dadney merchants', which were to lessen the Company's risk at
the *aurungs* and to secure a timely supply of goods etc., had now
become ineffectual. There is also a specific hint in the report that
many of the merchants were not in a position to pay back the
security money in case of their failure to supply goods against the
advance paid earlier. It is true that in the early fifties the
merchants were deficient in their supply of goods to the
Company but the deficiency in investment had nothing to do with
their financial solvency. It was only quite natural in the condition
through which Bengal was passing in the early fifties. The
authors of the report seem to have been confused and have made
contradictory statements in their enthusiasm for changing over
to the *gomasta* system which, one suspects, would have been more
beneficial to the Company servants' private trade. The report
advocated the change as the *dadni* merchants' terms for investment 'have reduced us to an absolute necessity of pursuing other
measures' which could only be by a 'new sett of merchants' or
employing *gomastas*. But 'to obtain a new sett of merchants is not
in our power'. One wonders why. Was it because of the power
and influence wielded by the *dadni* merchants led by the Setts and
Basaks? One would like to argue that if there was really any

[43] BPC, vol. 26, f. 165vo, Annex to Consult., 7 June 1753.

decline of the merchants of Calcutta, then how could the report of Manningham and Frankland talk of investment by 'new sett' of merchants? Did the Company's servants want to get rid of the *dadni* merchants, as the latter were too powerful to be coerced to assist in the servants' private trade?

Perhaps one can reasonably suspect that the Calcutta Council was tempted to make the change in the procurement system with the ulterior motive of augmenting the private trade interests of its members. The Company's servants in Calcutta were concerned about the trade decline from the early fifties. It was in 1753 that Manningham and Frankland wrote to Clive: '...the situation of trade since you left us has continued so bad.'[44] So one can reasonably argue that the change over to the *gomasta* system was the result of the Calcutta Council's attempt to resolve its commercial problems by cutting out the *dadni* merchants. The abuse of *dastak* [permit] increased considerably under the *gomasta* system and the private trade of the Company's servants, no doubt, increased after the abandonment of the *dadni* system.[45] It is too well known to emphasize how the *gomastas* became the main instruments of coercion in the post-Plassey period.

There is ample evidence to prove that there was no decline in the position of Bengal merchants, especially the *dadni* merchants of Calcutta. The Setts and Basaks were still the leading and dominant merchant families of Calcutta in the 1750s while Hari Krishna Roy was the influential Dutch broker at Chinsurah. The most important thing one has to remember in this connection is that despite all wars, depredations and troubles the credit market in Bengal was not at all destroyed because of the great financial resources of the Jagat Seths. There is evidence that this banking house used to finance extensively both the Asian and the European traders in Bengal. The financial solvency of the Jagat Seths was never in question even in the 1750s. The house also used to finance the *dadni* merchants of Calcutta.[46] Moreover, when merchant princes like Umichand and Khwaja Wazid were

[44] Eur. G37, Box 27, 1 Sept. 1755.
[45] N.K. Sinha, *Economic History of Bengal*, vol. 1, pp. 8-9.
[46] BPC, vol. 12, f. 263, 26 Sept. 1737; vol 22, f.345vo, Annex. to Consult., 26 Oct. 1749.

still operating in full swing and playing a dominant role in Bengal's commercial life, and who had extensive trade connections with Calcutta merchants, the thesis of the general decline of the Bengal merchants becomes wholly untenable.

The Bengal merchants were divided into hereditary occupational caste groups and it was usual for the mercantile families to serve the European companies for generations. Such were the Setts and Basaks of Calcutta, the Katmas of Kasimbazar and the Mullicks of Jugdea. Some of these merchants rose to their positions from weaving and other castes. It seems that because of the caste affiliation, the merchants could organize themselves into a strong 'combination' whenever necessary, especially for bargaining with the European companies or other Asian merchants. Such a 'combination' of merchants was to be found in all major trading centres. After the dismissal of the *dadni* merchants, the Calcutta Council noted on 23 June 1753 that 'it is certain the merchants have assembled themselves of a night lately'.[47] In a dispute regarding the sorting and pricing of silk in 1754, when the Council asked the Kasimbazar merchants to give their replies, 'they all sent us word separately that what the Punch/or Whole Body assembled/ agreed to, they would...'. [48] The best illustration of this sort of combination of merchants and the severe restrictions for adherence to the common agreement is to be found in the Kasimbazar Consultation of 21 October 1754. The Council noted:[49]

> Our merchants having entered into and signed a punch or agreement whereby they are bound not to allow of our taking the 10 percent penalty for the short delivery of goods in the year 1752, and that in case of our discharging any of them from our Employ, the whole body should quit our Business, and that any one or more, should for private ends violate these agreements, he or they should be liable to pay a penalty both to the merchants dismissed and to the Government with several other restrictions.

[47] Ibid., vol. 26, f. 181vo, 23 June 1753.
[48] Fact. Records, Kasimbazar, vol. 12, 21 Feb. 1754.
[49] Ibid., vol. 12, 21 Oct. 1754.

5.2 ROLE OF 'MERCHANT PRINCES'

The commercial life of Bengal and, to a great extent, its economy in the last three decades of the first half of the eighteenth century were dominated by the merchant princes namely, the famous banking house of the Jagat Seths, the well known Umichand and the Armenian merchant Khwaja Wazid. The Jagat Seths played a very prominent role in Bengal's economy from the early decades of the century. Umichand came into prominence in the thirties and Wazid in the forties. These merchant princes collectively predominated both the commerce and financial administration of Bengal. The Bengal money market which financed both trade and the government was closely controlled by them. They were able to dominate Bengal's trade and industry through their farming of leading commodities and commercial privileges. As financiers, traders and administrators, they played a crucial role for the European companies. Through their control of the credit market, their coinage of specie, provision of goods for exports and purchase of imports, the merchant princes had a close relationship with the Europeans. It is to be emphasized, however, that their position depended to a very great extent upon their influence at the nawab's court. Their commercial farms were political in nature, and seem to have been extended in the forties and fifties of the eighteenth century.

The Jagat Seths were least dependent on the European companies. The only direct link between the European companies and the Seths arose out of the latter's monopoly of the mint and the former's need for liquid capital for financing their investments. A major source of income for the banking house was the coining of the bullion and specie the European companies used to import into Bengal for paying for their export commodities. Another good source of income for the Seths was lending money to the Companies which were perenially in short supply of cash. The European companies freely borrowed money from the Jagat Seths' *kuthees* (agencies or branches) in Calcutta, Kasimbazar, Dhaka, Hughli, Patna etc. Robert Orme who was in Bengal in the early 1750s described the Jagat Seths as 'the greatest shroff and banker in the known world'.[50] Captain

[50] Orme Mss., India, VI, f.1455.

Fenwick, writing on the 'affairs of Bengal in 1747-48', referred to Jagat Seth Mahtab Rai as a 'favourite of the Nabob and a greater Banker than all in Lombard Street joined together'.[51] Luke Scrafton wrote to Clive in 1757 that 'Juggutseat is in a manner the government's banker: about two-thirds of the revenues are paid into his house, and the government give the draught [draft] on him in the same manner as a Merchant on the Bank'.[52] Referring to the merchant princes in general and the Jagat Seths in particular, Clive wrote: 'The city of Murshidabad is as extensive, populous and rich, as the city of London, with this difference that there are individuals in the first possessing infinitely greater property than any of the last city.'[53]

The financial credit and prestige of the house which migrated from Nagar in Marwar were raised to such a great height by Manickchand and Fatechand that the Mughal emperor conferred on the latter the title of Jagat Seth or 'Banker of the World' as a hereditary distinction in 1722. The house of Jagat Seth reached the zenith of its prestige and prosperity during the time of Fatechand who, after wielding great influence in the commercial, economic and political life of Bengal for nearly thirty years, died in 1744. He was succeeded by his two grandsons Jagat Seth Mahtab Rai and Maharaja Swaroopchand.[54] The major sources of the huge income, tremendous power and great prestige of the house of Jagat Seth were derived from their farms of Murshidabad and Dhaka mints, two-thirds of the province's revenue collection, their control over rates of exchange, interest rates, bill-broking and the provision of credit. By 1720 the Seths had established almost an absolute monopoly of the mint, obviously with the support of Murshid Quli, the subadar of Bengal. The Fort William Council wrote in 1721: '...Futtichund having the entire use of the mint, no other shroff dare buy an ounce of silver'.[55] The English East India Company was trying for a long time to have minting privileges and the Kasimbazar

[51] Ibid., f. 1525.

[52] Orme Mss., India XVIII, f. 5041.

[53] Quoted in J.H. Little, *The House of Jagatseth*, p. 2.

[54] Fact. Records, Kasimbazar, vol. 7, 3 Jan. 1745; BPC, vol. 17, f. 437, 4 Jan. 1745; C&B. Abstr., vol. 5, f. 28, para. 49, 9 Jan. 1745.

[55] BPC, vol. 4, f. 462vo, 9 Nov. 1721.

Council was asked to secure the privileges from the nawab. The Council negotiated with some high officials of the *darbar* but 'are informed that while Futtichund is so great with the Nabob, they can have no hopes of that Grant, he alone having the sole use of the mint nor dare any other shroff or merchant buy or coin a rupee's worth of silver'.[56]

As the minting of coin was a great source of income, the Jagat Seths were determined to maintain the privilege at all costs. As late as 1743 the Kasimbazar factors reported: ' ...but this [minting privilege] they can never hope while Futtichund subsists and has that weight with the government which his usefulness to them and great influence at Court naturally gives him.'[57] The European companies were thus most often forced to sell all their treasure—both bullion and specie—to the house of Jagat Seth, and under the circumstances they had no other alternative but to accept the price the banking house offered. So great was the control and power of the Jagat Seths over Bengal's money market that the rates of exchange fixed by the house were accepted by all concerned. Through his great influence on the Bengal administration which he gained by virtue of his steady financial support to the nawab, Fatechand could induce the government to take such measures and pass such regulations for the rate of money exchange as would favour the house. There are several instances of this in the Company records.[58] The *batta* [discount] on recoinage was another source of considerable profit to the house of Jagat Seth. According to Luke Scrafton's estimate in 1757, the Seths coined 5 million rupees a year and the profit on this account amounted to 0.35 million rupees.[59] The *batta* on

[56] Ibid., vol. 4, f. 438vo, 28 Aug. 1721. It has been recently suggested by Om Prakash that my assertion that the house of Jagat Seth had a virtual monopoly of the mint 'is in need of drastic revision' which I think is unwarranted in view of the evidence put forward here and in chapter 4, *c.f.* Om Prakash, 'On Coinage in Mughal India', *IESHR*, 25, 4, (1988), p. 487.

[57] Fact. Records, Kasimbazar, vol. 6, 16 March 1743.

[58] BPC, vol. 11, f. 349, 8 Nov. 1736; vol. 12, f. 17, 13 Dec. 1736; Beng. Letters Recd., vol. 21, f. 507, 13 Jan. 1750; BPC, vol. 25, f. 43, 3 Feb. 1752.

[59] Luke Scrafton to Clive, Orme Mss., India, XVIII, f. 5043, 17 Dec. 1757.

various foreign coins and coins from different parts of India was
also a source of great profit to the Seths. The house was the
receiver and treasurer of government revenues. It received land
revenue payments made by the zamindars and *amils* [collectors].
It also received other government collections. The Jagat Seths
gradually became secuiity for most of the renters.

The Seths charged an interest of 12 per cent per annum for
the sum they used to lend to the European companies. On 11
December 1740 the Calcutta Council was informed by Kasimbazar
that the Seths would be willing to reduce the rate of interest from
12 to 9 per cent if a request from the Company was made to do
so.[60] The Calcutta Council wrote to Jagat Seth Fatechand on that
very day requesting a reduction in the rate of interest. On 21
December the English Council at Kasimbazar borrowed Rs
60,000 at the new rate of 9 per cent.[61] From then onward, the
Company borrowed money at Calcutta, Dhaka, Patna, etc. at 9
per cent from the Jagat Seth's house. In one day on 29 March
1742 the Company borrowed a sum of Rs 200,000 at 9 per cent
interest of the Seths at Calcutta.[62] The Dutch and the French too
borrowed freely from the Jagat Seths. That the Jagat Seths could
reduce the interest rate is an indication of their total control over
the credit market in Bengal and northern India.

The house of the Jagat Seths became rather an institution at
least from the forties of the eighteenth century, and was a guide
to the conduct of the merchants, *shroffs* and bankers. The
Kasimbazar Council reported on 7 June 1742, after Jagat Seth's
retreat from Murshidabad because of the Maratha invasion, that
'no merchant or shroff of any consequence will think themselves
safe in the city till Juggutseat comes to reside there' and that the
nawab solicited Jagat Seth to return to the city, 'his presence
being as necessary to the Nabob as to the merchants' and 'his
conduct being the general guide to all of them'.[63] On 14 June it
noted that the merchants came back from their places of retreat

---

[60] BPC, vol. 14, ff. 317-17vo, 11 Dec. 1740.
[61] Ibid., vol. 14, f. 337, 26 Dec. 1740.
[62] Ibid., vol. 15, f. 84vo, 29 March 1742.
[63] Fact. Records, Kasimbazar, vol. 6, 7 June 1742; BPC, vol. 15, f.
188, 10 June 1742.

after Jagat Seth's arrival in the city.[64] Again, when Fatechand left Murshidabad in the wake of the Maratha incursion in 1743, the Kasimbazar factors wrote to Calcutta on 6 June: 'It is wholly impracticable to raise money there for never was known so great a scarcity occasioned by the retreat of Futtichund'.[65] They noted on 2 July that 'Futtichund is returned and money is more plenty here'.[66]

From the early eighteenth century the Jagat Seths were permanent members of the *darbar* and exerted an influence over the nawab and his administration that seems unparalleled in the history of Bengal. It may be said that from the time of Manickchand, the influence of the Seths 'was of chief importance in deciding the result of every dynastic revolution, and they were always in constant communication with the ministers of the Delhi Court'.[67] A striking example of the power of the Jagat Seths at Delhi was the manner in which they obtained *farmans* ratifying the appointment of Bengal nawabs. Fatechand did not exert his influence in Delhi to obtain an imperial *farman* for Sarfaraj, Murshid Quli's grandson. But he supported the cause of Shujauddin who succeeded Murshid Quli in 1727 and this facilitated the new nawab's confirmation by the imperial authority. Shujauddin was therefore more generous than Murshid Quli in his favours to Fatechand. In 1730 when the Kasimbazar Council tried to influence the government for the 'currency of their trade' through Haji Ahmed and Alamchand, the two most important persons in the *darbar* besides Jagat Seth, they 'answered the Nawab has such a regard for Futtichund, it was out of their power to serve us in opposition to him and continue to advise us to make up the affair with him as well as we can'.[68] Haji Ahmed told the Kasimbazar factors in 1730 that 'Futtichund's Estate was esteemed as the King's treasure and the Nabob was resolved to see him satisfied'.[69] Fatechand was one of the prime movers of the revolution of 1740 which brought Alvardi to

---

[64] Ibid., vol. 6, 14 June 1742; BPC, vol. 15, f. 194vo, 21 June 1742.
[65] Ibid., vol. 6, 6 June 1743; BPC, vol. 16, f. 181vo, 10 June 1743.
[66] Ibid., vol. 6, 2 July 1743.
[67] W.W. Hunter, *A Statistical Account of Bengal*, vol. IX, p. 254.
[68] BPC, vol. 8, f. 260, 13 July 1730.
[69] Ibid., vol. 8, f. 234vo, 2 June 1730.

power. It is well known that the Seths played a major role in the revolution of 1757 which brought about the downfall of Sirajuddaullah. Jean Law, the chief of the French factory at Kasimbazar, wrote: 'It is this family [Jagat Seth] who conducted all his [Alivardi's] business and it may be said that it had long been the chief cause of all the revolutions in Bengal.'[70]

As to the wealth of the house of the Jagat Seths, it is extremely difficult to form a correct estimate. Gholam Hossein, the author of *Seir Mutaqherin*, writes: 'Their wealth was such that there is no mentioning it without seeming to exaggerate and to deal in extravagant fables.'[71] 'As the Ganges pours its water into the sea by a hundred mouths,' wrote a Bengali poet, 'so wealth flowed into the treasury of the Seths.'[72] In the early sixties of the eighteenth century William Bolts estimated that the house possessed a capital of 7 *krors* [70 million] of rupees, 'as his countrymen calculate'.[73] N.K. Sinha thinks that in their heyday they must have owned at least 140 million rupees.[74] Luke Scrafton made an estimate of the annual income of the Jagat Seths in 1757 (Table 5.1).[75]

When the Marathas, guided by Mir Habib, led a lightning raid into Murshidabad in 1742, they succeeded in plundering Jagat Seth's house and carried away 20 million rupees (0.3 million according to Karam Ali, the author of *Muzaffarnama*) besides a quantity of other goods. The translator of *Seir Mutaqherin* was struck by the remarkable fact that this huge sum was all in Arcot rupees and added 'so amazing a loss which would distress any monarch in Europe, affected him so little, that he continued to give government bills of exchange at sight of full one cror at a time'.[76]

---

[70] S.C. Hill, *Three Frenchmen in Bengal*, p. 77.

[71] *Seir*, vol. II, p. 458.

[72] Little, *Jagatseth*, p.3.

[73] Bolts, *Considertaions*, p. 158.

[74] Little, *Jagatseth*, p. XVII.

[75] Luke Scrafton to Col. Clive, 17 Dec. 1757, Orme Mss., India, XVIII, f. 5043; Eur. G23, Box 37.

[76] Quoted in Little, *Jagatseth*, p. 120; J.N. Sarkar, *Bengal Nawabs*, p. 29.

Table 5.1
The Jagat Seths' Estimated Annual Income, 1757
(Rupees)

On 2/3 of revenue at 10%	10,60,000
Interest from zamindars at 12%	13,50,000
On recoining 50 lakhs at 7%	3,50,000
Interest on 40 lakhs at 37 $\frac{1}{2}$%	15,00,000
Interest from Batta or Exchange rates 7 to 8 lakhs	7,00,000
Total	49,60,000

[Source: Scrafton to Clive, 17 December, 1757]

The power and influence wielded by the house of Jagat Seths were so great that the Dutch Directors in Bengal always made it a point to recommend to their successors in office to have good relations with the house. Sichtermann wrote in his 'memorie' in 1744 that Jagat Seth Fatechand was the greatest banker of Hindusthan (voornaamsten wisselaar van geheel Hindosthan), his business was spread all over the 'kingdom' and though he did not take part directly in the governance, he had great influence over it. He suggested that the best way to keep him in good humour was to present him regularly small gifts like birds, spices and some curios.[77] The next Dutch Director, Jan Huijghens, wrote in 1750 in the instructions for his successor that the Company should maintain good relations with Baijnath, the *gomasta* of the Jagat Seths in Hughli, who could influence his masters in favour of the Dutch.[78] Similarly, Jan Kerseboom mentioned in his 'memorie' in 1755 that the business empire of Jagatseth Fatechand's heirs, Jagat Seth Mahtab Rai and Jagat Seth Swaroopchand, was growing more and more powerful and extensive because of the considerable sum they were lending to

[77] Sichtermann's 'Memorie', VOC, 2629, f. 967, 14 March 1744.
[78] Jan Huijghen's 'Memorie', VOC, 2763, f. 467, 20 March 1750.

the government. He recommended their friendship which was very important for the Company.[79] Louis Taillefert, the next Director, emphasized again that the Jagat Seths were the greatest bankers of Hindusthan. He wrote that the name of Jagat Seth Fatechand had been mentioned in Bengal letters for such a long period that the authorities in Holland might have begun to doubt whether such a person existed at all. He further pointed out that the *Kuthee* (office or agency house) of the Jagat Seths at Hughli was run under the name of Seth Manikchandji and Seth Anandchandji, in Dhaka under the name of Seth Manikchandji and Jagat Seth Fatechandji, and in Patna under the name of Seth Manikchandji and Seth Dayachandji. It is extremely significant that the house of the Jagat Seths made all the bankers and money changers in Bengal and many in Bihar subservient to them, and those who did not submit to them were gradually eliminated from the business with the connivance of the government. The *batta* or exchange rate and rates of the bills of exchange were manipulated entirely by the house which secured all these extraordinary privileges through the large sums of money it advanced to the government.[80]

Another merchant prince, the famous Umichand, played a major role in the commercial life of Bengal, especially in the last three decades of the first half of the eighteenth century. An upcountry merchant from Agra,[81] on being domiciled in Bengal in the second decade of the eighteenth century, he began his commercial operations in Calcutta under the aegis of Bishnudas Sett, a *dadni* merchant who was also at one time the broker of the English Company.[82] He had established himself as a leading merchant by the early 1730s. His activities were mainly in two

---

[79] Jan Kerseboom's 'Memorie', VOC, 2849, ff. 128-128vo, 14 Feb. 1755.

[80] Louis Taillefert's 'Memorie', VOC, 2849, f. 247vo-248vo, 27 Oct. 1755.

[81] Umichand and his brother Deepchand have been referred to as 'Agrawallah' dwelling in Azimabad in 1747, Fact. Records, Patna, vol. 2, 3 April 1742; In another document, Umichand was referred to as 'formerly of Agra', see BPC, vol. 17, f. 276vo.

[82] Sinha, *Economic History of Bengal*, vol. 1, p.6.

areas— Bihar whose economy was based in Patna, and the region centred round Calcutta with the Company's investments, financial activities and country trade. In 1731 he, along with the Company's broker Bishnudas Sett, was accused of malpractice in the *dadni* investment. But the Council did not think it prudent to dispense with Umichand's services and thought it proper to give him a small share of the *dadni* 'for fear he should leave us to go to the French or other European nations'.[83] In 1735 Umichand was again accused of indulging in fraudulent practices in the investment and the Calcutta Council decided not to 'let him have any more Dadney...and to record him disqualified ever to serve the Company as a merchant again'.[84] However, he was restored as a *dadni* merchant again in 1739 and provided investment for the Company until 1753, when the *dadni* system was replaced by the *gomasta* system. In 1747 he proposed to undertake one-third of the Company's total investment 'in equal proportion for ready money'. While most of the Council agreed to Umichand's proposal, John Jackson dissented stating that 'he thinks it imprudent to lift up any particular one too high above the rest'.[85] In reply to Jackson, John Forster of the Council noted that Umichand was 'not raised above them by this contract with us but was before their superiority, his natural and acquired capacity for business, his extraordniary knowledge of the Inland trade and his greater command of money all which qualities I think render him a proper person to deal with for ready money'.[86] Umichand was given the contract for one-third of the investment amounting to about 0.9 million rupees.[87]

Umichand was not only a *dadni* merchant but also did quite substantial business independently of the English Company. Like other merchant princes of the time, he tried to monopolize trade in certain commodities. As early as 1731 the English factors at Kasimbazar reported that 'Omichund's gomastah had by fraudu-

[83] BPC, vol. 8, f. 419, 21 July 1731; vol. 9, ff. 17vo-18, 23 March 1732.

[84] C & B. Abstr., vol. 4, f. 82, para. 144, 24 Jan. 1735.

[85] BPC, vol. 19, f. 277vo, 8 June 1747; Beng. Letters Recd., vol. 21, ff. 219-20; *FWIHC*, vol. 1, pp. 193-94.

[86] BPC, vol. 20, f.109-9vo, 15 Aug. 1747.

[87] Ibid., vol. 19, f. 298, 25 June 1747.

lent practices obtained an unlawful grant from the Phousdar of Rungpore, for engrossing all the opium of that place'. His brother and *gomasta* Samjee employed *vakil* (political agent) of his own at the *darbar* to represent their interest, and gave valuable presents to government officers.[88] It seems that Umichand also tried to monopolize the trade in grain.[89] The Court of Directors wrote from London in 1734 that Umichand 'is no longer worthy of our protection'.[90] But the Company could hardly do without transacting business wih Umichand, especially for Bihar goods. He was closely connected with Alivardi Khan's government at Patna from the late 1730s and in 1741 he farmed the mint at Patna.[91] His brother Deepchand controlled the *faujdari* of *sarkar* Saran which was the major centre of saltpetre production in Bihar.[92] The combination of Umichand, Deepchand and Khwaja Wazid had complete control of the Bihar trade and a similar domination over smaller traders and contractors. Umichand was mainly concerned with the saltpetre trade and opium business, and the latter he monopolized.[93] He was a major contractor with the Company for saltpetre. Through their influence over the Bihar administration and farming of the centres of saltpetre production, Umichand and Deepchand almost monopolized the saltpetre trade.

Umichand had also a close connection with the administration at Murshidabad. When his name was struck off the list of the Company's *dadni* merchants in 1735, Haji Ahmed, Alivardi's brother and one of the most influential persons at the court, sent word to the Company to reinstate Umichand as a *dadni* merchant and that he (Haji) would be security for any sum advanced to him.[94] Such strong support from Haji Ahmed only indicates the great extent of Umichand's influence on the administration. His farming of territories producing saltpetre and the mint at Patna,

[88] Ibid., vol. 8, ff. 400-400vo, 21 June 1731; vol. 9, f. 22vo, 3 April 1732.

[89] DB., vol. 105, ff. 453-54, para. 124, 11 Feb. 1732.

[90] Ibid., vol. 106, f. 182, para. 39, 29 Jan. 1734.

[91] C & B. Abstr., vol. 4, f.376, 11 Dec. 1741.

[92] BPC, vol. 17, f. 769, 16 Dec. 1744.

[93] Home Misc. Series, vol. 192, f. 64.

[94] Fact. Records, Kasimbazar, vol. 5, 21 Jan. 1736.

his monopoly of the opium trade etc., could only be procured and maintained through a strong connection with the ruling elite of the country. Clearly he was very influential at the court and could retain the affection of Alivardi with exotic presents.[95] He also won the confidence of the next nawab Sirajuddaullah. He has generally been portrayed as a villian for his role in the Plassey conspiracy. But there should be little doubt as to his capacity, independence and business acumen as a merchant. Orme, who knew him well, wrote:[96]

> Among the Gentoo merchants established in Calcutta, was one named Omichund, a man of great sagacity and under-standing, which he had employed for forty years with unceasing diligence to increase his fortune ... he was become the most opulent inhabitant of the colony. The extent of his habitation, divided into various departments; the number of his servants continually employed in various occupations, and a retinue of armed men in constant pay, resembled more the state of a prince than the condition of a merchant.

There can be no doubt that Umichand was a wealthy merchant. He could provide one-third of the Company's investment amounting to rupees 1 million even without receiving any payment in advance. In 1750 the Company owed him more than 1.6 million rupees.[97] At the time of Sirajuddaullah's sack of Calcutta in 1756, an amount of 0.4 million rupees in cash besides 'many valuable effects' were found in his treasury.[98] If the annual income of his brother Deepchand of Patna was at least 0.1 million rupees,[99] Umichand's earnings can only be guessed. He was the owner of most of the best houses and 'had many other interests' in Calcutta. 'The whole body of Omichand's peons and armed domestics' numbered three hundred.[100] In his will after distrib-uting about Rs 1,60,000 among the members of his family, he

[95] Hill, *Bengal in 1756-57,* vol. II, pp. 63-64.
[96] Orme, *Military Transactions,* vol.II, Sec. I, pp. 50-51.
[97] BPC, vol. 23, f. 186, 1 July 1750.
[98] Orme, *Military Transactions,* vol. II, Sec. I, p.78.
[99] BPC, vol. 17, f. 372vo, 1 Dec. 1744.
[100] Orme, *Military Transactions,,* vol. II, Sec. I, pp. 60, 128.

gifted away the entire residue as *debottur* to Sri Govind Nanakji.
After payment of Rs 37,000 to the Magdalen House and
Foundling Hospital in England, the estate was valued at 4.2
million rupees.[101]

Like Umichand, the Armenian Khwaja Wazid played a
significant role in Bengal's commercial life in the forties and
fifties of the eighteenth century. The Armenian merchant
prince's commercial empire was based in Hughli, the commercial
capital of Bengal. He had extensive business transactions with the
French and the Dutch, and through Umichand also with the
English. He seems to have been extremely devious and had a
passion to extend his commercial interests at any cost. His
allegiance was swung by the prospect of commercial advantages.
Through political influence, he seems to have consolidated his
commercial position throughout the 1740s. By virtue of his great
influence on the nawab, he managed to gain virtual control over
the trade and commerce of Bihar by the late 1740s. Backed by
the court, he had risen from being a leading Armenian merchant
to a monopolist in Bengal's two major extractive commodities—
saltpetre and salt.

Wazid obtained the saltpetre monopoly in 1753. The Fort
William Council reported on 2 April 1753 that Wazid procured
a licence to deal in saltpetre 'exclusive of any other purchasers'.[102]
The monopoly in the salt trade was even more lucrative and was
farmed in 1752 for Rs 25,000 or Rs 30,000 a year with Wazid
importing salt on favourable customs duties. Batson wrote in
1763 that 'Coja Wazeed of Hughly had the salt farm of Bengal
for many years for an inconsiderable sum'.[103] The anonymous
author of an English manuscript, writing in around 1752,
noted:[104] 'Salt on account of Coja Wazeed is exempted from these
duties and pays only:

[101] Home Misc. Series, vol. 420, ff. 25, 29; N.K. Sinha, *Economic
History of Bengal*, vol. I, p. 245.
[102] BPC, vol.26, f.110, 2 April 1753; Beng. Letters Recd., vol. 22,
para. 18, f. 410.
[103] Orme Mss. O.V. 134, f. 13.
[104] Mss. Eur., D. 283, f. 22.

Import: per 100 md. one rupee which is Rs. 0.8 percent
Export: per 100 md. one rupee which is Rs. 0.8 percent
Total: per 200 md. two rupee which is Rs. 1.0 percent'.

Wazid was also active in maritime commerce in the 1740s and greatly enhanced his position in the country trade by the acquisition of a fleet of trading vessels which dominated the maritime trade of Hughli in the 1750s. The Dutch Director Kerseboom and the Fort William Council referred to Wazid's trading house at Surat.[105]

Wazid operated his business with monopolistic design. He had tried, through his influence on the Bengal administration, to monopolize the trade of Bihar *suba*. As a merchant his influence and power were so great that he would never enter into any contract which would require other merchants to stand security for him.[106] The tremendous influence Khwaja Wazid exerted in the Murshidabad court, next only to that wielded by the Jagat Seths, is reflected in the fact that he often acted in the role of an intermediary between the Calcutta Council and the nawab, and this indicated the growing importance of the merchant princes in Bengal politics. There is little doubt that Wazid was closely connected with the Murshidabad *darbar*. In the course of the Calcutta Council's debate whether the saltpetre contract should be made with Khwaja Wazid, the owner of the commodity, or Umichand, Wazid's close link with the government was revealed clearly. Most of the Council members referred to him either as a *darbar* official or closely connected with it.[107] Orme described Wazid as 'the principal merchant of the Province'[108] while Watts and Collet of the Kasimbazar factory noted in 1756: 'Coja Wazeed the greatest merchant in Bengal...resides in Hughley and had great influence with the Nabob.'[109] Jan Kerseboom, the chief of the Dutch factory, wrote

[105] VOC, 2849, ff.105vo-106, 16 Feb. 1755; S C. Hill, *Bengal in 1756-57*, vol. II, p. 87.
[106] BPC, vol. 26, f. 132vo, 3 May 1753; C & B. Abstr., vol. 5, f. 424; Beng. Letters Recd., vol. 22, f. 412.
[107] BPC, vol. 26, ff. 131vo-132vo, 3 May 1753.
[108] Orme, *Military Transactions*, vol. II, Sec. I, p. 58.
[109] *Records of Fort St. George, Diary and Consultation Book, 1756.* vol. 86, p. 32; Orme Mss., O.V. 19, p. 104.

in 1755 that Khwaja Wazid was lately given the title of 'Faqqur Tousjaar' [Fakhr-ut-tujar] meaning 'supporter of the treasure'. He mentioned that Wazid was truly the maintainer of the riches of the rulers in the court of Nawab Alivardi Khan. He gave the nawab rich presents willingly, rather than under compulsion and the Dutch chief recommended that Wazid's friendship should be cultivated as he could prove very useful to the Company.[110] It is worth noting here that in that very year, Taillefert, who succeeded Kerseboom as Director in Bengal, significantly remarked, while commenting on the residents of the Company's village (in Chinsurah, a suburb of Hughli) that the Company should not have admitted 'respectable persons of so high standing as the Moorish merchant Coja Wazeed who trade overseas or who have such internal trade that in some respects they can be considered as competitors of the Company, and who deem themselves to be on an equal footing with the Directors [of the Dutch Company], if not their superiors'.[111]

Of the merchant princes involved in the Plassey conspiracy, Wazid was the last to join the bandwagon. He was a shrewd,

---

[110] Jan Kerseboom's 'Memorie', VOC, 2849, f. 128vo, 14 Feb. 1755.

[111] Taillefert's 'Memorie', VOC, 2849, f. 128vo, 14 Feb. 1755. It is obvious from this reference that Wazid lived in Chinsurah for some time. But this must have been for a short period because in early 1750, in a letter from Bengal, Wazid was referred to as 'the merchant who was removed' (from Chinsurah), VOC, 2732, f.9vo, Hughli to Heeren XVII, 11 Feb. 1750. It is of interest that in the Dutch records Wazid was frequently referred to as 'Moor Merchant' (Moors Koopman). There can be hardly any doubt that Wazid was an Armenian and there is no evidence that he was ever converted to Islam. It might have been possible that because of his close connection with the Muslim rulers, the Dutch referred to him as 'Moor merchant' or 'Khoja Mhamet Wazid'. There is evidence that the Armenian merchants changed their names often for the sake of convenience in trade. Thus in the early seventeenth century, Khwaja Philipos of New Julfa was known as Philippe de Zagly in Courlande while in Persia his name was Imam Kuli Beg (Robert Gulbenkian, 'Philippe de Zagly, merchand armenien de Julfa, et l'e'tablissement du Commerce persan en Courlande eu 1626', Revue des etudes armeniennes, n.s. 7, 1970, pp. 361-369). So it might be possible that Wazid also added 'Muhammed' to his name to enhance his business prospects.

talented and unscrupulous operator who belonged to Sirajuddaullah's inner circle of advisers. He had been a serious obstacle to the success of any coup until May 1757. He joined the conspiracy as he badly needed a revolution to restore the political backing for his commercial empire. But the gamble failed. The Plassey revolution brought about the downfall of the merchant princes—sooner or later. After 1757 both Khwaja Wazid and Umichand felt the consequences of an altered and hostile environment. With the Plassey revolution went the foundations of their commercial empires: court backing for trade monopolies and contracts for investments with the European companies.

5.3 MERCHANTS AND RULERS

In his unique narrative of the trading world of Asia in the early seventeenth century, J.C. van Leur emphasized the function performed by the small trader and the peddler in the distribution of commercial goods. Though he carefully distinguished between the small peddling trade and the large wholesale merchants to be found in India and China, yet at the same time he adds: 'But all that does not change the fact that there appears to be only one conclusion regarding international Asian trade....It was a small-scale peddling trade, a trade in valuable high quality products'.[112] Niels Steensgaard, in his excellent study of the overland caravan trade in the early seventeenth century, had reinforced the peddler thesis of van Leur and stressed that the ordinary entrepreneurial character of the Asian trade was a sum of peddling activities. He admits that the peddling trade could make use of fairly sophisticated commercial methods, but he concludes: 'Nevertheless the ordinary entrepreneur operates on the pedlar level, and there is nothing in the sources to indicate the existence of comprehensive coordinated organizations—of an Armenian, Turkish or Persian version of a Fugger, Cranfield or Tripp'.[113] As has been rightly pointed out by K.N. Chaudhuri, the activities of Armenian, Turkish or Persian merchants have

[112] J.C. van Leur, *Indonesian Trade and Society*, pp. 132-33, 197-201, 219-20.
[113] Niels Steensgaard, *Asian Trade Revolution*, p. 30.

not yet been studied in depth from original sources to believe uncritically in such a categorical statement. It can be proved from evidence in European sources that the existence of a man like Hovhannes or the *banjaras*[114] does not justify the conclusion that trade in India or the Middle East was carried on only at the peddling level. In India the true peddlers were those who were engaged mostly in local trade. They went from village to village with their pack bullocks collecting wares and selling them in a similar way. But the Armenian merchants were a different category. They were a group of 'highly skilled arbitrage dealers', ready to deal in any commodity that offered the prospect of a profit.[115] There were among them, as the case study of Bengal discussed earlier would endorse, merchants whose status was equal to that of the most successful merchants of London and Amsterdam. The cases of Khwaja Surhaud Israel[116] and Khwaja Wazid, the two prominent Armenian merchants in Bengal in the first half of the eighteenth century, will bear the point out.

The European trading companies in Bengal generally contracted for procurement of export commodities with substantial merchants who could handle a large volume of trade. The commercial empires and the trading world of Umichand and Khwaja Wazid, and most important of all, the business world of the Jagat Seths—as have been examined earlier—were not the ones which correspond to the world of Hovhannes but were the Indian equivalent of the business world of the Medici family or the Fuggers or the Tripps. We have seen earlier how extensive the trading activities of Umichand and Khwaja Wazid were and how they monopolized several sectors of Bengal's economy. The Jagat Seths were the most powerful economic force in the state. It is apparent that the business houses headed by such wealthy and influential merchants as the Jagat Seths, Umichand and

---

[114] Steensgaard refers to Hovhannes' journal which indicates only small scale transactions of the Armenian merchant, but he was actually a factor operating in India and Tibet for his principals in Ispahan; *banjaras* were grain merchants who traded in Indian villages while moving from one part of the country to another and were involved in small retail trade.

[115] K.N. Chaudhuri, *Trading World*, pp. 135-39, 145-51.

[116] For Khwaja Surhaud Israel, see, S. Chaudhuri, *Trade and Commercial Organization*, pp. 94, 96, 124, 131, 134, 135.

Khwaja Wazid were akin to a Fugger or Cranfield in their ability to undertake extensive and organized commercial ventures. Thus, it can be safely asserted that the Asian entrepreneurial structure included both great and small merchants, though in its organization it was perhaps more similar to the Venetian *fraterna* than the impersonal business form of joint stock companies.

The trading activities of the Asian merchants in Bengal, however, confirm van Leur's thesis that the merchant gentleman in Asia was a 'political animal'. His contention that the patrician merchants were closely connected with the ruling hierarchy and in some sense carried on political trade is corroborated by the experience of Asian merchants in Bengal. He writes: '...the wealthy merchant class was allied to the mighty who exercises social and political authority'.[117] This observation conforms well to the cases of the merchant princes of Bengal — the Jagat Seths, Umichand and Khwaja Wazid. We have seen earlier how the power and wealth of the merchant princes were closely allied with the favour from the *darbar*. The sources of the immense wealth and the great influence of the Jagat Seths, as observed earlier, were dependent on court support. So much was the ruling support necessary for the eminence of the Jagat Seths that when it was gradually withdrawn after the battle of Plassey, the house crashed headlong. Similar was the case with Umichand and Khwaja Wazid. One of the main props of their rise to such a great height of eminence in the commercial life of Bengal, especially in the forties and fifties of the eighteenth century, was the *darbar* backing.

This close alliance between the merchant princes and the ruling elite, and the great political influence enjoyed by them are entirely different in nature as evident from the findings of two recent studies on Gujarat in the sixteenth century and Surat in the first half of the eighteenth.[118] Both portrayed the merchant as an independent entity, with hardly any close connection with the ruling hierarchy. But the state in Bengal was quite concerned about the affairs of the merchants. That the state cared for the merchants and the latter could turn to the state for redressal of

---

[117] J.C. van Leur, *Indonesian Trade and Society*, p. 204.

[118] M.N.Pearson, *Merchants and Rulers*; Ashin Das Gupta, *Indian Merchants*.

their grievances will be borne out by the events of 1748-49. Two Armenian ships carrying goods of the Hughli merchants from Jedda and Basra were captured in 1748 by the English fleet. The Hughli merchants made a representation regarding this to nawab Alivardi Khan who directed the Company to compensate the merchants' losses and wrote: 'The Syeds, Mogulls, Armenians and merchants of Hooghly have complained....These merchants are the Kingdom's benefactors. Their imports and exports are an advantage to all men and their complaints are so grievous that I cannot forebear any longer giving ear to them'.[119] So great was the political influence and power of the merchants that in their letter to the Calcutta Council the Hughli merchants dared write: 'The skirts of the government are in our hands and we will not cease seeking their justice until we have full satisfaction.'[120]

The distinctive feature of the mercantile world in Bengal was the co-existence of big and small merchants of different castes and regions, operating side by side in various trade marts of the province. Alexander Hume made an interesting analysis of the merchants connected with the investment of the Ostend Company in 1730.[121] Of the 24 merchants enlisted by him, 21 were Hindus, 3 Muslims and 1 Armenian. The Hindu merchants belonged to different caste groups such as Sen, Datta, Majumdar, Khan, Nandy, Mullick—the last two, as he specifically mentioned, belonging to weaving castes. Again, among these merchants, several were quite substantial and big merchants like the Armenian Khwaja 'Mahmet' Fazel or the Gujarati Manikchand, while a few others like Muhammed Bakr or Ramjiban Sen were small dealers who worked mainly on *arrot* or commission, by sending their agents to different *aurungs* after receiving the advance from the Company. Hume's report also brings out clearly the close connection between the merchants and the government at Murshidabad. He categorically pointed out Khwaja Fazel's 'great influence over the Moors government'. Often the merchants were recommended to the Company by influential people. For example, Balaram Nandi was recom-

[119] BPC, vol. 22, f. 96, Annex. to Consult., 9 Jan. 1749.
[120] Ibid., vol. 22, ff. 134vo-135, Annex. to Consult., 20 Feb. 1749.
[121] Alexander Hume's 'Memorie', Stadsarchief Antwerp, GIC 5769.

mended to Hume by Fatechand's *gomasta* Baijnath. But Hume warned against appointing merchants recommended by *darbar* officials or persons connected with the government as, in that case, the Company might have to face great difficulty in realizing any dues from such merchants. The general practice in the commercial world of Bengal was that 'whoever recommends a man to any business is answerable for him'. Some of the merchants used their own capital for business while others borrowed money from the credit market and sometimes also from the ruling elite. Though generally the merchants dealt in most of the commodities, Hume's report suggests a certain amount of specialization among the merchants. While commenting on the Gujarati merchant Manikchand, he stated categorically that the Gujarati merchants in Bengal generally 'dealt in exchange, jewels, gold and silver, and silk, some of them in opium and other Patna goods but rarely in piece-goods'. This is also corroborated by later evidence that some of the merchants specialized in the trade of silk piece-goods (e.g. as we have seen earlier that the Kasimbazar factors reported in 1744 that only 3 substantial merchants of Murshidabad provided the Company with *taffetas* which 'the other merchants do not care to meddle in'), others in *garras* while even in the silk trade, only a few merchants dealt in Rangpur silk while 'Gujarat' or Kumarkhali varieties were traded by most silk merchants.

A common practice among the merchants in Bengal was to conduct business in their own names as also in the name of their relations or even children, often minor ones. This was done probably to keep the real identity of the owners a secret and thus reduce the possibility of political exactions. In an enquiry made by the English Company officials about charges of corruption and malpractice against the broker, Bishnudas Sett and his associate, Umichand, in 1731, it was revealed that these two supplied a large part of the *dadni* goods in their own names, in the name of their children and also under fictitious names.[122] Such practices, however, were not uncommon. That the merchants often took resort to such strategem is also evident from the Dutch report that in the early 1760s they succeeded in recruiting the Dhaka merchant, Santosh Roy, whose real name

[122] BPC, vol. 8, ff. 424-424vo, 26 July 1731.

was Raghunath Mitra, as their merchant for providing textiles. In 1762 he procured cloth for the Dutch not in his name but in the name of his son, Anandamoy Mitra.[123] At the same time the tradition among merchants was to help out others in the business who were not able to fulfil their contract obligations with the Companies for one reason or another. Thus in 1750, in addition to his own quota, Umichand supplied the English Company with textiles worth 0.03 million rupees which, according to the contract, were to be provided by Pitambar Sett, Gangabishnu 'Mendrew' (?) and their 'setts'.[124]

As regards the contention that the decline of the Bengal merchants in the early 1750s forced the East India Company to change its investment pattern from the *dadni* to the *gomasta* system, it can be safely asserted that there was really no decline of the merchants in Bengal, and the change in the investment system was due to other considerations. The prominent merchant families of Calcutta, the Setts and Basaks, and the Katmas of Kasimbazar were still prominent and quite substantial merchants in the early fifties. Moreover, merchant princes like the Jagat Seths, Umichand and Khwaja Wazid were in their heyday during these years. So long as these merchant princes were there, Bengal's credit market was as strong as ever, and there was no paucity of capital for smaller merchants to thrive in their trade. The fact of the matter was that the *dadni* merchants refused to contract for investment in 1753 except absolutely on their own terms. In view of the uncertainty of trade in the troubled times, they rejected the Company's terms, viz. that the *dadni* should not exceed 30 per cent which was generally 85 per cent earlier, the contract should be made on 'old musters' which were prepared in normal times, the penalty of 10 per cent to be levied on any deficiency of supply[125]—terms which the merchants thought, not without some justification, were extremely unreasonable. On the other hand, as the private trade of the Company's servants was dwindling in the early fifties, they saw an opportunity in the introduction of the *gomasta* system to augment their private trade interest.

---

[123] Louis Taillefert's 'Memorie', HR 246, ff. 93-95, 17 Nov. 1763.
[124] BPC, vol. 23, f. 185vo, 1 July 1750.
[125] Ibid., vol. 26, f. 164, Annex. to Consult. 7 June 1753.

Nor were the merchants in Bengal subservient in any way to the European companies. The Asian merchants trading in Bengal held fast to their ground in the first half of the eighteenth century and successfully resisted attempts by the East India Companies to dictate terms to them, let alone by individual Europeans.[126] Partnership or interdependence as distinct from a later period of subjugation was the keynote of the relationship between Asian merchants and European traders. This only confirms the views held by historians from case studies of different parts of India.[127] Throughout the first half of the eighteenth century the merchants maintained their traditional organization of commerce without any serious strain, though they had to extend the scope of methods generally practised. There was hardly any innovation to encompass the 'new situation' arising out of the expanded demand of the European companies for Bengal commodities. The commercial aptitude of the merchants in Bengal was no less inferior to that of the European traders. An analysis of the trading activities and methods of these merchants reveals the keenest competition among buyers and sellers, an eager search for exclusive information, the organization of rings and commercial monopoly which the European companies tried to foil but often with little success. But trade or business was the concern of individuals rather than of groups acting in common interest. Men tended to act as individual merchants, as members of families, at most one in a group thrown together in the course of business. Impersonal cooperation in the institution of business, as had already been developed in Europe by this time, was relatively uncommon. Even cooperation at a personal level was not easy to come by. As in other parts of India, a commercial venture was mainly the risk of an individual merchant or a very small group of merchants

[126] For such situations in the late seventeenth and early eighteenth century, and some of the important Bengal Merchants, see S. Chaudhuri, *Trade and Commercial Organization*, pp. 62-85; I. Ray, 'The French Company and the Merchants of Bengal', *IESHR*, VIII (1971), PP. 46-48.

[127] P.J. Marshall, *East Indian Fortunes*, pp. 44-45; S. Arasaratnam, 'Trade and Political Dominion in South India, 1750-1790: Changing British Indian Relationships', *MAS*, vol. 13, pt. I, Feb. 1979, pp. 21-22; Holden Furber, *Rival Empires*, pp. 315-16.

taking part in it.

The remarkable growth of the financial machinery for credit and exchange, thanks to the house of the Jagat Seths, and the specialized activities of a large class of merchants, undoubtedly point towards the fact that merchant capital and commercial organizaton were highly developed in Bengal in the first half of the eighteenth century. The general picture of merchant community and commercial organization that one finds in the European records is one of a long established and highly skilled tradition. The expertise in financial and trading methods was confined to closed commercial groups and was acquired through hereditary channels. But it appears that business transactions were not only confined within the same caste or communal group—these transcended, more often than not, caste or communal boundaries. It was not unusual to find a Hindu *bania* of a Muslim merchant or a Muslim associate of a Hindu or Armenian trader. The merchant community, especially in the urban areas, though probably organized on caste lines at the primary level, was a homogeneous group in general, acting in concert whenever necessary with little regard to caste or regional affiliations. Thus while the *dadni* merchants of Calcutta included high castes like Sen, Bose, Mitra, Roy, Chaudhury, Ghose, Dey, weaving castes like Sett, Basak, Nandy, Mullick and the so-called low castes like Seal, Telly, as also merchants from Gujarat, Rajasthan, the Punjab and northern India and the Armenians, they stood firm 'as a body' against the impositions of the English Company in 1753 — a unique instance of solidarity of the mercantile community. As the Company was quite conscious of the unity of the merchants, it became apprehensive that they might act 'as a collusive body' and 'may have power to give us much interruption in the execution of this plan'. So it instructed William Watts at Kasimbazar 'to be upon watch to learn if there is any disturbance given to it at the Durbar by our late Merchants and to put an immediate stop to it'.[128] The singular instance of the Setts refusing to contract in 1748 on the ground that three of the new merchants introduced into *dadni* in the previous year belonged to a 'different caste' seems to be only a subterfuge to exclude these merchants who were previously *dadni* merchants of

[128] BPC, vol. 26, ff. 163, 165-166, 7 June 1753, Annex. to Consult. 7 June 1753.

the Dutch, and hence it should not be taken as serious objections pertaining to caste considerations. It was basically an attempt to keep out the competitors in the field. Had it been otherwise, the Setts or other Calcutta merchants would not have contracted for the supply of goods to the English along with those merchants in 1750.[129]

The European companies hardly ever commanded the markets from time to time for particular commodities, nor did they even dominate the 'commercial outlook'. These were the exclusive prerogatives of the Asian merchants who, it appears, through their wealth, influence and business acumen controlled the entire wholesale trade within the area of their operations. The affluence and wealth as also the trading and commercial empire of the merchant princes—the Jagat Seths, Umichand and Khwaja Wazid—compare favourably with the credit and influence of Virji Vohra, Mulla Abdul Gaffur or the Parekhs of the seventeenth century Surat. It is interesting to note that the merchant princes of Surat were indigenous merchants belonging to the locality. But the merchant princes of Bengal, like the prominent merchants in Bengal in the second half of the seventeenth century,[130] were all outsiders. This is perhaps the historical evidence of the fact that Bengalis in general had seldom been keen about the profession of a merchant.

[129] Ibid., vol. 23, ff. 188-90, Annex to Consult. 29 June 1750.
[130] S. Chaudhuri, *Trade and Commercial Organization,* p. 98.

6

STRUCTURE AND ORGANIZATION OF TEXTILE INDUSTRY

The textiles produced in Bengal, especially the finer varieties, had received overwhelming appreciation for centuries. Even in the late 1760s the Dutch traveller Stavorinus stated that the Bengal muslins were made so fine that a piece of twenty yards in length or even longer could be put into a common pocket 'tobacco-box'.[1]   It was not only the visitors from the West who were surprised by the extreme fineness and exquisite beauty of the Bengal textiles, but even to Robert Orme, the official historian of the English Company who lived in Bengal in the early 1750s, it remained a puzzle 'how works of such extraordinary niceness can be produced by a people ...who must be deprived of such tools as seem absolutely necessary to finish such manufactures'. His 'surprise was heightened' when he found that at Dhaka 'where all the cloths for the use of the king and his seraglio are made' were of 'such wonderful fineness as to exceed ten times the price of any linens permitted to be made for Europeans, or any one else in the kingdom'. He tried to account for the exceptional quality of the fabrics by referring to the high skill of the Bengali weavers and comparing it with that of their European counterparts. He writes:[2]

---

[1] J.S. Stavorinus, *Voyages*, vol. 1, p.413. The 'tobacco-box' here actually meant snuff-box.

[2] Robert Orme, *Historical Fragments,* p.412.

As much as an Indian is born deficient in mechanical strength, so much his whole frame endowed with an exceeding degree of sensibility and pliantness. The hand of an Indian cook-wench shall be more delicate than that of an European beauty; the skin and features of a porter shall be softer than those of a *petit maître*.

Similarly the Danish report on the textile production in Bengal, written in 1789, also reflected on how 'through unwearying industry and with the help of a few paltry tools' the weavers in Bengal produced 'the prettiest and finest cloths without use of machines'.[3] In his famous report on the Dhaka cloth manufacture in 1800, John Taylor, the Commercial Resident of Dhaka, dwelt on the 'singular beauty of the Fabric' and 'the extraordinary skill requisite in manufacturing it'.[4] But one should not overlook the fact that Bengal had at the same time a traditional and flourishing trade and industry in ordinary and medium quality textiles which enjoyed a substantial market in many parts of India and Asia in general. The textile trade from Bengal to Coromandel, Ceylon, South-East Asia as also to West and Central Asia in the seventeenth and first half of the eighteenth century comprised mainly coarse and medium piece-goods while the trade with areas in the region of Agra, Lahore, Multan, the Persian Gulf and the Red Sea might have been mostly in finer qualities. The European companies however exported both ordinary and fine textiles throughout the period of our study.

6.1 BENGAL'S COMPARATIVE ADVANTAGES

Bengal had several advantages over other centres of textile production and trade in India of which the most important and distinct ones may be identified as a) abundance of highly skilled labour; b) remarkably low cost of production; c) cheap and highly flexible transport facilities in its riverine network and finally, d) a flourishing agriculture resulting in cheapness of staples like

[3] Ole Feldbaeck, 'Cloth Production in Bengal', *BPP*, vol. LXXXVI (July-Dec. 1967), p.126.
[4] Home Misc., vol. 456F, f.147.

rice, cotton yarn, silk thread etc. Besides, in common with other major centres of textile production like Gujarat, Coromandel and the Punjab, Bengal enjoyed for long an active regional and intra-Asiatic trade, the presence of an entrepreneurial class from all over Asia and locally produced raw materials like cotton and silk. But it should be noted that it was the comparative advantages of Bengal, listed above, over other centres of textile production that gave it the preponderance in textile trade and industry for centuries, including the period under review.

The whole process of textile manufacture was quite complex and involved the participation of a host of workmen. Right from the cultivation of cotton or mulberry plants, the spinning of cotton or reeling of silk, the warping, the fixing of the harness to the warp and the loom, and the final weaving and washing required highly specialized and technical skill. In its peasant-cultivators, spinners, reelers, weavers and washermen, Bengal had the special expertise needed for the complex craft of manufacturing cotton and silk textiles. The famous muslins of Dhaka and the silk piece-goods of Kasimbazar were specimens of the workmanship of the highly skilled labour force of the areas— a skill which was transmitted from one generation to another for centuries. And the Bengali workmen produced the finest quality of textiles with the simplest possible tools which provoked Orme to write: '...the tools which they use are as simple and plain as they can be imagined to be. The rigid clumsy fingers of an European would scarcely be able to make a piece of canvas with the instruments which are all that an Indian employs in making a piece of cambric.'[5]

That there was no dearth of the skilled work force, rather an abundance of it, in Bengal was because of the fact that textile production was primarily a domestic rural industry, the members of the whole family often participating in it. The spinning of cotton or the winding of silk was almost exclusively the monopoly of the women in the family who utilised their traditional and hereditary skill, taking time off the daily chores. The peasant-cultivator was often a weaver as well and whenever necessary

[5] Orme, *Historical Fragments*, p. 413.

could shift from one occupation to the other, part-time or full-time depending on the situation. It was almost a common feature in Bengal that even children contributed their part in the complex process of production of cloth. This abundance of labour together with the cheapness of staples like rice, wheat and yarn automatically kept the production costs lower in Bengal than in other regions. Again the staples were cheap because of the high productivity of the agricultural sector. There is hardly any need to emphasize the legendary cheapness of prices of provisions in Bengal which was attested to by all contemporary foreign travellers and observers.[6] To all this was added Bengal's unique advantage of having a cheap and an easy transport system in its numerous inland waterways. Almost every important producing area of Bengal textiles was easily accessible through navigable rivers and the cost of transportation from those areas to any trade mart of Bengal or main emporium of northern India or to the ports was probably the cheapest compared with that in any other region of India. So it is no wonder that Bengal enjoyed an unrivalled supremacy in textile trade and industry for centuries, and probably even more so for the period under review.

Distinct Features of Bengal Textile Industry

The textile industry in Bengal had several distinctive features. The first notable feature of Bengal's handicraft industry was that, as we have already noted, it was basically a domestic rural industry. There is no denying the fact that the industry thrived in urban areas of Bengal too, but the basic characteristic of the manufacture in Bengal was that it was mostly a rural and domestic industry. Orme's observation that in Bengal 'it is difficult to find a village in which every man, woman and child is not employed in making a piece of cloth' only brings out the predominantly rural character of the industry.[7] No doubt the European companies and to some extent, the Asian merchants, collected their cloth for export mainly at several trade marts and urban centres but that too through a network of intermediaries whose

[6] For some of the observations, see S. Chaudhuri, *Trade and Commercial Organization*, pp. 4-5, 241-46.

[7] Orme, *Historical Fragments*, p.409.

agents procured the wares from weavers or *hats* in the rural areas. Dhaka, Kasimbazar, Malda, Hughli, Radhanagar, Santipur, Jugdea etc. were mainly the emporia rather than prominent weaving centres. The Danish report cited earlier typically refers to this rural character of the industry when it notes that the district of Birbhum, the principal centre of *garra* (an ordinary calico) production, was 'almost solely inhabited by weavers'.[8]

That the textile industry in Bengal was primarily a rural domestic handicraft industry is borne out by the fact that the weaver was more often than not a peasant farmer. The specialized works such as spinning of cotton, winding of silk, were almost exclusively done by the women in the peasant family, and even the children of the family of the cultivator were involved in the process of manufacture. It was not only Orme who noted 'the assistance which a wife and family are capable of affording to the labours of the loom'[9] but among many others the Danish report too emphasized that the weaver bought cotton which 'he himself, his wife and family may clean and spin' and took the cloth after weaving to the market.[10] While describing the textile manufacture of Malda disrict in 1670, Henry Cansius of the Dutch Company stated that the hinterland of the *aurungs* in the district extended over as many as 350 villages.[11] In 1741 the English Council at Kasimbazar reported that the *garras*, one of the main staples of the European trade, were produced in the 'town and villages within the circuit of twenty miles round about Cutwah [Katwa] (which town is chief place to which they [merchants and weavers] bring said cloth when ready in order to send it away by boats or land carriage as the time of the year admits)'.[12] Even as late as 1757 the Dhaka factors, while considering the proposal of making contracts with weavers through *gomastas* excluding the *dalals* and *paikars*, noted that the 'extent of the different aurungs is so very considerable' that it would require an 'infinite number

---

[8] Ole Feldbaeck, 'Cloth Production in Bengal', *BPP*, p.128.

[9] Orme, *Historical Fragments*, pp. 409-10; Ole Feldbaeck, 'Cloth Production in Bengal', *BPP*, p. 126.

[10] Ibid., p. 126.

[11] Report of Henry Cansius on Malda, VOC, 1278, ff.2173-2174, 7 Sept. 1690.

[12] Fact. Records, Kasimbazar, vol. 6, 16 Oct. 1741.

of servants to overlook the weavers'.[13] Orme was perhaps not exaggerating the rural character of the textile industry in Bengal when he wrote that 'the weavers live entirely in villages' and the weaver was generally 'living and working with his wife and several children in a hut'.[14] This is rather in sharp contrast to the character of the industry in some other parts of India. Though in the Coromandel the textile industry was mainly a rural domestic handicraft industry like that of Bengal, in western and northern India it was urban-based or situated close to the main cities.[15]

Another distinct feature of Bengal's textile industry was its extremely diffused nature. As it was basically a rural domestic industry, the natural corollary was its extraordinary diffusion. An important factor contributing to the decentralization of the industry was the extensive and comparatively cheap means of Bengal's riverine transport system. As a result, the textile industry in Bengal could be highly decentralised and spread over a wide area, which was not the case in northern or western India. It should be noted that the 'vital qualitative difference between production for a purely local market and production for export and inter-regional trade'[16] was blurred to a considerable extent in so far as textile production in Bengal was concerned. So whether it was the traditional Asian merchants or the newcomers in the trade —the European companies in the seventeenth and the eighteenth centuries— all had to procure their wares through a network of intermediaries from areas widely dispersed all over Bengal. One of the main reasons why the Companies were not able to purchase textiles from the weavers directly was, besides their ignorance of the local language and market conditions, this widespread diffusion of the industry in Bengal.

A third distinctive feature of Bengal textile industry was its localization. Not only Orme but other travellers like Stavorinus as well emphasized the fact that every distinct kind of cloth was the product of a particular district.[17] Each and every locality

---

[13] Fact. Records, Dacca, vol. 3, 30 Nov. 1757.
[14] Orme, *Historical Fragments,* p. 410.
[15] K.N. Chaudhuri, *Trading World,* p. 249.
[16] Ibid., p. 241.
[17] Orme, *Historical Fragments,* p. 413; Stavorinus, *Voyages,* p. 474.

producing textiles had its special characteristic imprinted in the product so much that, according to Calcutta Council's report of 1752, the piece-goods could not be packed in one and the same bale as 'fabric of every aurung had its peculiar qualities'.[18] The main factors contributing to this localization and concentration of artisans in a particular area were the availability of the relevant raw material and 'the cumulative effect created by a hereditary concentration of craft skills'. It appears that the location of these centres of production was 'neutral with respect to transport costs' or other important mercantile considerations because not only the manufacture of luxury cloth was localized, but the same was the case with even coarse and medium quality calicoes. That is why while muslins were produced mostly in Dhaka and silk fabrics in Kasimbazar, places like Birbhum which were not-quite-so-near the port of shipment area produced ordinary textiles like garras and Malda which was a more distant place from the consideration of transport and shipment produced both fine and coarse textiles.

In most cases, the proximity to the supply of suitable raw materials was one of the main factors behind localization of textile industries in Bengal. The most famous and the finest muslins were manufactured in Dhaka district where the finest cotton in the world was produced. Similarly the areas around Kasimbazar held the monopoly of manufacturing silk piece-goods as most of the quality silk was produced in the vicinity of this famous trade mart. This localization (and of course specialization too) was so much an integral part of the textile industry in Bengal that some of the well-known aurungs were named after the particular product of that manufacturing centre. Two illustrations from contemporary records will suffice to establish the point. While referring to the Maratha invasions, the Kasimbazar Council noted in 1741 that before the Marathas had left, they burnt all the 'Taffaty aurungs'.[19] The manufacturing centres of garras in Birbhum and Burdwan were referred to as 'garra aurungs' in the Company records. The English factors at Kasimbazar wrote in 1742 that they were facing extreme difficulty in providing the garras as there were hardly 'four or five merchants that had any

[18] BPC, vol. 25, f. 299, 17 Nov. 1752.
[19] Fact. Records, Kasimbazar, vol. 6, 26 May 1742.

gomastas at the Gurrah aurungs'.[20] Numerous such references are to be found in the Company records which refer to such localized (and specialized too) *aurungs*. The very name *aurung*, the localized centres of production, emphasizes the localization of the industry.

There were, however, additional factors contributing to such localization. The Fort William Council wrote to the Court of Directors in 1732 that it was almost impossible to make the *garras* within the factory bounds because 'every piece [of *garras*] would be double the price, it is at the particular aurungs where the cotton grows and rice much cheaper' that *garras* were made.[21] Not that all the *aurungs* or districts where cloth was manufactured produced their own cotton. As John Taylor informs us, several of the districts which were big manufacturing centres of textile 'grew little or no cotton', drawing their supplies from other parts of the province or the country.[22] Notable examples were the districts of Birbhum and Burdwan. While Birbhum needed about 100,000 maunds of cotton, its annual production did not exceed 80,000 and Burdwan imported at least about 50,000 maunds a year.[23] The coarse cotton textiles like *garras* and *dosooties*, produced mainly in the above two districts, were generally made of Surat cotton, and the fluctuation in the import of cotton from Surat often affected the prices of these fabrics.[24] So it appears that along with the twin considerations of availability of raw materials and concentration of hereditary skill, the prices of staples like rice, cotton and silk as also the tradition of making a particular variety in a particular area explain the localization of the textile industry in Bengal.

Finally, another remarkable aspect of the Bengal textile industry was the extent of specialization it had reached during the period under review. Not only in every district but even in almost every *aurung*, textiles were manufactured on a specialized basis. While in general most varieties were produced in most of

[20] Ibid., 3 April 1742.

[21] C & B. Abst., vol. 3, f. 180, 25 Feb. 1732.

[22] Home Misc., vol. 456F, f.117.

[23] N.K. Sinha, *Economic History of Bengal*, vol. I, p. 104.

[24] Beng. Letters Recd., vol. 23, ff. 51, 60; *FWIHC*, vol. I, pp. 917-18, 923.

the places, it is significant that there was not only regional specialization but often products of every *aurung* had their own distinctiveness which differentiated them from the product of another *aurung*. That was the reason why the same types of piece-goods and of the same size produced in one *aurung* varied in price from that produced in another *aurung*, depending of course on the fineness of quality and workmanship. Though the same types of textiles were produced in several *aurungs* of different districts, they were generally identified by the names of the *aurungs*, and not just by the name of the textile. Our points will be amply clear from Table 6.1 which illustrates the different types of two principal muslins namely, *khasa* and *mulmul*, and their respective prices at which the English Company contracted for their supply with Calcutta merchants in 1742.

TABLE 6.1

Different Types and Prices of Muslins
(*Khasa* and *Mulmul*), 1742

Name of Piece-goods	Length x breadth (in covid)	Prices per Piece (Rs)	(As)
Khasa Malda fine	40 x 3	17	8
" " flowered	40 x 3	22	5
" Cogmaria	40 x 3	9	8
" "	40 x 2 1/4	7	6
" Orrua	40 x 2 1/4	7	12
" " flowered	40 x 2 1/4	12	8
" Serry	32 x 1 3/4	3	3
" Burron	40 x 2	4	12
" Kumarkhali	40 x 2	4	12
Mulmul Santipur	40 x 3	10	-
" " fine	40 x 3	16	8
" "	40 x 2 1/4	7	12
" "	40 x 2	6	12
" Cossajura	40 x 2	11	-
" " fine	40 x 2	19	-
" " "	40 x 2 1/4	22	8
" " "	40 x 3	30	-
" Serry	36 x 1 3/4	4	2

[Source: BPC, vol. 15, pp. 233-34, Annex to Consult. 31 March 1742; 1 *covid* = 18 inches]

Though the whole district of Dhaka was known for the production of muslins which were the finest variety made in Bengal, the best type of muslins was actually produced in three *aurungs* namely, Junglebarry, Bazetpur and Sonargaon. The finest plain muslins called 'mulboos khas' (royal clothing) were produced exclusively in these three *aurungs* during the Mughal period. But here again there was difference in the quality of the produce of these *aurungs* which only brings out the degree of specialization. While the weavers of Junglebarry and Bazetpur excelled in manufacturing muslins of a close texture, Sonargaon specialized in making thin and clear muslins.[25] It was not only in weaving but also in spinning, washing etc. that specialization was a typical feature of Bengal's textile industry. The best thread was spun at Junglebarry and Bazetpur, 'the fabrics of which arangs, from the great skill with which the thread is prepared, possess a peculiar softness'.[26] As the Danish report informs us, there were 'certain washermen in all weaving districts, whose washing can be imitated nowhere'.[27] John Taylor noted that the art of making *jamdanies*, of embroidering cloth in loom, was the monopoly of the weavers of the Dhaka *aurung*. These weavers who specialized in producing *jamdanies* were called 'jamdani weavers'.[28] Similarly *jamawars*, an expensive variety of silk piece-goods, were manufactured by weavers who specialized in that particular kind of work.[29]

The theoretical concept of 'important economies of concentration',[30] was somewhat blurred by the distinctive features of the textile industry in Bengal. The assumption that production for local consumption and local market should be distinguished from production for export and inter-regional trade can hardly be applied to the Bengal situation. There is little doubt that the main consideration for manufacturing cloth for local consumption was the availability of cotton or yarn while the consideration of

[25] Home Misc., 456 F, f.135.

[26] Ibid., f.129.

[27] Ole Feldbaeck, 'Cloth Production in Bengal', *BPP*, p. 132.

[28] Fact. Records, Kasimbazar, vol. 12, 20 Dec. 1753; NAI, Home Misc., vol. 16, para. 61, ff. 183-84, Fort William Council to Court, 4 Feb. 1751; f.250, para. 70, Fort William Council to Court, 28 August. 1751.

[29] K.N. Chaudhuri, *Trading World*, p.241.

[30] Ibid.

distance, both between manufacturing and consuming areas, and between production centres and the point of final shipment, naturally comes in as the cost of transport is vital for the profitability of the enterprise. Besides, the merchants or the middlemen had to organize proper inspection through agents to ensure the quality of the finished goods as per specifications. If all these considerations were applicable to Bengal, it would have been difficult to explain why cheap and ordinary calicoes like *garras*, a staple of the European trade, were produced only in Birbhum and Burdwan districts, and both coarse and fine cloth manufactured in Malda since both the areas, especially Malda, were quite far away from the port of shipment. Similarly, if the spatial pattern in the production of muslins in Dhaka and *taffetas* in Kasimbazar can be explained on the ground of special geographical factors and concentration of hereditary craft skills, how can one explain that Dhaka and Kasimbazar also produced coarse calicoes like *baftas*, *salampuris*, *garras* and *guinees* for export?[31]

Moreover, the idea that muslins and silk piece-goods were 'high-cost luxury products consumed in the richer households' and hence the location of the production centres of these textiles was 'neutral with respect to transport costs' hardly conforms to fact.[32] Of course, muslins or silk piece-goods in general were more expensive than ordinary cloth like *garras* or *baftas*. But there were different varieties and qualities of muslins and silk textiles with varying range of prices depending on fineness, workmanship and the *aurung* where they were produced. Sometimes there was not much of a difference in the prices of several types of muslins, silk piece-goods, fine calicoes or ordinary textiles. Again within the same variety, the prices could vary widely depending on the quality of fineness, workmanship and the place of production. The cost prices of some of these textiles procured in different areas of Bengal by the Dutch Company in 1752/53 and 1754/55 will clearly illustrate these points.

---

[31] It is clear from the export invoices of the Dutch ships from 1752/53 to 1754/55 when an area-wise breakdown of cargoes is available that the Dutch procured *baftas* from Dhaka and *garras*, *salampuris*, and *guinees* from Kasimbazar.

[32] K.N. Chaudhuri, *Trading World*, p. 241.

TABLE 6.2
Cost Prices of Textiles Procured by the Dutch Company
1752/53 & 1754/55

Name of Piece-goods	Category	Production area	Price per piece (in Florin)
Khasa Junglebarry	Muslin	Dhaka	72-73
" ordinary	"	Hughli	13-15
Mulmul "	"	Hughli	11-13
Duriyas	"	Dhaka	46-51
"	"	Hughli	25-29
Humhum	"	Hughli	11-12
Bethilas	Fine calico	Hughli	11-12
Chowtars	"	Hughli	12-12.5
Bandanas	Silk	Kasimbazar	8-9
Armosin (Taffeta)	"	Kasimbazar	8.5-9.5
Dheris	"	Kasimbazar	17-18
Baftas	Coarse calico	Dhaka, Hughli	8.5-9
Guinees	"	Hughli, Kasimbazar	13-14

[Source and note: Collected and computed from Dutch export invoices in VOC records. Guinees were of the size 75co x 2 1/4 co while other piece-goods were generally 40co x 2 1\4 co. 1 Rupee = 1.5 Florin]

The bewildering varieties of textiles produced in Bengal—150 different names are to be found in the first ten years of the eighteenth century in the English Company records—make their classification into different categories such as muslins, fine and coarse calicoes, silk and mixed piece-goods an extremely difficult task. Any attempt to do that can hardly be foolproof. John Taylor noted that in Dhaka alone there were more than 100 varieties of cloth manufactured.[33] And as we have seen from Table 6.2, it is equally difficult to state in general terms that muslins and silk piece-goods were high-cost luxury items. Except for certain well-

[33] Home Misc., vol. 456F, f.173.

known varieties of muslins such as *jamdanies, nainsooks* or silk
textiles like *jamawars*, most of the ordinary muslins or silk piece-
goods were not really very expensive items. That is why both the
Dutch and the English Companies exported a large quantity of
both these varieties. Though the finest and the best muslins were
most expensive, it was not only the fineness of quality which
accounted for the high price. As Taylor reported that the same
kind of *jamdanies* which used to cost Rs 250 in nawab
Sirajuddaullah's time (1756-57) was made at the rate of Rs 450
per piece for Muhammed Reza Khan, the *naib nazim* of Dhaka
in the 1760s, not because of 'any superior fineness of thread' but
expensive patterns.[34] But the *jamdanies* exported by the Dutch and
the English in 1752/53 cost only between Rs 31-43. Some of the
costlier varieties of textiles exported by the Companies are to be
found in Table 6.3 with their respective prices.

Table 6.3
Expensive Textiles Exported by the Companies
1752/53

Piece-goods	Category	Dutch Cost Price (Rs)	English Cost Price (Rs)
Nainsooks	Muslin	43	31-36
Jamdanies	"	-	21-22
Allibalies	"	36	16-25
Duriyas	"	18-31	12-27
Jamawars	Silk	-	30

[Sources: For Dutch exports, prices calculated from export invoices in
VOC records. Prices for English exports calculated from Bengal General
Journals and Ledgers, Range 175, vol. 54.]

[34] Ibid.

6.2 PRODUCTION ORGANIZATION

Mughal Practice

The detailed description by John Taylor of the working of the royal *karkhanas* where high-quality cloths were produced exclusively for the royalty and nobility brings out some interesting elements in the production organization of the textile industry in the eighteenth century. He noted that under the Mughal government, 'mulboos khas cooties' (factories or sheds for making 'royal clothing') were established in Dhaka, Sonargaon and Junglebarry. These 'cooties' were supervised by the officials called *darogas* whose duties were to inspect the manufacture of all the cloth made for royal use. Sheds were erected in the 'cooties' of Sonargaon and Junglebarry for the weavers and their looms. The best weavers were selected, registered and compelled to attend regularly at the appointed hours. On behalf of the *darogas*, officials called 'mokeems' (*mukims*) daily inspected the thread which the weavers brought for the looms and 'none was permitted to be used until it had been previously compared with' established samples. Peons were set on the weavers if they did not attend and punished if they attempted to abscond. Taylor also commented that none of the weavers worked willingly 'on account of the inadequate profit which the cloths yielded them' and the constant practice of weaving such cloth 'must have highly advanced the skill of the weavers'.[35]

Several important features of the organization of the textile industry emerge from the above. First, it is of significance that even in the royal *karkhanas*, the weavers brought their own yarn. If that was so, in case of private or commercial manufacture it is beyond doubt that the weavers bought their own yarn. So even in the *dadni* or advance system, which possibly became more widespread in the eighteenth century, there was certainly no advance in yarn or raw material; only a cash advance was made to the weavers. Secondly, the implication of the statement that the weavers had 'inadequate profit' in the royal *karkhanas* was that the weavers were not wage workers even there.

[35] Ibid., f. 163-169.

It follows logically from Taylor's description that in all probability the cloth produced by the weavers was bought by the *daroga* of the *karkhana* for the royalty or nobility. In the process however the weaver did not get the proper price of his produce, quite a bit of which was pocketed by the *daroga*, *mukim* and other officials. The fact of the matter is confirmed by Taylor who stated that during Sirajuddaullah's time, while the *jamdanies* were charged Rs 250, the weavers actually received Rs 150 only, the rest being appropriated by the officials. Another important feature of the structure of textile industry that emerges from Taylor's report was that even in the case of *jamdanies* made for the imperial household in the 'sadar malboos khas cootie' at Dhaka, advances in cash were paid to the weavers.[36] This only confirms the fact that *dadni* was very much a traditional system — it was nothing new which could be associated with the increase in the European demand in the second half of the seventeenth and first half of the eighteenth century.

Dadni System

The production of textiles in Bengal, especially for inland, inter-regional and long distance trade, it seems, was hinged to a great extent on the system of advance or *dadni* given to the weavers by the merchants through a host of intermediaries like *dalals*, *gomastas* and *paikars*. The goods thus bought were called *patan* or *patni* goods. But at the same time one comes across *khush khareed* or goods bought with ready money even towards the close of the eighteenth century. However, in all probability, most of the textiles for inter-regional and long distance trade were produced mainly against advances paid and contracts made under the *dadni* system. It may be noted here that rich weavers often used their own capital—something that will be obvious from a contemporary observer[37] quoted below, though this was perhaps an exception rather than the rule.

It was common practice for respectable families of the weaver-caste to employ their own capital in manufacturing

[36] Ibid., ff. 171-73.
[37] Mss. Eur. D. 283, f.21; William Bolts, *Considerations*, pp. 193-94.

goods, which they sold freely on their own accounts. At Dacca in one morning 800 pieces of muslin brought by the weavers of their own accord have been purchased at the door of one gentleman.

The basic *raison d'être* of the *dadni* system has been explained in various ways.[38] The common argument with varying degrees of emphasis is that it was necessitated by three important considerations. First, the weaver's need for finance; the *dadni* provided him with the cash to buy his raw materials for the manufacturing process and to sustain himself and his family for the period, extending sometime up to six months that took him to finish his work. Secondly, it gave him the necessary security for the purchase of the goods ordered. Thirdly, while on the one hand it played an important role in securing large enough quantity for the merchants who advanced *dadni*, on the other it was also a way of binding-up the producers in the face of competition from other buyers in the market of whom there was no dearth in the seventeenth and first half of the eighteenth century. Though a traditional system, it seems that the *dadni* system was quite extended during this period to meet the requirements of 'an expanded and expanding market'. But the suggestion that 'the need to operate through the system of contracts increased considerably' with the European demands for specific size, quality, design etc. can hardly be taken for granted.[39] For long Bengal had been supplying her traditional markets in different parts of India, South-East Asia, West and Central Asia, the Persian Gulf and Red Sea areas, and North Africa with varying degrees of standard, size and quality, and hence standardization was not something absolutely new. Nor was the volume of this traditional trade in any way less than that of the European trade during the period under review.

The *dadni* or advance system was however somewhat different from the *verlaggsystem* of the sixteenth and seventeenth

[38] K. N. Chaudhuri, *Trading World*, pp. 256-57, 260-61; T. Raychaudhuri, *Cambridge Economic History of India*, vol. I, pp. 281-82; Om Prakash, *Dutch Company*, pp. 88-89; S. Arasaratnam, 'Weavers, Merchants and Company', *IESHR*, vol. XVII, no. 3, pp. 268-69.

[39] Om Prakash, *Dutch Company*, p. 98.

century Europe. In the putting-out system of Europe, most of the artisans were supplied with necessary raw materials and the cash payment made out to them was only an advance against their wages. In the *dadni* system in Bengal however the weavers were in almost all cases given cash advance; advance in raw material is extremely rare to come by. As we have seen earlier, even in the royal *karkhanas*, the weavers brought their own yarn. But more importantly, while in Europe, at all stages of production the output belonged to the merchant-financier, in Bengal the producer appears to have retained considerable independence. He had control over his produce until it changed hands and was still the owner of the means of production, though his freedom to fix the price of his goods was not unrestricted. The merchant-middleman who paid the advance to the weaver had the first claim on the goods and it might be that debt obligations often exposed the artisan to coercive control of the merchant-financier. However, he was still, in Max Weber's terminology, not reduced to the position of a 'wage-earner'.[40] So the weaver in the pre-colonial period retained the ownership of his means of production — his loom, bought his own yarn independently and at least in theory was the owner of his product. The suggestion that 'this was no more than an illusion of ownership'[41] is perhaps not wholly appropriate. The transactions under the *dadni* system were still in the form of sales with the artisans retaining considerable independence. At most, the system promoted the control of merchant capital over the producer and not the process of production itself. It was only under the English Company after 1757 that the weavers had virtually become wage workers in terms and conditions over which they had no control.[42]

Basic Unit of Production

The assertion that the traditional system of production in Bengal remained virtually unchanged is quite doubtful, though perhaps

[40] Max Weber, *General Economic History*, pp. 99-101.

[41] A.I. Chicherov, *Economic Development*. pp. 167, 175.

[42] N.K. Sinha, *Economic History of Bengal*, vol. I, pp. 157-60; Hameeda Hossain, *Company Weavers*, pp. 108-39; D.B. Mitra, *Cotton Weavers*, pp. 79-87.

there was no fundamental change in the production organization.[43] The basic unit of production in the traditional organization was the weaver, operating as an independent artisan with his wife and children. He owned the hut he was living in with his family and the loom he was working with. As the family was the working unit, his home was the typical workshop. This traditional system was in vogue even in the mid-eighteenth century. This was clearly emphasized by Orme when he wrote that it was difficult to find a village where every man, woman and child were not employed in making cloth.[44] Even in the family unit there was the division of labour — the weaver mostly busy with weaving, the wife with processing of cotton including spinning and the child helping as an apprentice in the whole process. The weaver also bought his yarn for weaving from the local *hat* or weekly market whenever necessary with the capital from the surplus over his consumption. In this traditional unit of production, the fixed capital requirements were minimal and working capital was derived from the surplus of sale proceeds. Even in the early nineteenth century, the fixed capital cost of a weaver's unit was estimated at Rs 20 for a shed, a loom and other implements.[45] The rudimentary character of technique with emphasis on simple instruments and low ratio of fixed to working capital implied a minimal concentration of labour and capital in individual units of production.

A significant aspect of Bengal handloom industry was that weaving was often a subsidiary occupation to agriculture and the farmer could easily move from the plough to the loom during the slack season or the other way round. James Taylor reported in the early nineteenth century:[46]

A ryot [peasant] quitting his plough to work at the loom or leaving the latter in order to resume the former is a common occurrence, especially among those who make coarser cloths

[43] K.N. Chaudhuri, *Trading World,* p. 260, 262.

[44] Orme, *Historical Fragments,* p. 409.

[45] Buchanan Hamilton, *Dinajpur,* p. 246 quoted in Hameeda Hossain, *Company Weavers,* p. 61.

[46] James Taylor, *Topography and Statistics of Dacca,* p.73.

in many parts of India but in Dacca this is seldom the case,
weaving being there a distinct trade, to which those practising
it devote their whole-time attention.

But in the early eighteenth century, even in Dhaka, the artisans
were found to be engaging themselves in agriculture. In 1736 the
Dhaka factors reported that many female spinners and 'men that
served weavers' were obliged to 'apply themselves to agriculture
in order to pay their rents' which were then reported to have
gone up considerably.[47] In his description of Dhaka cloth
production, John Taylor noted that towards the end of the
eighteenth century, a number of manufacturers of Dhaka cloth
for which the demand had gone down considerably had discon-
tinued weaving and turned to other occupations, presumably
agriculture.[48] That the production of manufactured goods by the
peasant-cultivator for the consumption of his family was a long-
established tradition in Bengal is borne out by the fact that the
seventeenth century poet Mukundaram mentioned that women
in peasant households produced the yarn for weaving cloth.[49] It
is quite likely that even before the eighteenth century the
peasants manufactured cloths in their homes both for their own
use as well as for the market. The literature of the period will
testify that the peasant-cultivators took their cloth to the weekly
hats for sale and bought their raw materials and victuals with the
sale proceeds. Hence no clear line of demarcation can be drawn
between agricultural and manufacturing activities. Even for the
subsistence-farmer, production of cloth for the market was not
an uncharacteristic activity. It appears that the same peasant caste
carried out the functions of all the early stages of silk production—from mulberry cultivation to the winding of cocoons—
except perhaps the finishing process which was a highly specialized activity.

Along with this small peasant-weaver family as the basic unit
of production, we come across in the sources occasional refer-

[47] BPC, vol. 11, ff.288vo-89, 28 Aug. 1736.
[48] Home Misc., vol. 456 F, f. 219.
[49] T. Raychaudhuri, *Cambridge Economic History of India*, vol. I, p.
279.

ences to weaving shops and head weavers. The Dhaka factors reported in 1736 about such weaving shops where spinners and men who helped the weavers were working.[50] While discussing the profit of weavers in the mid-eighteenth century, John Taylor referred to head weaver who bought thread for weaving cloth.[51] Though the head weaver is known to have functioned in Hughli in the 1670s, had acted as an intermediary between the weavers and merchants and exercised some authority over members of his community, his functions and precise status are not clear from the sources.[52] However it appears that he was not so common a feature of the weaving village in Bengal as he seems to have been in the Coromandel Coast.[53] If he were, we should have come across him in our sources where he is rare to come by. Taylor reported that the production of cloth was carried out in Dhaka by master-weavers possessing two or three looms and employing usually an apprentice (*nikari*) and a journeyman (*kareegar*).[54] At the same time it is interesting to note that in the mid-eighteenth century it was common for respectable families of the weaving community to employ their own money in manufacturing goods which they sold freely on their own accounts.[55] Some of the weavers in Dhaka were even reported to have advanced money to 'a number of most skilful spinners' for the supply of the finest thread.[56]

In all probability, the bulk of the production for medium and long distance trade was done through the advance contract or *dadni* system though the Asian merchants seemed to have bought quite a large amount of textiles in the spot markets. But it is not clear as to what extent in the two sectors—the basic family unit of production with marginal presence of rich weavers investing their own money for production and the *dadni* contracts—there was an overlapping of functions or whether duality of production

[50] BPC, vol. 11, ff.288 vo - 89, 28 Aug. 1736.

[51] Home Misc., vol. 456F, f.145.

[52] Om Prakash, *Dutch Company*, p.107.

[53] S. Arasaratnam,' Weavers, Merchants and Company', *IESHR*, vol. XVII, no. 3, pp. 265-266, 277.

[54] J. Taylor, *Cotton Manufacture*, p. 78, quoted in D.B. Mitra, *Cotton Weavers*, p. 39-40.

[55] Eur. Mss. D. 283, f. 21; William Bolts, *Considerations*, p.194.

[56] Home Misc., vol. 456F, f. 153.

was maintained to cater to the demands of trade. Yet what emerges from a close scrutiny of the sources is that there was an increasing division of labour based on caste and occupational differentiation in Bengal textile industry in the seventeenth and eighteenth centuries. Almost every stage connected with the production of textiles—from cotton-carding, spinning, unwinding and rewinding the thread, formation of the cloth on the loom, washing, bleaching, dyeing etc.—virtually became an independent manufacturing activity. The observation of Robert Orme is appropriate in this context. He emphasized that unlike other industries where the craftsmen could perform singly all the different stages of production, the textile industry required the combined skills of several separate groups of craftsmen before the finished cloth could reach the consumer.[57]

The weaving of cloth was a complex process and called for a thorough knowledge of the preparation and treatment of the natural thread before it could be made ready for weaving. The following description of weaving *mulmul* in Dhaka by John Taylor would give an idea of the complicated process and the precise schedule of work involved.[58]

> Preparation of warp yarn consisted of sorting the thread from different parts of the warp. Approximately eighteen days were taken to soak, rinse and dry the yarn several times before it was sized in rice starch and wound on reels. The warp was next laid by two men over bamboo sticks which had been fixed at regular intervals in the open ground. The warp was fixed to the loom by two men while the reel was attached to the warp by two. It took two men ten to thirty days to fix the warp. Weaving required one or two persons, though for the *jamdani* variety of *mulmul*, which was embroidered in the loom, a third weaver worked on the flowering. Ordinary assortments were made in 10-15 days, the fine variety required twenty days and the superfine thirty days.

The production of cotton yarn and spinning, two important aspects in the manufacture of textile, appears to have been always

---

[57] Orme, *Historical Fragments*, p. 411.
[58] Home Misc., vol. 456F, ff. 223-25.

independent manufacturing activities and a secondary occupation in weavers' families. Cotton yarn was also produced in peasant households by a subsistence-oriented system. There are also frequent references suggesting that the weavers producing for the market were buying yarn spun by independent spinners. Spinning yarn for cloth manufacture was a small-scale part-time activity of all classes of women in Bengal. It is significant that though weaving was a caste-based hereditary occupation in Bengal, there was no caste bias so far as spinning was concerned and even women of high castes including Brahmins spun yarn, as did the women of weaving castes like *jugis, tantis, juluhas* etc. In the spinning of thread again a high degree of specialization is discernible. Yarn for coarse quality cloth was spun by wheels while for the fine varieties it was done by spindles. Though thread was made at all *aurungs*, the greatest quantity and with a few exceptions the best in Dhaka district was produced at Junglebarry and Bazetpur. The thread of these *aurungs*, possessed a peculiar softness because of 'the superior skill with which the thread was spun'. Around 1800 there were only thirty spinners of this category in Dhaka.[59]

Spinning yarn was highly labour-intensive. Only small quantities of thread could be produced by long and strenuous work but because of several factors the hours of work could not be extended. The spinning could be done for a few hours in the early morning and in the evening when it was not too hot; otherwise the mid-day heat would ruin the thread. According to John Taylor, a spinner of the best quality yarn could produce 'eight annas weight' (i.e. half a rupee weight) of thread in a month if she devoted all her time to spinning. But as the spinners generally had other domestic duties to attend to, they could hardly devote more than three hours a day to spinning and therefore the average quantity from each spinner was estimated at no higher than a quarter of a 'sicca weight' (i.e. weight of a sicca rupee which is equivalent to about 2/5 of an ounce) in a month.[60] Again as spinning of yarn involved strain for the eyes, the women were restricted by the declining capacity for work after the age

[59] Ibid., ff. 129-31.
[60] Ibid., ff. 131-35.

of thirty. Moreover as the earning was comparatively low, there was hardly any incentive to work for long hours. Yet the growing demand for yarn and the need to supplement income, no doubt, encouraged the spinners to engage in commodity production.

The division of labour as also the extreme specialization that characterized Bengal textile industry in the eighteenth century is apparent in other stages of cloth production too. Washing, for example,was done by a separate group which specialized in the art as is observed in the Danish report on textile production: 'Now the pieces [*garras*] are to be washed, for which purpose there are certain washermen in all weaving districts whose washing can be imitated nowhere.'[61] Similarly, the darning of broken threads, after washing and bleaching, was undertaken by *rafugars* while remaining spots and stains were removed by *dagh dhobis* or washermen specialized in that art. The embroidery work like *kashida* in which *tasar* or *muga* silk was used for embroidering fine cloth like *duriya* and *mulmul,* was done mainly by women and the great demand for such work drew into regular employment groups of women in Dhaka. In the late 1730s and the early 1740s the Dhaka factors were finding it difficult to get *kashida* work done as most of such workers 'were ruined' and as 'it was chiefly done by women in the Junnannaes [i.e. under *purdah* or seclusion] who on no account would be prevailed to come to do it in the factory where they may be properly overlooked'.[62]

6.3 WEAVERS, WAGES AND MOBILITY

Position of Weavers

Though it is difficult to get a clear picture of the social and economic position of the weavers in the first half of the eighteenth century, the assertion of a distinguished authority that they formed 'the hinge of Bengal economy' does not seem to be

[61] Ole Feldbaeck, 'Cloth Production in Bengal', *BPP*, vol. *LXXXVI*, July-Dec. 1967, p. 132.

[62] Fact. Records, Dacca, vol. 2, 10 Feb. 1737; BPC, vol.12, f.137, 16 April 1737; vol. 14, f.158vo, 27 Jan. 1740; C & B. Abstr., vol. 4, f.380, para. 65, 11 Dec. 1741.

far from the truth. Given the fact that Bengal textile trade and industry were perhaps at their zenith during the period under review and the Bengal piece-goods were the main export commodity both for the European companies and Asian merchants, bringing in their train an incessant flow of bullion and silver into the country, there can be little doubt that the weavers played an important role in the economy. Traditionally a caste-based and hereditary occupation as weaving was, it is difficult to ascertain from the meagre evidence available whether the expanding demand during this period broke down the caste barriers and brought in others from higher or lower strata of the caste hierarchy into the organization of production. The general assumption is that as the demand for textiles expanded, additional labour was brought into the industry to increase the output and as such weaving was not confined to any particular caste any more.[63] The only evidence we have on this question is of the late-eighteenth century and of a contradictory nature. Colebrooke wrote in the 1790s that the view that 'professions are confined to hereditary descent' was 'unfounded' and that 'professions are not separated by an impassable line' or 'every profession, with few exceptions, is open to every description of persons'.[64] On the other hand, the Danish report of 1789 states categorically that 'a weaver cannot become a member of another caste'.[65] As such, it is difficult to suggest anything definitive on the caste mobility in the textile industry. Yet it is significant to note in this context what Orme observed in the 1750s: 'A weaver amongst the Gentoos is not a despicable cast[e]. He is next to the scribe, and above all the mechanics. He would lose his cast[e], were he to undertake a drudgery which did not immediately relate to his work.'[66]

If that be so, and as weaving could be carried on side by side with agriculture and above all, as the small-scale family-based unit of production does not seem to have been 'displaced from its

---

[63] P.J. Thomas, 'The Indian Cotton Industry about 1700 A.D.', *Modern Review*, Feb. 1924, pp. 45, 134-35; D.B. Mitra, *Cotton Weavers*, p.39; Hameeda Hossain, *Company Weavers*, pp. 47, 174.

[64] H.T. Colebrooke, *Remarks on the Husbandry*, pp. 170-71, 174.

[65] Ole Feldbaeck, 'Cloth Production in Bengal', *BPP*, vol. *LXXXVI*, July-Dec. 1967, p. 126.

[66] Orme, *Historical Fragments*, p. 410.

position of primacy', weaving in general remained in all probability primarily a caste-based hereditary occupation even in the mid-eighteenth century. At the same time the peasant-cultivators who belonged to most of the castes might have been drawn into the industry as and when the situation demanded. But unfortunately we do not have any evidence to determine the proportion of such extra labour drawn from agrarian and other groups to the main weaver castes engaged in weaving. The fact that spinning was not confined to any caste group and that even high caste women participated in this commodity-production only lends support to the hypothesis that labour from other occupations could be easily drawn to weaving if and when necessary.

Again, though most of the occupations were mainly caste-based, in all probability the system was not extremely rigid. The most remarkable instance of upward economic mobility is that most of the *dadni* merchants in Calcutta in the first half of the eighteenth century, especially the Setts and Basaks, belonged to the weaving caste. In Kasimbazar, as in Calcutta, the *dadni* merchants included such names as Pramanick (barber), Nath (weaving caste), Telly (oil grinder) etc. along with high castes like Basu, Sen, etc. However, it is difficult to ascertain whether these were exceptions rather than the rule. As to the weavers' corporate organizations which according to some scholars, who even talk of 'weavers' guild', existed in the early eighteenth century also,[67] our sources maintain conspicuous silence, while we hear so much of merchants' *panchayats* (corporate body) during the period. Even if such bodies existed, these were probably caste-based associations in urban areas and their functions were not primarily economic. This is perhaps because of the fact that handloom industry was still basically a rural cottage industry in Bengal.

Mobility

As regards the geographical mobility of the weavers, we have little evidence to show that there was a marked difference from

[67] P.J. Thomas, 'Indian Cotton Industry', *Modern Review*, Feb. 1924, p. 134-35.

the situation in the second half of the seventeenth century when the weavers were often found reluctant to move from their habitual place of residence despite economic inducements.[68] But what is noticeable during this period was that the weavers, whenever faced with extortions or oppressions, wars or aggressions, or in order to escape from their creditors, often ran away from their villages. It was difficult to use force or compulsion on the weavers. As Orme pointed out: 'If guards were placed upon the [weaving] village which is the only method of compulsion that can be used, the alarm would be taken; and half of the country, by the retreat of these people [presumably weavers], would be depopulated in a day's time.'[69] That the desertion of the weavers from their villages was not uncommon is clear from the records of the English Company. The English factors at Jugdea reported in 1751 that several of their weavers and washermen had fled the village for 'dread of the nawab's extortions'.[70] Again Thomas Hyndman who was sent to Chandpur to procure *khasas* reported to Dhaka in 1754 that many of the weavers there had left their habitation to escape their indebtedness to the *dalals* and *paikars* who 'have thrown more money into their hands than they were able to account for'.[71]

Similar references abound in the Company records. In the wake of the Maratha invasions, many weavers from western parts of Bengal, which were more affected than other parts, migrated to established centres of textile industry in northern Bengal.[72] The *dadni* merchants of Calcutta insisted on a rise in the prices of textiles in 1745 because 'the late troubles in the country [the Maratha invasion] and the extortion of the government had ruined numbers of weavers and made them fly another parts'.[73]

---

[68] See S. Chaudhuri, *Trade and Commercial Organization,* p. 151, how the English found it difficult to bring weavers from Kasimbazar to Hughli in the 1660s and failed totally to get them to Madras 'for their caste and lineage is such that they shall lose their birth right if they come upon salt water'.

[69] Orme, *Historical Fragments*, p. 411.

[70] Beng. Letters Recd., vol. 22, f.298, para. 80, 18 Sept. 1752; *FWIHC*, vol. I, p. 606.

[71] Fact. Records, Dacca, vol. 3, Annex. to Consult., 17 Nov. 1754.

[72] N.K. Sinha, *Economic History of Bengal*, vol. I, p.157.

[73] BPC, vol. 17, f. 495, 21 March 1745.

Again when the Fort William Council asked the *dadni* merchants
in 1752 the reasons for demanding 'such extravagant prices and
proposing to contract for so few goods', the latter replied that it
was 'on account of dearness of cotton, rice and oil and everything
in general at the aurungs, and most of the weavers being obliged
to fly from their place of residence on account of the government
and troubles in the country'.[74] There are instances also, though
a few, when weavers left their villages for lack of work. The
English factors at Jugdea wrote to Dhaka in 1750 that unless they
were supplied with adequate funds to keep the weavers engaged
in their works, they apprehended that the weavers would 'leave
the aurungs for want of work'.[75] In 1751 the *dadni* merchants
reported that they would not be able to supply any *jamawar* as 'the
weavers who used to work in Jamawars were gone from thence',
presumably for lack of sufficient orders.[76] All these instances,
however, do not indicate much of geographical mobility in
response to more lucrative economic incentive, the reason
perhaps being that textile industry in Bengal remained chiefly a
caste-based domestic rural industry. It was only in the 1750s that
the English were able to lure the weavers to settle in the bounds
of the Company's establishment at the Fort William but that too
on a very limited scale.[77] In this respect the Bengali weavers seem
to be less mobile than their Coromandel counterparts as has been
indicated in a recent study.[78]

Bargaining Power

The weavers in Bengal however did not lack ingenuity. Even the
Court of Directors wrote in 1721 that the Bengali weavers 'are
ingenious enough to make very near imitation' of any kind of
piece-goods.[79] But this they would do only at the inducement of

---

[74] BPC, vol. 25, f. 125vo, 25 April 1752.

[75] Beng. Letters Recd., vol. 21, f. 25, para. 59, 23 Aug. 1750.

[76] NAI, Home Misc., vol. 16, ff. 183-84, para. 71, Letter to Court,
4 Feb. 1751.

[77] BPC, vol. 29, f. 157vo., 11 August 1757.

[78] S. Arasaratnam, 'Weavers, Merchants and Company', *IESHR*,
vol. XVII, no. 3, p.274.

[79] DB, vol. 100, f. 586, para. 29, 26 April 1721.

a higher price. Any change in the pattern or increase in the dimension would follow a consequent rise in price. If this was not allowed, the Company's factors would find that 'the people cannot be persuaded to alter their method' or 'they are so inept'.[80] The English Council at Fort William found in 1739 that the cloths sent from Balasore were much 'worse and dearer' than those in the previous years. When asked to explain the reason for this, the Balasore factors wrote that 'the cloth being one covid and half increased in length occasions the dearness' and that the weavers told them that 'they cannot make it cheaper or better at the price and say they will not receive the dadney for this year's investment'.[81] The merchants in Kasimbazar told the English Council there in 1744 that they could not undertake the investment of *Lungee romalls* because 'the weavers were formerly beat down in the price so much that they could not go on with them and had turned their hands to making other sort of Romalls that yielded more profit'.[82] In the same year the Company found it difficult to contract for *dosooties* because the merchants told them that the weavers were reluctant to produce them as they took more time than making *garras* and 'yielded them less profit'.[83]

All this only shows that the Bengali weavers were not ignorant of the market forces and they enjoyed some bargaining power which vanished completely in the post-Plassey period. Again, despite the fact that he had accepted *dadni* from several merchants, the weaver was not completely tied down and had some freedom of selling his goods. Occasionally what he would do was to produce cloth which did not conform to the specifications and when it was rejected by the merchant/*dalal* he had taken an advance from, he would sell the rejected goods to other buyers in the market. The *dadni* merchants reported to the Fort William Council in 1727 that despite advances given to the weavers by their *gomasta*s, the demand at all *aurungs* was so very great that they were apprehensive 'the weavers would make it late before

---

[80] C & B. Abstr., vol. 4, f. 81, para. 138, 24 Jan. 1735; f.241, para. 58, 31 Dec. 1737.

[81] BPC, vol. 13, f. 473vo, 6 Feb. 1739.

[82] Ibid., vol. 17, f. 129, 11 June 1744.

[83] Ibid., vol. 17, f. 151, 12 July 1744.

they could be able to give their goods [since] they had taken money of the Dutch, French and other people so that the prices were not only risen but the goods as soon as they were made were immediately divided, some to one nation and some to another'.[84] When the prices offered were not lucrative enough, the weavers would even desist from taking orders. This is clear from Thomas Hyndman's report from Chandpur in 1754 when he stated that the weavers assured him that the rate at which the piece-goods were priced by the Company did not afford them a sustenance. The great difficulty he had in procuring a very small quantity of textiles there convinced him that there was some measure of truth in the complaints of the weavers.[85] The state of things in Dhaka in the pre-Plassey period is best described by John Bebb who was Commercial Resident there in 1789:[86]

> The manufacturer in treating for the sale of his material and labour could say 'you do not offer me the price sufficient therefore I will not sell this assortment to you' and the purchaser was in a position to say 'you demand too much therefore I will not buy of you unless you will be more reasonable.

What was true of Dhaka was also largely true of the rest of Bengal before 1757. The assertion that the weavers in the pre-colonial period used to manufacture their goods freely and 'without oppression, restrictions, limitations and prohibition' is more or less a correct assessment of the situation in the pre-Plassey days.[87] This is well borne out by the responsible officials of the Company who referred to 'diffusion of commerce', 'general opulence', 'readiness of sales' and to the encouragement of the artisans before the revolution of 1757.[88]

---

[84] Ibid., vol. 6, f. 348, 9 Jan. 1727.
[85] Fact. Records, Dacca, vol. 3, Annex. to Consult., 17 Nov. 1574.
[86] Quoted in N.K. Sinha, *Economic History of Bengal,* vol. I, p. 25.
[87] Ibid., p. 159.
[88] Verelst's letter to the Court of Directors, 5 April 1769, *FWIHC,* vol. V, pp. 19, 546-548.

Artisans' Earnings

Regarding the wages or earnings of the weavers and other artisans engaged in the textile industry, we find only meagre evidence in our sources. The only significant information that one comes across is for 1736 when the Dhaka factors reported that women spinners and 'men that served weavers' worked for 'a pun [one *pun* of *cauris*] and their rice'.[89] Taking the price of rice at this time around 2 maunds for a rupee[90] and assuming that the artisans received 2 seers of rice per day, the money value of the rice part of his wage for a month would be 48 *pun* of *cauris* and his money wage 30 *pun* a month, making the artisan's total wage for a month at 78 pun or 19.5 annas i.e. Re 1.3 $^1/_2$ annas.[91] This tallies more or less with the estimate of John Taylor who states that around the mid-eighteenth century the earning of an ordinary weaver was from Re 1 to Re 1.5.[92] A significant fact that emerges from the above is that the spinners working full-time earned as much as the helper-weaver or ordinary weaver.

There are various estimates however of the earnings of the weavers, spinners and washermen in the late eighteenth century. John Taylor stated that the net profit from weaving a *mulboos khas* (royal clothing—one of the finest textiles) at Sonargaon in Dhaka district which took about 6 months for 3 persons—the head weaver who bought the thread, the weaver who made the cloth and the journeyman who helped the weaver—amounted to Rs 47 (it was actually Rs 41 but the weavers using different quality of thread could raise it to Rs 47). The weaver and the journeyman were employed by the head weaver at a monthly rate of Rs 3 to

[89] BPC, vol. 11, f. 289, 28 Aug. 1736.

[90] The Dhaka factors reported that the price of rice in 1738 was 2 maunds 20 seers to 3 maunds for a rupee (*Bengal and Madras Papers*, vol. II, p. 34, Fort William Consultations, 11 Dec. 1752; BPC, vol. 26, f. 214, 11 Dec. 1752; James Long, *Unpublished Records*, (ed.), M.P. Saha, p. 40, doc. no. 103. Making allowance for the possible exaggeration by the Dhaka factors who were trying to justify the high price of the textiles provided by them by referring to the rise in price of rice, it is safe to take the price of rice at 2 maunds for a rupee.

[91] 4 *pun* of *cauris* = 1 anna, 16 annas = 1 Rupee.

[92] Home Misc., vol. 456F, f. 205.

Rs 3.5 and Re 1.5 to Re 1.75 respectively. Taylor was careful to note that this 'profit' was 'less even than what the weavers are understood to make by several other high priced assortments of this province'.[93] The above earnings were of those weavers and artisans engaged in the production of high quality fabrics and hence should not be taken as the average wage of the artisans during this period. Taylor himself clarified this when he mentioned later that the wage of a weaver, presumably not of high quality cloth, was about Rs 2.5 to Rs 3.5 and that of his assistant from Rs 1 to 2.[94] Though the maximum rates in the above two estimates of Taylor are almost the same, the minimum rates differ to some extent, suggesting probably that the earnings of ordinary artisans even in Dhaka were lower than those who possessed higher skills.

The interesting point which is not clear from Taylor's report is the precise status of the head weaver. If he had to give away Rs 19.5 in wages for 6 months to the weaver and Rs 9.60 to the journeyman (at the medium rate of Rs 3.25 and Re 1.60 respectively), making a total of Rs 29.10 out of his profit of Rs 47, his own share for 6 months would be Rs 17.90. In other words, his monthly income in making that particular cloth comes to around Rs 3, which is less than the wage of the weaver. So the question that crops up is: was he a weaver-entrepreneur himself employing several workers or a rich peasant-farmer engaging weavers and journeymen or just a merchant entering into production in a limited way? From the available indications in the sources which are admittedly scanty, it is reasonable to assume that he was perhaps the head of the weaving community of the village, and though himself a weaver, employed other people to work for him so that he could afford to have a profit which was lower even than the wage of a weaver who actually did the weaving.

The Danish account of 1789—a period later than ours but still quite relevant for the period under review—gives a detailed account of the earnings of the *garra* weavers of Birbhum which is worth quoting here at length:[95]

[93] Ibid., f. 145-47.

[94] Ibid., f. 205.

[95] Ole Feldbaeck, 'Cloth Production in Bengal', *BPP*, vol. LXXXVI, July-Dec. 1967, p. 130.

The weaver's wages differ according to whether the demand for cloths in the aurungs is great or small; during the weaver's bad season—December, January, February—his pay for one piece of gurrah is generally no more than 10 annas; normally it is 11 to 12 annas and sometimes slightly more; if the weaver is an able worker he might finish his piece in five and a half to six days; but when his feast days are deducted he is able at most to produce four and a half to five pieces per month, by which he is generally estimated to earn three sicca rupees and—when times are best—three and a half rupees at most; if his family is able to help him, especially with cleaning and spinning the cotton, this is estimated at one fourth of his earning, but no more. Three to four rupees per month are thus the best weaver's highest earnings if he is fully employed.

It is instructive from the above that the weaver's earnings depended on several factors—the time of the year, state of the competition in the market at the given time, help from the family and above all his own diligence. Though the *garra* weavers were not regarded as highly skilled, the estimate of John Bebb in 1787 of the earnings of the weavers manufacturing *soot romals*, a higher quality cloth than *garras*, in Golaghar puts the rate of earnings much higher than those of the *garra* weavers. According to it,[96]

The earning of an "indifferent" weaver per month — Rs 3
The earning of a "middling"   weaver per month — Rs 5
The earning of a "good" weaver per month   — Rs 7.5

This seems rather an overestimation because, as we have seen earlier, even the highly skilled weaver of Sonargon was estimated by Taylor to have earned only Rs 3.5 at the maximum towards the end of the eighteenth century. But here it should be noted that the price of yarn was an important factor that was responsible for the wide fluctuation in the remuneration of weavers. As the weaver himself bought the thread for weaving,

[96] Proceedings of the Board of Trade, 24 Feb. 1787, quoted in N.K. Sinha, *Economic History of Bengal*, vol. I, p. 176.

TABLE 6.4

Manufacturing Costs of *Khasas* and *Baftas* in Burron, 1788 & 1789

(Cost in Rup. Anna. Pie; Cloth measured in covid)

Type of Cloth	1788				1789				Decrease in Profit from 1788
	Total Cost	Yarn Cost	Weavers' Profit	Profit as Percentage Share of Cost	Total Cost	Yarn Cost	Weavers' Profit	Profit as Percentage Share of Cost	
Khasa Burron (40x2)	6.1.6	4.0.0	2.1.6	34	6.1.6	4.12.0·	1.5.6	17	- 0.12.0
Khasa Kumarkhali (40x2)	5.3.6	3.8.0	1.11.6	35	5.3.6	4.4.0	0.15.6	22	- 0.12.0
Khasa Kumarkhali Ordinary (37x17/8)	2.14.0	2.0.0	0.14.0	34	2.14.0	2.10.0	0.4.0	19	- 0.10.0
Khasa French (40x21/4)	12.13.0	8.0.0	4.13.0	31	12.13.0	9.0.0	3.13.0	10	- 1.0.0
Baftas fine (25x2)	3.5.9	2.5.2	1.0.9	37	3.5.9	2.14.0	0.7.9	30	- 0.9.0

[Source and note: Home Misc., vol. 393, ff. 261-62; 1 Rup. = 16 Annas; 1 Anna = 12 pie].

any bad harvest and consequent rise in the price of yarn would invariably result in a sharp decline in his earning, which is well illustrated by the report from Burron in 1789 (Table 6.4).

It is clear from Table 6.4 that while in normal years the percentage share of the weavers' earnings in the total cost of manufacturing a particular type of cloth varied between 31 and 37 per cent, it could go down to as low as 10 per cent when the price of cotton yarn rose sharply. It is important to note that the official of the Company who prepared the estimate stated that 'the profit of weaver... for last year (i.e. 1788) did not appear more than was actually necessary to afford an ordinary subsistence'.[97] A significant fact that emerges from the above table is that the share of the weaver's profit is more for weaving a coarse cloth like *bafta* than the finer varieties like *khasa*. Even with the sharp rise of yarn price, his earnings while weaving *bafta* did not decline so markedly as did in the case of better quality fabric like *khasa*. That the percentage share of the weaver's profit in the 1780s was generally between 30 to 40 per cent of the total manufacturing cost of most textiles is also corroborated by the estimate in the Danish account which is presented here in Table 6.5.

Table 6.5.
Cost of *Garra* Production & Weavers' Earnings in Birbhum, 1787
(In Rupees)

Textile Type	Total Cost	Yarn Cost	Washing Cost	Weaver's Profit	Profit as Percentage Share of Cost
Garra	95 (for 20 pcs.)	55	2	38	40

[Source: Ole Feldbeack, 'Cloth Production in Bengal', *BPP*, vol. LXXXVI, pp. 128,130.]

At the same time it should be taken into account that the percentage share of the weaver's profit depended also on the

----

[97] Home Misc., vol. 393, f. 261.

type of cloth and the technique used. This will be quite apparent
from the estimate of the production cost of different types of
taffetas in Kasimbazar in 1756 (Table 6.6).

Table 6.6 shows that the calculation of percentage share of
the weavers' earnings is no indication of his actual income
because while his share in weaving *taffetas* of various colours
could vary from 9.6 to 13.5 per cent, his remuneration remained
the same at Re 1.4 an. per piece. It cannot be a fact, which is
obvious from what we have analysed so far, that the weavers
would earn less by weaving *taffetas*, a silk piece-good, than by
weaving *garra*, a coarse textile or his earnings were less in the mid-
eighteenth century than what they were in the late eighteenth
century. The most important facts that we need to know are how
many pieces of what type of cloth the weaver could produce in
a month/year and his profit in manufacturing each piece of cloth
so that we could have a rough idea of his monthly/yearly income.
But unfortunately we do not have any such information for the
eighteenth century. This makes the task of making any precise
estimate of the earnings of the weavers during the period under
review extremely difficult.

Similarly, we can have only a very rough idea of the earnings
of other artisans engaged in the textile industry. The spinners,
mainly women drawn from almost all sections of the society and
working mostly part-time, undoubtedly played a vital role in the
organization of production. As we have seen earlier, women
working full-time as spinners were not altogether unknown
during the period, though all evidence will generally indicate that
spinning was a part-time activity in most weaving and peasant
households. But in all probability, as was the case in the late
eighteenth century, the finest thread was spun by women who
worked full-time and had their domestic work done by servants.[98]
According to John Taylor's estimate towards the end of the
eighteenth century, the best spinners of Dhaka could earn
around 12 to 14 annas per month, working about three hours a
day.[99] However in an estimate of 1790, a highly skilful and
industrious woman was said to have earned about Rs 3 per

[98] N.K. Sinha, *Economic History of Bengal,* vol. I, p. 184.
[99] Calculated from Taylor's report, Home Misc., vol. 456F., ff. 131-
33.

TABLE 6.6.
Production Cost of Taffetas in Kasimbazar, 1756
[In Rup. An. Pie]

Taffeta	Cost of Silk	Winding Cost	Twisting Cost	Patash & Straw	Blue & other agent	Other Dyes	Tying Broken Threads	Weaving	Total Cost	Weaver's Profit in Percentage of Total Cost
Pucca Green	6.10	0.4.6	0.4.0	0.2.0	0.10.6	3.12.6	0.1.0	1.4.0	13.0.6	9.6
Pale Green	6.10	0.4.6	0.4.0	0.2.0	0.10.6	0.11.0	0.1.0	1.4.0	9.15.0	12.5
Blue	6.10	0.4.6	0.4.0	0.2.0	0.10.6	-	0.1.0	1.4.0	9.4.0	13.5

[Source: Fact. Records, Kasimbazar, vol. 12, 15 Jan. 1756; BPC, vol. 28, f. 386, 22 Jan. 1756]

month.[100] Probably in this case the woman-spinner was working full-time. There is evidence that such highly skilled spinners were in great demand and received advances from weavers even in the late eighteenth century.[101] If that was so, there is every reason to infer that the same kind of spinners would have earned at least the same amount, if not more, in the first half of the eighteenth century when there was a greater demand for such fine threads which were essential for the manufacture of muslins and fine calicoes.

Here again the earnings of the spinner depended on her skill and the type of thread she spun. It has been estimated that in the late eighteenth century women who spun yarn used in the medium and fine muslins earned about Rs 2 per month while those who spun thread for coarser cloths could earn only 12 to 14 annas per month, presumably working full-time.[102] From this one can have a rough idea of the remuneration of the spinners in the early eighteenth century which was perhaps higher than that in the late eighteenth century. As regards the washing charges, the only information we have is from the Danish account where it is stated that a washerman could earn Rs 2 for washing twenty pieces of *garras*.[103] Other artisans like *kashida* workers, *rafugars* etc. worked mainly on contract basis and as a result we do not have any precise idea about their earnings.

Alleged Poverty of Weavers

Whatever might have been the earnings of the weavers, the records of the period persistently refer, as they did for the second half of the seventeenth century[104], to the alleged poverty of the

[100] Proceedings of the Board of Trade, 2 July to 31 Aug. 1790, quoted in N.K. Sinha, *Economic History of Bengal*, vol. I, p. 184.

[101] Fact. Records, Kasimbazar, vol. 16, 23 April 1751; Home Misc., 456 F, f. 153.

[102] N.K. Sinha, *Economic History of Bengal*, vol. I, p. 184.

[103] Ole Felbaeck, 'Cloth Production in Bengal', *BPP*, vol. XXXVI, p. 132.

[104] See S. Chaudhuri, *Trade and Commercial Organization*, pp. 237-38. Basing on these I have argued there, which now seems wrongly, that 'the lot of the poor weavers' remained the same 'despite the increase in production and competition amongst buyers'.

weaver in the first half of the eighteenth century. One frequently comes across such expressions as 'weavers are too poor to be trusted with [advance] money' or 'none of the weavers worth any money' or 'necessitous circumstances of the weavers' or 'the poverty of the weavers obliges the gomastah to be very careful in the advance of money' in the records.[105] Most of these, however, were references to what the merchants or *gomastas* stated often in justification of the higher prices they were asking for. However, the officials of the Company also occasionally referred to the poverty of the weavers. Yet it is difficult to reconcile this alleged poverty with the huge demand for the products of the loom or the bargaining position of the weavers. In this context the observation made by Orme is very pertinent:[106]

> ... the dread of extortion or violence from the officers of the district to which he [the weaver] belongs, makes it prudence in him to appear, and to be poor; so that the chapman who sets him to work, finds him destitute of everything but his loom, and is therefore obliged to furnish him with money, ... in order to purchase materials, and to subsist him until his work is finished....

If that be so, was the weaver's poverty only a pretence and not a fact?

At this stage of our knowledge, it is extremely difficult to make a definitive assertion on the point. The argument of a recent authority that 'the poverty of the weavers remains an unidentified historical concept' seems to be quite appropriate.[107] It is indeed difficult to reconcile the alleged poverty of the weavers with the huge demand for textiles or the artisans' bargaining power which we have already referred to. The records in the Company archives leave no doubt that the weaver-

---

[105] BPC, vol. 11, f. 289, 28 Aug. 1736; Fact. Records, Kasimbazar, vol. 6, 12 June 1743, 2 July 1743, 1 March 1744; Fact. Records, Dacca, vol. 3, Annex to Consult., 17 Nov. 1754; *FWIHC*, vol. I, pp. 811, 824, 919.

[106] Orme, *Historical Fragments*, p. 9.

[107] K.N. Chaudhuri, *Trading World*, p. 270. Also see his general argument on the subject, pp. 268-71.

artisans were not completely ignorant about the markets for their products or the competition among numerous buyers for textiles, or when the prices offered did not 'afford them a sustenance' or even when to 'raise the value of their work' to compensate for the rise in prices of rice, cotton and other staples.[108] They were even reported to have turned to weaving a different variety of cloth when the one they were used to be manufacturing was not yielding enough profit or if some other variety proved more profitable.[109] Another important fact that one has to take into consideration in this context is that the weaver, despite accepting advance, was free to buy his own yarn whereby he can adjust the price offered for his cloth and the actual cost of weaving it to allow him a reasonable subsistence. That the weavers often took recourse to such measures even while making high quality fabrics for the royalty and thus enhancing his profit from Rs 41 to Rs 47 is reported by John Taylor.[110] Moreover, as Sir John Child argued in 1689, if the weavers were so poor that they could not afford to provide cloth without advance being given, they were perhaps 'not all so poor' as to supply goods against ready money.[111] And it was a fact that the buyers, especially the Asian merchants, purchased textiles against cash payment besides those procured through advance contracts.

But still as we cannot be so sure about the point, given somewhat contradictory evidence in the records, how can one explain the alleged poverty of the weavers, if it were true at all? An important fact to emphasize here is that one has to remember that the weavers, like the peasantry, were not a homogeneous group—there was every possibility of stratification within the community itself. It could be reasonably expected, as is indicated clearly in our sources, that there were different categories of weavers like the head weaver under whom worked the weaver and the journeyman, and the weaver who undertook weaving on an individual basis working mostly full-time in his occupation.

[108] For example, see BPC, vol. 16, f. 371, 14 Dec. 1743; Fact. Records, Kasimbazar; vol. 6, 6 Dec. 1743; Fact. Records, Dacca, vol. 3, 17 Nov. 1754.

[109] BPC, vol. 17, f.129, 11 June 1744; f. 151, 12 July 1744.

[110] Home Misc., vol. 456 F, ff. 145-49.

[111] DB, vol. 92, f. 69, 11 Sept. 1689.

This latter category of weavers, unlike the peasant-weaver, could not always fall back easily on an alternative source of employment, if and when necessary. It was probably this section of the weaving community which is alluded to in the sources as being 'poor'. Whether the alleged poverty of the weavers was the actual reflection of the reality or not, there are indications that a number of weavers, probably working full-time as individuals, were indebted to the *dalals* and *paikars* from whom they received advances. This made the situation difficult for them. It was not only the merchants but even Company officials often referred to the indebtedness of weavers to intermediaries.[112]

At the same time there is little doubt that quite a large portion of the weaver's profit was appropriated by the merchant-middlemen and others operating in the trade. It was very seldom that the weaver would receive the full amount of advance which the Companies or Asian merchants gave to different agents while entering into contract for procurement of textiles. As he was mostly working in his rural isolation in the society, the weaver was vulnerable to the deception of the middlemen whether in regard to the advances or to the final price to be paid. He was also often a victim of exploitation by the bureaucracy which would snatch a part of his profit. This is well illustrated by John Taylor when he mentioned that even in royal *Karkhanas*, the weaver received only 75 per cent of the value of his cloth, the rest being appropriated by the officials in administration.[113] The weavers' bargaining power could not always be that effective because mostly isolated as he was within his rural community and caste barriers, he lacked the collective bargaining power of a group combined against the exploiters. But what seems most likely and for which we have enough evidence in the sources is that the situation was not so bad in normal years when, as Orme says, 'his natural indolence...is satisfied in procuring by his labour, his daily bread'.[114] There is no indication that he ever thought of bad days or about his future. The Danish account clearly reflects this

[112] Fact. Records, Dacca, vol. 3, Annex. to Consult., 17 Nov. 1754; 30 Nov. 1757.

[113] Home Misc., vol. 456F, f. 137.

[114] Orme, *Military Transactions*, vol. II, Sect. I, p. 9.

attitude of the artisan[115]: 'In Bengal...the spinner and the weaver require and expect no more than is necessary to pay for the material, procure enough to eat and to have a little leisure; when times are good they even flourish in this way.'

Be that as it may, there is little doubt however that the weaver was in a much better position during this period than he was in the post-Plassey period. Whatever freedom or bargaining power he had enjoyed earlier, he lost them completely in the second half of the eighteenth century under the repressive and exploitative machinery of the Company and its servants who were assisted in the process by their Indian *gomastas*. Several recent works have shown graphically how the weavers were put under almost inhuman oppression and ruthless exploitation by the Company and its servants in the second half of the eighteenth century.[116] The anonymous author of an early nineteenth century English manuscript thus described the position of weavers under the Company:[117]

> The whole inland trade of the country and the provision of the company's investment ... became one continued scene of oppression, the baneful effects of which was felt by every weaver and manufacturer in the country, every article produced being made a monopoly in which the English arbitrarily decided what quantities of goods each manufacturer should deliver, and the prices he should receive for them.... Generally a number of weavers are registered in the books of the company's gomastahs, and *not permitted to work for any other persons, being transferred from one gomastah to another as so many slaves, subject to the tyranny and roguery of every succeeding gomastah. The English with great strictness monopolised the weavers; their hardship is scarcely to be described.*

It has been estimated in a recent study that while costs of

[115] Ole Feldbaeck, 'Cloth Production in Bengal', *BPP*, vol. XXXVI, p. 126.

[116] N.K. Sinha, *Economic History of Bengal,* vol. I, pp. 157-181; D.B. Mitra, *Cotton Weavers,* pp. 49-87; Hameeda Hossain, *Company Weavers,* pp. 108-39.

[117] Mss. Eur. D. 283. ff. 37-38. Emphasis mine.

manufacture and other charges had gone up considerably between 1747 and 1800, the weaver's proportion of earning showed hardly any increase during the period. But meanwhile the prices of food increased and so it can be assumed that the weaver's earnings from the loom were hardly sufficient any more to provide for his basic needs.[118] The pathetic condition of the weavers in the late eighteenth century is well reflected in the Bengali records of Dhaka factories. When a weaver of Titbadi, one of the famous *aurungs* in Dhaka, died, he left behind for his wife and child daughter a little yarn, his paltry tools, one stone tureen, one waterpot of brass, one rupee due from a spinner and a 'servant' (apprentice?) while his debt amounted to Rs 13.5.[119] When another weaver of Sonargon, the famous *aurung* of muslin production, died, his wife and three year old daughter had few earthly belongings while the debt amounted to Rs 141.5.[120] Any such instance of the weaver's extreme poverty could hardly be found in the early eighteenth century. As such, it can reasonably be argued that the weavers and artisans were in a much more enviable position in the first half of the eighteenth century than their counterparts in the second half of the century.

6.4 PROBLEMS OF TECHNOLOGY

Historians have tried to explain the absence of any technological innovation in the textile industry in various ways. Some explained it in terms of a 'low-level equilibrium trap' by which the availability of surplus labour and hence low wages enabled an increase in output without any rise in per unit productivity, and too much of specialization in the industry which would have required 'very great incentives to introduce any change in technology'. Others have tried to trace it to the existence of a numerous class of artisans and craftsmen able to live at very low wages which mitigated against any labour-saving techniques. Yet others pointed out the rigidity of the caste system and tyrannical

---

[118] Hameeda Hossain, *Company Weavers*, p. 61.

[119] Beng. Mss. I.O. 4046, f.100. It is significant that in a note in this document it is stated that the custom there was that the servant (*nafar*) may be sold if necessary.

[120] Beng. Mss. I.O. 4045, ff. 146-47.

administration where there was little incentive for any innovation.[121] It appears that most of these arguments were advanced
on the assumption that in the seventeenth and early eighteenth
century the European demand was so huge, compared with the
earlier situation, that it called for technological change in the
industry. The explanation given so far as to how Bengal could
meet the extra demand of the European trade without any
fundamental change in the technique of production was that this
was done either by picking up the slack in the economy — by
drawing in more labour force to the industry, turning more part-
time workers to full-time activity in the weaving process, and to
some extent by increasing the individual output.[122]

There is little doubt that the European export of Bengal
textiles was quite large in the second half of the seventeenth and
the first half of the eighteenth century. But the big question is
how significant quantitatively this European demand was compared with the purchases of the traditional Asian merchants for
supplies to various parts of India and Asia, and especially in
proportion to the total production in the country. We have shown
recently and argued here also[123] that the European trade was
certainly not the most important factor in the commercial life of
Bengal even in the mid-eighteenth century. Even during this
period, the volume of Asian export from Bengal, especially of the
key commodities like silk and textiles, was larger than that of the
Europeans. In an estimate of the late eighteenth century[124], the
total production of cloth for local consumption in the province
was valued at Rs 60 million. If that was so, it can be assumed that
the amount of textile production for local consumption was at

---

[121] K.N. Chaudhuri, *Trading World*, pp. 274-275; T. Raychaudhuri,
Cambridge Economic History of India, vol. I, p. 295; Irfan Habib, 'The
Technology and Economy of Mughal India' *IESHR*, vol. XVII, no. 1,
pp. 32-33.

[122] S. Chaudhuri, *Trade and Commercial Organization*, p. 234; Om
Prakash, *Dutch Company*, p. 101.

[123] S. Chaudhury, 'Asian Merchants and Companies in Bengal's
Export Trade, circa. mid-18th Century', revised version of the paper
presented at the International Seminar on 'Merchants, Companies and
Trade', M.S.H., Paris, 30 May - 1 June 1990. Also see chapters 7 and
8.

[124] H.T.Colebrooke, *Remarks on the Husbandry*, p. 105.

least the same, if not more (considering the great famine of 1770 and the high mortality following it[125]), in the first half of the century. As against this, the textile export by Asian merchants ranged, in all probability, between Rs 9 to 10 million while that of the Europeans was around Rs 5 to 6 million. So the European export was only a small proportion of the total output and as such could be easily met without a fundamental change in the technique of production. If the European demand had been significantly high compared to the total output so as to put severe strain on the supply side, only then the question of meeting the extra demand without technological change would have arisen. But as it was only a small part of the total produce, it could be met by stretching the existing structure of the industry a little. In other words, the question of technological innovation in response to 'huge' or 'phenomenal' increase in European trade becomes superfluous.

But if we take into account the combined amount of Asian and European export, then the position, however, becomes different. It is said that with the Mughal conquest of Bengal in 1575 and the resultant peace and stability, the 'outer world' came to Bengal and Bengal went to the 'outer world'.[126] Though perhaps an overstatement, there is little doubt that one of the benefits of the 'Mughal peace' was the expansion in trade and industry. By the early decades of the seventeenth century, Bengal's trade with Upper India and areas beyond seem to be quite considerable. And the trade of the European companies in Bengal boomed from the 1680s. So if we add the Asian export with that of the Europeans, then the total amount of export becomes quite considerable and forms a substantial part of the total production. In this context the absence of technological change comes in.

It is perhaps true that there were several inhibiting factors which stood in the way of technological innovations. So it is imperative to try to identify these deterrents to innovatory techniques in the industry. It should be emphasized, however,

---

[125] The famine is said to have wiped off 1/3 of the population of Bengal, see *BPP*, XXIX, 37, quoted in D.B.Mitra, *Cotton Weavers*, p.212.
[126] J.N.Sarkar, ed., *History of Bengal*, vol.II, p. 188.

that the textile industry as a whole did not remain altogether
static throughout the seventeenth and eighteenth centuries.[127] If
not so much in techniques, there were certainly changes in the
organization of manufacture, though in a limited scale and
without signalling a break with the past. The technology
remained simple and capital inputs were minimal; yet the
industry could achieve a substantial increase in the total output
through the familiar instruments of *dadni*, taking up the slack in
the economy, increased localization, a high degree of specialization and minute differentiation of functions based on a distinct
division of labour. The organization of production showed a
remarkable capacity for adaptation and response to expanding
demand. These were, however, qualitative developments within
the limits of familiar pattern and did not signify any break with
the traditional system. But the changes in organization were more
fundamental than those in technology.

Still there was no emergence of a rich artisanate class as yet
and that only indicates a limited range of forms of organization
even in the mid-eighteenth century. Though one occasionally
comes across 'respectable family of weavers' or 'head weavers'
employing a number of artisans, they seem to be exceptions
rather than the rule and only peripheral to the system of
production. Nor were the merchants or other affluent groups
involved in any way in the production process. Hence the
initiative for introducing any innovation in the technology could
have only come from the weaver-artisans who lacked the
incentives to pioneer such things. Having no access to mercantile
profit, no scope for upward social mobility, exploited and
abused— though occasionally—by officials and merchants alike,
and given the relatively low remuneration even for high skill,
they had little reason to initiate any change in the traditional
technology.

As such, the extreme simplicity of tools used and a general
indifference to any labour-saving device characterized the technology of textile industry in the early eighteenth century as it did
in the former period. The Danish report aptly remarked: "...the
country's way of production—so different from the European
way—which is generally managed with certain funds, by help of

[127] For the controversy on the issue, see Morris *et al*, *Indian Economy*.

machines, and under supervision of professional entrepreneurs. In Bengal, on the other hand, no machines shorten the work of the artisan'.[128] There is no denying the fact that the continuation of the age-old technology was only possible by the monopoly Bengal textiles enjoyed in the world market. The absence of any competition whatsoever, availability of cheap labour and hence low cost, easy access to raw material which was cheaper than in any other parts — all this made the quest for technological innovation redundant.

Yet it is worthwhile to identify the major elements which inhibited or restricted the process of change. The most dominant element in this respect, the disclaimer of a late-eighteenth century writer notwithstanding, was probably the rigour of the caste system within which the weaver-artisans had to function. The Danish account portrayed this vividly:[129]

> Always poor, without even thinking of better conditions, they [the weaver-artisans] work solely for their subsistence; they have no prospects of improving their work or of changing the organization or the tools they use; and as a weaver cannot become a member of another caste or tribe than his father was, he is bound to follow his father's trade and will never become anything else than a weaver; therefore he does not think ahead, as long as he has enough money or advance to buy a few seers of cotton which he himself, his wife and his family may clean and spin, and as long as he may take his pieces of cloth to the market in the weaving district....

The Dutch traveller Stavorinus corroborates this when he wrote in the late 1760s that the weaver or artisan 'can never expect to rise above the station in which they are born'.[130] Hence the weaver/artisan's vested interest was naturally inclined to continue the labour-intensive techniques which he inherited for generations from the past.

[128] Home Misc., vol. 456 F, f. 126.
[129] Ibid.
[130] Stavorinus, *Voyages,* p. 411.

7

EXPORT OF TEXTILES— COMPANIES AND ASIAN MERCHANTS

Bengal textiles enjoyed a unique place and an indisputable supremacy in the world market for centuries before the invasion of the machine-made fabrics in the early nineteenth century, following the Industrial Revolution of the West and political control of the sub-continent by the English East India Company. There is hardly any need to emphasize that the products of the Bengal handloom industry reigned supreme all over the accessible Asian and north African markets in the Middle ages, and later became one of the major staples of the export trade of the European companies from about the third quarter of the seventeenth century. Most travellers from Europe starting with Tomé Pires, Varthema and Barbosa in the sixteenth century to Bernier, Tavernier and many others in the seventeenth especially singled out textiles of Bengal for comments on their extraordinary quality and enchanting beauty. But it was not only in the field of high quality cloth that Bengal enjoyed a predominant position; it was also an emporium of ordinary and medium quality textiles. Long before the advent of the Europeans, the Asian merchants from different parts of the continent and Indian merchants from various regions of India derived a lucrative trade in Bengal textiles. During the period under review, the calicoes of Bengal were the major item in the export list of the European companies which were engaged in an extensive trade in the commodity from Bengal while the merchants from various parts of India and Asia were still carrying on quite a substantial trade in Bengal textiles.

7.1 COMPANIES IN TEXTILE EXPORT

In the initial stage of their trade in the seventeenth century, the European companies were not interested in the export of textiles from India. Their main concern was to procure spices in the East Indies, the so-called spice islands in the Indonesian archipelago. They went there to buy spices with silver, the supply of which became abundant with the discovery of the 'new world'. But to their great surprise, they found that it was not silver which was favoured as exchange against spices but Indian textiles, mainly cheap coarse varieties, which were the most sought-after items in the spice islands. Hence the Companies turned their attention to India for cheap cotton piece-goods. In India again their attention was focused mainly on the Coromandel Coast but subsequently when political instability, wars and famines made the Coromandel trade uncertain and expensive, both the Dutch and the English Companies turned their attention to Bengal which was not only an inexhaustible source of supply of cheap cotton textiles but also a rich producer of high quality and inexpensive raw silk.[1]

But the export of Bengal textiles did not assume any significant proportion in the Companies' total exports from Asia till around the middle of the seventeenth century. It was actually from the early 1680s that there was a sudden boom in the textile export from Bengal which made revolutionary changes in the pattern of the Asiatic trade of the European companies. From then onward Bengal became the chief partner of the Companies' export trade to Europe from Asia which was conducted mainly by the Dutch and the English East India Companies, and this trend continued till the middle of the eighteenth century. It was only after the revolution of 1757 in Bengal that there began an altogether different story when the English Company and its servants, by virtue of the total control over Bengal polity and economy, were intent on practically eliminating all the other European and Asian competitors from any worth-while trade.[2]

---

[1] For details, see S. Chaudhuri, *Trade and Commercial Organization*, pp. 11-26.

[2] Glamann, *Dutch Asiatic Trade*, p. 144.

Of the two major European companies, the Dutch had a definite lead over their rivals, the English, in the export of Bengal textiles to Europe (even excluding the Dutch export to various Asian markets) from the middle of the seventeenth up to the first decade of the eighteenth century. Though the Dutch maintained the lead even towards the close of the seventeenth and early years of the eighteenth century, the competition was severe and it was a near thing. The position altered somewhat in the second decade of the eighteenth century (Table 7.1) when the English established the lead in the period from 1710/11 to 1713/14 while in the next quadrennial period, 1714/15 to 1717/18, the share of the two Companies was almost equal.

TABLE 7.1

Quadrennial Total and Average of Dutch and
English Textile Exports
1710/11—1717/18

Years	Dutch		English	
	Total (pieces)	Average (pieces)	Total (pieces)	Average (pieces)
1710/11—1713/14	745,995	186,497	1,056,587	264,147
1714/15—1717/18	925,254	231,313	915,918	228,980

[Source: Dutch exports computed from Om Prakash, *Dutch Company*, p. 195; English exports from S. Chaudhuri, *Trade and Commerce*, p. 258]

The question that crops up is how to explain the big boom in the demand for and the consequent export of Bengal textiles to Europe. In general historians are apt to come up with the obvious economic explanation for this phenomenon namely, that the Bengal textiles were much cheaper and of better quality than any other varieties available in the world market. The reasons for cheapness and fine quality of Bengal piece-goods were that both labour and provisions were much cheaper in Bengal than anywhere else and the Bengal artisans and manufacturers had a long tradition of high skill in weaving both fine and ordinary textiles. All this is true but only necessary, not sufficient, factors to explain the sudden boom in the European demand for Bengal textiles. The phenomenal increase can only be explained satisfactorily by the revolutionary change in the consumer taste in the European society during the period. The 'Indian craze' or 'Indiennes' is well reflected in contemporary European, especially English, literature of the time. That the fashion rather than the cheapness of Indian cloth worked as an active economic factor in the textile export to Europe is revealed in several pamphlets of the time.[3] The race for procuring constant novelties went to such an extent that the Court of Directors instructed Bengal factors in 1681 to change the fashion and design in all flowered silks every year as much as possible because the English, French and other European ladies 'will give twice as much for a new thing not seen in Europe before though worse, than they will give for a better silk of the same fashion worn the former year'.[4] Of course, there can be little doubt that the low cost of Bengal textiles acted as a factor in the popularity of the new fashion. An important contributory factor in the expansion of textile export from Bengal, especially plain white piece-goods, was the rapid growth of the cotton printing industry in England and other parts of Europe in the early eighteenth century.[5]

The great importance of textiles in the export lists of the Companies will be apparent from the percentage share of the commodity in the total export value from Bengal throughout the first half of the eighteenth century (Table 7.2). In fact, throughout this period textiles formed the largest single item in the Companies' export bills. In the early years of the eighteenth century the share of the textile value in the total export value from Bengal was 54 per cent for the Dutch Company while for the English it was 71 per cent. Towards the end of our period the share of the Dutch Company ranged between 74 and 78 per cent whereas the English share varied between 80 and 92 per

[3] J. Cary, *Discourse*, p. 4. India Office Tracts, vol.83, Tract No.7,p.50. Extracts from these are quoted in S. Chaudhuri, *Trade and Commercial Organization*, pp. 223-25.

[4] DB, vol. 89, f. 352, 20 May 1681.

[5] Serigo Aiolfi, *Calicos und gedrucktes Zeug*, Stuttgart, 1987, pp. 130-204; R.E. Hartkamp-Jonxis, *Sits: Oost-West Relaties in Textiel*, pp. 30-42, 54-64.

cent. This only confirms the fact that textile was the most important item in the export trade of the European companies throughout the first half of the eighteenth century.

TABLE 7.2
Share (Percentage) of Textile Value in the
Total Export Value: Dutch and English:
Select Years, 1700-1755

Years	Dutch Export	English Export
1701/02	54.19	71.00
1702/03	54.19	71.00
1748/49	N.A.	88.98
1749/50	N.A.	91.91
1750/51	N.A.	87.42
1751/52	N.A.	80.07
1752/53	N.A.	79.55
1753/54	78.42	88.11
1754/55	74.07	80.82

[Source: Dutch share, 1701/02 and 1702/03 taken from Om Prakash, *Dutch Company,* p. 72 and 1753/54 and 1754/55 collected and computed from Dutch export invoices in VOC records. English share, 1701/02 to 1702/03 taken from S. Chaudhuri, *Trade and Commerce,* p. 254; 1748/49 to 1752/53, collected and computed from Bengal General Journals and Ledgers, vols. 46,48,50,52,54 and 1753/54 to 1754/55 calculated with one-year lag from K.N. Chaudhuri, *Trading World,* pp. 510, 545.NA = Not available.]

The huge demand for Bengal textiles in Europe is also reflected in the orders sent out from Europe to Bengal. These orders were generally sent out about two years ahead for the shipment of goods in a particular year. The fluctuations in the demand for different varieties of textiles in Europe are reflected in these orders. The annual list sent out to Bengal generally contained the name of every type of textiles, the quantity of each type to be supplied and sometimes also the price range within which to buy a particular type. But despite all these detailed instructions, an interesting feature of the export trade from Bengal was that often some of the textiles sent were vastly in excess of what actually was ordered from Europe, while some other varieties fell far short of the quantity asked for. The reasons for this were the inflated demand from Europe on the one hand, and on the other hand factors like the supply condition in Bengal, the reluctance of the *dadni* merchants to bring in goods which did not yield them a handsome profit as also their attempts, in collusion with the Company servants, to dump the Companies with some textiles which they procured cheap. The most glaring example of oversupply of goods, some of which were not even ordered from Europe, presumably in connivance with the Indian merchants, was by the Fort William Council in 1727-28 for which the chief of the Council, Henry Frankland, was dismissed from the Company's service.[6] The problem was not confined only to the English; the Dutch too faced the same with oversupply of several varieties which the Heeren Seventeen had to sell in auctions at considerable loss.[7]

The list of textiles ordered from Bengal (Table 7.3) also makes it clear that the English were far ahead of the Dutch in the textile export from around 1720, something which, as we shall see later, will also be borne out by the actual exports of the two Companies during the period under review.

Quite a few interesting features of the textile trade emerge from a comparative study of the orders sent to Bengal by the two Companies. First, the most noticeable thing is the predominance of ordinary calicoes, the cheapest Bengal textile, in the orders of both the Companies. This only indicates that there was not only a greater demand for these varieties, but it was perhaps more profitable to export these categories than the rest as maximum profit in sales and/or re-exporting these goods would have been the prime consideration of the joint stock companies. Secondly, the demand for ordinary calicoes was growing steadily except for the Dutch Company in 1750 when it reduced the orders for this particular category to a great extent—cutting it down to about 1/3 of what was ordered in 1740. Thirdly, the orders for muslins,

---

[6] K.N. Chaudhuri, *Trading World*, p. 253.
[7] Glamann, *Dutch Asiatic Trade*, pp. 145, 150.

TABLE 7.3
Orders for Textiles from Europe
Number of Pieces Ordered in Select Years (1720-1750)

Textile Categories	1720 Dutch	1720 English	1733 Dutch	1733 English	1740 Dutch	1740 English	1750 Dutch	1750 English
Ordn. Calicoes	127,600	157,000	138,400	339,400	241,500	317,000	87,000	400,000
Fine Calicoes	39,400	59,000	43,200	139,500	45,300	138,700	85,200	93,600
Muslins	121,500	153,000	36,660	98,200	57,360	209,900	89,400	262,300
Silk Pc.- Goods	51,000	38,000	33,160	28,000	37,500	36,800	56,400	41,000
Mixed Pc.- Goods	28,000	94,000	19,700	45,000	8,300	48,100	19,900	31,700
Total	367,500	501,000	271,120	650,100	389,960	750,500	337,900	828,600

[Source and note: Dutch orders collected and computed from the Resolutions of Heeren XVII, VOC, vols. 117, 120, 122, 126 and English orders from DB, vols. 100, 106, 108, 111. In the Dutch orders for 1720, only the minimum amount ordered for a particular type is computed here. For example, while 3,000 to 3,500 fine *humums* were ordered, we took the minimum i.e., 3000 in our computation. When the maximum amount is taken into consideration, the total number of pieces ordered would amount to 376,000, and not 367,500 as shown in the table. But this occurs only in the order for 1720 and not for other years computed here. For the basis on which the classification is made, see f.n.8.]

TABLE 7.4
Share of *Garras* and *Khasas* in the Total Textiles Ordered Select Years (1720 - 1750)

Years	Dutch Orders				English Orders			
	Garras pieces	Share per cent	*Khasas* pieces	Share per cent	*Garras* pieces	Share per cent	*Khasas* pieces	Share per cent
1720	60,000	16.33	33,000	8.98	80,000	15.97	58,000	11.58
1733	60,000	22.13	16,400	6.05	202,000	31.07	39,700	6.11
1740	80,000	20.51	25,000	6.41	144,000	19.19	59,600	7.94
1750	10,000	2.96	27,000	7.99	185,000	22.33	146,000	17.62

[Source and note: Same as in Table 7.3]

the finest and most expensive of all Bengal textiles, generally speaking, was next only to those for ordinary calicoes. The priority of these two categories of textiles was maintained throughout the period and like the ordinary calicoes, the order for muslins too was growing steadily except for 1733 when both the Dutch and the English ordered fewer quantities of muslins than in 1720. In fact the Dutch order for muslins was the highest in 1720 out of the four years for which the orders are presented in Table 7.3. Next, what becomes apparent is that the orders for three other varieties namely, fine calicoes, silk and mixed piece-goods were much smaller compared with the first two categories, and they fluctuated quite a bit depending mainly on the amount ordered for the first two categories.[8] Finally, while the total

[8] It should be made explicitly clear that it is extremely difficult and in some cases almost impossible to classify the textiles into various categories because of their numerous varieties, some of which were extinct long back. So the classification made is only tentative though based on contemporaneous accounts like, Taillerfert's 'memorie' (Hoge Regering van Batavia, 246), John Taylor's Description of Dhaka Cloth Manufacture (Home Misc. 456 F), references in Dutch and English Company records, the price of different varieties worked out from export invoices of the Companies and contracts with merchants as well as modern works like John Irwin, K.N. Chaudhuri, Hameeda Hossain, etc. The different types, especially those exported by the Companies during the period under review, in each category are mentioned in alphabetical order:

Muslins: *adaties, allabalies, dimities, duriyas (dooreas), humhums, jamdanies, kepers, khasas, mulmuls, milmils, nainsooks, sarbatis, seerbands, seerhaudcanas, shalbafts, tanjebs, terrindams,* etc.

Fine Calicoes: *bethilas, chowtars, dysooksies, handcerchieves* (cotton), *kamkhani, rumals* (cotton), *sologazis, sanus* (sanoes), etc.

Ordinary Calicoes: *atchiabanies, baftas, chilas, chints, coopies, dariabadies, dosooties,* (Dutch *zeijlkleden*), *emerties* (Dutch *amritijs*), *garras* (gurrahs), *guinees, gunnies, fotas* (photaes), *lakhories, parcallas, salampuris, tuckeries,* etc.

Silk Piece-Goods: *alcatives, allegias, armosins, bandanas, chandrabanies, chapalens, chapasaris, choukutas, cottabani, dheris, dotanies, fulla chetas, foelies, jamawars, kakatoestaff,* (silk) *lungies, mohunbanies, momtanies, maypoost, ragiabanies, restas, rudrabanies,* (silk) *rumals, taffachelas, taffetas,* etc.

Mixed Piece-Goods:*alliabanies charkanies, chuklas,cushtas, elatchies, ginghams, handkerchief, kharadaries, nillaes, peniascoes, seersuckers, soosies, tepoys, sichterman's rumal, sichterman's sai,* etc.

number of pieces ordered by the Dutch Company remained more or less steady during the period except a decline in 1733, the English orders show a steady increase throughout.

What is not reflected in the Table (7.3) but which is of considerable interest is the importance of several types of textiles in the orders from Europe. The two single items that were in great demand were *garras*, an ordinary calico and *khasas*, a relatively more expensive muslin, throughout the period under review.

Table 7.4 clearly shows the predominance of *garras* and *khasas* in the list of orders from Europe, especially in consideration of the fact that every year at least 50 to 55 different types of piece-goods were ordered from Bengal.

It is not difficult to relate the predominance of plain white cotton piece-goods in general, and *garras* and *khasas* in particular, in the orders sent out from Europe to the domestic situation there. The wool and silk weavers in England succeeded through their protests in having an Act passed in 1700 which prohibited the import into England of 'all wrought silks, Bengals and stuffs mixed with silk or herba, of the manufacture of Persia, China and the East Indies and all calicoes painted, dyed or printed or stained there'.[9] This resulted in an increase in the export of plain cotton and muslin rather than other varieties from Bengal. At the same time another important factor that accounted for an increase in the import of plain cotton and muslin in the early eighteenth century was the rapidly growing cotton printing industry in Europe, especially in England around London.[10] The preference for *garras* among all the plain calicoes or muslins was obviously because of their cheapness. The cotton printers, unlike craftsmen of the old type, were industrial entrepreneurs and were always eager to expand their production by lowering the prices of their products. More expensive plain muslin like *khasa* was also welcome by the printers because, after printing, these could be sold to rich people at home and also could be re-exported profitably. In 1720 another Act was passed according to which

[9] S. Bhattacharyya, *East India Company*, p. 158.
[10] Glamann, *Dutch Asiatic Trade*, p. 151. For the growth of cotton printing industry in London, see S. Aiolfi, *Calicos*, pp. 192-203.

the use of any calico was prohibited in England.[11] But this too
failed to prevent the Company from ordering larger quantities
of textiles from Bengal, something which would be obvious from
Table 7.3. This was because, on the one hand, the Company tried
to keep up its supply so as to cope with the buoyant demand of
the cotton printing industry while on the other it continued the
old policy of re-exporting Bengal textiles with handsome profit.
Even in the 1730s the Dutch merchants were buying textiles
imported by the English Company.[12]

Regarding the actual exports of the two Companies to
Europe, if the total number of pieces exported from Bengal is any
indication, the English had established a decisive lead over the
Dutch from the early 1730s, which was maintained steadily till the
mid-eighteenth century, completely reversing the situation of the
second half of the seventeenth and first decade of the eighteenth
century. Table 7.5 illustrating the total pieces of textiles exported
by the two Companies from Bengal will bear this out.

TABLE 7.5
Quinquennial Total and Average Annual Textile Exports
Dutch and English, 1730-1755

Years	Dutch Exports		English Exports	
	Total (pieces)	Average (pieces)	Total (pieces)	Average (pieces)
1730/31-1734/35	835,357	167,071	3,026,154	605,231
1740/41-1744/45	1,021,899	204,380	3,026,405	605,281
1750/51-1754/55	1,342,789	268,558	1,951,952	390,390

[Source and note: Dutch exports collected and computed from export
invoices in VOC records; English exports computed from detailed data
provided by K.N. Chaudhuri. For Dutch ships *Lis* (1743-44), *Spanderswout*
and *De Snoek* (1754-55), though the invoice value is available, the
breakdown of the cargoes could not be traced. Interpolated data is used
for missing cargoes of these ships.]

[11] S. Bhattacharyya, *East India Company*, p. 159.
[12] Glamann, *Dutch Asiatic Trade*, p. 150.

Several interesting features of the exports by the two Companies emerge from the above Table (7.5). Throughout the period, the Dutch exports show a steady increase culminating in the early 1750s when the wide gap with the English exports of the 1730s and 1740s was greatly reduced. This was of course because of the fact that while on the one hand the Dutch exports increased steadily, the English exports on the other were reduced dramatically in the early 1750s. The average annual English exports were strikingly almost at the same level in the first five years of the 1730s and the 1740s while in the 1750s they declined sharply by about 35 per cent of the earlier levels. Interestingly enough, the orders from Europe during these years (Table 7.3) show that while the Dutch orders fluctuated within a limited range, the English orders show a steady annual increase of around 0.1 million pieces for each of the four years we have tabulated earlier.

The obvious question that arises is why the English exports dropped in the early 1750s though the orders from England by far surpassed those for earlier years. The general assumption is that the Maratha invasion in the 1740s was so disastrous for the economy that it resulted in the decline of trade in general and the textile trade in particular, and as such the reduction in English exports too.[13] But that does not explain the situation fully. There is little doubt that the Maratha incursions created serious dislocation in the economy but it was mainly local in character and only a temporary phenomenon. The economy and production recovered from the shock soon so that the impact of the invasions was not so devastating as it was generally assumed to have been. Had it been really so, the Dutch exports would not have gone up so steadily in the 1740s and 1750s as is evident from Table 7.5. The decline in the total number of pieces exported by the English Company in the 1750s can be explained to some extent by the fact that there was a relative shift in the different types of textiles exported during these years. As will be evident from Table 7.7, while the percentage share of cheaper varieties like ordinary calicoes was around 46 per cent in the early 1730s, it

---

[13] K.K. Datta, *Alivardi*, pp. 92, 157-59; K.N. Chaudhuri, *Trading World*, pp. 253, 308, 310; P.J. Marshall, *Bengal*, pp. 71-73.

came down to about 31 per cent of the total volume of textile export during the first five years of the 1740s and 1750s. But the share of the expensive items like muslins went up from 24 per cent in the 1730s to 34 per cent in the 1740s and to 39 per cent in the 1750s. The reason for this was two-fold; first, the orders from England too show a sharp increase in the demand for muslins like *khasas* (from 7.94 to 17.62 per cent) while for the coarse calicoes like *garras* the increase was only marginal (19.19 to 22.33 per cent).[14] Secondly, the decline was also due to the fact that the procurement of ordinary calicoes like *garras* and *dosooties* which were produced mainly in Birbhum, Burdwan and Kasimbazar areas became extremely difficult from around the mid-1740s as a result of the Maratha invasions which affected those areas most.[15]

Moreover, as the muslins were comparatively more expensive items than ordinary calicoes like *garras*, the larger export of the former would only mean much greater decrease in the export of the latter if the total value of the textile exports was to be the same. It was because of this that there was no proportionate decline in the total number of pieces exported and the total value of the textile exports in the early 1740s and early 1750s. That the Maratha invasions did not affect either the production of most of the varieties or the total value of the textile exports to any considerable extent will be evident from a comparative study of the total volume and the total value of the textile export by the English Company in the quinquennial periods from 1740/41 to 1744/45 and 1748/49 to 1752/53. The above dates are suitable for such an analysis because the Maratha invasions began in April 1742 and ended by May/June 1751. As such, they include the years prior to, during and immediately after the incursions. Another important reason for selecting the period up to 1752/53 is that from 1753 the investment pattern was changed from *dadni* to *gomasta* system, something which could have some impact on exports from 1753/54 and it was really so.

[14] See Table 7.7.
[15] Fact. Records, Kasimbazar, vol. 6, Consult., 2 July 1743, 1 March 1744; vol. 10, Consult., 23 April 1751; BPC, vol. 16, f. 211, 14 July 1743.

TABLE 7.6

Volume and Value of English Textile Exports, Quinquennial
Period, 1740/41 to 1744/45 and 1748/49 to 1752/53

Years	Total (pieces)	Average (pieces)	Total Value (Rs)	Average Value (Rs)
1740/41—1744/45	3,026,154	605,231	15,410,680	3,082,136
1748/49—1752/53	1,856,780	371,356	15,147,699	3,029,539

[Source & note: Figures for 1740/41 to 1744/45 computed from K.N. Chaudhuri, *Trading World*, p. 545 with one-year lag and converting the value from pound sterling to Rupees @ £ 1 = Rs 8. Figures for 1748/49 to 1752/53 collected and computed from Bengal General Journals and Ledgers, vols. 46,48,50,52,54]

Here a possible argument that could be advanced is that the total value of English textile export did not alter very much despite the substantial reduction in the total number of pieces exported in the quinquennial period from 1748/49 to 1752/53. This is possibly because of the fact that the unit price of textiles had gone up considerably during the period. But as we would show later, the cost prices of textiles did not reveal any marked increase during the period under question, except a marginal rise in the prices of some ordinary piece-goods.

There are also interesting differences in the composition of the different categories of textiles exported by the two Companies which will be evident from Table 7.7 which shows the percentage share of different categories in the total textile exports during the period under review[16].

---

[16] For the basis of classification, see, f.n.8. *Doreas*, a staple variety, in the export of the Companies is included here under the category of muslins though both Irwin and K.N.Chaudhuri think that it was a mixed piece-good. Taylor stated, no doubt, that *dorea* meant 'double threads'(Taylor, *Topography*, p.173) but it is possibly a corrupt form of Bengali 'dure' which means striped and this 'dure' cloth (mainly cotton *sari*) is still in vogue. Despite Buchanan-Hamilton's assertion of *duriyas* made in Bhagalpur in 1812 being mixed piece-goods, the reference in *Ain-i-Akbari* (vol.1,p.95) includes it among cotton fabrics (Irwin, p.63).

TABLE 7.7
Percentage Share of Different Categories of Textiles
Exported by the Companies, 1730-1755
(First Five Years of Each Decade)

Textile Categories	Dutch Exports			English Exports		
	1730s	1740s	1750s	1730s	1740s	1750s
Ordn.Calicoes	46.40	39.85	55.69	46.02	30.60	30.80
Fine Calicoes	14.99	19.89	12.66	20.30	22.49	19.17
Muslins	20.23	26.22	17.79	24.44	34.08	39.26
Silk Piece-Goods	10.44	10.08	11.19	3.18	4.56	66.36
Mixd. Piece-Goods	7.94	3.96	2.67	5.98	7.88	3.72
Miscellaneous	-	-	-	0.08	0.39	0.69
Total	100	100	100	100	100	100

[Source: Dutch exports collected and computed from export invoices in VOC records; English exports computed from detailed data provided by K.N. Chaudhuri]

The price of *dorea* in the early 1750s would clearly indicate that it was not only muslin but one of the more expensive varieties in this category. While *doreas* procured in Hughli area cost between f 25 to f 29, the price of Dhaka *doreas* ranged from f 46 to f 51. The price of ordinary mixed piece-goods like *allibany* was f 8.9 while the more expensive variety like *seersuckers* cost f 15 to f 18 during the same period (computed from the invoices of ships *Bevalligheid* and *Ruijskenstein*, VOC,2794,ff.7vo-8; 2829,ff.134vo-135vo;ff.185-85vo). Moreover that *doreas* were produced also in Dhaka which hardly produced any mixed piece-goods would indicate that *dorea* was a muslin. Similarly *kamkhani* which was exported only in very small numbers is not included under muslins though both Irwin and Om Prakash identified it as such. Taillefert describes it as muslin from Bihar but makes it clear that it was of a coarse quality. Though Bihar produced muslins like cossa (*khasa*) and *mulmuls*, these were of ordinary quality, generally coarse and much cheaper than Bengal muslins. The price of *kamkhani*, for example, works out to be around f 4.5 only (VOC 2617, HB 24 Jan. 1745, Invoice of ship *Hofwegen*) while the price of muslins during this period would have been at least f 15 to 20 (VOC 2629, HB, 4 January 1744, ff.199-218, Contracts with merchants).

What is clearly reflected in the above Table (7.7) is that the lion's share of the Dutch export was of ordinary calicoes while in case of the English, muslins constituted the major category of textiles exported. The share of coarse calicoes in the Dutch exports during the period varied from about 40 to 56 per cent, the percentage share being 46, 40 and 56 in the first five years of the three decades (1730-1755) respectively. In the English exports, while the share of coarse calicoes was 46 per cent in the 1730s, both in the 1740s and 1750s it remained lower at 31 per cent. The share of the fine calicoes did not vary much, constituting 13 to 20 per cent of the Dutch exports and 19 to 22 per cent of the English exports. In case of muslins, while the Dutch share fluctuated between 18 and 26 per cent, the English exports show an increase of 10 per cent in the 1740s and 5 per cent in the 1750s. On the other hand, the Dutch share of silk piece-goods remained almost steady between 10 and 11 per cent while the English share shows an increase of about 1 to 2 per cent during these years. So far as the mixed piece-goods are concerned, the Dutch figures show a steady decline and the English share fluctuated quite a bit. What all this means in analytical terms is that the two most important categories of textiles exported by both the Companies throughout the period were the cheapest ordinary calicoes on the one hand and muslins, the most expensive of all the categories, on the other. So it was not a fact that the Companies exported only the cheap varieties or the more expensive ones — they exported both the categories in much larger quantities than the medium priced fine calicoes, silk or mixed piece-goods. The major factors behind this pattern of export in the textile trade were probably that the Companies were catering to the printing industry as also to the poor and rich sections of the European society. As we have noted earlier, the most suitable textiles for printing came mainly from the two categories namely, ordinary calicoes and muslins.

In the light of the percentage share of the different categories in the total exports, it would be interesting to see how the total value of the Dutch and English textile exports compared during this period. But for the lack of data on the value of the Dutch textile exports for most of the years, it is not possible to make such a comparative study for the whole period. However, we are able to make such an analysis for two years, 1753/54 and 1754/55, for which we have breakdown of the total value of textile

exports in the Dutch records. The comparative volume and value
of the Dutch and English exports of textiles in these two years
can be seen in Table 7.8.

TABLE 7.8

Volume and Value of the Dutch and English Textile Exports
1753/54 and 1754/55

Years	Dutch Exports		English Exports	
	Total (pieces)	Value (Rs)	Total (Pieces)	Value (Rs)
1753/54	279,800	1,670,336	345,267	2,287,128
1754/55	226,432	1,328,188	381,543	2,660,520
Total	506,232	2,998,555	726,810	4,947,648
Average	253,166	1,499,278	363,405	2,473,824

[Source & note: Dutch exports collected and computed from export
invoices in VOC records. English exports computed from K.N. Chaudhuri,
Trading World, p. 545, with one-year lag. Florin and pound sterling
converted to rupees @ Re 1 = 1.5 Florin and £ 1 = Rs 8]

It will be clear from the above Table (7.8) that though the
average annual export of the English for these two years was
110,239 pieces more than the Dutch export, the average annual
value of the English exports was Rs 974,546 more than that of
the Dutch, making the average unit price of textiles Rs 8.6 for
this difference. But the actual unit price of the textiles for the
Dutch exports was around Rs 6 and for the English about Rs 6.8
during these two years.[17] This was only because of the fact that
in the Dutch exports for these years the share of the cheap
ordinary calicoes was much higher while the largest share in the
English exports was taken by the more expensive muslins (Table
7.7). The main implication of the above analysis is that in any

[17] Calculated from Dutch export invoices in VOC records and K.N.
Chaudhuri, *Trading World*, p. 545.

computation regarding the price of textiles, the most important factor, among others, that should be taken into account is the total pieces of a particular type of cloth exported and their total value. From that only we can have a rough idea of the unit price of a particular textile. Other important factors in finding out the unit price are the actual measurement of the textile, the *aurung* in which it was produced and its quality such as ordinary, medium, fine, superfine etc. Any generalization such as arriving at the unit price just by deflating the total value by the total number of pieces could be highly misleading.[18]

7.2 DUTCH COMPANY'S INTRA-ASIATIC TRADE IN TEXTILES

In the second half of the seventeenth century, intra-Asiatic trade was an important part of the Dutch Company's operations in Asia. And in this intra-Asiatic trade of the Company, Bengal textile was an important component, especially in the last decades of the seventeenth and the first decade of the eighteenth century. It appears that the major centres of Dutch textile export from Bengal were (in descending order of total pieces exported) Batavia (mainly for distribution in the Indonesian archipelago), the Persian Gulf and Japan while the share of places like Malabar, Ceylon, Coromandel etc. was not so significant.[19] It is worth noting here that though the maximum number of pieces, which was even larger than that during any period in the second half of the seventeenth century, was exported in the first decade of the eighteenth century, in the second decade there was a sharp decline in textile export which will be evident from Table 7.9.

However, the declining trend in the Dutch Company's exports to Asian markets was completely reversed from at least the early 1730s, if the total pieces exported could be taken as an indication. The significant fact is that the Dutch export of Bengal textiles for intra-Asiatic trade reached its peak in the first half of the 1730s after which there was again a gradual decline both in the first five years of the 1740s and 1750s, as will be evident from

---

[18] For such tabulation of unit price of textiles, see K.N. Chaudhuri, *Trading World*, pp. 544-545.

[19] Om Prakash, *Dutch Company*, pp. 138-39, 146-47, 168-69, 178-80.

TABLE 7.9
Dutch Asiatic Trade (Textiles)
Quinquennial Total and Average (Pieces)
1705/06-09/10 & 1713/14-1717/18

Destination	1705/06—1709/10		1713/14—1717/18	
	Total (pieces)	Average (pieces)	Total (pieces)	Average (pieces)
Batavia	240,191	48,038	163,726	32,745
Persian Gulf	188,749	37,750	104,449	20,890
Japan	145,614	29,123	39,667	7,933

[Source & note: Om Prakash, *Dutch Company*, pp. 139,147,180. As the figures for the Persian Gulf are not available for 1705/06 and 1706/7, the figures for 1702/3 and 1703/4 are included in the period 1705/6-1709/10]

Table 7.10. The trends which clearly emerge from this Table (7.10) are as follows : first, throughout this period, the largest number of pieces was exported to Batavia, its share in the total volume of Dutch exports to Asia increasing from 54 per cent in early 1730s to 67 per cent in the first quinquennial period of the 1740s and finally to 87 per cent in the early 1750s, though there was a general decline in the Dutch textile export to different Asian markets. Secondly, though Japan came next to Batavia in the 1730s having a share of 21 per cent, it lost its place to Persia in the 1740s when its share went down to 6 per cent while the latter's share rose to around 11 per cent from 6 per cent in the 1730s. However in the 1750s Japan recovered its position though its share decreased to 5 per cent as Persia's share declined to 3 per cent. Among other places, Coromandel and Malabar had an almost equal share of around 5 per cent in the 1730s while in the subsequent period their shares declined considerably, the former having only 1.5 per cent and the latter 2 per cent in the 1730s and both almost drawing a nil in the 1750s. In the case of Ceylon, while the share was about 3 per cent in the 1730s, it went up to over 12 per cent in the 1740s but slided to 4 per cent in the 1750s. The share of other markets like Siam, Cochin, Malacca, Mocha,

TABLE 7.10

Dutch Intra-Asiatic Trade in Bengal Textiles: Quinquennial Total, Average and Share Percentage: 1730-1755 (first five years of each decade)

Destination	1730/31 - 1734/35			1740/41 - 1744/45			1750/51-1754/55		
	Total (pieces)	Average (pieces)	Share (%)	Total (pieces)	Average (pieces)	Share (%)	Total (pieces)	Average (pieces)	Share (%)
Batavia	584,022	116,804	54.23	432,007	86,401	67.19	371,884	74,377	86.78
Japan	230,648	46,130	21.42	36,086	7,217	5.61	20,344	4,069	4.75
Persian Gulf	65,382	13,076	6.07	68,650	13,730	10.68	14,175	2,835	3.31
Coromandel	55,463	11,093	5.15	9,460	1,892	1.47	400	80	0.09
Malabar	55,214	11,043	5.13	13,930	2,786	2.17	0	0	0.00
Malabar	28,084	5,617	2.61	80,081	16,016	12.46	16,835	3,367	3.93
Ceylon	23,980	4,796	2.23	0	0	0.00	1,200	240	0.28
Siam	21,280	4,256	1.98	1,818	364	0.28	120	24	0.03
Cochin	8,100	1,620	0.75	0	0	0.00	2,360	472	0.55
Malacca	3,220	644	0.30	0	0	0.00	0	0	0.00
Mocha	1,600	320	0.13	0	0	0.00	1,200	240	0.28
Macassar	0	0	0.00	893	179	0.14	0	0	0.00
Cape of Good Hope									
Total	1,076,993	215,399	100	642,925	128,585	100	428,518	85,704	100

[Source: Collected and computed from Dutch export invoices in VOC records.]

Macassar and the Cape of Good Hope was almost negligible except for the first two in the 1730s when their share was around 2 per cent each.

Looking at the total number of pieces exported, the Dutch Company's textile exports to Asian destinations seem quite impressive, especially compared to its exports to Europe, the annual average being 215,399, 128,585, and 85,704 pieces for Asia and 167,071, 204,380, and 268,558 pieces for Europe for the first quinquennial periods of the 1730s, 1740s and 1750s respectively.[20] But what is hidden in these numbers is the actual category of the different textiles exported to Asia and Europe— a fact on which the total value of the exports really depended, especially when we do not have any precise data on the value exclusively of the textile exports for most of the years under review. For such an analysis we select here the three major centres of the Dutch Asian exports namely, Batavia, Japan and Persia for which we tabulate below (Table 7.11) the share of different categories of textiles they received during this period.

What significantly emerges from Table 7.11 is that Batavia which claimed 54, 67 and 87 per cent respectively of the total textile exports in the first quinquennial periods of 1730-1755, actually imported the largest amount of *gunnies* and *gunny* bags which constituted 45, 60 and 62 per cent of its total textile imports from Bengal in the three quinquennial periods of 1730s to 1750s respectively. The second largest share of textile export to Batavia was of ordinary calicoes, being 47, 22 and 29 per cent respectively in the three quinquennial periods while the share of the more expensive item, muslins, was 5, 13 and 5 per cent respectively. These are important facts in terms of the value of the total exports to Batavia. For, *gunnies* which were strong coarse calicoes used for sacking and as covering for bales as also exported as piece-goods were the cheapest even among ordinary calicoes, their cost prices ranging from *f* 0.25 to 0.33 (Rs 0.16 to 0.20) in the early 1750s while even the cheap variety of coarse calicoes like *chintz* would cost *f* 3.76 (Rs 2.4) at that time.[21] So it is reasonable to assume that though the volume of textiles exported to Batavia was quite large, in terms of value it was not very significant as the

[20] See Tables 7.5 and 7.10

[21] Computed from invoices of ships *Brouwer* (VOC 2821, ff. 457-59, HB, 20 March 1753) and *Anna* (VOC 2829, f. 275 vo, HB, 15 Dec. 1754).

TABLE 7.11

Percentage Share of Different Textile Categories Exported by the Dutch to Batavia, Japan and Persia 1730-1755 (first five years of each decade)

Categories	Gunnies	Ord. Calicoes	Muslins	Silk	Mixed	Others	Total
A. *BATAVIA*							
(1) *1730s*							
Total Pieces	263,375	277,284	29,985	(#)	(#)	13,414	584,022
% Share	45.10	47.48	5.12			2.30	100
(2) *1740s*							
Total Pieces	258,961	96,641	53,986	(#)	(#)	22,419	432,007
% Share	59.94	22.37	12.50			5.19	100
(3) *1750s*							
Total Pieces	228,955	109,668	16,915	(#)	(#)	16,346	371,884
% Share	61.57	29.49	4.54			4.40	100
B. *JAPAN*							
(1) *1730s*							
Total Pieces	0	27,299	(#)	120,989	72,862	9,488	230,648
% Share		11.84		52.46	31.59	4.11	100
(2) *1740s*							
Total Pieces	0	2,980	(#)	21,359	10,370	1,377	36,086
% Share		8.26		59.19	28.74	3.81	100

(Contd.)

Table 7.11 (Contd. from page 199)

Categories	Gunnies	Ord. Calicoes	Muslins	Silk	Mixed	Others	Total
(3) 1750s							
Total Pieces	0	7,086	(#)	9,381	2,200	1,677	20,344
% Share		34.83		46.11	10.81	8.25	100
C. PERSIA							
(1) 1730s							
Total Pieces	14,000	22,972	13,760	(#)	10,060	4,590	65,382
% Share	21.41	35.14	21.05		15.39	7.01	100
(2) 1740s							
Total Pieces	32,363	3,582	23,036	(#)	6,069	3,600	68,650
% Share	47.14	5.22	33.56		8.84	5.24	100
(3) 1750s							
Total Pieces	0	3,300	8,275	(#)	0	2,600	14,175
% Share	0.00	23.28	58.38		0.00	18.34	100

[Source & note: Collected and computed from Dutch export invoices in VOC records. (#) indicates small number which is added in the category "Others".]

total share of the cheapest variety, *gunnies* and coarse calicoes, constituted 92, 82 and 91 per cent of the total export in the three quinquennial periods we are analyzing here.[22]

The exports to Japan, the next major export area, show a different pattern altogether. Silk piece-goods constituted the major category exported to this area, their share being 52, 59 and 46 per cent during the first quinquennial periods of 1730s, 40s and 50s respectively. Next came mixed piece-goods made of silk and cotton, which had a share of 32 and 29 per cent respectively in the early 1730s and 1740s while in the 1750s it went down to 11 per cent when the share of ordinary calicoes shot up to 35 per cent from the earlier figure of 12 and 8 per cent in the 1730s and the 1740s respectively. Though silk fabrics were comparatively more expensive than ordinary calicoes or even mixed piece-goods, the major varieties generally exported to Japan comprised cheaper items like *chandrabani, rudrabani, ragiabani* (prices around *f* 6.5 in the early 1750s), *taffeta* (price around *f* 4.5) etc. which were much less expensive than certain types of *armosins* (price of 'effene dubbelde' *armosin* being *f* 17.8) or *dheris* (striped *armosins*, price being *f* 17.93) which were exported only in limited quantities.[23]

In the case of the Persian Gulf, the pattern was somewhat different from that of Batavia and Japan. While the share of ordinary calicoes was quite considerable in the early 1730s (35 per cent) and 1750s (23 per cent), it was as low as 5 per cent in the 1740s. *Gunnies* made up for 21 and 47 per cent in the 1730s and 1740s respectively though they drew a blank in the 1750s. In other words, the cheapest coarse calicoes (*gunnies* and ordinary calicoes) constituted 56, 52 and 23 per cent of the total exports to this area in the first three quinquennial periods of the three decades respectively. The share of muslins, however, increased gradually from 21 per cent in the 1730s to 34 in the 1740s and 58 in the 1750s. But as the total number of pieces exported declined considerably in the 1750s (to only 14,175 pcs. from 65,382 in the 1730s and 68,650 in the 1740s), in terms of value again the amount could not have been very significant. What is

---

[22] These figures are arrived at by adding the shares of *gunnies* and ordinary calicoes in Table 7.11.

[23] All the prices computed from the invoice of the ship *Brouwer*, VOC 2821, ff. 457-59, HB, 20 March 1753.

clear from the above analysis is that though the total number of
pieces exported by the Dutch to various Asian destinations was
quite large to start with in the 1730s and showing a gradual
decline in the subsequent period, the total value of these exports
does not seem to be very substantial. An illustration of this fact
which we can compute from our sources is that the average
annual value of the Dutch exports to Japan, the second major
area of the Dutch export of Bengal textiles in Asia and where the
largest number of comparatively more expensive silk piece-goods
was exported, amounted only to Rs 28,650 in the first five years
of the 1750s. As such, it can be reasonably argued that the
importance of the Dutch Company's intra-Asiatic trade in Bengal
textiles, in terms of value, was only marginal compared with its
export to Europe during the period under discussion.

7.3 ASIAN MERCHANTS AND TEXTILE EXPORT

There has been a surprising consensus among historians for long
that the European East India Companies, especially the English
and the Dutch, were the major exporters from Bengal in the first
half of the eighteenth century. And as textiles formed the single
largest item in the export list of the Companies, the assumption
was that the European export of Bengal textiles (as also of raw
silk) was the most important factor in the commercial economy
of Bengal during the period under review. The above implies
that the exports by Asian merchants from Bengal, both of textiles
and raw silk, was not at all significant compared with the volume
of exports by the Europeans. Two illustrations from recent
studies will suffice to establish the great emphasis put so far on
the European trade in Indian textiles. It has been stated in a
recent study that[24]:

> The development of European trade with Bengal in the late
> seventeenth century had the effect of shifting the balance
> radically in favour of the seaborne trade. During the first half
> of the eighteenth century *Europe was unquestionably Bengal's
> chief trading partner* and its textile industry had not only

---

[24] K.N. Chaudhuri, *Trading World*, p. 24, emphasis mine.

expanded at a rapid rate to keep pace with the increased demand but had also fully adjusted its output to the special specifications required for selling in Europe.

Though another authority was describing the situation in the Coromandel, his observation on European trade and textile industry is extremely significant.[25]

Before the Europeans came into the textile market, trade in textiles was *erratic, seasonal and highly unpredictable....* In such a demand situation,, the weaver could work at leisure and weaving could be carried out side-by-side with cultivating the fields. This in itself contributed to keeping down the price of textiles. The *increased and regular demand caused by the entry of Europeans* into the market *created more and steady work* for weavers....

Further it was asserted recently by another scholar that the Dutch and the English trade in Bengal generated a significant increase of 'income, output and employment' and that it created the equivalent of 100,000 new jobs in the textile industry.[26] The main reason for such assertions is not only the paucity of quantitative data regarding the export trade of the Asian merchants from Bengal but also possibly the Euro-centric view of the historians in general working in the field.

There is no denying the fact that the Europeans were the dominant factor in Bengal's seaborne textile trade but that does not necessarily imply they were far ahead of the Asians in textile export from Bengal as a whole. The above does not take into account Bengal's export trade by overland routes which had always been extremely significant. It is generally assumed that with the fall of the great empires — Mughal, Persian and

[25] Arasaratnam, 'Weavers, Merchants and Company', *IESHR*, vol. XVII, no. 3, p. 262, emphasis by me.

[26] Om Prakash, *Dutch Company*, pp.242-48, 256. For a critique of this, see S.Chaudhury, 'European Companies and the Bengal Textile Industry in the Eighteenth Century : The Pitfalls of Applying Quantitative Techniques', *MAS*, May 1993, pp. 321-40; For Om Prakash's reply, see the same issue of *MAS*, pp.341-56.

Ottoman — and the consequent decline of important ports like Surat, the overland trade was doomed. The reason for this sort of assumption, it seems, was mainly owing to the lack of data compared with the abundance of quantitative material in the Company archives on European exports from Bengal. But from the qualitative as well as quantitative evidence we have now, admittedly not very exhaustive (hopefully we would be able to unearth more material on this aspect from European and indigenous sources), it can be shown that the share of the Asian merchants in the textile export from Bengal even in the mid-eighteenth century was in fact higher than that of the Europeans.

Let us first examine the position of the Asian trade in Bengal textiles around the 1670s i.e. prior to significant penetration of Bengal's textile markets by the European companies. The descriptive material both in the Dutch and the English archives leaves little doubt that there was a thriving trade carried on by the Asian merchants in textiles. A Dutch report on Malda, one of the several important centres of textile production, in 1670 states that textiles worth Rs 0.8 to Rs 1 million were sold in the district for export to places like Pegu, Agra, Persia, etc. Henry Cansius who prepared the report gives a detailed breakdown of the *aurungs* or production centres in the district and the value of the amount produced in each *aurung* for export.[27] This is the nearest to quantitative data one gets in the Dutch records of the textile export by the Asian merchants from an important centre of textile production in Bengal before the large scale European participation in this sector of Bengal's export trade.

A similar report by Richard Edwards of the English East India Company in 1676, a few years before the establishment of the English factory in Malda, states that the 'chief trade' in the district was carried by the 'factors of Agra, Gujarat and Benares merchants who yearly send them 15 to 25 *pattellas* (a large flat bottomed boat) whose lading consists of cossaes, mulmuls... mundils and elatches of all sorts, valued at about [Rupees] 1 lakh each *pattella* and about the half of that amount by landing said goods and raw silk'.[28] In other words the textile export by Asian

[27] Report by Henry Cansius on Malda, 7 Sept. 1670, VOC, 1278, ff. 2173-74.
[28] Fact. Records, Misc., vol. 14, ff. 334-36.

merchants from Malda by riverine routes is estimated at Rs 1.5 to 2.5 million and about Rs 0.75 to 1.25 by land (including silk in the latter case).[29] Even assuming that the value of the silk export (though silk was not an important product of Malda as compared to textiles) was half of the total value of the export by land (i.e. the share of silk and textiles being Rs 0.375 million to 0.625 million each), the value of the total textile export, combining the export by riverine and land routes, stands at between Rs 1.9 and Rs 3.1 million. So the value of textile exports by Asian merchants from Malda, according to Edwards' estimate, could have been around Rs 2 to 3 million, which is no doubt higher than the estimate of Cansius. In the light of the two divergent estimates, though it is difficult to arrive even at a rough figure, perhaps it will be safe to assume that the textile exports by the Asian merchants from Malda alone could have been anything between Rs 1 and 3 million in the 1670s.

Here one has to take note of the fact that Malda, though an important centre of textile production, was not certainly the major one. The honour goes to areas around Hughli, Dhaka and Kasimbazar. In an account of the textile export from Dhaka in 1747, the annual export from the district was estimated at Rs 2.85 million.[30] Though Dhaka was famous from the Roman time for the production of legendary muslin, it also produced fine and ordinary calicoes in large quantity.[31] Similarly Kasimbazar, though famous for its silk piece-goods, also produced mixed piece-goods and coarse textiles. Even in the late 1740s and early

---

[29] It is strange that Om Prakash makes a complete misreading of the document. As he writes: 'The Edwards estimate is somewhat problematic in so far as it talks of 15 to 25 boats each carrying goods worth about Rs 100,000, but at the same time seems to imply that only half of this value was accounted for by textiles and raw silk.' Om Prakash 'On Estimating the Employment Implications of European Trade for the Eighteenth Century Bengal Textile Industry', *MAS*, May 1993, p.393. It is absolutely clear from the report that Edwards first talks exclusively of textile export (even specifying the types of textiles as cossaes, mulmuls, etc.) by riverine routes (and hence says 'pattellas'or boats) and then by land routes ('landing' is nothing but land) as opposed to export by rivers.

[30] Home Misc., vol. 456F, ff. 93-95.

[31] Ibid., f. 175.

1750s the Asian merchants exported silk textiles from Bengal worth around Rs 0.63 million a year on an average.[32]   Besides, there were other important traditional centres of textile production like Birbhum, Hughli, Balasore, Santipur in Nadia and Radhanagar in Midnapore, etc. So if the value of textiles exported by the Asians from Malda alone was valued at Rs 1 to 3 million in the 1670s, the value of the total amount of textiles exported from several other important production centres could be anybody's guess.

We have no definitive evidence that the supply for the 'huge' demand in European markets from around the 1680s seriously affected Bengal's traditional exports to other regions or that Bengal met the European demand by diverting the supplies from her traditional buyers. So it can be assumed that even in the late seventeenth or first half of the eighteenth century, Bengal continued to supply her traditional markets while at the same time meeting the new European demand. This seems to be quite evident from the presence of merchants from various parts of Asia in different textile *aurungs* of Bengal, procuring cloth side by side with the agents/merchants of the Companies. In the European records, there are regular references to the stiff competition faced by the Companies from Asian merchants in Bengal's textile market. The quantitative evidence that we have for Asian textile export, though meagre, also indicates that the Asian merchants had a definite edge over the Companies even in this sector of Bengal's export trade. In the estimate of the total textile exports from Dhaka in 1747, the Asian share including that of the Armenians stood at two-third of the total compared to one-third of the Europeans including European private trade.[33] The Asian lead in the textile trade in general is confirmed by the Dutch sources which refer to advances given for investments in textiles (which was about 50 per cent around this time[34]) to the tune of Rs 7.6 million by the Asians and Europeans excluding the Dutch, of which the combined English and French share could

---

[32] W. Aldersey's report, BPC, Range 1, vol. 44, Consult. 19 June 1769.

[33] Ibid, ff. 93-95.

[34] See chapter 5.

not have been more than Rs 3 million.[35] Hence the Asian share would have been about Rs. 4.5 to 5 million. This seems quite plausible in view of the fact that from among several important centres, the export by Asian merchants from only two (Malda and Dhaka for which we have some quantitative data) even was quite substantial. Moreover the Dutch report refers to the month of June when most of the European companies which procured their export commodities mainly through the advance system had already contracted for their required amount. Though the Asians too bought their wares through *dadni*, it seems that they collected quite a large amount of textiles from the spot markets in the same manner as they did buy most of their silk without giving out advances.[36] So even if we ignore the Dutch account which is used here mainly as a corroborative evidence despite its vagueness, our main hypothesis will remain unaltered.

It would be interesting to note here that in the Danish account of the 'Cloth Production and Trade' in the late eighteenth century Bengal, when the trade of Asian merchants declined considerably for reasons explained later, the total production of *garras*, one of the staple piece-goods of export from Bengal, was estimated at 400,000 pieces of which only 160,000 pieces were reported to be annually exported to Europe.[37] The significant fact one should remember is that areas

---

[35] Taillefert's 'Memorie', VOC, 2849, 27 Oct, 1755, ff. 188vo-189. Taillefert talks of Rs 6 million sent to textile centres for some years but mentions categorically to the June resolution of 1741 where it referred to Rs 7.6 million as the amount given as advance by various buyers other than the Dutch. We accept the latter sum because first, it is mentioned in the official resolution; secondly, Taillefert in all probability spoke of (while mentioning Rs 6 million) the late 1740s and early 1750s when textile trade and industry was to some extent disrupted as a result of the Maratha invasions. The official resolution of 1741, on the other hand, referred to the period prior to the Maratha incursions when things were normal, and trade and industry flourished as usual. It should be noted however that both the figures could have been mere guesses, given the diffusion of the industry and the presence of numerous buyers in Bengal.

[36] See chapter 8.

[37] Ole Feldebeck, 'Cloth Production and Trade in late Eighteenth Century Bengal', *BPP*, July-Dec. 1967, pp.127-29.

like Hughli, Kasimbazar, Malda and Patna actually produced more medium and ordinary piece-goods (and these were the main staples of Bengal textile export) than Dhaka for export to different parts of Asia and Europe. As a matter of fact the Dutch Company (probably the same would would be the case, more or less, with the English too[38]) exported more than 50 per cent of the total value of its textiles from the Hughli area (possibly including Malda where piece-goods were procured through the *dadni* merchants of Calcutta), 25 to 38 per cent from Kasimbazar and 8 to 12 per cent from the Patna area while the share of Dhaka varied from 5 to 10 per cent in the mid-eighteenth century. This will be apparent from an analysis of Dutch textile exports for 1753/54 and 1754/55 for which we could find area-wise break-down.[39]

Fortunately we have been able to find precise information regarding the export of silk piece-goods from Bengal by the Asian merchants. This was included in the report of W. Aldersey on silk trade in Kasimbazar in 1769. According to this report, the total value of silk textiles exported by the Asians in the five years from 1749 to 1753 amounted to Rs 0.63 million and Rs 0.43 million from 1754 to 1758 on an average in a year. In this context one has to note that though Bengal produced fine quality silk fabrics, it was especially various types of cotton and mixed piece-goods which were the main attractions for both the European and Asian buyers. But even in the export of silk piece-goods, the Asians had a decisive lead over the Europeans in the mid-eighteenth century, which will be apparent from the comparative study of the volume (piece-wise) of Asian and European exports of this category of textiles for 1750/51 to 1754/55, the five years for which such an analysis is possible.

[38] See for instance the geographical analysis of orders for piece-goods from London in the early 1680s, S.Chaudhuri, *Trade and Commercial Organisation*, p.201, f.n.166.

[39] See Table 3, Geographical Distribution, Unit Price and Share of Different Areas in the Total Value of Dutch Textile Export from Bengal to Holland, 1753-54 and 1754-55 in my article 'European Companies and Bengal Textile Industry' in *MAS*, vol. 27, pt. II, May 1993, p. 339.

TABLE 7.12

Quinquennial Total and Average of Silk Textile Exports
Asians and European Companies
1750/51 to 1754/55

Years	Asians (Pieces)	European Companies		
		Dutch (Pieces)	English (Pieces)	European Total (Pieces)
1750/51	124,675	12,890	12,760	25,650
1751/52	92,475	39,628	20,041	59,669
1752/53	89,978	27,777	32,615	60,392
1753/54	74,978	29,029	24,663	53,692
1754/55	75,062	40,883	34,160	75,043
Total	457,168	150,207	124,239	274,446
Average	91,434	30,041	24,848	54,889

[Source: Asian export, BPC, vol. 44, Consult. 19 June 1769; Dutch export collected and computed from export invoices in VOC records; English export computed from data provided by K.N. Chaudhuri].

Though Table 7.12 does not take into account the French export for lack of any precise data on that, it can well be assumed that the French share could not have been more than half of the Dutch or English export[40] i.e. between 12,000 and 15,000 pieces at the uppermost limit. Thus the average annual European export of silk textiles would have been around 67,000 to 70,000 (the total of Dutch and English being 54,889, Table 7.12) pieces

[40] Marshall also estimated from Martineau that the French Company's purchases 'may have been half of those of the Dutch and the English, P.J. Marshall, *Bengal*, p. 66.

while the Asian export was more than 91,000 pieces. It is to be
noted in this connection that silk textiles was perhaps not a staple
variety in the Asian export from Bengal. It was cotton piece-
goods—ordinary, medium and fine—which comprised the bulk
of the Asian export to the Middle East and Central Asia.

That the demand in these areas was for the latter categories
of textiles is evident from an analysis of the Dutch exports to the
Persian Gulf region where in the first quinquennial period of the
1740s and 1750s the share of silk textiles was nil[41]. This only
substantiates our point that the Asian textile export even in the
mid-eighteenth century was quite substantial and much higher
than that of the European companies.

If that is so, and considering the rough estimates of textile
export from Malda and Dhaka, and also that the Asians advanced
about Rs 4.5 to 5 million for textiles though they also bought a
large amount from the spot markets, perhaps the total value of
Asian textile export could have been in the range of Rs 9 to 10
million. That this is not an overestimation can be established from
other indirect evidence and assumptions. If the share percentage
of the textiles exported by the Dutch and the English from Dhaka
ranged between 5 and 10 per cent in the early 1750s (which we
have pointed out earlier), the share of Dhaka textiles in the Asian
exports could be assumed to have been not more than 10 per
cent. From the estimate of the textile export from Dhaka in 1747,
the value exclusively for Asian export to different areas can be
computed at Rs 1.15 million[42]. That means that the total value of
the Asian textile export from Bengal could have been around Rs
11.5 million. As against this, the total value of textile export by
the European companies would not have been more than Rs 5
to 6 million at the most. It is generally believed that the European
private trade was quite substantial though we do not have any
definite idea about its size. But the share of the European private
trade in the export from Dhaka was only about 5 per cent of the
total value of the export. That will only indicate that perhaps

---

[41] See Table 7.11.

[42] Leaving aside the amount sent for the emperor at Delhi, the
breakdown is as follows: Upper Provinces Rs 100,000; Pathans Rs
150,000; Mughals for foreign consumption Rs 400,000; Armenians to
Basra, Mocha and Jedda Rs 500,000.

private trade still constituted only a small portion of Bengal's export trade as a whole[43]. Here one has to bear in mind that these are crude estimates and subject to a wide margin of error. But still they give us a clear indication of the comparative position of the Asians and Europeans in Bengal's textile export trade in the mid-eighteenth century.

If, along with the above facts, we consider some other relevant evidence on the textile trade and production in Bengal, the picture becomes much clearer. It has been reported that in some years between 1738 and 1747 the production of cloth at Dhaka was worth as much as Rs 4 million[44]. An estimate of the late eighteenth century puts the value of cloth production in Bengal for local consumption only at Rs 60 million. That could well have been the amount locally consumed, if not more, in the mid-eighteenth century, especially considering the great famine of 1770 and the high mortality following it. Moreover, there is an abundance of qualitative evidence on the predominance of the Asian merchants in Bengal's textile markets during the pre-Plassey period. Harry Verelst, a responsible official of the English Company, wrote mainly referring to this period that besides 'the large investment of the European nations, the Bengal raw silk, cloths etc. to a vast amount were dispersed in the West and North inland as far as Guzzrat, Lahore and even Ispahan'.[45] Two other English officials, William Bolts and Luke Scrafton, emphasized how caravans, consisting of 'many thousands' of merchants from various parts of India and Asia, resorted to Bengal for the 'produce of the province', of which the two most important ones, as is well-known, were textiles and raw silk.[46] So all the pieces of evidence we have analyzed so far only indicate that the European export of Bengal textiles was a small fraction of the total output and hence should be placed in its proper perspective.

[43] Taylor's report, Home Misc. Series, 456F.

[44] Proceedings of the Board of Trade, vol.156, quoted in N.K.Sinha, *Economic History of Bengal*, vol.III, p.4.

[45] Verelst to Court of Directors, 2 April 1769, BPC, vol. 44, f.324, para. 6.

[46] Bolts, *Considerations*, p. 200; Scrafton, *Reflections*, p.20.

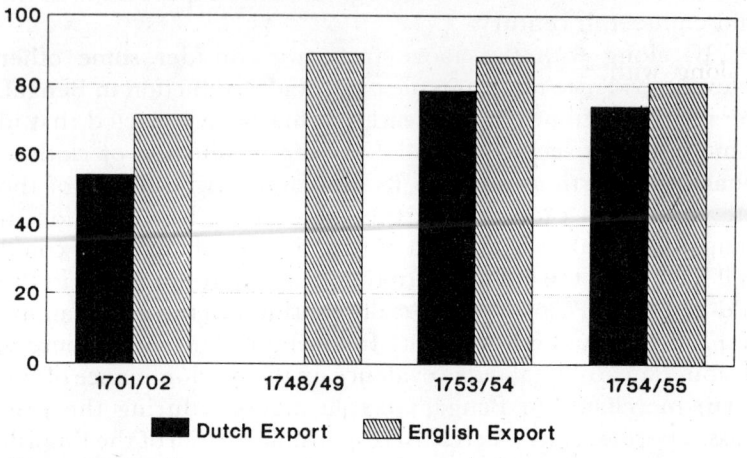

Figure 7.1 Dutch and English Share of
Textile Value in Total Export Value
[1701/02 - 1754/55]

[Source: Table 7.2]

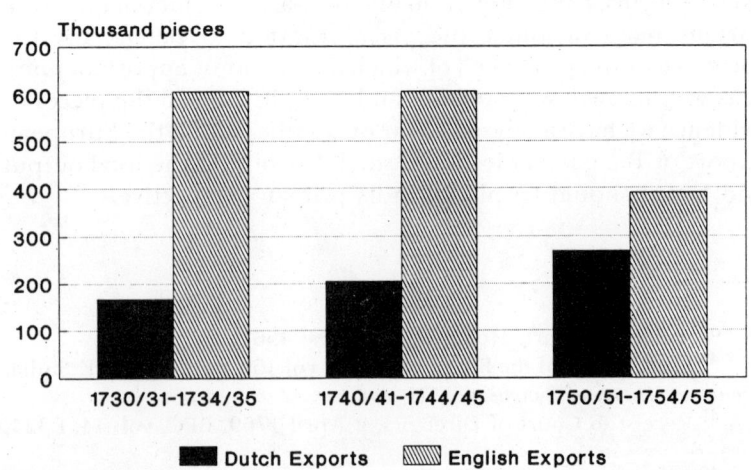

Figure 7.2 Dutch and English Textile
Exports, 1730-55 (Annual Average)

[Source: Table 7.5]

Figure 7.3 Volume and Value of English Textile Exports 1740-1753

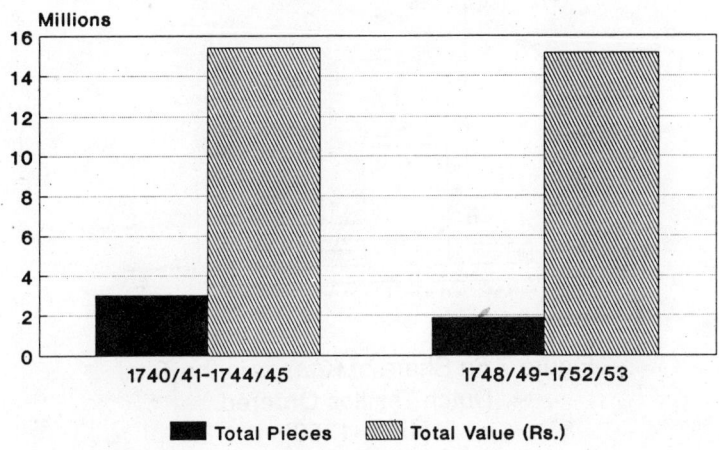

[Source: Table 7.6]

Figure 7.4 Share of Different Categories of Textiles in Dutch & English Exports 1730-1755

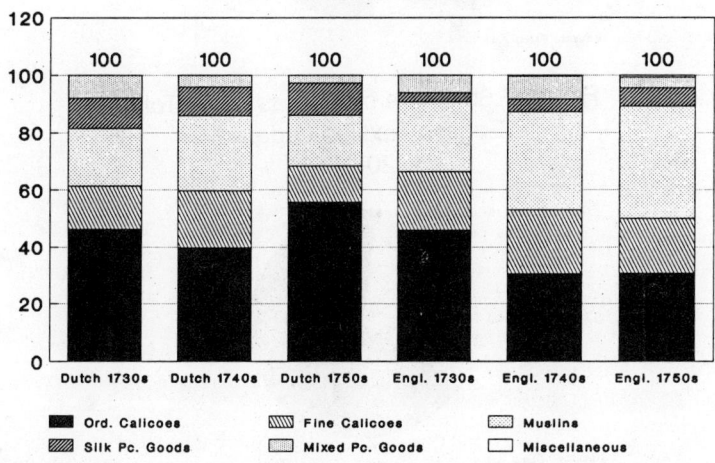

[Source: Table 7.7]

Figure 7.5 Volume and Value of Dutch & English Textile Exports 1753-55

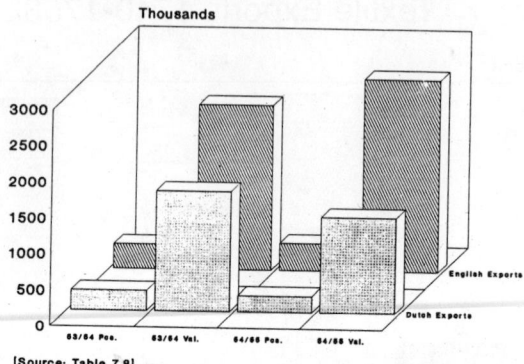

[Source: Table 7.8]

Figure 7.6a Share of *Khasas* in the Total Dutch Textiles Ordered [1720-1750]

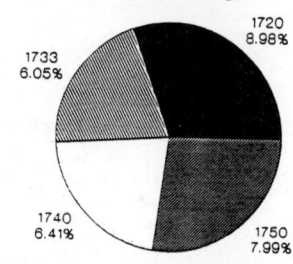

[Source: Table 7.4]

Figure 7.6b Share of *Khasas* in the Total English Textiles Ordered [1720-1750]

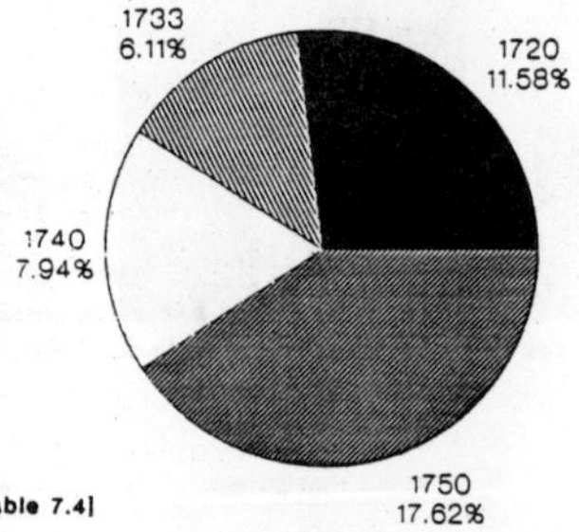

[Source: Table 7.4]

Figures 7.7a, b and c
Share of Different Textile Exports
to Batavia 1730s (Dutch)

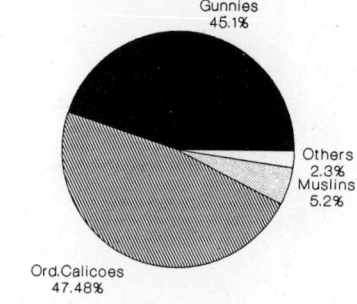

Gunnies
45.1%

Others
2.3%
Muslins
5.2%

Ord.Calicoes
47.48%

[Source: Table 7.11]

1740s (Dutch)

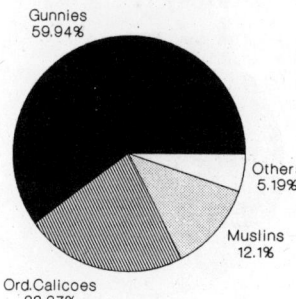

Gunnies
59.94%

Others
5.19%

Muslins
12.1%

Ord.Calicoes
22.37%

[Source: Table 7.11]

1750s (Dutch)

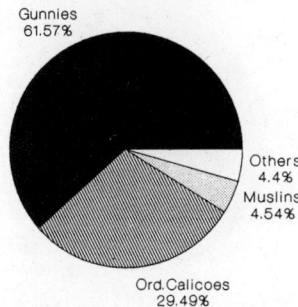

Gunnies
61.57%

Others
4.4%
Muslins
4.54%

Ord.Calicoes
29.49%

[Source: Table 7.11]

Figures 7.8a, b and c
Share of Different Textile Exports to
Japan 1730s (Dutch)

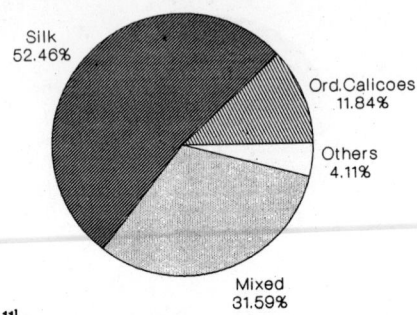

[Source: Table 7.11]

1740s (Dutch)

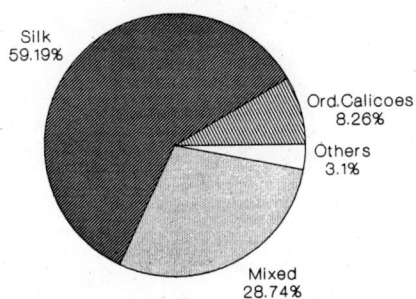

[Source: Table 7.11]

1750s (Dutch)

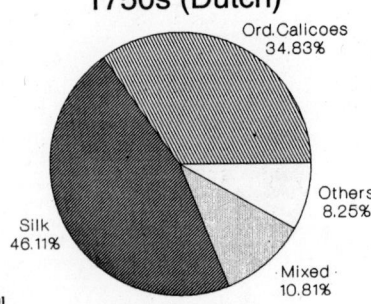

[Source: Table 7.11]

Figures 7.9a, b and c
Share of Different Textile Exports to Persia 1730s (Dutch)

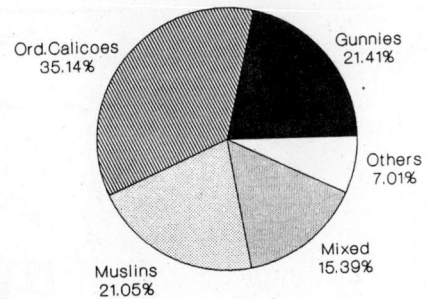

[Source: Table 7.11]

1740s (Dutch)

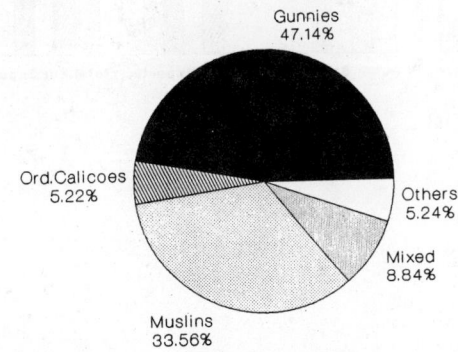

[Source: Table 7.11]

1750s (Dutch)

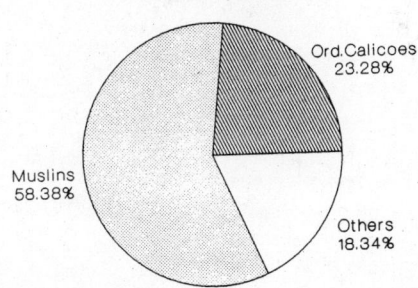

[Source: Table 7.11]

Figure 7.10 Export of Silk Textiles by Asians and Europeans, 1750-1755

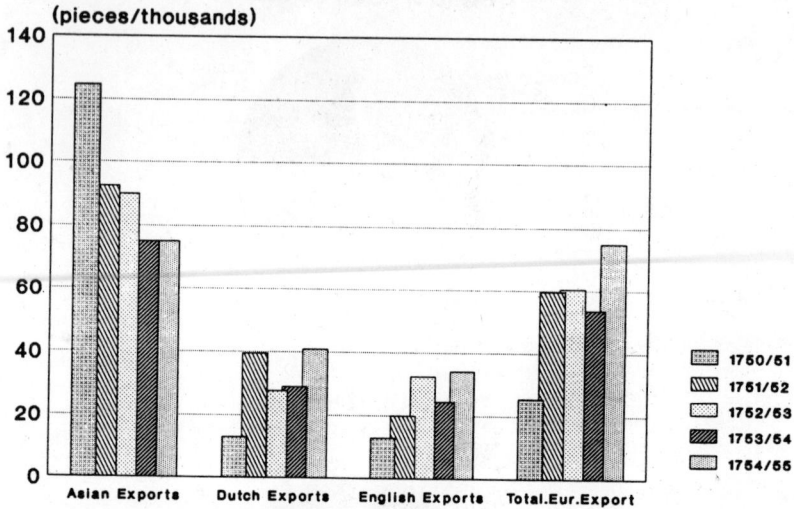

[Source: Table 7.14]

8

SILK TRADE AND INDUSTRY

Raw silk was one of the most important articles, next only to textiles in terms of value, exported by the European companies from Bengal throughout the first half of the eighteenth century. It was from about the middle of the seventeenth century, after the misadventure in the trade of Persian and Chinese silk, that both the Dutch and the English Companies turned their attention to the rich potentials of trade in Bengal silk.[1] Though the English Company started exploring the possibility of trade in Bengal raw silk from about the third decade of the seventeenth century, it was only with the establishment of a factory in 1658 in Kasimbazar, the most important centre of silk trade and industry in Bengal, that marked the beginning of a long period of English export of silk from Bengal.[2] But in the early years, English trade in silk was not very significant and it was from around the mid-seventies of the century that the English began to pursue silk trade from Bengal on an extensive scale.[3] From then onward, Bengal raw silk was an established and a valuable item in the Company's list of exports from Bengal. Despite some fluctuations

---

[1] For a detailed discussion of the Dutch and the English experiments in Chinese and Persian silk trade, and the shift in their interest to Bengal silk, see S. Chaudhuri, *Trade and Commercial Organization*, pp. 178-80; Bal Krishna, *Commercial Relations*, 97-98; Glamann, *Dutch Asiatic Trade*, 112-13; K.N. Chaudhuri, *Trading World*, 343-47; Om Prakash, *Dutch Company*, 208-9.

[2] The early English interest in Bengal silk and the various attempts to explore the silk trade in Bengal is discussed in details in S. Chaudhuri, *Trade and Commercial Organization*, p. 179.

[3] For early English trade in Bengal silk, see Ibid, pp. 181-85.

in the early years of the eighteenth century, the volume of English export of Bengal silk increased steadily till the 1730s when it reached the peak, followed by a gradual decline in the next two decades. The Dutch too began the trade in Bengal silk in the right earnest from about the middle of the seventeenth century, though they were aware of the possibilities of a profitable trade in that commodity much earlier.[4] They procured Bengal silk mainly for the Japanese and the Dutch markets, the former playing a major role in the Dutch export of the commodity. Until the 1670s, Persian silk was a dominant component of the Dutch export to Europe while most of the Chinese and Bengal silk was diverted to Japan. But the situation changed completely in the last two decades of the seventeenth century when because of the decline in Japan trade and the lower price of Bengal silk compared to that of the Chinese silk, Bengal became the main supplier of silk to Holland.[5]

The main advantage of Bengal silk was that it was much cheaper than both the Persian and the Chinese silk but fetched a price about the same as the former and slightly lower than the latter. Commercially, the high rate of profit and the increasing demand in Europe acted as stimulus to the steady growth of silk export from Bengal by the Companies. The Dutch Company realized a gross profit of about 200 per cent on the silk exported from Bengal in 1653/54, though this rate fluctuated quite a lot in the second half of the seventeenth century.[6] For the English too, the trade in Bengal silk was quite profitable; one consignment in 1695/96 brought by the ship *Martha* fetched a gross profit of over 250 per cent.[7] As was the case with the Dutch, there was high fluctuation in the rate of profit for the English too, though the evidence undoubtedly points to a substantial profit earned by this commodity. The fact that Bengal silk could be used as a substitute for Italian silk widely used so far in silk industries of Europe and at a much cheaper cost price than the latter made it a lucrative item for the Companies' export to Europe. Though

[4] Glamann, *Dutch Asiatic Trade*, pp. 122-23, where he explains the reason for belated Dutch trade in Bengal silk.

[5] Om Prakash, *Dutch Company*, p. 208.

[6] Glamann, *Dutch Asiatic Trade*, p. 122. For the fluctuations in the rate of profit, see Om Prakash, *Dutch Company*, pp. 187, 196, 199.

[7] S. Chaudhuri, *Trade and Commercial Organization*, p. 181.

the quality of Bengal silk was a little inferior to other var~
the world market, its low price more than compensated t~
former and the quality proved quite suitable for silk industries
in Europe. Bernier aptly observed: 'The [Bengal] silks are not
certainly so fine as those of *Persia, Syria, Sayd* and *Barut*, but they
are of a much lower price; and I know from indisputable
authority that, if they were well selected and wrought with care,
they might be manufactured into most beautiful stuffs'.[8]

It should be noted here that it was not only the Companies
but merchants from various parts of Asia as well as from different
provinces of India were active in Bengal's silk market throughout
the first half of the eighteenth century. Long before the arrival
of the Europeans on the scene, these merchants were carrying on
a substantial inter-regional and international trade, mainly
through the overland route, in Bengal silk. Though the principal
group among these merchants appears to be mainly from
Gujarat, there were numerous other groups of merchants from
Central Asia, Multan, Lahore, Agra, Benaras, Hyderabad,
Gorakhpur, etc. What is of great significance is that these Asian
and Indian merchants carried on an extensive trade in silk from
Bengal even in the mid-eighteenth century and were not
displaced from their predominant position by the Europeans till
after the battle of Plassey in 1757.

8.1 PRODUCTION AND ORGANIZATION

The major centre of silk production in Bengal was Kasimbazar
and its neighbourhood in Murshidabad district. Streynsham
Master noted in 1676 that mulberry trees, the leaves of which
were the essential food of the silk worms, were cultivated in 'all
the country or great part thereof about Kasimbazar'.[9] The
extensive cultivation of mulberry trees was indeed a typical
feature of the rural scene in Murshidabad and naturally provided
employment to many people. The great importance of silk
production in the economic life of Murshidabad is reflected in
a common saying prevalent for long in the area that 'the
mulberry is a greater source of wealth and happiness than one's

[8] Bernier, *Travels*, p. 439.
[9] Master's *Diaries*, vol. 2, p. 28.

son'.[10] Raw silk was however also produced in some parts of north Bengal such as Rangpur and in Kumarkhali near Nadia. But there is little doubt that Murshidabad, of which Kasimbazar was only a suburb, was the most important production and manufacturing centre of Bengal raw silk in the seventeenth and eighteenth centuries. Hardly any information regarding the total annual production of raw silk is to be found in the sources. The assertion of Tavernier that Bengal produced around 22,000 bales of 100 lbs. each in a year in the 1660s and 1670s has recently been discounted as 'gross exaggeration' in view of the fact that his figure of 6000-7000 bales exported annually by the Dutch was vastly in excess of the actual Dutch export.[11] But given the fact that the Asian merchants exported around 24,000 maunds of silk in 1751,[12] the period when silk production as also trade was greatly hampered by the Maratha invasions and assuming that the Asian merchants then were probably more active in this trade than in the mid-eighteenth century, Tavernier's figure of total annual production, though perhaps a little exaggerated, was possibly not very wide off the mark.

The silk industry can be divided into two parts — the production of raw silk and its manufacture. The production of sericulture proper was agricultural-cum-home industry. The peasant-farmers grew mulberry trees along with other agricultural crops and reared silk worms on the mulberry leaves at their homes. The rearing of the cocoons was a domestic industry inasmuch as while the male members of the family worked for mulberry cultivation in the fields, the women were engaged in rearing the silk worms indoors. J. Geoghegan, writing on the silk industry in the early nineteenth century stated, on the basis of other authorities, that special houses were needed for rearing of silk worms.[13] A suitable room for such a purpose should be 24 ft. long, 15 ft. wide and 9 ft. high with a raised platform of 3 ft. and a thick earthen wall, with two windows at the top of the wall and a roof of thick compact thatch. A room of this specification

---

[10] Quoted in H.R. Ghosal, *Economic Transition*, p. 57, f.n. 126.

[11] Tavernier, *Travels*, vol. II, p.2; K.N. Chaudhuri, *Trading World*, p. 354; Om Prakash, *Dutch Company*, p. 57.

[12] BPC, vol. 44, Annex. to Consult. 19 June 1769.

[13] J. Geoghegan, *Silk in India*, pp. 15-16.

could accommodate 200 *kahans*[14] or 2,56,000 worms spread out on *dalas* or shelves of 5 1/2 ft. x 4 1/2 ft., plastered with cow dung[15] and placed upon *manchas* or platforms. These platforms were supported by bamboo pillars resting on small earthen saucers filled with water to obstruct the passage of insects. Among other things, each cultivator needed several spinning mats, knives, baskets (to carry mulberry leaves), a few gunny bags on which to spread the cocoons in the sun, and a number of *kalsis* or earthen pitchers to store water for the saucers. And the whole establishment would have cost about fifty to sixty five rupees in the early nineteenth century.[16]

Though Speed's description pertains to the early nineteenth century, it can well be projected back to the eighteenth since the main features of the silk industry do not seem to have changed much in the intervening period. He noted that in the first and second stages of rearing, the silk worms were fed twice a day and every six or eight hours in the last two stages. As soon as the worms were ready to spin, 'they turn from a greenish-cream to a mellow light orange colour ... with a transparent streak down the back, passing, as is observed, the emission from tail to head, which forms the silk'.[17] They were then put on the mat, placed in the open air facing the sun when it was not too scorching and brought under cover at night. The worms continued spinning for about 56 hours. Four or five days later the cocoons were ready for reeling, except in the rainy season when they took longer time to dry. The peasant-cultivators either sold the cocoons immediately to silk *paikars* or other merchants, or the cocoons were steamed and reeled into silk thread in the peasant's house.[18]

The spinners wound off the cocoons in the first instance into a thread called 'putney' or 'pattany' which was an assortment of fine and coarse threads.[19] Orme perhaps did not exaggerate

[14] 1280 worms make one *kahan* or 16 *pans*.

[15] Cow dung makes the *dalas* durable and its odour is congenial to the worms.

[16] D.W.H. Speed, 'Notes on the Culture of Silk in Bengal in the East Indies', *Transactions of the Agricultural and Horticultural Society of India*, vol. III, 1837, pp. 14-15.

[17] Ibid. p. 22-23.

[18] J. Geoghegan, *Silk in India*, pp. 6-7, 15-16.

[19] Ibid., pp. 15-16.

when he wrote about the high skill of the silk spinners in the 1750s:[20]

> The women wind off raw silk from the pod of the worm. A single pod of raw silk is divided into twenty different degrees of fineness; and so exquisite is the feeling of these women, that whilst the thread is running through their fingers so swiftly that their eyes can be of no assistance, they will break it off exactly as the assortments change, at once from the first to the twentieth, from nineteenth to the second.

Buchanan, writing around 1807, gave an elaborate description of working the cocoons where he emphasized that the process was mainly handled by women.[21]

One of the important features of silk production in Bengal was that there were three harvests, called bands, in a year. The November band silk was of the best quality, the next being March band and the July band silk was generally of a coarse quality. The superiority of the November band silk was because of the fact that the silk worms throve best in cool conditions and it was the time when the mulberry trees had the softest leaves to provide ample food to the worms. As the weather became warmer by February and mulberry leaves harder, the March band silk was of an inferior quality while the adverse conditions of rain, heat and storm made the July band silk coarse and worst of the three seasonal varieties. It is obvious from the above that as the silk production depended so much on weather conditions, the total annual output could vary to a great extent and as such also the price, given the great demand and competition in the silk market. The Dutch Director, Jan Kerseboom, noted in 1755 that the first two kinds of silk accounted for about two-thirds of the total output in a year and the filaments did not lose their natural softness and yellowish colour even in storage.[22] He however enlisted four types of silk produced in a year which he termed Baishaki band (harvested in April and May), Assari band (produced in June and July), Saoni band (to be had in August)

[20] Orme, *Historical Fragments*, p. 412.
[21] F. Buchanan, *Bhagalpur*, p. 613.
[22] VOC, vol. 2849, f.119 vo-110.

and finally Assin band (gathered in September and October).[23] Alexander Hume, the chief of the Ostend Company, on the other hand described in 1730 five varieties that were produced in a year. He stated that the best silk in the country was 'Agni' which was gathered from November to the latter half of February while the other varieties were 'chita' (March), 'Baishaki' (April or May), 'Assary' (June), 'Saony' (July) and 'Assiny' (September).[24] The first three varieties we mentioned earlier seem to be the major ones, the latter being sub-varieties within those.

The two main types of raw silk exported by the Dutch Company during the period under review were *tanny* and *tanna-banna*. These were raw silk reeled from *pattany* filaments—*tanny* being by far the superior variety which used a larger number of cocoons per unit of output.[25] In the early stage of their trade, the Dutch export consisted mainly of *tanna-banna* silk, in which there were three sub-qualities, *cabessa*, *bariga* and *pee* which corresponded to 'head', 'belly' and 'foot' of the English records. The *tanny* silk first emerged in the order for 1676 and in a short time surpassed other sorts and became most marketable of all Bengal varieties.[26] From the 1730s till the mid-eighteenth century, *tanny* silk was the predominant variety in the Dutch export. During this period, there was yet another variety, exported by the Dutch, called *adapangia* which was described as 'kleene gestrengde' (short skein) while the variety *tanna-banna* was mentioned as 'groote gestrengde' (long skein). Another variety of silk in the Dutch export list, though in small quantity, was the *mochta* silk (in all probability the half-silk known now as *matka*) or floretta yarn.

The best and most expensive raw silk produced in Kasimbazar was the variety called 'Gujarat', probably named after the most dominant group in the Bengal silk market, the Gujaratis from western India. The English Company did not export 'Gujarat' silk in any large quantity before the 1730s. The main reason for this was that this variety was considered too fine for English 'throwsters' and hence had to be sold at a low profit. But from about 1735 the 'Gujarat' silk became so popular with the buyers

[23] Ibid., f.110.
[24] Stadsarchief Antwerp, GIC 5769.
[25] Om Prakash, *Dutch Company*, p.55.
[26] Glamann, *Dutch Asiatic Trade*, p. 124.

in England that the Court directed the Bengal factors not to fail in purchasing this variety in which private trade of the Company servants was prohibited.[27] It is probable that the increased demand for the finer variety of 'Gujarat' silk resulted from the improvement in silk-twisting techniques in England which took place in the first half of the eighteenth century.[28] However, the 'Gujarat' silk does not seem to have enjoyed an eminent position among the varieties of silk exported from Bengal. The English Company began to export Kumarkhali and Rangpur silk from about the early thirties of the eighteenth century. And in fact it contracted for greater quantities of November band, Kumarkhali and Rangpur silk than 'Gujarat' variety. This will be apparent from the contract with the silk merchants of Kasimbazar for 1733 which also indicates the price of different varieties in the market.[29]

November band	-	2,400 mds. at Rs 5-12 ans. per seer
Gujarat	-	780 mds. at Rs 6-6 ans. per seer
Kumarkhali	-	600 mds. at Rs 5-2 ans. per seer
Rangpur	-	800 mds. at Rs 4-6 ans. per seer
Total	-	3,580 mds.

It seems interesting that though the Kumarkhali variety was possibly coarser than the November band and 'Gujarat' silk, as is obvious from the fact that it was cheaper than the other varieties, it acquired more importance among the several varieties exported by the English from Bengal. In 1740 the Kasimbazar Council contracted for Kumarkhali (1800 mds.), November band (1350 mds.), 'Gujarat' (420 mds.) and Rangpur silk (150 mds.). The same trend is to be found in 1741 when the silk investment was reduced to a great extent (from 3,720 mds. to 2,590 mds.). The Company contracted for Kumarkhali (1270 mds.), November band (990 mds.) and 'Gujarat' (330 mds.).[30]

[27] DB, vol. 106, para. 31, f.411, 31 January 1735.

[28] K.N. Chaudhuri, Trading World, p. 349.

[29] Fact. Records, Kasimbazar, vol. 5, Consults. 7 March, 19 March, 3 Sept. 1733; 28 Jan., 6 March 1740.

[30] Ibid., 6 March, 9 March 1741.

Even in the early 1750s when silk production in Bengal was affected by the Maratha inroads of the 1740s and when the Company's silk investment was considerably reduced, the Kumarkhali and November band silk predominated among the varieties exported from Bengal.[31] It is only from 1752 that 'Gujarat' silk came back as a prominent item from Bengal when the Kasimbazar Council contracted for 1,000 mds. of November band and 800 mds. of 'Gujarat' variety.[32] From then onwards it appears that these were the two main varieties that were exported by the English Company. The probable reason for this was that the Company was finding it difficult to contract with merchants for Kumarkhali and Rangpur silk at reasonable prices. This will be borne out by the fact that the silk merchants in Kasimbazar refused to contract for Kumarkhali and Rangpur silk in 1752 as they alleged that 'thereby they gain a little'.[33] The procurement of Rangpur silk proved a difficult task even in the early 1740s. In 1741 the Kasimbazar Council was told by Balai Katma, the late broker of the Company, and other principal silk merchants that 'they chose not to meddle with this article' and 'those that had ever done any for the Company had always been great losers by it'. The price of Rangpur silk in that season rose sharply 'greatly occasioned by the Guzzeratt and Hydravad merchants who have bought up great quantities to send up [to Delhi and Agra?] with the King's treasure'. When the Council asked the merchants to reduce the price they were demanding for Rangpur silk, they answered in the negative stating that only six or seven among them had 'ever traded to said aurung...and that they ever lost very considerably by this Rangpore Silk Business'.[34] Ultimately the Council sent Edward Eyles to Rangpur to have 'intelligence regarding prices there, procure putney and see how the price comes out by winding off putney'.[35] After 1753, the picture of the English silk investment in Kasimbazar becomes extremely hazy—the Council making contracts for small lots with mer-

---

[31] Ibid., vol. 10, Consult. 17 March 1741; Beng. Letters Recd., vol. 22, para. 64, ff. 175-76; C&B. Abstr., vol. 5, f.299.

[32] BPC, vol. 25, f.86vo, 16 March 1752; f.127vo, 27 April 1752.

[33] Ibid.

[34] Fact. Records, Kasimbazar, vol. 6, Consult. 9 Dec. 1741.

[35] Ibid., Annex to Consult. 18 Jan. 1742.

chants, experimenting with sending 'cottah banians' or Company servants to silk *aurungs* for procuring *pattany* and finally asking Warren Hastings, a junior factor in Kasimbazar, to go to the 'putney aurungs' and make all necessary enquiries with regard to silk trade and industry in the country.[36]

8.2 MARKETS, MERCHANTS AND PRICE

It can be established beyond any doubt that the silk market in Bengal was extremely competitive during the period under review. The presence of very many groups of Asian merchants—besides the major group, the Gujaratis, there were merchants from Lahore, Multan, Delhi-Agra, Hyderabad, Gorakhpur, Benares as also from Central Asia—and the European companies in Bengal silk marts resulted in a keen competition among the buyers of the commodity. But the significant fact to underline is that it was not the Companies as a whole but the Asian merchants who controlled the silk market in Bengal throughout this period. It may be noted in this connection how John Kenn of the English Company pointed out the close link between the silk and money markets in Kasimbazar and those in north India when he wrote in 1661: 'According as this silk sells in Agra, so the price of silk in Kasimbazar riseth and falleth. The exchange of money from Kasimbazar to Patna and Agra riseth and falleth as the said silk findeth a vent in Patna and Agra.'[37]

The frustration of the Companies for not being able to control the silk market or the silk price is amply clear from their records. As early as 1733, the English Council at Kasimbazar wrote that it is 'not in their power to command the [silk] market which will rise according to the demand there is'.[38] In 1744 the Kasimbazar Council referred to this inability on its part in no uncertain terms: 'Though this price is so much higher than the last year, it is not in our power to help it as we cannot command the market which has been much higher lately.'[39] Besides the

[36] BPC, vol. 28, f. 302, 24 Nov. 1755; Fact. Records, Kasimbazar, vol. 12, Annex. to Consult. 21 Nov. 1755.

[37] B.M. Addl. Mss., 34,123, f. 42; Wilson, *Early Annals*, vol. I, p. 376.

[38] C&B. Abstr., vol. 3, f. 337, para. 36, 26 Dec. 1733.

[39] Fact. Records, Kasimbazar, vol. 6, Consult. 23 Jan. 1744.

competition among numerous buyers in the market, a major
factor affecting the price of silk was the weather conditions which
determined the total output of the harvest in a given year. Heavy
rains, storms, drought or excessive heat would invariably cause
a poor harvest and, with so many competitors in the market,
result in an increase in the price of raw silk. The Kasimbazar
Council reported in 1726 that the 'heavy rains which has
destroyed such numbers of the mulberry trees will be lessening
the quantity [and] very much influence the price of silk'. In a
rather pre-emptive bid, it contracted for November band silk at
Rs 4.11 ans. per seer before the 'extraordinary demands' made
by the Gujaratis raised the price 'any higher'.[40] The very next
year it wrote to the Fort William Council that the 'silk is grown
very dear, occasioned by the unusual mortality among the
worms'.[41] In a characteristic reply in 1728 to the Court which
complained of bad quality and high price of silk sent from
Bengal, the Company officials referred to the heavy rains and
consequent flood destroying the mulberry trees and silk worms
so much so that hardly one third of the 'wanted quantity of silk'
was produced. This scarcity, they argued, resulted in high price
and bad quality of the silk.[42]

It was not only the Company servants that gave such reasons
for the rise in silk price. Queries in the local market also revealed
the same as the main causes for the scarcity of silk and consequent
rise in the price of the commodity. Edward Eyles, who was sent
to Rangpur in 1742 to enquire into the silk market and price
there, reported from Daudpur that the 'reasons given for its
[pattany] being so dearer than usual are because a good many of
the worms dyed last year in the Rains which occasioned a great
scarcity of Putney and because it has been much more in demand
than any former years'.[43] The Kasimbazar Council, however, was
quite vigilant in having the 'intelligence' of the price of raw silk
in the open market. In 1753 it noted that despite the 'considerable rise' in the price of pattany because of heavy rains in the last

[40] BPC, vol. 6, f. 172, 21 Feb. 1726.

[41] Ibid., f. 498 vo, 11 Sept. 1727

[42] Ibid., f. 668, 28 Oct. 1728.

[43] Fact. Records, Kasimbazar, vol. 6, Annex. to Consult. 31 Jan.
1742.

season, it was successful in contracting with the merchants for raw silk at the previous year's rate. It claimed that it acquired 'undoubted proof' of the dearness of the *pattany* by checking the 'day books' of several of the merchants, sending money secretly to the *aurungs* and through 'intelligence' it received from several merchants who were not connected with the Company's investment. And one of the definite proofs, it argued, was that Tawarjee Acharjee, one of the 'most considerable merchants' of the Company, refused to contract for silk, 'throwing up' the Company's service. Several other merchants, including the prominent ones like Munshiram and Gopal Babu, too absolutely declined to accept *dadni* for silk. The Council maintained that these merchants would not have done so, had there been 'any view of profit'.[44] There were, however, constant complaints from the Court of Directors, especially in the 1750s, regarding the bad quality and high price of the silk sent from Bengal. In a long note in 1755 the Kasimbazar Council tried to justify the above:[45]

> As to the causes of the scarceness and consequently the dearness of raw silk, they are various. But for these three years past it is evidently owing to the extraordinary heavy rains in the years 1752 and 1754 which occasioned the Mulberry leaves to grow so sank as to be unfit for the young worms which also requiring warmth and sunshine to bring them to maturity were in great numbers destroyed by the dampness of the air, they being so very tender that the least alteration of weather ... proves fatal to the worms and particularly last year the stormy weather which we had in the month of October was very destructive to the worms from which the Novemberbund putney is produced and which occasioned the silk to be so very dear.

A new and disturbing element affecting the production of raw silk and its price was added in the 1740s when the Maratha invasions became almost an annual event. One of the major industries that was badly affected by these incursions was the silk industry as most of the silk *aurungs* were situated in the areas

[44] Fact. Records, Kasimbazar, vol. 12, Consult. 19 March 1753.

[45] BPC, vol. 28, f. 270vo-71, 30 Oct. 1755; Fact. Records, Kasimbazar, vol. 12, Consult. 24 Oct. 1755.

badly ravaged by the Marathas. The impact of the Maratha raids on the silk industry is almost monotonously repeated in the Company records as one of the main factors enhancing the scarcity and consequent rise in the price of raw silk during the period. In 1746 when the Kasimbazar Council asked the merchants the reasons for demanding 'so extravagant a price', they replied shrewdly and categorically:[46]

> The Marattoes having entered this province and plundered three of the principal places (out of four)[47] where the putney is produced has occasioned so great a scarcity and what has been produced being bought up at a great price by the Armenians, Guzerattees and other merchants early in the season whereas it is now very late and little or no putney remaining to be purchased except at great price...

They added further that another reason for the excessive price of November band silk was because of the fact that 'half the crop of March band is consumed for want of rain'.

Again, faced with the challenge of resisting the Marathas, the state apparatus in Bengal seems to have become more exacting than before with the ostensible purpose of raising extra funds for maintaining an army, and this in turn affected the silk market too. As the Kasimbazar factors reported in 1752, the merchants demanded higher price for silk 'alleging the dearness of rice and the government's exactions on the [silk] winders'.[48] The Court of Directors however suspected, not without much ground perhaps, that the high price of raw silk was due to the 'malpractice' of the Company servants in Bengal. The Fort William Council wrote back in 1752 that it had directed the factors in Kasimbazar to make 'strict enquiry' into the causes for high price of raw silk but the latter replied that 'it was owing to the Marathas constantly entering Bengal, plundering and burning the people's houses

---

[46] Ibid., vol. 7, Consult. 3 April 1746; BPC, vol. 18, f. 173, 19 April 1746.

[47] I have tried to trace in the Company records which these four principal centres referred to here were but in vain.

[48] Fact. Records, Kasimbazar, vol. 11, Consult. 6 March 1752; BPC, vol. 25, f. 86 vo, 16 March 1752.

and destroying the chief aurungs from whence the workmen have fled to distant parts', but not to any malpractice of the servants there.[49] Perhaps the main factors affecting the supply and price of raw silk were well summed up by the merchants when they told the Kasimbazar Council in 1751 that they wanted a higher price because the samples 'were wound off' from 'the finest quality of November band *pattany* of which only a small quantity was produced because of the want of rain, the late troubles in the country [Maratha invasions] and other misfortunes [exactions of the state?]'. Besides, whatever silk was available was being bought up by the Dutch, French, Gujaratis and other merchants at a very high price [referring to the highly competitive market], as a result of which they were apprehensive that the price would go up further in a few days' time.[50]

All this was true to some extent, no doubt, but one should also take note of the fact that the merchants were prone to give such excuses to enhance the price as much as possible in the bargain. Similarly, the reports of the Company servants too can only be accepted with some caution as on the one hand many of them were engaged in private trade in raw silk[51] while on the other there was every possibility of collusion between them and the merchants which, as we have seen, was the suspicion of even the Court of Directors in London. In all probability, the effects of the Maratha invasions on the production and price of silk seem to have been exaggerated by both the merchants and the Company officials to serve their respective vested interests—for the merchants to enhance the price, for the servants to justify the high price and bad quality of silk sent by them. Otherwise it is difficult to reconcile the fact that even during the years of these invasions, the export of raw silk by the Asian merchants was quite substantial, the highest being 23,740 mds. in 1751.[52] If the

[49] C & B. Abstr., vol. 5, f. 324; Beng. Letters Recd., vol. 22, f. 222; NAI, Letters to Court, 1751-53, s. no. 2, ff. 76-77, para. 49, 2 Jan. 1752; *FWIHC,* vol. I, p. 548.

[50] NAI, Letters to Court, 1751-52, s. no. 2, pp. 22-23, para. 62, 20 Aug. 1751; Beng. Letters Recd., vol. 22, para. 64, ff. 175-76; C & B. Abstr., vol. 5, f. 299; *FWIHC,* vol. I, 510-11.

[51] See for example the reference to the private trade, BPC, vol. 28, f. 270vo, 30 Oct. 1755.

[52] BPC, vol. 44, Annex. to Consult. 19 June 1769.

Maratha incursions had been so disastrous for the silk industry as the merchants of the Company and its servants would have us believe, then it is surprising as to how the Asian merchants had exported such a large amount of raw silk in the period from 1747 to 1757. Again, an important point to note here is that, as we shall see in due course of our analysis, unlike the Europeans, the Asian merchants never bothered much about the price as long as they could get the commodity in the market.

It was indeed in the silk market that the European companies faced the stiffest competition from various groups of Asian merchants operating in Bengal. Of the many Asian buyers active in the market, there is little doubt that the Gujaratis were the most important group and it can be safely asserted that their operations acted as a 'general indicator' of the trends.[53] This is evident even from the Company records of the early years of our period. As we have noted earlier, the Kasimbazar Council entered into contracts with merchants in a hurry in 1726, apprehending the 'extraordinary demand' of the Gujaratis would raise the price further. It is little wonder that the Gujaratis were the largest exporter of Bengal silk in the first half of the eighteenth century, since from the sixteenth century, if not earlier, it was the raw silk of Bengal which kept the looms busy as far away as Gujarat and Chaul. Tavernier wrote in the 1660s that the greater part of the silk from Kasimbazar was exported to Surat and Ahmedabad.[54] Besides the Gujaratis, other important groups of Asians active in the silk market were the merchants from Multan, Lahore, Agra-Delhi, Gorakhpur, Benares, Hyderabad and Jangipur in Murshidabad, the last ones acting as *gomastas* or agents of Benares merchants. And of course there were the Armenians too, and another group, possibly from northern India, called 'Burdellwallys' in the Company records.[55]

[53] K.N. Chaudhuri, *Trading World*, p. 354.

[54] Tavernier, *Travels*, vol. II, p. 2.

[55] Numerous references to these merchants are to be found in the Company records. To refer to a few only: BPC, vol. 6, f. 337, 4 Jan. 1731; vol. 8, ff. 381-81vo, 22 March 1731; vol. 10, f. 190vo, 23 Dec. 1734; vol. 12, f. 86vo, 26 Jan. 1737; vol. 13, f. 689vo, 2 Nov. 1739; vol. 15, 33vo, 25 Jan. 1742; vol. 26, f. 52, 19 Feb. 1753; Fact. Records, Kasimbazar, vol. 6, 9 Dec. 1741; 25 Jan. 1742; 12 March 1744; 3 April 1746; vol. 12, 7 Feb. 1753; vol. 12, 12 Sept. 1753.

It is significant to note that sometimes the demand by these groups of merchants, excluding the Gujaratis, had considerable impact on the market and enhanced the price of raw silk. Warren Hastings reported from Powa, one of the silk *aurungs* on the other side of the river *Padma,* in 1756 that the prices of *pattany* or unspun silk suddenly rose there not because of the purchases of the Gujarati merchants but 'the arrival of every considerable foreign merchants at the aurungs'. He identified these merchants as 'Calwars' (from Agra-Delhi), Gorakhpuris and Jangipuris (who are reported to have bought 'upwards of six or seven lack of rupees for the provision of putney, especially the finest sorts which they are daily buying up notwithstanding its dearness').[56] An intelligent person as he was, Hastings tried to analyze as also rationalize the behaviour of these indigenous merchants who were buying up silk with the least regard for price. He wrote:[57]

> For the two former [Calwars and Gorakhpuris] coming from the distance of Delhi and Benares are in a manner necessitated by the long journeys they had taken for this commodity, to take it at such a rate as the market affords; nor are the latter [Jangipuris] less free in this respect, for tho' Jungapoor lies but a few days' journey from hence yet as they are most of them gomastas and their constituents living otherwise as far off as Benares they are obliged to comply with whatever orders they receive from thence, let the price be ever so great.

Further reflecting on the remarkable behaviour of the merchants from Delhi-Agra region and how it affected the silk market, he adds:[58]

> ... the Calwars by their eager manner of purchasing serve not a little to encrease the expectations of the country people and consequently the price of Putney in general tho' they provide only the finest sorts of all, for wherever they meet with any silk that strikes their fancy, they spare no price for it.

[56] Fact. Records, Kasimbazar, vol. 12, Annex. to Consult. 27 Jan. 1756.
[57] Ibid.
[58] Ibid.

Naturally, one can easily guess the severe competition in the Bengal silk market among the various indigenous merchant groups and the European companies. Even a good crop in a given year was no guarantee that the prices would be low and stable. The events in 1731 will bear out the point. Though there had been a good harvest of November band silk in that year, the Kasimbazar Council reported to Calcutta that by mid-March no silk was procurable, the reason being that the Lahore merchants had already bought up to the tune of Rs 3 lakh and the Burdelwalis 2 lakh while the Gujaratis had not bought 'so much as usual'. A lot of silk was stocked by a few *paikars* in the expectation that prices would go up further. Many buyers, including the Gujaratis, were waiting for the March band silk to be out in the market, hoping that it would ease the price of November band silk. The Dutch in Kasimbazar was in the same difficult situation, declaring publicly that they were not buying silk. But the English Council there was 'well assured' that the Dutch broker bought *pattany* which was 'frequently seen to be carried' into the Dutch factory'.[59]

The competition in the silk market was all the more intense because most of the groups active in the procurement of Bengal silk were intent on buying almost all the varieties of raw silk produced in the country. The Kasimbazar Council reported in 1737 that the Kumarkhali silk was in great demand among the Gujarati and Lahore merchants.[60] Again it noted in 1741, as we have mentioned earlier, that the price of Rangpur silk had gone up because the Gujarati and Hyderabad merchants had bought up a 'great quantity' to send up with the convoy of the King's treasure. Edward Eyles reported from Daudpur in January next year that the *gomastas* of the merchants from Gujarat, Hyderabad, Benares and 'other merchants' had already bought 700 mds. of November band Rangpur silk and some of those *gomastas* were still there 'buying daily'.[61] The silk merchants of Kasimbazar were extremely reluctant to contract for Rangpur silk in 1744 because of the enhanced price of the commodity resulting from the great

[59] BPC, vol. 8, ff. 381-81vo, 22 March 1731.

[60] Ibid., vol. 12, f. 86vo, 26 Jan. 1737. The contention of K.N. Chaudhuri (p. 357) that the 'products bought by the Gujaratis did not directly compete with those shipped to Europe' is hardly tenable.

[61] BPC, vol. 15, f. 33vo, 15 Jan. 1742.

demand of the Benares merchants, 'there being no less than eleven Families come from thence and are buying up all the Putney they can lay their hands on'.[62] When the Kasimbazar Council asked the merchants why they demanded 'an extravagant price' for the November band silk in 1746, the latter replied that the silk production was greatly affected by the Maratha inroads and the 'great part of the crop' that was available was bought up at a high price early in the season by the Armenians and the Gujaratis.[63] Even the silk rejected by the Kasimbazar Council in 1753 was bought at a higher price by the *gomastas* of the Gujarati merchants in Kasimbazar.[64] Warren Hastings reported from Chuncapara, an important silk *aurung* on the other side of the river *Padma*, that the *gomastas* of Gujarati, Lahore, Kasimbazar and other merchants 'continually reside at the aurungs, besides others who come here occasionally at this season of the year particularly'.[65] All this only indicates clearly that the Asian merchants were much more active in Bengal silk market than the Europeans.

8.3 COMPANIES AND PROCUREMENT OF SILK

As raw silk was one of the most profitable and valuable articles in the export list of the Companies—its low bulk making it possible to reduce the transport cost compared to other commodities—the organization of silk procurement was of great concern to these foreign monopolistic Companies. All of them had their factories in Kasimbazar for active supervision of the silk investment. It was also easy for them to send the silk cargo from Kasimbazar down the river either to Hughli, Calcutta or Chinsurah. The easy accessibility to the main silk producing areas made it convenient for them to send their servants to the silk *aurungs* so as to investigate the different aspects of silk trade and industry in the country. The usual practice for the Companies was to contract for silk with the merchants and rarely with *paikars*,

[62] Fact. Records, Kasimbazar, vol. 6, Consult. 12 March 1744.

[63] BPC, vol. 18, f. 173, 19 April 1746; Fact. Records, Kasimbazar, vol.7, Consult. 3 April 1746.

[64] Ibid., vol. 12, Consult. 19 Sept. 1753.

[65] Ibid., vol. 12, Consult. 28 Nov. 1755.

generally from January till April when the best *pattany* was out in the market. A common feature preceding the contract every year was the prolónged bargaining and wrangling between the Companies and merchants. The Companies always preferred forward dealing to buying from the merchant-middlemen at the shipping season, obviously because the latter would have involved payment of a higher price as also the uncertainty of having the required quantity for Europe-bound ships.

The merchants were generally given an advance at the rate of 80 per cent for November band and Kumarkhali silk, and 85 per cent for 'Gujarat' silk.[66] But as the problem of liquid capital plagued the Companies, they were not always able to pay the amount of *dadni* to the merchants who had either to invest their own money or borrow from the local credit market. Often the amount of advance given was ridiculously low as in 1748, when the English Company advanced only 3 1/4 per cent.[67] What the Companies did was to pay the merchants by bills of debt which the latter pawned to the *shroffs* and got the required capital.[68] Sometimes the problem of liquid capital became so acute that the merchants refused to contract for silk until and unless they received the balance for the previous year's supply—hardpressed as they were by the demands of the *shroffs* from whom they borrowed money.[69] In 1750 the merchants were even ready to lower the price of raw silk by 4 annas per seer if they were sure of receiving 'some money advanced' at the time of contracting so that they would not have to borrow money at 'a very high interest'.[70] The Kasimbazar Consultation of 29 March 1743 depicts the situation clearly:[71]

In the latter end of January several of the most substantial merchants represented ... that the Company's dadney being

[66] Ibid., vol. 6, Consult. 21 Feb. 1744.

[67] BPC, vol. 20, f. 303vo, 20 Jan. 1748.

[68] Fact. Records, Kasimbazar, vol. 7, Consult. 2 June 1748; 1 Nov. 1748; vol. 10, Consult. 15 March 1751.

[69] Ibid., vol. 7, Consult. 2 June 1748; BPC, vol. 22, f. 330vo, 31 Oct. 1749.

[70] Fact. Records, Kasimbazar, vol. 9, Consult. 23 June 1750.

[71] BPC, vol. 16, ff. 91vo-92, 29 March 1743.

commonly given out late in the season / and this year there
being no probability of its being otherwise / that the true and
pure Novemberbund putney / of which but a small quantity
is produced this year / would be all bought up by other people
before their dadney would be delivered out and that they
must be great sufferers by employing their own money or
taking it up at interest of the shroffs....

At the time of making the contracts, the prices of different
varieties of silk were fixed according to samples, though many
deductions were made by the Companies later on delivery. Prices
once fixed in the beginning of the season had to be maintained
even if the market price went up later. The merchants often
grudged this since the failure of a crop or the presence of too
many buyers frequently resulted in the prices going up later in
the season. On 19 January 1745 the merchants agreed to contract
at a certain price but towards the end of February asked for an
increase in price stating that they could not contract otherwise.
The Kasimbazar Council thus records the meeting with the
'assembly of merchants' which reveals several interesting features of silk trade in Bengal.[72]

> We told them the price being already agreed, it was not in
> our power to alter it, and if they would not undertake the
> investment we must look out for other merchants that would,
> to which they replied we might do as we pleased, but they
> were sure no merchants could contract cheaper than them-
> selves, who had been bred up in silk business from their
> childhood, but that they could not give us their labour
> without some profit of which they saw no prospect at the
> price we kept....

It is evident from the above that there was some sort of
specialization among the merchant groups of Kasimbazar. These
silk merchants of the Company were specialist dealers of that
commodity and were ready to deal in the goods only when there
was some guarantee of a profit. Moreover, this sort of 'ring' or
combination of merchants was a common aspect of the commer-

---

[72] Fact. Records, Kasimbazar, vol. 7, Consult. 19 Jan., 28 Feb. 1745.

cial life of Kasimbazar.

The Katma family of Kasimbazar was the mainstay of the English Company's silk investment. In the thirties and the early forties, before they moved over to Calcutta, the Katmas supplied most of the silk to the Company. The members of the family who successively held the position of 'chief merchant' or broker of the Company in Kasimbazar led the silk merchants in contracting with the Company. Justifying the appointment of Hatu Katma as broker and his confirmation in the post, the Kasimbazar Council wrote in 1731: '... the necessity of their affairs greatly requiring such a person to make proper dispositions for beginning their investment and this being the properest time for buying the Novemberbund silk ... they confirmed him as broker.'[73] His successor, Balai or Balaram Katma, appointed broker in 1737, was in the same way instrumental in the Company's silk investment through the merchants. The Council wrote to Calcutta that he had been of 'great use' as a 'curb' on the merchants in 1739. When the merchants refused to lower the price of March band silk, it was he who contracted for 1/4 of the total quantity, thus breaking up the 'ring' of the merchants. The Council also noted that he had been 'useful in the great reduction of price' in 1740 again and that 'his goods in general are as good as any of the merchants, some sorts better'.[74] When he was kept in confinement by the nawab, the Council felt helpless and requested him to ask some of his family to contract for 'the remainder of our silk and silk piece-goods'. The Company's total dependence on the Katmas is well illustrated in a Kasimbazar Consultation: '... for if some of that family will not assist us on this occasion, we find it on several Tryalls impossible to get any of our other merchants to agree for more silk or piece-goods'.[75]

In the early years of its trade, it does not seem that the Company insisted on security being given by the merchants for the advance paid to them for silk investment. In 1741 the Kasimbazar Council took proper security from only 4 merchants out of 25 who contracted for raw silk, 'the rest being substantial

[73] BPC, vol. 8, f. 337, 4 Jan. 1731.
[74] Ibid., vol. 14, f. 47, 4 Feb. 1740.
[75] Fact. Records, Kasimbazar, vol. 6, Consult. 10 March 1742.

persons'.[76] But the Court of Directors did not approve of it and wrote to Bengal: '... this is by no means satisfactory, the more substance a man has, he may the readier produce Bonds/Men, and ... it [is] necessary to take security of every one of your Merchants.'[77] From about 1744 the Kasimbazar Council insisted on security from every merchant but at the same time noted that 'as this method is entirely new to them, it occasions a delay in settling their investment'.[78] Interestingly enough, in the trading world of Kasimbazar, even such security was no guarantee for the contract to be honoured and the person who stood security thought himself not liable for the deficiency of the merchant in question or even tried to ignore such obligation through his strong connection in the court. The point is well illustrated by the case of Debiprasad, a silk merchant and his security Ramkrishna Babu in 1753. The Kasimbazar Council found the said Debiprasad deficient and his solvency in doubt. It had also reason to believe, as it claimed, that he did not even employ the money advanced to him. He could not return the advance he had taken. So the Council confined him in the factory on 7 September 1753 and sent word to his security, Ramkrishna Babu, that he should pay the amount due to the Company or he too would be confined.[79]

Ramkrishna, himself a silk merchant of the Company and the adopted son of Chain Rai, an important official at the *darbar*, attended the Council and acknowledged that he was Debiprasad's security but maintained that 'he does not think himself answerable for another person's deficiency'. The Council confined him too 'till he gives some security' for the money advanced to Debiprasad. But Ramkrishna did not sit idle and the Council was informed by its *vakil* at the court that the former was trying to get his release 'by means of his friends at the Durbur'. On 24 September, Kissendeb, the deputy of the influential *pachotra daroga*, Hakim Beg, informed the Council that 'a powerful solicitation' had been made from Raja Kiratchand, the *diwan* and his deputy Umid Ray, along with several *mutsuddies* on behalf of

[76] Ibid., vol. 6, Consult. 5 March 1741.
[77] DB, vol. 108, f. 624, para. 56, 4 Feb. 1743.
[78] BPC, vol. 17, f. 15vo, 23 Feb. 1744.
[79] Fact. Records, Kasimbazar, vol. 12, Consult. 16 Aug., 6 Sept., 7 Sept. 1753.

Ramkrishna. He also acquainted the Council of his apprehension that the nawab was likely to demand Ramkrishna if he was not released in a day or two and he might even 'set forces' on the English factory. So he advised the Council to deliver Ramkrishna to his 'charge' to 'forestall such happenings'. Either the Council got scared or wise counsel prevailed on it so that it handed over Ramkrishna to Kissendeb who promised to get a security bond from the former for his appearance at the Council whenever he was asked to.[80] The case reveals undoubtedly the strong connection between the merchants and the ruling elite in Bengal during the period under review.

The combination or 'ring' of the silk merchants for hard bargaining with the Companies or other Asian merchants was a familiar feature of the commercial life in Kasimbazar. We have already noted how the silk merchants entered into an agreement among themselves in 1743 to resist the pressure of the Company from, what they thought, unwarranted impositions on the part of the latter.[81] What is significant is that these 'rings' or 'combinations' cut across the caste or regional barriers as the merchants who entered into the said agreement not only belonged to different castes but several of them were from different parts of India.[82] The event of 1754 again will underline the solidarity of the silk merchants of Kasimbazar which the

[80] Ibid., vol. 12, Consults. 12 Sept., 19 Sept., 24 Sept., 1753.

[81] See chapter 5.

[82] Of the 42 merchants with whom the Company contracted for raw silk and silk piece-goods in Kasimbazar in 1753, as many as 10 to 12 appear to be non-Bengalis, probably from Gujarat, Rajasthan, the Punjab and north India while among the Bengali merchants such high castes as Bhaduri (brahmin), Sen etc, were to be found along with lower castes like Telly. The names of the merchants were: Allumchand Gainchand, Manickchand, Myachand, Suchi Baral, Kashinath Sarma, Harish Chaudhury, Titu Sarma, Meherchand Mahter (Mathur or Mehta?), Sibaprasad Sarma, Gopal Babu, Ramkrishna Babu, Jugal Bhaduri, Nimu Sen, Chaitan Charan Poddar, Odit Baral, Ram Saran Ghose, Ballabh Biswas, Radhakrishna Sarkar, Bishnu Charan Nandy, Anup Coppree (Kapur?), Kali Charan Sarma, Gokulchand Dharamchand, Gopi Thakur, Dulal Sarkar, Krishna Chand Katma, Radhamadhab, Jayram Lochund (?), Nandalal Ramgutty, Jitu Telly, Ram Saran Sarma, Nishi Roy, Chaitan Bridgmohan, Narain Sarma, Shyam Mohan Sarma, Ramdurlabh Conjoo (?), Radha Charan Sarma, Raghuchand Sarma,

Council found extremely difficult to break up. The dispute arose when the Council offered lower prices for the silk brought in by the merchants or asked them to take away the silk after paying the amount of *dadni* advanced 'with the penalty'. The merchants left the factory 'in a body' and decided to go to Murshidabad to lodge a complaint against the Company. The Council took serious note of it and decided to write to Hukum Beg, Ghulam Hussain Khan and other *darbar* officials to 'prevent any complaint being heard', because it was 'ill-grounded'. It was informed the same day that the merchants were camping at Suncally [Sonakhali?] near Murshidabad and 'forming a petition against us to deliver to the nawab'.[83] The advice from Calcutta was to prevent such a complaint being made at the *darbar* by informing the merchants that they would forfeit their employment with the Company if they carried the matter to such a length.[84] Accordingly, the Kasimbazar Council tried 'every possible means' to stop the complaint being made and threatened the merchants with dismissal from the Company's service, 'which they seem to make very slight of'. Completely ignoring the threat of the Council, the merchants did complain to the court but the Council, it seems, through a present to the powerful Hukum Beg, somehow manipulated the strings at the court. The merchants were persuaded by the Council 'with greatest difficulty' to return to the factory and drop the complaint.[85]

Meanwhile as the dispute dragged on and the proper time for silk investment was running out, as also finding the merchants 'refractory and refusing' to contract for silk, the Council decided to try the merchants employed by the Gujaratis and the Dutch. It first contacted 'one of the most considerable of the merchants' employed by the Gujaratis. He was willing to contract for silk but

Podolochund (?), Jagmohan Dhar. That Babu (Baboe) was the title of Marwari merchants is clear from Alexander Hume's 'memorie' where he speaks of one Nainsook Baboe, who was a near relation of Jagat Seth Fatechand, c.f. Hume's 'memoire', Stadsarchief Antwerp, GIC 5769. However, N.K. Sinha refers to one prominent silk merchant, Bostom Chand Babu, who was a nephew of Kantu Babu, the famous *banyan* of Warren Hastings (*Economic History of Bengal*, vol. I, p. 112).

[83] Fact. Records, Kasimbazar, vol. 12, Consult. 23 Feb. 1754.
[84] Ibid., vol. 12, Consult. 12 March 1754.
[85] Ibid., vol. 12, Consults. 25 March, 28 March, 2 April 1754.

his rate was considered quite high (November band Rs 7.7 ans.
and 'Gujarat' Rs 8 per seer). Moreover, he would not allow any
'ferret' or usual deductions for *dastur* and brokerage. He also
insisted that the silk should be 'prized in the bundles, without
being untied or sorted skein by skein', the latter being the usual
English practice. His samples, which were not fine enough, as also
his terms were totally unacceptable to the Council.[86] The Dutch
merchants responded well, quoted their prices (Rs 8. 7 ans. for
November band and proportionately for 'Gujarat') and were
willing to contract with the English Company but 'they would not
come to the factory till they are under some certainty of our
employment, lest such a step should prejudice them with their
present Employers'. But their price was considered too high and
hence rejected by the Council.[87] Ultimately the Council had to
turn to its own merchants, the dispute with them having been
settled by early April. But they demanded Rs 8 per seer for
November band and Rs 8. 9 ans. for 'Gujarat' which was thought
to be 'very extravagant' by the Council which noted rather in
despair that it had 'no hopes of reducing it lower as the
Merchants seem rather desirous to decline than engage in this
article even at this exorbitant price'.[88] Having failed to persuade
the merchants to agree to a reduction in price, the Council took
resort to a novel stratagem. It wrote to Calcutta on 31 May that
it sent a small amount of money to the *aurungs* to make a show
as if it was determined to provide silk investment by itself. This
had the desired effect. Some of the merchants thought that the
Company was resolved not to allow 'any advanced price' and had
at last agreed to contract on the basis of the previous year's
price.[89]

The Kasimbazar Council's deliberations on the silk investment for 1755 clearly bring out some of the ramifications of the
silk trade and industry in Bengal. As suggested by Calcutta, the
Council refrained from buying *pattany* which the Gujaratis were
also doing in order to lower the price. But this had little effect
either on the market or on the price. As the Council failed to
bring the merchants to any 'reasonable' terms, it decided to send

[86] Ibid., vol. 12, 6, 10 March 1754.
[87] Ibid., vol. 12, 12 March 1754.
[88] Ibid., vol. 12, 22 April 1754; *FWIHC*, vol. I, pp. 815-16.
[89] Fact. Records, Kasimbazar, vol. 12, 31 May 1754.

Rs 20,000 through the two 'cottah banias' to the *aurungs* to buy
pattany and find out the price. Meanwhile the merchants told the
Council that as the November band *pattany* was 'scarce and dear'
they would not be able to provide it at less than Rs 8. 4 ans. per
seer. The Council too noted that it came to know from the 'best
enquiry' that the price of *pattany* was the highest in the last three
years and the merchants could hardly make any profit even at
their price.[90] But when it asked the merchants to lower the price
a little and contract for silk on 4 March 1755 the latter replied
that they could not then afford to contract at the price quoted
earlier as the price of *pattany* had gone up considerably from what
it was. The Council admitted that the merchants could hardly
contract at the last three years' price, they suffered heavy loss for
the last two years by silk contracts, the *pattany* procured and
wound off at the factory would only strengthen the merchants'
case for a rise in the price.[91] The merchants now demanded Rs
9. 3 ans. for November band and proportionately for 'Gujarat'
but the Council contracted for small lots with several merchants
and no formal contract was made for silk investment of 1755.[92]

It would be interesting to note the cost price of 'Gujarat' raw
silk for which the Company bought the *pattany* and wound it off
at the factory in 1755.[93]

'Exact Calculation of the Cost and Charges' of 1 seer 'Gujarat'
Silk

	Rs.	As.	Ps.
Pattani bought at the aurungs per seer...	6	6	9
Curka or coarse pattani in a bundle which amounts to 1 sr. 12 ch. in a maund and being unfit for winding off, sold at a loss...	0	2	0
Batta being the difference between Dasmasha rupees and Sicca rupees (pattani bought			

(contd.)

[90] NAI, Letter to Court, s.no. 4, 1755-57, f. 135, 6 Jan. 1755; Fact.
Records, Kasimbazar, vol. 12, Consults. 12, 13, 19 Feb. 1755.
[91] Ibid., vol. 12, Consults., 4,10,17,19 March 1755.
[92] Ibid., vol. 12, Consults., 26 March 10, 11, 24 April, 1755.
[93] Ibid., vol. 12, Consults., 12, 23 June 1755.

Contd. from page 244	Rs.	As.	Ps.
in Dasmasha rupees)...	0	2	3
Charges for winding...	0	6	0

Fullun and Dull, the first being the very coarse
threads which are found in the very best pattani
and thrown out being of little or no use; the
latter being the gum which washes out of the
pattani as it is soaked in water before winding;
both together resulting in a loss of 2 sr. 8 ch.
per maund and to be added on the price of raw
silk...   0   7   9

Inferior pattani taken out of Gujarat to be used
for 5 lettered silk not being fine enough for the
former: which in consequence must be priced
lower and added to the price of Gujarat silk...   0   1   0

A deduction being usual in our [English] pricing
of silk of 4 ans. from A to B and so on to D,
of 6 ans. from D to E, 8 ans. from E to F, the A
must be valued higher to allow for this...   0   14   9

The poor being likewise priced 2 ans. less than
the assell occasions a further deduction to the
price of the A assell of...   0   0   9

Dastur and Brokerage 5:11 percent brought to
the Company's credit since abolishing the
office of broker...   0   7   9

| The net price of A assell Damasha Rupees | 9 | 1 | 0 |

The reports of Edward Eyles and Warren Hastings in 1742
and 1756 respectively (who were sent by the Kasimbazar Council
to the different silk *aurungs* on the other side of the river *Padma*
to enquire into the state of silk trade and industry) reveal quite
a few interesting aspects of silk trade and industry in Bengal.
Edward Eyles reported from Daudpur in Rangpur district that
the amount of *pattany* produced in Rangpur in the early 1740s

was around 4,000 maunds, of which the breakdown was as
follows:[94]

November band	-	1,000 mds.
March band	-	700 mds.
July band	-	2,300 mds.
Total	-	4,000 mds.

He added that in earlier years generally one thousand
maunds more *pattany* were produced 'by reason of a greater
increase of silk worms'. The customary method of silk winding
in Rangpur was by employing a *dalal* who charged 2 per cent for
his trouble and risk for any deficiency in silk delivered to the
winders. But he observed that 'it was impossible to wind off large
quantity of silk to make it come out exactly at the same price and
of the same goodness of a muster by reason it is wound off by
so great a number of different hands and because it is uncertain
what the lower sorts will fetch here'. He also gave an account of
the charges of the silk sent from Rangpur.[95]

Charges for winding	- 6 ans. per seer
Dallaly	- 2 per cent
Packing, Cooly hire, Way charges to Kasimbazar	- 6 ans. per seer.

Hastings was sent to 'the other side' of the *Padma* in 1755 for
collecting the 'best information' about the prices of various kinds
of *pattany*, the total quantity produced in the *aurungs* and the
different buyers in the market. He first reported from Chuncapara
on 28 Nov. 1755 that though there was a prospect of a very
'plentiful season' of November band *pattany*, it was difficult to
'foretell' what effect it would have on the prices. He further
noted that the *gomastas* of Gujarati, Armenian, Lahore, Kasimbazar
and other merchants 'continually reside' at the *aurungs* besides
those 'who go there occasionally at that time of the year' and

[94] BPC, vol. 15, f. 27, 18 Jan. 1742, f. 33vo, 25 Jan. 1742; Fact.
Records., Kasimbazar, vol. 6, Consults. 18 Jan. 1742, 25 Jan. 1742.
[95] Ibid., vol. 6, Consult. 25 Jan. 1742.

there was likely to be a greater number of buyers than usual.[96] On 19 December he wrote from Powa, another silk *aurung*, about the high price of 'Mulluck' *pattany* which he thought was because of the 'unusual concourse of purchasers at Mulluck in expectation of November band which is in season at that place three weeks or a month sooner than in any other'. Lakhipur *pattany*, he added, would not be 'so dear'. He also tried to explain the rise in prices of *pattany* in those *aurungs* for the last few years.[97] One of the reasons, as he noted, was that the country on that side of the river *Padma* was in general very low and marshy, especially those places which were situated 'at the greatest distance from the river so that any extraordinary inclemency of the rainy season is much more sensibly felt there than in any other place'. The excessive rainfall three years ago, as he wrote, had entirely overwhelmed a large tract of land about 25 miles to the east of this place' and 'dispersed or destroyed the greatest part of the inhabitants whose livelihood depended entirely on the breeding of the silk worms'. Another reason for the hike in the price of silk, as he pointed out, was the difference between 'the land tax now and five years ago' which had been more than doubled during these years. He then remarked: 'The effects which these circumstances must necessarily produce in the price of the principal produce as well as the only merchandise of this country are too obvious to mention.'[98] Hastings' report underlines the fact that the increase in the price of silk in the 1750s was more because of natural calamities than the effects of the Maratha invasions since the areas on the other side of the *Padma* were not at all affected by these raids.

Almost throughout the period of our study, the Court of Directors often complained that the silk sent from Bengal was of uneven quality, some of the skeins being more like pack thread

---

[96] BPC, vol. 28, f. 302, 24 Nov. 1755; Fact. Records, Kasimbazar, vol. 12, Consult. 21 Nov. 1755; Annex. to Consult. 28 Nov. 1755.

[97] BPC, vol. 28, ff. 348-48vo, Hastings' Letter from Powa, 19 Dec. 1755; Fact. Records, Kasimbazar, vol. 12, Annex. to Consult. 22 Dec. 1755.

[98] BPC, vol. 28, ff. 348-48vo, Annex. to Consult. 29 Dec. 1755. However it is difficult to substantiate Hastings' statement about the increase in land tax.

than silk and full of knots. The main fault of Bengal silk was that
the threads in the same skein were often a part single, part double
and in some cases even more. Unless carefully reeled, the
'country wound' silk thread had several defects and impurities.[99]
When the Kasimbazar Council tried to make the merchants
'sensible for the Company's complaint with regard to the winders
twisting two broken ends of the silk together instead of tying
them in a knot', the merchants replied that by this method the
silk would turn out much dearer as the winders could not then
be able to wind off more than two thirds of what 'they do now'.[100]
It was only in 1755 that the Council carried out an experiment
of winding the filament on a wheel which seems to be an
European innovation. The Fort William Council noted in
February of that year that it received from Kasimbazar a parcel
of *tanny* silk 'even spun upon a wheel which they wound off in
the factory from the pods'. It was informed by Kasimbazar in
January that 'this manner of winding off silk was entirely foreign
to the winders of these parts, and it was with some difficulty [that]
they could get proper hands to work the machine'. At the same
time the Kasimbazar Council noted: 'As this method obliges the
workmen to more labour and attention than the usual method,
the silk turn out very dear though even.' But the factors were
confident that if they were allowed to continue the method for
a season or two, they would be able to reduce the price and
contract with the merchants for silk 'wound off in the same
manner'.[101]

In August 1755, the Kasimbazar Council wrote to Calcutta
that the 'several evils in our raw silk' as pointed out by the Court
of Directors could be remedied by 'no other method than
winding off the silk within our walls'. It came to the conclusion
that the buildings of the factory could not accommodate more
than 300 winders with their machines, and at the rate of 3
chataks[102] per day per winder (which was the usual output per

[99] Mohsin, *Murshidabad*, p. 45.
[100] BPC, vol. 26, f. 52, 19 Feb. 1753; Fact. Records, Kasimbazar, vol.
12, Consult. 7 Feb. 1753.
[101] Beng. Letters Recd., vol. 22, f. 710, para. 11, 3 Feb. 1755;
FWIHC, vol. 1, p. 860; NAI, Home Misc., vol. 18, ff. 118-19, 22 Aug.
1755.
[102] 1 *chatak* is 1/16 of a seer.

person), it would not be able to wind off more than 500 mds. in a year, which was not even one fourth of the amount ordered from England.[103] So it asked Calcutta for permission to build such outhouses as might be necessary for the purpose. But the Fort William Council did not approve any expenses for new buildings and asked Kasimbazar to find room to wind off the silk without putting the Company to fresh charges on that account.[104]

The silk winders of Bengal, however, were not reluctant to learn the new technique of winding. As Hastings reported from Powa, the method of winding silk there was very different from that in the English factory at Kasimbazar 'with which these people cannot be supposed to be acquainted' but 'they will easily fall into any new method which shall be shown them'.[105] So when the Court of Directors, induced by the silk manufacturers of England, sent Richard Wilder to Kasimbazar to examine the causes of the defects in Bengal silk and suggest improvements, his task was not too difficult.[106] Until his death in 1761, he remained in Kasimbazar and rendered valuable services to the silk industry by improving the method of silk winding and teaching the art of improved reeling to the local artisans.[107] For some time he also resided on the other side of the *Padma* in order to instruct the winders in those areas. The new silk winding machine which he introduced was found very useful by the Kasimbazar Council and it considerably improved the defective winding.[108]

8.4 SILK EXPORTS—COMPANIES AND ASIAN MERCHANTS

It has been well established that throughout the second half of the seventeenth century, the Dutch export of Bengal raw silk was

---

[103] Fact. Records, Kasimbazar, vol.12, Consults. 7 Aug., 27 Aug. 1755.

[104] BPC, vol. 28, ff. 400-401, 2 Feb. 1756.

[105] Fact. Records, Kasimbazar, vol. 12, Consult. 19 Jan. 1756.

[106] J. Long, *Selections*, vol. I, p. 84, paras. 140,146, Letter from Court to Bengal, 25 March 1757.

[107] Mohsin, *Murshidabad*, p. 56.

[108] NAI, Public Letters to Court, s. no. 6, f. 17, para. 41, 29 Dec. 1759.

much larger than that of the English Company.[109] Even in the first
two decades of the eighteenth century, the Dutch lead was
maintained. This will be apparent from Table 8.1.

TABLE 8.1
Quinquennial Total and Annual Average of Dutch and
English Exports: Raw Silk, 1700-1720

Years	Dutch Exports			English Exports	
	Total (Dutch lb.)	Average (Dutch lb.)	Average (Eng.lb.)	Total (Eng.lb.)	Average (Eng.lb.)
1700/01-1704/05	754,648	150,930	164,514	476,283	95,256
1710/11-1714/15	751,054	150,211	163,730	259,292	51,858
1715/16-1719/20 (Dutch for only 3 years 1715/16-1717/18)	625,653	208,551	312,827	635,225	127,045

[Source: Om Prakash, *Dutch Company*, p. 218 for Dutch exports; S.
Chaudhuri, *Trade and Commercial Organization*, pp. 254-55 for English
exports. All calculations are in English small pounds. The Dutch pond
is converted at the rate of 1 Dutch pond = 1.09 lb. avoirdupois]

But as the Dutch trade in general declined in the 1720s, the
English export of raw silk from Bengal surpassed that of the
Dutch towards the end of 1720s.[110] As a matter of fact, the English
export of raw silk reached its peak in the 1730s and Table 8.2
will indicate the average annual export by the English Company
which fell sharply from around the mid-1740s, reaching its nadir
in the early 1750s in the whole period from 1730 to 1755.

[109] Glamann, *Dutch Asiatic Trade*, pp. 126-130; Om Prakash, *Dutch Company*, pp. 217-19.
[110] Glamann, *Dutch Asiatic Trade*, p.131.

TABLE 8.2

Ouinquennial Total and Annual Average of English Exports,
Raw Silk, 1730-1755

Years	Total (grt.lb.)	Average (grt.lb.)	Average (small lb.)	Average (maunds)
1730/31-1734/35	702,907	140,581	210,872	2812
1735/36-1739/40	714,004	142,801	214,201	2856
1740/41-1744/45	596,051	119,210	178,815	2384
1745/46-1749/50	300,001	60,000	90,000	1200
1750/51-1754/55	286,620	57,324	85,986	1146

[Source & note: Compiled and computed from K.N. Chaudhuri, *Trading World*, p. 534. 1 great lb. = 1.5 small lb. In Bengal silk was weighed in maunds and seers, 40 seers making a maund. One Bengal maund was equivalent to 75 lb. i.e., lb. avoirdupois or what was called small lb.]

It is evident from the above Table 8.2 that the maximum annual average of raw silk exported by the English Company was 2856 mds. or 0.21 million lbs. in the peak period of the 1730s and never crossed 3000 mds. or 0.23 million lbs. Indeed from the mid-1740s till the mid-1750s, the average annual English export was even less than half of that in the boom period of the 1730s.

As against this, the Dutch export of raw silk was more or less steady from the 1730s through the 1750s, with a marginal decline in the 1740s and recovering again in the early 1750s. This will be evident from Table 8.3.[111]

[111] Floretta yarn or *mochta* silk was not included in the computation as it was not really regarded as raw silk, was of a much inferior variety and cheaper quality than the varieties like *tanny, adapangia*, Gujarat, *tanna banna* etc. Even in the sale of the different chambers in Holland, this was not advertised as raw silk like *tanny, cabessa* etc., but as floretta yarn (c.f., Notice of Auction, 16 Sept. 1755, Resolutions of Heeren XVII, VOC 7380). Om Prakash (pp. 202,218) too dealt raw silk and floretta yarn separately. But even if we include floretta yarn in our computation, it hardly alters the picture because in the early 40s the average annual export of floretta yarn was only 84 mds. while in the early 50s it was 184 mds. (computed from Dutch export invoices) on an average in a year.

TABLE 8.3

Quinquennial Total and Annual Average of Dutch Exports,
Raw Silk, 1730-1755

Years	Total (Dutch lbs.)	Average (Dutch lbs.)	Average (Eng. lbs.)	Average (maunds)
1730/31-1734/35	335,319	67,064	73,100	975
1740/41-1744/45	308,448	61,689	67,241	897
1750/51-1754/55	333,210	66,642	72,640	969

[Source: Collected and computed from Bengal export invoices in the VOC records.]

It is clear from the above Table 8.3 that the Dutch export of Bengal raw silk in the period between 1730 and 1755 never crossed 1000 mds. or 0.08 million lbs., though it was probably higher than the figure for the late 1720s and certainly much lower than the average annual export in the first two decades of the eighteenth century.[112] In other words, in the crucial period of the late 1740s and the early 1750s, the total average annual export of Bengal raw silk by the two major European companies, involved actively in Bengal trade, certainly did not exceed 2500 mds. or 0.19 million lbs., even taking the English export at 1500 mds. and the Dutch at 1000 mds.[113] Adding to this the export of raw silk by other European companies which could not have been more than 1000 mds. at the maximum,[114] the total European

[112] See Table 8.1.

[113] The Dutch export of Bengal raw silk to Japan, which was an important branch of trade of the VOC in the second half of the 17th century (see, Om Prakash, p. 126) was only 6154 Dutch lb. on an average in the quinquennial period 1740-45 while in the 5 year periods from 1730 to 1735 and 1750 to 1755, it was nil. I have collected and computed all this evidence from the Bengal export invoices in the VOC archives.

[114]Among other European companies, only the French were of some importance. The Ostend Company had to abandon its trade in 1744 while the Danish Company was permitted to establish its factory only in 1755. Though the French private trade increased remarkably in the early 1750s, the volume of their corporate trade seems to have been much smaller than that of the English or the Dutch. Even assuming, as

export of raw silk would have been 3500 mds. or 0.26 million lbs. in a year on an average at the most.

The important question that crops up is what was the amount of raw silk exported by the Asian merchants from Bengal as against the European export. We are fortunate enough to unearth a complete list of silk export by the Asians from Bengal from 1749 to 1767 from the records at the India Office Library. The report was prepared by W Aldersey, who was chief of the Kasimbazar factory in 1769, in response to an official query as to the causes of the decline in silk trade and industry in Bengal. Aldersey specifically mentions that he collected the information from Murshidabad customs house and it included the raw silk exported by 'natives only on which Duties have been collected'.[115] From his list, we compute here the quinquennial total of silk export by the Asians from 1749 to 1758 for a comparative study of the Asian and European exports of raw silk (see Table 8.8 & Figure 8.1), the full details of which are given in Tables 8.5 and 8.7.

TABLE 8. 4

Quinquennial Total and Annual Average of
Silk Exports by Asians, 1749-1758

Years	Total (mds.)	Average (mds.)	Average (lb.)	Total Value (Rs)	Average Value (Rs)
1749-53	99,016	19,803	14,85,240	2,77,24,365	55,44,873
1754-58	74,692	14,938	11,20,380	2,09,13,345	41,82,669

[Source: Bengal Public Consultations, Range 1, vol. 44, Annex. to Consult., 19 June 1769; for the complete list, see, Table 8.7]

did P.J. Marshall (*Bengal*, p.66), that the volume of the French Company's trade was about half of that of the English or the Dutch trade, the French export of raw silk would have been around 500 mds. at the most. And raw silk does not seem to be a staple commodity in the European private trade to Western India, Red Sea or Persian Gulf area (VOC 2304, f.211, HB. 30 Nov.1734). Hence it could be reasonably assumed that the export of raw silk by other Europeans (i.e. excluding the English and the Dutch Companies) could not have been more than 1000 mds. at the maximum on an average in a year in the early 1750s.

[115] BPC, Range 1, vol. 44, Annex. to Consult., 19 June 1769. This is more or less corroborated by other English and indigenous sources.

The above Table 8.4 clearly indicates that the Asians were far ahead of the Europeans in the export of raw silk from Bengal. While the export by the Asian merchants in the late forties and early fifties amounted on an average to 19,803 maunds or about 1.5 million lbs. in the mid-fifties, the Europeans exported only about 3500 mds. or 0.26 million lbs. in a year on an average during the same period. In other words, it can be said that the European export was less than 1/5 of what was exported by the Asian merchants around this time. Again the total value of the European export of raw silk, taking it to be 3500 mds. a year and at the rate of Rs 7 per seer (40 seers making a maund), which is the rate at which the Asian export is valued in the said English Company records, would have been around only Rs 0.98 million. On the other hand, the total value of the silk exported by the Asian merchants is estimated at around Rs 5.5 million on an average during the period from 1749 to 1753 and Rs 4.1 million in the next five years i.e. from 1754 to 1758. So far as the total value of the raw silk exported by the Europeans and Asians is concerned, the European share was thus only between 1/5 and 1/4 of the Asian share. If that was so, the last part of the Dutch Director Jan Kerseboom's observation in 1755 that the silk would remain as expensive as it used to be in Kasimbazar because of the 'imposition' of the government, high prices of provisions and as the orders of the European nations far surpassed the quantity 'the country yields' become superfluous.[116]

It would be worthwhile to investigate the direction/destination of the exports by the Asian merchants, especially of raw silk because it was exported in such huge quantity even in the late 1740s and the early 1750s. However one has to keep in mind that evidence of such nature is hard to come by in our sources.[117] We

See for example, Mss. Eur. D. 283, f. 21; Verelst's letter to the Court of Directors, 5 April 1769, *FWIHC*, vol. v, pp. 18-19. For the indigenous account, see N.K. Sinha, *Economic History of Bengal*, vol. 1, p. 112.

[116] Jan Kerseboom's 'Memorie', VOC, 2849, f. 112.

[117] I do not think that for my present thesis it is absolutely essential to show where the silk was exported to. Contrary to an opinion expressed in private conversation by a distinguished historian of the period that my thesis "stands or falls on this very question" of identifying the destination of the raw silk exported from Bengal, I maintain, as some experts in the field do, that so far as I know the volume and value of

are extremely fortunate to find some data regarding the direction/destination of raw silk exports by the Asian merchants from Bengal during 1775-77. By reading back from the evidence of the 1770s, it is possible to provide some idea of the direction/ destination of the Asian silk trade in the pre-Plassey period. One has to remember in this connection that in the 1770s there was a precipitate decline of the Asian merchants' trade under the ruthless repression of the English Company and its servants backed by political power—a process which started immediately after 1757-58. The decline of the Asian merchants' trade is evident from the report of Aldersey which we quoted earlier and the following Table 8.5 from his report will bear out our point.

TABLE 8.5

Volume and Value of Raw Silk Exported by Asian Merchants, 1759-67

Year	Volume (in maunds)	Value (in rupees)
1759	14,394	40,30,387
1760	13,056	36,55,791
1761	10,562	29,57,229
1762	5,953	16,66,845
1763	6,601	18,48,333
1764	8,326	23,31,193
1765	7,191	20,13,525
1766	5,180	14,50,307
1767	6,599	18,47,832

(The total quantity for the quinquennial period 1763-67 amounts to 33,897 maunds and the average 6779 maunds. For this Table the source is the same as in Table 8.7).

raw silk exported by the Asian merchants, it is more than sufficient for my present thesis. However I agree that it is worth investigating the destination of the raw silk exports from Bengal so that we can have a comprehensive idea of the silk trade as a whole.

It is apparent from Table 8.5 that the average annual export of the Asian merchants during the quinquennial period from 1763 to 1767 stood at 6779 maunds which tallies more or less with the figure of export from 1775 to 1777 which was on an average 7025 maunds. The destination as well as the total amount of silk export by the Asian merchants from 1775 to 1777 is recorded in the Patna Customs House Register and for the three years combined, the totals are as follows:

TABLE 8.6

Destination/Direction and Triennial Total of Silk Exported
by Asian Merchants, 1775-1777

Destination / Direction (in descending order of total qnty.)	Total Quantity (in maunds)
Mirzapore	12,568
Lahore	3,851
Multan	1,649
Aurangabad	1,471
Agra	598
Benares	511
Delhi	427

(Average annual export = 7,025 mds.)
(Source: Board of Revenue, Misc. Proceedings, Range 98, vols. 18,20,22, IOR.)

From the Table 8.6, it is quite clear that during this period the maximum amount of silk from Bengal went to Mirzapore which was a distribution centre rather than a manufacturing one, and it can be assumed that this silk was re-exported from Mirzapore to northern and western directions. The next highest amount was destined for Lahore while Multan and Aurangabad came third and fourth in descending order of total quantity exported. If this was the destination/direction of Bengal silk exported in the mid- 1770s, it can be reasonably assumed that the destination/direction of Bengal silk exported by the Asian merchants in the late 1740s to mid-1750s would have been almost similar.

TABLE 8.7

"Extracts from Customs Office Receipts at Murshidabad, 1749-58"
Volume and Value of Raw Silk Exported by Asian Merchants

Year	Volume (in maunds)	Volume (in Engl.lbs.)	Value (Rupees)
1749	20,037	15,02,775	56,10,423
1750	19,571	14,67,825	54,79,786
1751	23,740	17,80,500	66,47,095
1752	17,615	13,21,125	49,32,221
1753	18,053	13,53,975	50,54,840
1754	15,249	11,43,675	42,69,594
1755	12,269	9,20,175	34,35,310
1756	7,635	5,72,625	21,37,762
1757	21,347	16,01,025	59,77,045
1758	18,192	13,64,400	50,93,634

After this table there is a note which runs as follows:

"The above account includes only the Trade on which Duties were really paid to the pachotra Daroga [Royal Customs House] but besides this there was formerly carried on a very considerable trade in these articles by Juggutseats House and others who had interest with the Nizamat for these goods to pass Duty free.... The above is the trade of Natives only on which Duties have been paid."

[Source: Bengal Public Consultations, Range 1, vol. 44, Consult. 19 June 1769, IOR. The figures in the Table are rounded off to the nearest digit.]

After all this, there could be little doubt that the Asians had a predominant position in Bengal's silk trade and even in the mid-eighteenth century their exports of raw silk from Bengal by far surpassed those of the European companies. The supremacy of the Asian merchants is also confirmed by one Sadananda

Bandopadhyay who was the *gomasta* of a Gujarati merchant in Kasimbazar and was himself in silk business for thirty years, who stated, referring to the 1750s in all probability, that there were ten merchants in Murshidabad who exported Bengal raw silk to the tune of 13,000 to 20,000 maunds annually.[118] It was Louis Taillefert, the Dutch Director in Bengal, who clearly pointed out in 1763 that the procurement of raw silk by the *gomastas* of traders from Lahore and Multan had gone up to a great extent since the beginning of the eighteenth century.[119] That there was an incessant flow of large caravans from different parts of India and Asia to Bengal mainly for its textiles and raw silk in the pre-Plassey period is attested in unequivocal terms by responsible Company officials like Harry Verelst, William Bolts and Luke Scrafton.[120]

But this predominant position of the Asian merchants was subverted systematically by the English Company and its servants in the post-Plassey period, as a result of which there was a precipitate decline in the trade of the Asian merchants in the second half of the eighteenth century.

TABLE 8.8

Comparative Position of Asian and European Silk Exports (Average Volume and Value), 1749-58

Years	Asian Exports		European Exports	
	Quantity (lbs.)	Value (Rs)	Quantity (lbs.)	Value (Rs)
1749-53	1.5 million	5.5. million	—	—
1749-58	—	—	0.26 million	0.98 million
1754-58	1.1 million	4.1 million	—	—

(Source: Asian Exports computed from Table 8.7 and European Exports from Tables 8.2 & 8.3)

[118] Proceedings of the Board of Trade, 13 March 1791, quoted in N.K. Sinha, *Economic History of Bengal*, vol. I, pp. 111-112.

[119] Taillefert's 'Memorie', HR, 246, f. 141, 17 Nov. 1763.

[120] See chapter 7.

Figure 8.1

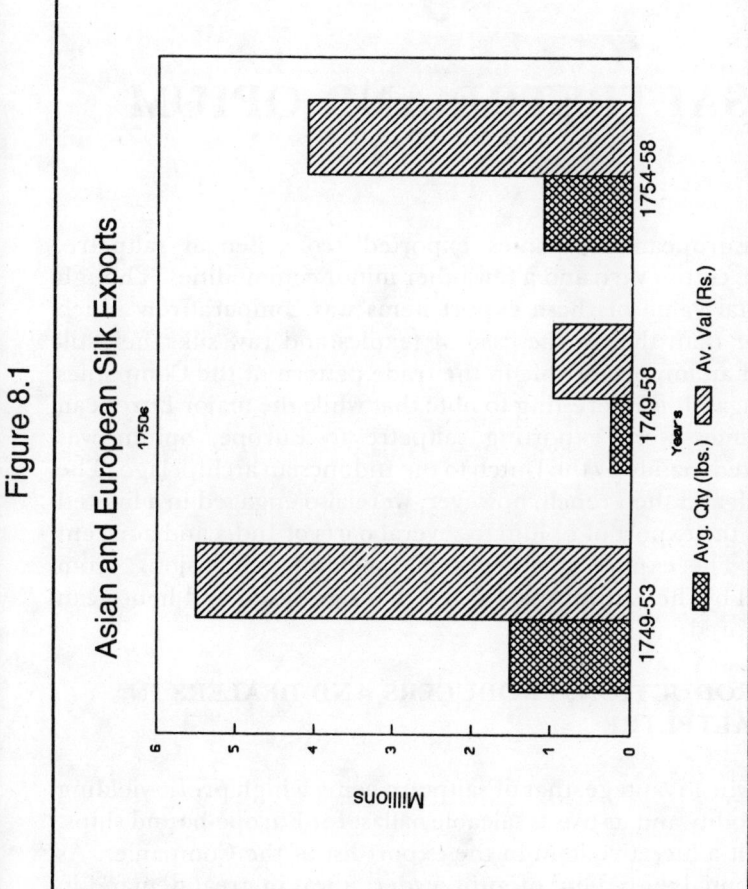

Table 8.8   Table 8.8   **Table 8.8**   Table 8.8   Table 8.8

9

SALTPETRE AND OPIUM

The European companies exported from Bengal saltpetre, opium, cotton yarn and a few other minor commodities. Though the total value of these export items was comparatively much smaller than that in the case of textiles and raw silk, they still played an important role in the trade pattern of the Companies in Bengal. It is interesting to note that while the major European companies were exporting saltpetre to Europe, opium was exported mainly by the Dutch to the Indonesian archipelago. The English and the French, however, were also engaged in a limited way in the export of opium to several parts of India and adjacent areas. The export of other items, including provisions, from Bengal by the Europeans was not that significant and hence can be ignored.

9.1 PRODUCTION, PRODUCERS AND DEALERS IN SALTPETRE

The twin advantage, that of saltpetre being a high profit-yielding commodity and its use as saleable ballast for Europe-bound ships, made it a lucrative item in the export list of the Companies. As an essential ingredient of gunpowder, it was in great demand in Europe even in the first half of the eighteenth century, though this fluctuated periodically depending on the prospects of war and peace in Europe. The trade in saltpetre had the added attraction that it could be used to ballast home-bound ships of the Companies which otherwise had to take the uneconomic method of using iron as ballast. As such, all the European companies took particular care to export saltpetre to Europe throughout the period under review.

Saltpetre was produced mainly in Bihar, especially in the region around Patna where it was available in abundance. The most important centres of production as also of collection of saltpetre in Bihar were Singia, Chapra and Mouw. The saltpetre produced in these areas was generally known as Bihar or Patna saltpetre which was considered the best in quality for the manufacture of gunpowder. Saltpetre was also produced in Bhagalpur and Purnea districts of Bihar, and some parts of North Bengal but these varieties were of a much inferior quality and produced in much smaller quantity.[1] According to a Dutch report of 1688, the total amount of saltpetre produced in the 28 *parganas* of Bihar amounted to 226,200 maunds which, when refined, stood at 127,238 maunds. Of this, 11,200 maunds were consumed in the province while the rest amounting to 105,238 maunds were left for export.[2] It seems that the total annual output was maintained at the same level throughout the first half of the eighteenth century. In his 'memorie' both in 1755 and 1763, Taillefert estimated that the annual production of saltpetre was between 120,000 and 140,000 maunds, of which the Dutch exported around 60,000 maunds a year during this period.[3]

Generally there were three varieties of saltpetre in Bengal — the refined one called *kalmi* or *dobara-cabessa*, the twice boiled or *dobara* and the raw variety called *katcha*. The Companies exported mainly the refined variety from Bihar as the raw saltpetre could not be used for making gunpowder. The export of raw variety was also uneconomic as it increased the freight charges while customs duties remained the same for all the varieties.[4] In the second half of the seventeenth century, both the Dutch and the English Companies refined saltpetre in their own factories but it appears that in the first half of the eighteenth century they

[1] Alexander Hume's 'Memoir', 1730, Stadsarchief Antwerp, Generaal Indische Compagnie, 5769.

[2] Instructions by Adrian van Ommen and Heck, VOC, 1454, ff.748vo-749vo, HB, 30 June 1688.

[3] Louis Taillefert's 'Memorie', VOC, 2849, f.201, 27 Oct. 1755; HR 246, f.186, 17 Nov. 1763. The actual Dutch export to Europe was, however, about 47,000 mds. in the first quinquennial period of 1740-45 while in that of 1750-55, it was around 31,000 mds. (See Table 9.1). The lb. avoird. is converted into mds. at the rate of 72.5 lb. per md.)

[4] DB, vol. 95, f. 232.

abandoned the practice.[5]

Saltpetre was produced by a particular group of people called *luniahs* whom the Dutch called saltpetre 'ackerbouwers', and bought in small quantities from them by *paikars* or *assamies* ('voorkoopers' in Dutch records) who generally undertook the refining.[6] The *luniahs* paid a duty called 'attrophy' in English records to the administration which was often farmed by others. Occasionally, the Europeans also were involved in the farming of the duty. In 1719 the English Company servants, Browne and Barker, farmed a part of this tax together with an *assamy* named Shaikh Gholam Muhammed, and in his explanation to the President of Fort William Council, Barker stated that they did it for the 'protection of the assamies from any trouble from the government'.[7]

Of the main saltpetre production and trade centres, the two most important ones were Chapra and Singia. Chapra enjoyed a slight edge over Singia as will be apparent from the saltpetre contracts of the European companies in the 1720s and 1730s. Out of the total Dutch contract for 31,400 mds. of *dobarra-cabessa* in 1731, the share of Chapra was 13,400 mds., Singia 12,700 mds. and Mouw 5,300 mds.[8] The position was the same with the English who contracted for 18,580 mds. of saltpetre in Chapra in 1732.[9] But in the early 1750s, Singia supplied more saltpetre than Chapra as we find that out of the total of 30,000 mds. sent by the Dutch from Patna in 1751, Singia supplied 14,000 mds., Chapra 12,000 mds. and Mouw 4,000 mds.[10] It is interesting to note that there were quite a few Muslims among the saltpetre merchants who were so conspicuous by their absence in the textile or silk contracts of the major European companies. One comes across very rarely any Muslim merchant contracting for silk or

[5] VOC, 2783, pt. I, f. 261, HB, 31 Jan. 1751; for the refining by the Europeans, see S. Chaudhuri, *Trade and Commercial Organization,* pp. 162-63; Om Prakash, *Dutch Company,* pp. 112-13.

[6] Taillefert's 'Memorie', VOC, 2849, ff. 198vo-200vo, 27 Oct. 1755.

[7] BPC, vol. 4, ff. 156, 172, Consults. 9 Nov., 8 Dec. 1719.

[8] VOC, 2195, ff. 281-82, HB 10 March 1731.

[9] BPC, vol. 9, f. 199, 19 Nov. 1722

[10] VOC, 2783, pt. I, f. 261, HB 31 Jan. 1751. All lbs. converted into maunds at the rate of 72.5 lbs. = 1 maund, at which the calculations were made in Dutch records.

textiles with the Companies. In the saltpetre trade again, Muslim *assamies* were more to be found in Singia and Mouw than in Chapra. In the Dutch Company's contracts in the 1730s, out of 9 merchants only 1 was Muslim while in Singia, out of 10 *assamies*, as many as 3 were Muslims and in Mouw, 2 out of the 3 merchants were Muslims.[11] The English Company's contract for 34,438 mds. of saltpetre in 1720 included 6 Muslims out of the total of 22 merchants.[12] Some of these merchants were, as the Company records noted, quite substantial and powerful people. Hugh Barker, who was the chief of the English factory in Patna at the time, especially mentioned one Mier Ishaqullah who was also a prominent salt merchant as 'the most considerable merchant in the city and of great weight in the durbar'.[13]

The Companies realized that the cheapest and the best way to provide saltpetre was to buy the commodity in Patna and send it directly to Calcutta or Hughli. Though some quantity was always available in Hughli, it was often inadequate for the large fleet of European ships, of an inferior quality and much more expensive. In Patna the Companies had to pay advances to the *assamies* to ensure the supply of the required quantity for export. Alexander Hume, the chief of the Ostend Company, emphasized in 1730 that if saltpetre was not contracted for before the arrival of Europe-ships, there was every possibility that the return ships would invariably be delayed for lack of saltpetre, even if other cargoes had already been procured.[14] So throughout the period of our study, the main rivalry for the procurement of saltpetre was between the two major Companies namely, the Dutch and the English, and this often enhanced the price of the commodity. In 1725 the *assamies* of Chapra were formed into a 'Company' serving both the Dutch and the English in order to maintain a steady supply of saltpetre and not to bid up the prices by competition with each other. Though Hugh Barker claimed that the 'confederacy was formed by the assomies among themselves' and that it was 'the work of the assomies alone' in which he had

---

[11] VOC, 2195, ff. 281-82, HB, 10 March 1731.

[12] BPC, vol. 4, f. 199vo, Annex. to Consult., 24 March 1720.

[13] Ibid., vol. 9, f.204-04vo, 27 Dec. 1732; vol. 10, ff. 60-61vo, 7 June 1734.

[14] Hume's 'Memorie', Stadsarchief Antwerp, GIC 5769.

'no hand',[15] there is little doubt that the 'Company' was formed under the aegis of the English and the Dutch in Patna.

This 'Company' of the 14 Chapra merchants dealing in saltpetre was the first successful attempt to organize the merchants into joint stock which the English tried in vain in Bengal in the 1680s in line with the successful experiment in the Coromandel Coast.[16] So it would be interesting to have a close look at the agreement entered into by the *assamies* of Chapra in 1725 which runs as follows:[17]

> We fourteen assomies of the English Company ... do agree to unite ourselves for the joint purchasing of saltpetre, to divide what quantity shall be procured and each person to pay in such summes of money as shall become due from him in proportion to his Dividend of saltpetre. If any person of the confederacy shall have a dispute with the Dutch or their assomies, the expense of it shall be paid out of the Joint Stock and all the saltpetre provided shall be on the general account. Whatever have been bought of saltpetre since November last shall be brought into the confederacy and if any person shall pay in more money to the stock than his proportion, he shall be allowed for it 2 percent interest.

The formation of this 'Company' was quite a significant development in the commercial organization of the period since the Patna factors thus commented on the prospects of forming a joint stock of merchants there in the 1680s: 'We much doubt of bringing our old or new petremen to it, we knowing by experience, they are unwilling to trust their own brothers, much less to be securities for one another which makes us fear, the abler sort will not be brought to it.'[18]

The English Company regarded the formation of the joint stock of the *assamies* as very advantageous because this provided

---

[15] BPC, vol. 9, f. 204, 27 Dec. 1732.

[16] For details, see S. Chaudhuri, *Trade and Commercial Organization*, pp. 84-85; S. Arasaratnam, 'Indian Merchants and their Trading Methods (circa 1700)', *IESHR*, March 1966, vol. 3, no. 1, p. 86.

[17] BPC, vol. 9, ff. 250-50vo, Annex. to Consult. 1 Feb. 1733.

[18] Fact. Records, Hughli, vol. 10, ff. 165, 182-83, 185.

a flexible means of varying the quantity to be procured without
having to take into account the level of Dutch purchases all the
time. In 1728 when the Fort William Council asked Patna to stop
buying any more saltpetre as the orders from England decreased
considerably, the Patna factors wrote back that as 'at present their
assomies and those belonging to the Dutch are formed into a
Company', if they now desisted from employing these *assamies* as
usual, 'the Dutch would readily embrace such an advantage and
secure it as their orders for petre yearly are unlimited'. They
further pointed out that if they stopped buying saltpetre through
these *assamies*, it would be extremely difficult to procure large
amount at reasonable prices later. As such, they were permitted
to provide 10,000 mds. so that they could procure larger amount,
if and when necessary, through the *assamies*.[19] As a matter of fact,
the need for a huge quantity arose when the Court of Directors
ordered for a very large amount in 1731, and the Fort William
Council asked Patna to provide 40,000 mds. of saltpetre in 1731/
32.[20] But by that time it appears that the 'confederacy' had broken
up.

9.2 COMPANIES AND EXPORT OF SALTPETRE

Apart from the rivalries among the European companies which
became more pronounced in the 1740s and 1750s, one of the
major difficulties that they had to contend with was the
interference in the trade by people connected with the administration. As in the second half of the seventeenth century when
the saltpetre trade was often monopolized by the ruling elite,[21]
during this period a few persons connected with the *darbar* often
used to buy a certain amount of saltpetre which they would then
impose on the European companies at a considerable profit. One
such person who meddled with the saltpetre trade was Haji
Ahmed, the elder brother of Alivardi Khan, the Bengal nawab
from 1740 to 1756, and an important member of the triumvirate

---

[19] BPC, vol. 6, f. 640vo, 6 Sept. 1728; C&B. Abstr., vol. 3, f. 135,
para. 42, 2 Feb. 1729.

[20] BPC, vol. 8, f.457, 20 Sept. 1731.

[21] S. Chaudhuri, *Trade and Commercial Organization*, p. 166.

which ruled Bengal for most of Shujauddin's reign from 1729 to 1739. Haji or his agent would occasionally buy saltpetre in Patna at a cheaper rate and would then sell it to the Europeans at a higher price. The Companies even complained that sometimes there were orders from Murshidabad prohibiting the Europeans from purchasing saltpetre and ordering the *assamies* to deliver all the saltpetre to the nawab.[22] In 1736 the Patna factors reported that Ali Hasan Khan, the Patna nawab's son-in-law, bought about 8 or 9 thousand maunds of saltpetre which he was planning to send down to Hughli where he expected to sell it at a high premium.[23] Haji Ahmed was putting pressure on the English Company in 1737 to buy his saltpetre which was lying in Hughli. The Company ultimately bought the saltpetre on condition that he would not meddle in the trade in future.[24] However, there was no large scale attempt at monopolization of saltpetre trade during the period under review as was done by Mir Jumla, Shaista Khan and Prince Azim-us-Shan in the earlier period.

In order to obviate all these difficulties, the three major European companies — the English, the Dutch and the French — entered into an agreement in 1736 to buy saltpetre jointly and then distribute it among themselves. According to this agreement, the three Companies 'should expressly prohibit the servants of their several factories and all private traders, Indians or Inhabitants of their colonies to buy or cause to be bought directly or indirectly any parcell of saltpetre that came from Patna, Pournea or any aurung so high as Maulda of any person whatsoever Moor or Gentue, even if they offer it to sale at an underprice'. The agreement was not to be abrogated within the space of two years.[25] But only after a few years the agreement broke down, and the Dutch and the English were involved in a bitter conflict over the saltpetre trade in Patna in 1740.[26] The

---

[22] Fact. Records, Kasimbazar, vol. 5, 31 Jan. 1736.

[23] BPC, vol. 11, ff. 251vo-252, 17 July 1736.

[24] Ibid., vol. 12, ff. 226, 27 June 1737; f. 226 vo, 228vo-29, 4 Aug. 1737; f.251, 19 Sept. 1737; f. 272vo, 7 Oct. 1737; f. 278, 11 Oct. 1737; f. 229vo, 13 April 1738.

[25] Ibid., vol. 11, ff. 254-54vo, 22 July 1736.

[26] C&B. Abstr., vol. 4, f. 344, para. 86, 3 Jan. 1741; BPC, vol. 14, ff. 121vo-22, 24 March 1740.

difference was only patched up in 1743 when the three
Companies again entered into another agreement for the joint
purchase of saltpetre, of which the French was to receive 15 mds.
for every 100 mds. received by the Dutch and the English. But
this also broke down in 1745.[27] The English Company complained in 1743 that the Dutch had farmed an important *pargana*
called Bissera and despite remonstrances from the English
concerning the 'fatal consequences of such farming', the Dutch
persisted in their design. It also accused that the Dutch, by means
of one of their black servants, had farmed 17 *parganas* of *sarkar*
Sirang (Saran) on the Chapra side of the country.[28] The Dutch
and the French, on the other hand, alleged that the English were
trying to buy saltpetre through Umichand and his brother,
Deepchand, and that Umichand had sent money to Deepchand
in Patna for that purpose.[29] However, there was no more
agreement among the Companies for joint purchase of saltpetre
during the rest of the period under study.

It is hardly surprising that the lucrative trade in saltpetre for
which the Companies competed among themselves would draw
the world of high finance and politics into it. The Calcutta
merchant, Umichand, who played a significant role in Bengal
trade and politics in the 1740s and 1750s was the first to get
involved in saltpetre trade when in 1734 he was reported to have
given out advances for 3,000 mds. of saltpetre from Bhagalpur
for the French. He also sent his *gomasta*, Meerchand, to Munger
to buy saltpetre.[30] In the early 1740s, he was said to have farmed
17 *parganas* producing saltpetre. In collaboration with his
brother, Deepchand, and aided and abetted by the Armenian
merchant Khwaja Wazid, Umichand virtually monopolized the
saltpetre trade from around the mid-1740s. Through his influence at Murshidabad *darbar* and his close connection with Bihar
administration where he was mint master in 1741 (he actually
came from Patna and signed his name as Umichand Agarwal,

[27] Ibid., vol. 16, ff. 55-56, 58vo, 18 Feb. 1743; vol. 17, f. 462, 21 Jan.
1745.

[28] Ibid., vol. 16, ff. 55-56, 18 Feb. 1743.

[29] Fact. Records, Patna, vol. 2, 10 May 1745.

[30] BPC, vol. 10, f. 26vo, 7 March 1734; f. 68, 1 July 1734; f. 92vo,
15 July 1734.

resident of Azimabad i.e. Patna), he and his brother established a stranglehold on saltpetre trade of Bihar.[31] In 1745, Deepchand received from nawab Alivardi Khan the *faujdari* of *sarkar* Saran, 'the principal place in the country for the produce of saltpetre'.[32] He had his saltpetre refineries (*karkhanas*) and warehouses at Saran, Chapra and Fatepur which clearly indicate the extent of his control over the saltpetre trade of Bihar in the late 1740s.[33] The Dutch chief at Patna, Drabbe, alleged in 1747 that Khwaja Wazid and Umichand were supplying money to Deepchand 'prompting him not to spare trouble nor cost to be master of all petre in Bihar' and that the latter had been granted by the nawab 'the farm of all the petre' in Bihar.[34] The English factors also reported in early 1748 that Deepchand had farmed 'the whole petre business' in Bihar.[35] Thus it appears that around 1747, the combination of Umichand at Calcutta, Khwaja Wazid at Hughli and Deepchand at Patna had managed to gain a virtual monopoly of the saltpetre trade, and could easily dictate their terms to the European companies which could ill afford to despatch their ships without saltpetre from Bengal.

Saltpetre was an extremely important commodity in the export list of the Companies. It is reflected in the fact that the Dutch Directors always made it a point to dwell on the situation in the saltpetre trade in Bihar. In his 'Memorie', Sichtermann emphasized in 1744 that the rise in the price of saltpetre was owing mainly to the competition between the English and the Dutch. He also pointed out that though advance payment was not required in earlier times when the European demand was comparatively small, but 'now because of the huge demand', it became essential for procuring a sufficient amount of saltpetre. But he was of the opinion that even paying advance did not

[31] Fact. Records, Patna, vol. 2, 3 April 1747; BPC, vol. 17, f. 664, 26 Aug. 1745; vol. 18, f. 458, 26 Nov. 1746; vol. 21, f. 142vo, 7 July 1748; C&B. Abstr., vol. 4, f. 376, 11 Dec. 1741.

[32] BPC, vol. 17, f. 572, 20 May 1745.

[33] Fact. Records, Patna, vol. 2, 31 March 1747.

[34] C&B. Abstr., vol. 5, f. 87, para. 68, 22 Feb. 1747; Beng. Letters Recd., vol. 21, f. 112, para. 68; ff. 264-65, para. 129; ff. 270-71, para. 143.

[35] BPC, vol. 21, f. 16vo, 4 March 1748.

reduce the price to any considerable extent as the difference was only from 1/8 to 1/4 of a rupee per maund.[36] Huijghens, the next Director, blamed the English for the failure of the 'confederacy' of the European nations for buying saltpetre jointly, and alleged that Deepchand, who was then the *faujdar* of Chapra, was trying to monopolize saltpetre trade and supplying the commodity to the English Company.[37] Jan Kerseboom wrote that in 1750 the Dutch were able to buy, at the instance of Jankiram, the *naib suba* of Bihar, more than 50,000 maunds of saltpetre from Deepchand at the reasonable price of Rs 3.5 per maund while in 1747 they had to buy 42,000 mds. which were sent by Deepchand to Khwaja Wazid at Hughli, whom the former authorized to sell it at the rate of Rs 6 per md. He also alleged that because of the 'intrigues' of Deepchand who had 'rented' most of the saltpetre producing districts, the Dutch could not buy the commodity from the open market and were compelled to buy it from him. The Dutch, however, tried to keep Deepchand out of the trade by paying Rs 45,000 to Haji Ahmed but not with much success.[38]

The interesting change in the scenario of saltpetre trade was the emergence of the Armenian merchant Khwaja Wazid with the monopoly right in the trade of the commodity around 1753. It appears that Wazid received the exclusive right of saltpetre trade from the Murshidabad court in 1753. Jan Kerseboom reported, almost in utter despair, that the trade in saltpetre 'had fallen entirely in his [Wazid's] hands and under his control' and that the Dutch 'did not have courage to oppose it'.[39] Wazid managed the saltpetre trade through his agent Mir Afzal and his brother Khwaja Ashraf, both of whom were stationed in Bihar.

---

[36] Sichtermann's 'Memorie', VOC, 2629, ff. 931-43, 14 March 1744.

[37] Huijghens 'Memorie', VOC, 2763, ff. 455-56, 20 March 1750.

[38] Jan Kerseboom's 'Memorie', VOC 2849, ff. 103vo-106, 14 Feb. 1755. It has been wrongly stated by K.N. Chaudhuri that Wazid was the agent or *gomasta* of Deepchand. The word used in Dutch is 'gemagtigden' which literally means 'empowered one'. By this time, Wazid was too substantial and powerful a merchant to be a *gomasta* of Deepchand. It appears that there was a mutual agreement that Umichand and Deepchand would send the saltpetre to Wazid at Hughli where it could be sold at a higher price to the benefit of all three.

[39] Kerseboom's 'Memorie', VOC, 2849, f.105vo, 14 Feb. 1755.

Another Dutch Director, Bisdom, wrote that Wazid received the privilege by paying only Rs 25,000 to the nawab. He also stated that the Dutch tried, 'in imitation' of Khwaja Wazid, to farm some districts in Bihar which would yield an annual amount of 60,000 mds. but only in vain. The significant point is that despite the monopoly of Wazid, the Dutch were able to buy saltpetre from his agents at the very reasonable price of Rs 3.5 per maund even in 1756.[40] The combination of Umichand and Wazid was still active in saltpetre trade, for we find Umichand supplying saltpetre, which belonged to Wazid, to the English Company till 1758 when the Company appropriated to itself the monopoly right to trade in the commodity from the puppet nawab Mir Jafar.[41]

The Dutch Company had definite lead over the English in the export of saltpetre in the first two decades of the eighteenth century and maintained the same even in the early half of the 1730s. But the position changed in the first quinquennial period of the 1740s when the English exported a larger amount of saltpetre than the Dutch. In the early 1750s, however, the average annual export of both the Companies was almost equal, the Dutch having a slight edge over their rival. This will be clear from the Table below (Table 9.1) giving the quinquennial total and average annual volume of export by the Dutch and the English from 1730-1755.

It is interesting to note that the first five years of the 1740s was the peak period of saltpetre export for both the Companies and in the early 1750s the volume of export declined considerably for both. While the Dutch export declined by 35 per cent, for the English Company it was 45 per cent. However, so far as the value of the total Dutch exports from Bengal was concerned, the highest figures were achieved in the 1750s though the volume of saltpetre export was the lowest during these years. On the other hand, the value of the total English exports was the highest

[40] Bisdom's letter to Jacob Mossel, VOC, 2850, 10 Jan. 1756; Bisdom's 'Memorie', VOC, 2977, f. 801vo, 11 Nov. 1760.

[41] Taillefert's 'Memorie', HR 246, f. 174, 17 Nov. 1763; C&B. Abstr., vol. 5, f.423, 3 Sept. 1753; vol. 6, f. 88, 8 Dec. 1755; Beng. Letters Recd., vol. 23, f. 63, 8 Dec. 1755; BPC, vol. 28, ff. 400-400vo, 2 Feb. 1756; vol. 29, f. 99vo, 6 June 1757; NAI, Public General, Letter to Court, s. no. 5, p. 95, para. 34, 10 Jan. 1758.

Table 9.1

Quinquennial Total and Average Annual Volume of Saltpetre
Export: Dutch and English, 1730-55

Years	Dutch		English	
	Total (lb. avrd.)	Annual Average (lb. avrd.)	Total (lb. avrd.)	Annual Average (lb. avrd.)
1730/31- 1734/35	14,292,566	2,858,513	10,165,904	2,033,180
1740/41- 1744/45	17,042,214	3,408,443	20,747,216	4,049,443
1750/51- 1754/55	11,108,438	2,221,688	11,090,240	2,218,048

[Source and note: Dutch exports collected and computed from export invoices in VOC records. English exports computed from K.N. Chaudhuri, *Trading World*, p. 532 with one-year lag. The Dutch bought saltpetre in maund which, as they stated, was equivalent to 72.5 lb. and hence the lb. in Dutch invoices was almost equal to lb. avoirdupois, *cf.*, VOC, 2241, f. 718, HB 3 March 1732; 2261, f. 142, HB 12 Jan. 1747].

in the first quinquennial period of the 1740s and the lowest in the early 1750s. This is also reflected to some extent in the volume of their saltpetre export from Bengal. What all this means in analytical terms is that there was not always a co-relation between the total volume and value of the goods exported and the volume of saltpetre export from Bengal.[42] Though one of the main incentives for the export of saltpetre was the ballast requirements of the Europe-bound ships, the demand condition in Europe seems to have been a more important consideration in deciding the amount of the commodity to be exported.

[42] For the total value of the average annual export by the Dutch and English Company in the first quinquennial period from 1730-1755, see chapter 3.

9.3 PRODUCTION, BUYERS AND COMPETITION
IN OPIUM TRADE

Unlike saltpetre which was mainly exported to Europe by the
Companies, opium was a lucrative commodity in the intra-Asiatic
trade. Of the Companies again, it was the Dutch East India
Company which exported a substantial amount of opium to
Batavia, and it appears that the English or the French Company's
share in the trade was quite small in the early years. However, a
small amount of opium was exported on account of the English
and the French private traders. So the Dutch Company did not
face much competition from their European rivals in opium
trade as they did in the textile and silk market until the battle of
Plassey in 1757, after which the English tried to monopolize the
opium trade in Bengal. The Dutch first exported opium to
Malabar from the Malwa region, procured at Surat. But as the
price of this variety began to increase at an alarming rate, they
turned their attention to Bengal opium.[43] Though the Dutch
Company exported a large amount of opium from Bengal to
Malabar in the 1660s and 1670s, gradually it was the Indonesian
archipelago which became the biggest consumer of Bengal
opium. A Dutch estimate of 1683 put the annual demand in the
entire archipelago at around 116,000 Dutch ponds.[44]

In Bengal opium was produced mainly in Bihar, though
there is reference that it was also produced in Rangpur in North
Bengal. According to an estimate of 1688, 8,700 maunds of
opium were produced in 48 *parganas* of Bihar in a normal year,
of which about 5,400 mds. were of very good quality. Of the total
produce, about 10 to 12.5 per cent was consumed in Bengal and
Bihar, 34.5 to 46 per cent sent to Agra and Allahabad region, and
the remaining 41.5 to 55.5 per cent was exported to other
national and international markets. The Dutch export around
this time amounted to 1,000 mds.[45] The total production

[43] Om Prakash, *Dutch Company*, p. 145.

[44] Ibid., p. 153; for Dutch trade in opium in the 17th century, see
ibid., pp. 145-56.

[45] VOC, 1454, ff. 764vo-768vo, 30 June 1688; Om Prakash, *Dutch
Company*, pp. 57-58.

remained more or less the same in the first half of the eighteenth
century, though the Dutch export increased considerably by this
time. The Dutch Director Sichtermann stated in his 'Memorie'
in 1744 that if there was a good harvest, the total output would
be 4000 chests or 8,000 mds. of which 2 to 3,000 mds. were
bought by the Indian merchants and the rest, 5 to 6,000 mds.,
left to the Europeans, the Dutch order never exceeding 1,800
chests or 3,600 mds.[46] Towards the end of our period, Taillefert
also mentioned in 1755 that in a normal year the total production
of opium in Bihar amounted to 8,000 mds. which does not take
into account the output in Bhagalpur and Purnea. Of this amount
the distribution pattern was as follows:

TABLE 9.2
Total Production and Distribution of Bihar Opium, 1755

Indian Merchants bought:	2,000 maunds
Local Consumption (Bengal & Bihar):	1,000 maunds
English and French bought:	1,600 maunds
Dutch bought:	3,400 maunds
Total	8,000 maunds

[Source: Taillefert's 'Memorie', VOC, 2849, f. 196, 27 Oct. 1755]

The best quality opium, as Taillefert reported, was produced
in the districts of Arra, Munir (Munger?), Patna, Bihar and
Saran. The seeds were generally sown in October and November,
and in a good year the yield per *bigha* could amount to 11 to 12
pounds, which the opium growers made into 2 or 3 cakes. He also
stated that the opium produced in Bhagalpur and Purnea was of
a bad quality and could not be compared with the Bihar opium.[47]
In his instruction to the next Director, Sichtermann also advised
not to buy Bhagalpur or Purnea opium.[48] Later on, in his

[46] Sichtermann's 'Memorie', VOC, 2629, ff. 946-49, 14 March
1744.
[47] Taillefert's 'Memorie', VOC, 2849, f. 193, 27 Oct. 1755.
[48] Sichtermann's 'Memorie', VOC, 2629, f. 949, 14 March 1744.

'Memorie' of 1763, Taillefert made a further categorization of the opium produced in Bihar. The best quality opium which was known as Bihar opium was produced mainly in the districts of Bihar, Jahanabad, Futwari and Kashmar while the opium from Mogra, Barbigha, Saran, and Munir was also good but of a quality inferior to the so-called 'Bihar' opium.[49]

Though the Dutch were the main buyers of opium, it was difficult for them to control the supply market. The competition from other Europeans and Indian rivals often raised the price of opium in Patna. There was also the occasional attempt by big Indian merchants, especially those active in Bihar trade, to monopolize the opium trade. The English Company reported as early as 1731 that the Calcutta merchant Umichand tried to monopolize the trade of the commodity through an 'unlawful grant' from the *faujdar* of Rangpur.[50] But it was the Armenian merchant Khwaja Wazid of Hughli who virtually controlled the opium trade in Bihar from at least the late 1740s. He managed his opium business, like his saltpetre trade in the early 1750s, through his agent Mir Afzal and his brother Khwaja Ashraf who were operating in Bihar. The Dutch Director Huijghens reported in 1750 that the Company could procure only 1,479 mds. of opium at Rs 115 per md. through a bribe of Rs 1,000 to the Bihar administration which prevented Khwaja Ashraf from collecting all the opium he had contracted for by December the year before. Wazid showed his displeasure over the incident by insisting on payment by the Dutch in Patna against a bill for Rs 25,000.[51]

The main difficulty of the Dutch in opium procurement was the shortage of liquid capital. Huijghens emphasized in his 'Memorie' the need for ready cash for buying opium because it was not possible to buy it on credit due to the keen competition in Patna. Sometimes the situation was quite bad for the Company. In January 1750 the Dutch got hold of 900 mds. of opium but were required to pay for it in cash. Though the Company servants got permission to draw bills of exchange for Rs 200,000

[49] Louis Taillefert's 'Memorie', HR 246, ff. 158-59, 17 Nov. 1763.
[50] BPC, vol. 8, ff. 400-400vo, 21 June 1731.
[51] Huijghen's 'Memorie , VOC, 2763, f. 458, 20 March 1750; VOC, 2732, f. 9vo, HB, 11 Feb. 750; f. 79, 27 Jan. 1750.

in the name of the Company in Hughli, they could only collect Rs 20,000. So the Company made a request to the house of Jagat Seth for two bills of exchange for Rs 100,000 and Rs 25,000 each payable in Patna after 41 days at the rate ['agio'] of 3 $1/_4$ per cent.[52] The Dutch generally entered into contract with the *paikars* who were given an advance for buying opium. But Sichtermann reported in 1744 that the practice was abandoned because of the 'bankruptcy' of the *paikars* who would generally tend to deliver opium when it was not properly dried. So the Company had to take the extra trouble of drying the commodity. From then onward, it appears that the Dutch bought opium against ready money from the dealers in the market.[53]

The competition from Indian merchants and other European rivals often raised the price of opium and stood in the way of procurement of the full amount specified in the Dutch order from Bengal. In 1741 the Dutch reported that they could collect only 1,6000 mds. of opium which was only 2/3 of the amount ordered for that year. The main reason, according to the factors, was the purchase by the Marwari and other Indian merchants which raised the price to about Rs 124 per maund. But next year when the Marwari merchants and the English were not that active in the opium market, the price came down by 9 to 10 per cent.[54] In 1744 Sichtermann reported that the Dutch could buy the previous year 2,600 mds. of opium for the price of 2,000 mds. which was the amount ordered, by waiting for the price to come down and then buying in the open market. He suggested that the best way to beat down the price was not to let the dealers know the amount the Dutch required. If they came to know that, they would artificially manipulate the price. The English and the French, according to Sichtermann, exported Bengal opium to Coromandel, Malabar, Surat and Malacca. The Dutch tried to stop their trade but to no avail.[55] The comparative position of the

[52] VOC, 2732, ff. 78-79, HB, 27 Jan. 1750.
[53] Sichtermann's 'Memorie', VOC, 2629, ff. 948-49, 14 March 1744.
[54] VOC, 2518, f. 166vo, HB, 26 Nov. 1741; 2556, ff. 167-69, HB, 16 Dec. 1742.
[55] Sichtermann's 'Memorie', VOC, 2629, ff. 946-47, 14 March 1744.

different buyers in the opium trade can be gauged from a Dutch
report of 1747 which outlined the share of different rivals in the
five years from 1741 to 1745.[56]

TABLE 9.3
Total Opium Production and Share of Different Buyers
[in Maunds]
1741-45

Year	Total Production	Dutch	English & French	Indian Merchants
1741	4,280	1,600	1,725	955
1742	4,796	3,200	846	750
1743	4,516	2,600	1,316	600
1744	4,669	1,600	1,000	1,869
1745	3,380	1,210	240	720

[Source: VOC 2661, ff. 143-144, HB 12 Jan. 1747]

9.4 DUTCH EXPORT OF OPIUM

Unlike most commodities in the Dutch export from Bengal, the
export of opium shows a secular upward trend from the early
1730s to the early 1750s, though rising very slowly but steadily.
While the average annual export in the first five years of the
1730s amounted to 148,003 lbs. or 2041 mds., it was 156,774 lbs.
or 2,162 mds. in the first quinquennial period of the 1740s, rising
to 192,782 lbs. or 2,659 mds. in the early 1750s.

[56] The amount is given in 'Kisten' (chests) in the report, each 'kisten'
weighing 2 mds., c.f., VOC, 2165, Pt. II, f. 84, HB, 30 Nov. 1730; 2829,
f. 65vo, HB, 31 Aug. 1754.

TABLE 9.4
Dutch Opium Export to Batavia
Quinquennial Total and Annual Average
1730-55

Years	Total (lb.)	Average (lb.)	Average (md.)
1730/31-1734/35	740,015	148,003	2,041
1740/41-1744/45	783,870	156,774	2,162
1750/51-1754/55	963,911	192,782	2,659

[Source: Collected and computed from export invoices in VOC records]

What emerges from Table 9.4 is quite interesting because while the intra-Asiatic trade of the Dutch Company in general and to Batavia in particular was marked by a gradual decline throughout the period from 1730-55,[57] the trade in opium to Batavia was steadily increasing during the same period. This only indicates that opium was a high profit-yielding commodity in the intra-Asiatic trade—the reason why the English Company and its servants monopolized the opium trade after the Plassey revolution. The Dutch Director Taillefert described in 1763 how the British were eliminating the Indian and other European merchants from the opium trade and the manner in which they were forcing the producers and dealers to sell opium to them at a very low price.[58]

[57] For the value of the Dutch intra-Asiatic trade from Bengal to different parts of Asia in the first quinquennial period from 1730-55, see chapter 3.

[58] Taillefert's 'Memorie", HR 246, ff.163-67, 17 Nov. 1763.

10

PRICE TRENDS

There has been complete unanimity among historians that prices of commodities in Bengal from 1720 to 1760, especially from the early 1740s, show 'a fairly sustained and marked increase' which was 'particularly strong for raw silk and Bengal textiles' as also for rice.[1] With the help of such sophisticated devices as 'weighted moving-average' of price series, histogram and, polynomial and linear trend of prices of several commodities, these authorities conclude that 'the general synchronic trends are clearly visible' and that there was a gradual rise in prices over the period as a whole.[2] But the general emphasis so far has been on the 'sharp increase' in prices from around the 1740s. The significant point to note is that the 'secular upward' trend in the movement of prices is linked to the 'phenomenal increase' in the European export trade from Bengal and the consequent influx of bullion into the country. Along with this, as the authorities hold, the contributory factors for the rise in prices during the period were the Maratha invasions which seriously disrupted the economy, and the keen competition among the European companies for the export commodities.

---

[1] For example, see K.K. Datta, *Bengal Suba,* pp.463-69; Brijen K. Gupta, *Sirajuddaullah,* p.33; K.N. Chaudhuri, *Trading World,* pp. 99-108; P. J. Marshall, *East Indian Fortunes,* p. 35; *Bengal,* pp. 73,142-43, 163-64, 170.

[2] K.N. Chaudhuri, *Trading World,* pp. 99-108, 159.

10.1 'MARKED AND SUSTAINED' INCREASE?

It is clear from the above that for the supposed upward trend in price movement, a lot of emphasis has been put on the European trade which brought in its train bullion into the province. It has been stated clearly that the 'foreign demand for export goods, which were all paid in cash, stimulated domestic demand for food grain and other consumer products' which ' in its turn could have exerted some pressure on prices'.[3] There is no denying the fact that there was a significant increase in European trade and a consequent inflow of bullion in the first half of the eighteenth century. It is also probable that as a result of this, there was an expansion in the economic activity of Bengal and increase in money supply. But the extent of the impact of these on the overall economy and the price movements over the period are yet to be determined precisely. Moreover, as we have argued earlier,[4] even in the mid-eighteenth century, the European trade was not the most important factor in the commercial life of Bengal; the volume of the export trade carried on by the Asian merchants from Bengal was much larger than that of the Europeans. The Europeans were not the only importers of bullion and for that matter, not even the largest at that. The Maratha incursions, no doubt, resulted in dislocation in the economy but it was not so serious as it was mainly local in character and only a temporary phenomenon. The competition among the European traders as also among the European and Asian merchants was certainly there but this need not be overemphasized.

Even taking for granted for the sake of argument that the price of export goods such as textiles and raw silk registered a rise over the period under review, it may be argued, as has been done by a recent authority, that 'such a sectoral rise might only reflect a failure of the supply of these goods to increase as fast as the demand for them, and may not necessarily indicate a general price rise in the economy'.[5] In order to prove the latter, we have to look for movements in the price of the so-called wage-goods. The most important among these are staple food items

[3] Ibid., p.108.
[4] See chapter 7.
[5] Om Prakash, *Dutch Company*, p. 250.

like rice and wheat. But at the present state of our knowledge, such an exercise is fraught with the danger of a wide margin of error because of the lack of precise information in the face of numerous varieties of staple food items, especially rice. One suspects that such an attempt might only lead to extremely erratic behaviour of the prices of provisions, as has been demonstrated in a recent study of Bengal prices on similar lines for the period 1650-1720.[6] Further, the explanation based on the quantity theory of money that the increasing European demand for export commodities which were paid in cash enhanced the demand for staple food like rice and other consumer goods has recently been subjected to doubt. A recent authority explains the phenomenon in a different way.[7] Though the extent of increase in the velocity of money circulation as a result of European trade cannot be precisely determined, the increasing European trade implied that the 'monetized transactions as a proportion of total transactions in the economy would have gone up'. Besides, over the period of more than 35 years from 1720 to 1757, 'natural increase in population would have necessitated a secular rise in output and transaction if the per capita output and availability were not to go down'. All these factors, it has been pointed out, would gravitate towards checking a general rise in prices which could have been the result of an increase in the supply of money following the influx of bullion connected with the European trade.[8]

10.2 PRICE OF TEXTILES

Be that as it may, as pointed out earlier, we should look into the prices of major food grains, especially rice, the staple food of Bengal, to determine whether there was any sharp rise in prices in general over the period, not the prices of major export commodities like textiles and raw silk where the great demand for such goods on the part of Asian merchants and Europeans

[6] Ibid., pp. 251-53. K.N. Chaudhuri, however, shows with histogram a steady increase in the price of rice during the period under review.

[7] Ibid., 253.

[8] The whole question is discussed in details by Om Prakash, pp. 253-256.

might have resulted in such a rise. But as even the latest studies emphasize this aspect to prove a general rise in prices and as 'evidence of a sustained and marked increase in prices',[9] let us examine how far and if at all, the prices of these commodities show a secular upward trend during the period under review. One has to take into account here that even earlier authorities pointed out a 'sharp increase' in the prices of textiles and raw silk, and asserted that between 1738 and 1754, prices of these goods increased by no less than 30 per cent.[10] The latest study on the period, quoting earlier authorities, also came to the same conclusion.[11]

The main and the only basis of the above conclusion by earlier authorities regarding the steep rise in the price of textiles is a complete misreading (and out of context too) of an entry in the Bengal Public Consultations under December 1752.[12] The particular Consultation refers to a letter of 4 December 1752 from Dhaka wherein the Dhaka factors were trying to answer the allegations from Calcutta regarding the bad quality of textiles sent by them, pointing out that the sample of 1738 was not 'fit standard for judging' the quality of cloth sent from Dhaka in the previous year. The reasons for the inferiority of the quality of cloth, as the Dhaka factors wrote, were:[13]

> ... as the Copass [kapas—cotton] or country cotton has not been for *the two years past* under 9 or 10 rupees and the price of rice at the same time very dear, whereas in 1738 the Coppas did not exceed Rs. 2 or Rs. 2-8 and the rice very cheap, mostly 2 maunds 20 seers to 3 maunds for a rupee to which may be added which is well known to all the purchasers

---

[9] K.N. Chaudhuri, *Trading World*, p. 102; following him, P.J. Marshall, *Bengal*, p. 73. Chaudhuri depends on polynomial and linear trend of textile and silk prices (pp. 103-4, 107-8) which shows a 'strong and gradual' rise in prices but as we shall see the method followed is susceptible to wide margin of error.

[10] K.K. Datta, *Bengal Suba*, p. 464; Brijen K. Gupta, *Sirajuddaullah*, p. 33.

[11] P.J. Marshall, *East Indian Fortunes*, p. 35; *Bengal*, p. 73.

[12] BPC, vol. 26, f. 214, Consult. 11 Dec. 1752; *Bengal and Madras Papers*, vol. II, p. 34; James Long, *Unpublished Records*, p. 40, doc. no. 103.

[13] All emphasis mine.

of cloth that the prices of all sorts of cloths have risen *near 30 per cent*, some more, since the year 1738, and that they now labour there and has done so *for these two years past* under the inconvenience of a French factory continually emulating the Hon'ble Company's trade and have advanced the price of all cloth both coarse and fine and obliged them to be less severe with their dellols in prizing their cloth....

It is amply clear from the above that this is a desperate bid on the part of the Dhaka factors—scrupulousness not being their strong point, something that was true also of other Company servants working in India at that time—to justify the inferiority of cloth and hence the emphasis on 30 per cent increase in the price of cloth between 1738 and 1752. As the 'muster' (sample) of 1738 had been the standard, 1738 became the year of reference—for no other reason. Moreover, if one carefully examines the above passage, one could seldom miss the stress on 'these two years past' which signifies that the quality of cloth sent by them deteriorated mostly in those two years and not really for the whole of the period from 1738 to 1752. There is the specific reference to 'near 30 per cent' increase in the price of cloth during the period but, if at all true, that applies to Dhaka only, and could hardly be taken as an evidence of a general phenomenon of price increase throughout Bengal. Besides, one can rightly suspect the validity of the evidence which was produced in self defence in the face of the allegation of malpractice. One who has gone through the Company records carefully can hardly fail to observe that throughout the period, whenever an allegation was made regarding 'badness' of investments, the factors always answered in the same vein—that it was because of the high price of staples like rice and cotton, competition from other Asian and/or European merchants, and the general increase in the price of export commodities. One should accept such 'evidence' or 'excuses' with due caution.

Still the fact remains that a distinguished authority has demonstrated with diagrams, polynomial and linear trends as also time series that 'a fairly sustained and marked increase [in prices] is particularly strong for raw silk and textiles' during the period under review.[14] How can one reconcile this with the fact, as we shall see shortly, that the increase in prices of these two main export commodities was hardly so spectacular as has been presumed to be? The answer is not far to seek. The weighted average, diagrams, polynomial and linear trends etc., so well illustrated by the said scholar, do not however take into account the most crucial factors which determined the price of either textiles or raw silk. There were numerous varieties of textiles and even within the same category (e.g. muslins or fine calicoes), there were different types (e.g. in muslin, there were *khasas*, *mulmuls* etc.) and the price of each type (e.g. *khasa*) depended on several factors such as the size, quality, the *aurung* in which it was produced, etc. which will be evident from the following table.

TABLE 10.1
Dutch Company's Contract with Merchants for Textiles,
24 June 1752

Name of Piece-goods	No.of Pieces	length (co.) x breadth (co.)	Price per Piece (Rs.Ans.)
Khasa	3000	40 x 3	14:11
"	840	40 x 2 3/8	12:11
" Jagannatpur	6000	40 x 2 1/4	10:13
" Hendial with gold head	2000	40 x 2 1/4	11:6
" Jagannatpur	2000	40 x 2	9:8
" Hendial	2000	40 x 2	9:8
" Jagannatpur	2960	40 x 1 4/5	8:7
" "	1200	40 x 1 1/2	7:6
" fine Hendial with gold head	500	40 x 3	18:15
" " " "	1500	40 x 2 1/4	14:3
" Nadona	1000	40 x 2 1/4	7:2
" "	2000	25 x 2 1/4	4:6
" Bourang	4000	38 x 1 7/8	6:10

(contd.)

[14] K.N. Chaudhuri, *Trading World*, pp. 100-108, 533-34, 544-45.

Table 10.1 (contd.)

Name of Piece-goods	No.of Pieces	length (co.) x breadth (co.)	Price per Piece (Rs.Ans.)
Mulmul fine	200	40 x 3	17:10
" "	300	40 x 2 1/4	13:11
" " Haripal	100	40 x 2 1/4	12:4
" " "	350	40 x 1 3/4	10:4
" " "	50	40 x 1 1/2	8:13
Mulmul (assorted)	1000	40 x 3	14:11
"	400	40 x 2 5/8	12:11
"	4500	40 x 2 1/4	10:12
"	500	40 x 1 3/4	8:7
"	1200	40 x 2	9:8
"	400	40 x 1 1/2	6:12
Mulmul Ordinary	4000	40 x 2·1/4	7:6
" "	1200	40 x 2	6:12

[Source : VOC 2821, HB, 20 Feb.1753, ff. 91-95, Contract. dt. 24 June 1752]

The same was the case with raw silk, the price of which depended on the particular variety (e.g. 'Gujarat', 'Kumarkhali' etc.), fineness and racolta (*band*—Indian term for the harvest).[15] If all these factors are not taken into consideration in minute details while working out the cost price, the results are bound to be misleading. Just by deflating the total cost price by the total quantity exported to find out per unit cost price does not reveal the real picture as has happened in this case.[16] Hence even with such scientific tools of analysis used by K.N. Chaudhuri, the results—showing a secular upward trend—can hardly be taken for granted.

[15] See chapter 8.
[16] K.N. Chaudhuri, *Trading World*, pp. 506, 546.

For any precise study of the movement of textile prices, one has to take into account very meticulously the number pieces of a particular type of cloth exported, their length and width, the *aurung* where they were produced and their prices. From that only one can get the exact picture of the price movement. To give an illustration, if we are looking into the price of *khasa*, just taking into account the total number of pieces of *khasas* exported and their total price to find out the unit price of *khasa* could be quite erroneous. We have to know whether the *khasa* was ordinary, fine or superfine (i.e. the quality), whether its measurement was 40 co. x 3 co.[17] or 40 co. x 2 3/4 co. or 40 co. x 2 1/2 co. etc. (i.e. its actual size), whether it was produced in Jagannatpur or Cogmaria or Orrua (i.e. the *aurung* in which it was produced) etc. Because the price of *khasa* will depend on all these factors and hence we have to take all these variables into consideration. This is almost an impossible task as in all the export invoices, whether of the Dutch or the English Company, what we get is the total number of *khasas* exported with their total cost price without any indication whatsoever about their size, quality or *aurung*. Again, if the unit price of the textiles in a particular year is arrived at just by dividing the total cost price by the total number of pieces exported by the Companies, without taking into account the composition of different categories such as muslins, fine calicoes, ordinary calicoes etc. which varied over the period, then the picture of price movement could be very much distorted. Thus the steady upward trend in K.N. Chaudhuri's time series can be explained by the fact that while the share of the more expensive category of textiles, muslins, (as also silk piece-goods) steadily increased in the first quinquennial period of 1740s and 1750s, that of the cheapest variety, ordinary calicoes, remained the same during this period, [18] and not because of any real increase in the price of textiles. That the unit price of textiles could vary widely depending on the category of textiles and place of procurement is amply clear from the unit price of the textiles exported by the Dutch Company in 1753/54 for which such break-up is available. Thus,the unit price of textiles sent from Patna, mostly ordinary calicoes, worked out to be *f* 6.13 and from Dhaka, mostly muslins

[17] co. is covido, measuring 18 inches.
[18] See chapter 7, Table 7.7 and Figure 7.4.

and fine calicoes, *f* 20.04, from Hughli, mostly medium quality, *f* 9.56 and from Kasimbazar, silk piece-goods and ordinary calicoes, *f* 7.85.[19]

The only evidence from which we can get an exact picture of the price movement in textiles is the contract the Companies entered into with the *dadni* merchants for supply of goods every year. In these contracts we find the particular details of the size, quality and the *aurung* of each type of cloth, which are absolutely essential for a proper scrutiny of the movement of price of textiles. Until and unless we know these details of the variables, nothing definitive can be said about price movement. As is well known, the prices were arrived at after days of bargaining and wrangling between the Company and the merchants. Though the Companies sometimes tried to pay lower prices for cloth delivered by the merchants, it was mainly on the ground of inferior quality supplied than agreed for in the contract, and the original contract price was never altered. So let us see the general trends as revealed in these contracts over the period for which we select six years namely, 1732, 1741, 1744, 1751, 1752 and 1754. These particular years are chosen for such an analysis for the following reasons : 1732 was a normal year without any political disturbance or natural calamity; 1741 was the year just prior to the Maratha invasions; 1744 was the year when the impact of these incursions which began in 1742 could naturally be expected to be reflected in the price movement. The Maratha invasions stopped in 1751 and 1752 was the year immediately after the peace with the Marathas while 1754 was the normal year after the famine of 1752. As such these years would give us a broad spectrum of the period with its ups and downs, whether political or economic. For our present analysis, we first take up the Dutch contracts for these six years and see how the prices of the two main types of muslins—*khasas* and *mulmuls* which were the staples in the export list of the Europeans—moved (Table 10.2).[20]

[19] Collected and computed from export invoices in VOC records, VOC, 2811, ff, 6vo-7, 20-20vo, 46-46vo, 99-99vo; 2821, ff.635-36; 2840, ff.39, 441-42.

[20] For the wide variation in the price of the same type of textiles, e.g., *khasa* and *mulmul*, depending on size, quality and *aurung*, see, Table 10.1.

TABLE 10.2

Contract Prices of *Khasas* and *Mulmuls*
1732—1754 (Select Years), Dutch Company

Textile Type	Measure (covid)	1732 Price Rs.As	1741 Price Rs.As	1744 Price Rs.As	1751 Price Rs.As	1752 Price Rs.As	1754 Price Rs.As
Khasa Ordn.	40 x 3	15.00	15.00	15.00	14.11	14.11	14.11
" fine	" · "	18.00	x	x	x	x	x
" ordn.	40 x 2 $^5/_8$	13.00	13.00	13.00	12.11	12.11	12.11
" "	40 x 2 $^1/_2$	11.00	11.00	11.00	x	10.13	10.13
" "	40 x 2 $^1/_4$	x	x	x	10.13	x	x
" "	40 x 2	9.12	8.00	9.12	9.8	9.8	9.8
" "	40 x 1 $^3/_4$	8.10	7.00	8.10	8.7	8.7	8.7
" "	40 x 1 $^1/_2$	7.8	x	7.8	7.6	7.6	7.6
" Nadona	25 x 2 $^1/_4$	3.14	3.14	3.14	4.6	4.6	4.6
Mulmul ordn.	40 x 3	15.00	15.00	15.00	x	x	14.11
" fine	40 x 3	18.00	18.00	x	17.10	17.10	17.10
" ordn.	40 x 2 $^5/_8$	13.00	13.00	13.00	12.11	12.11	x
" "	40 x 2 $^1/_4$	11.00	11.00	11.00	10.12	10.12	10.12
" fine	40 x 2 $^1/_4$	14.00	14.00	14.00	13.11	13.11	13.11
" ordn.	40 x 2	9.12	9.12	9.12	9.8	9.8	9.8
" "	40 x 1 $^3/_4$	8.10	8.10	8.10	8.7	8.7	x
" "	40 x 1 $^3/_4$	10.8	x	x	10.4	10.4	10.5
" ordn.	40 x 1 $^1/_2$	x	7.00	7.00	x	6.14	6.14
" fine	40 x 1 $^1/_2$	x	9.00	x	8.13	8.13	8.13
" ordn.	40 x 1 $^1/_4$	7	x	x	6.14	x	x

[Source: Contracts with Merchants, VOC 2241, ff. 649-661; VOC 2537, ff. 1427-28; VOC 2629, f. 218; VOC 2783, ff. 236-37; VOC 2821, ff. 91-95; VOC 2840, ff. 715-16]

It is quite evident from the above Table 10.2, that between 1734 and 1754, there was absolutely no increase in the prices of the 20 different types of *khasas* and *mulmuls* that were noted in the list of contract, except for *khasa* Nadona which seems to be, from its price, a medium or low quality *khasa*. What is extremely significant, as is apparent from this Table, is that the price of all the different *khasas* and *mulmuls*, except *khasa* Nadona, actually went down in the period 1751-54 from the level between 1732 and 1744. In other words, the prices of *khasas* and *mulmuls* in the period from 1732-1754 will negate the thesis of a 'fairly marked and sustained' increase in the prices of textiles in general during the period. But one might argue that *khasas* and *mulmuls* were finer varieties of calicoes, and perhaps the price rise was reflected in not-so-fine and medium types of textiles. So let us see how the prices of these varieties of textiles moved during the years under consideration. In Table 10.3 we note the contract prices for several types of textiles coarser than muslins and which were prominent in the export list of the Dutch Company.

TABLE 10.3
Contract Prices of Coarser Textiles
1732-1754 (Select Years), Dutch Company

Textile Type	Measure (in *covid*)	1732 Price Rs.As	1741 Price Rs.As	1744 Price Rs.As	1751 Price Rs.As	1752 Price Rs.As	1754 Price Rs.As
Sanoes	24 x 2	4.8	4.8	4.8	4.15	4.15	4.15
Kharadaries	18 x 2 1/4	4.00	4.00	4.00	4.3	4.8	4.8
Aliabanies	24 x 3	4.12	4.12	x	5.7	5.12	5.12
Ginghams (plain)	18 x 2 1/4	3.8	3.8	3.8	3.7	3.7	3.7
Ginghams (check)	18 x 2 1/4	4.12	4.12	4.12	4.7	4.7	4.7

[Source: same as in Table 10.2]

The price trend that emerges from Table 10.3 is undoubtedly different from the one in Table 10.2. Out of the 5 types of coarser textiles, the price of 3 went up by about 10 to 20 per cent while the price of two others actually show a downward trend from the period 1732-1744 to 1751-54. Though it is difficult to explain such mixed trends in prices of these textiles, one possible explanation could be that most of these piece-goods were produced in the areas around Hughli, which was one of the worst affected by the Maratha raids. Secondly, the competition among the buyers, whether Asians or Europeans, was more severe for these coarser varieties than in finer muslins. But then we cannot explain, at the present state of our knowledge, the slide in the prices of the two types of *ginghams* in the period 1751-54 from the level in 1732-1744. Still what is apparent from the prices of the coarser types of textiles is that there is hardly anything which can be termed 'a marked and sustained increase' in prices over the period.

TABLE 10.4

Contract Prices of Coarsest and Cheapest Textiles
1732-54 (Select Years), Dutch Company

Textile Type	Measure (in *covid*)	1732 Price Rs.As per corge	1741 Price Rs.As per corge	1744 Price Rs.As per corge	1751 Price Rs.As per corge	1752 Price Rs.As per corge	1754 Price Rs.As per corge
Garras	36 x 2 1/2	x	x	x	84	84	84
Garras	30 x 2 1/2	x	x	x	70	70	70
Garras	30 x 2 1/4	45	48	x	x	x	x
Garras	24 x 2 1/2	x	x	x	56	56	56
Guinees	75 x 2 1/2	x	x	x	175	175	175
Guiness	75 x 2 1/4	118	121.8	x	x	x	x
Salampuris	371/2 x 2 1/2	x	x	x	87.8	87.8	87.8
Salampuris	371/2 x 2 1/4	x	60.12	x	x	x	x

[Source and note: same as in Table 10.2 and VOC 2783, ff. 248-49; 2840, f. 680. Per *corge* means per 20. Generally the coarset textiles were contracted per *corge*.]

So far as the prices of coarsest textiles are concerned, no clear picture emerges from the Dutch contracts (Table 10.4). Though at the first glance it seems that the prices went up considerably, it is extremely difficult to measure the increase in prices over the period because the measurement of the textiles procured by the Dutch varied over these years, and there is no precise data as to how the prices of any of the coarsest textiles of exactly the same length and width rose during the period (Table 10.4). Here it is important to note that in Bengal, the price of the same type of textile often jumped when the traditional measurement was even slightly altered—a fact which is borne out by numerous references in the Company records. Yet, it is possible that the price of the coarsest textiles went up to some extent though it is not obvious from Table 10.4. The explanation for this probable rise in the prices of coarsest textiles is not far to seek. Most of these textiles were produced in Birbhum, Burdwan and Kasimbazar areas which were the most affected by the Maratha invasions. Besides, as we have seen earlier,[21] the keenest competition in the market was for this variety which was the reason why the merchants were most reluctant to contract for these textiles which, as they alleged, brought them little or no profit, while they were extremely eager to contract for finer varieties. Often the Companies had to impose the contract for these ordinary calicoes on the unwilling merchants.

Taking up the contracts of the English Company, it can be asserted that no uniform and precise trend is to be found in the prices of muslins like *khasa* and *mulmul*. While an upward trend is discernible in the cheaper varieties of muslins, the prices of finer varieties actually went down. For example, in case of more expensive *khasas* like *khasa* Cogmaria (40x3), while the price was Rs 11.8 in 1732, it came down to Rs 9.8 in 1741 and 1742 but rose again to Rs 10.8 in 1744 and remained at the same level up to 1751. Similarly in case of *khasa* Cogmaria fine (40x2 $^1/_2$), the price came down from Rs 8.00 in 1740 to Rs 7.6 in 1741 and remained at Rs 7.12 from 1744 to 1751 (Table 10.5). Similarly, in case of *mulmul* Santipur fine (40x3) while the price was Rs 17.8 in 1740, it came down to Rs 16.8 in 1741 and 1751. Again *mulmul*

---

[21] See chapter 7. In the pages that follow, the prices of textiles, raw silk and rice are given in Rupees and Annas; e.g. Rs. 10.8 would mean Rupees 10 and 8 Annas.

Balasore (20 yd x 1 yd) was priced at Rs 11.00 in 1744 and 1750 while in 1751 it was Rs 10.8 (Table 10.5). What is clear from Table 10.5 is that there was sharp increase in the prices mainly of the cheaper varieties of *khasas* and *mulmuls*. Thus while the price of *khasa* Burron (40x2) was between Rs 4.12 to Rs 5 from 1732 and 1741, it went up to Rs 5.12 in the period from 1744 to 1751. The same upward trend is visible in the case of *khasa* Kumarkhali (40x2) (Table 10.5). More or less the same picture is to be found in the price of cheaper *mulmuls*. For example, while *mulmul* Santipur (40x2 $^1/_4$) cost Rs 7.12 in 1741, the price was Rs 9.12 in 1750 and 1751. The increase in price is more marked in the case of *mulmul* Santipur (40x2) over the period (Table 10.5). In other words, though there was a sharp increase in the prices of cheaper types of muslins, the prices of more expensive types actually went down. So it is difficult to maintain that there was a marked and sustained increase in the prices of textiles as a whole over the period.

TABLE 10.5
Contract Prices of *Khasas* and *Mulmuls*
1732-1751 (Select Years): English Company

Textile Type	Measure (covid)	1732 Price Rs.As	1740 Price Rs.As	1741 Price Rs.As	1744 Price Rs.As	1750 Price Rs.As	1751 Price Rs.As
Khasa Orrua	40 x 2$^1/_4$	8.00	8.00	7.12	8.14	8.14	8.14
" "	40 x 2	x	7.2	6.12	7.14	7.14	7.14
" Cogmaria	40 x 3	11.8	9.8	9.8	10.8	10.8	10.8
" " fine	40 x 3	15.8	x	x	x	x	x
" " "	40 x 2$^1/_2$	x	7.10	7.10	8.2	8.2	8.8
" " "	40 x 2$^1/_4$	x	8.00	7.6	7.12	7.12	7.12
" Burron	40 x 2	5	4.12	4.12	5.12	5.12	5.12
" Kumarkhali	40 x 2	x	4.12	4.12	5.12	5.12	5.12
" Malda F. Goldh.	40 x 2$^1/_2$	x	19.00	19.00	x	x	x
" " " "	40 x 3	x	x	x	17.8	17.8	17.8

(contd.)

Table 10.5 (contd.)

Textile Type	Measure (covid)	1732 Price Rs.As	1740 Price Rs.As	1741 Price Rs.As	1744 Price Rs.As	1750 Price Rs.As	1751 Price Rs.As
" Serry	32 x 1^3/$_4$	x	57p.c.	64p.c.	x	x	x
Mulmul Santipur	40 x 3	14	x	10.00	x	11.00	x
" "	40 x 2^1/$_4$	x	x	7.12	x	9.12	9.12
" " fine	40 x 3	x	17.8	16.8	x	x	16.8
" " "	40 x 2^1/$_2$	x	x	9.8	9.12	x	x
" " "	40 x 2^1/$_4$	x	x	8.4	8.4	x	x
" "	40 x 2	x	x	6.12	x	8.4	8.8
" Balasore	20yd x 1yd	x	x	x	11.00	11.00	10.8
" Cossajura	40 x 2	x	11.0	x	x	x	x
" " fine	40 x 2	x	19.0	x	x	x	x
" " "	40 x 2^1/$_4$	x	21.0	22.8	x	x	x
" " "	40 x 3	x	30.0	30.0	x	x	x
" Serry	36 x 1^3/$_4$	x	55p.c.	55p.c.	x	x	x
" " fine	36 x 1^3/$_4$	x	82.8p.c.	82.8p.c.	x	x	x

[Source and note: BPC, vol. 9, f. 61; vol. 14, ff. 91-92; vol. 15, ff. 89, 233-34; vol. 17, f. 70; vol. 23, ff. 186-87; vol. 24, ff. 238-39. From 1744 onward, the 'medium price' is noted here. For 1752 no such price is available while the contract system was abolished in 1753; p.c. means per *corge* or per 20.]

There was, however, a marked and, to some extent, sharp rise in the price of coarse calicoes in the contract of the English Company. It will be apparent from Table 10.6 that the price of *photaes* fine (20x2^1/$_4$) went up from Rs 3.12 in 1740 and 1742 to Rs 4.8 in the period from 1744 to 1751. More marked was the rise in the price of *garras*. While the price of *garras* fine (72 x 2^1/$_4$) was Rs 106 per 20 pieces in 1740, it rose to Rs 112 in 1742 and to Rs 160 in 1750 and 1751. Similarly, *garras* fine (36x2^1/$_2$) cost Rs 53 and Rs 56 per 20 pieces in 1740 and 1742 respectively but the price moved up to Rs 80 in 1750 and remained so in 1751. This only indicates clearly that there was an increase in the price of coarse textiles in the contracts of the English Company—a trend which was not so very clear in the Dutch contracts. But as we have explained earlier, the coarse categories of textiles were produced mostly in the areas which were badly affected by the Maratha inroads. Moreover, there was always the keenest competition among various groups of merchants for the coarser textiles for which the demand was great and which often pushed up the prices. Still, what is obvious from the contract prices in the Dutch and the English records is that though prices of certain types of textiles went up, especially in the late 1740s and early 1750s from the level of the 1730s, there is nothing to establish that the prices of textiles in general went up sharply during the period under review.

TABLE 10.6
Contract Prices of Coarse Calicoes
1732-1751 (Select Years): English Company

Textile Type	Measure (covid)	1732 Price Rs.As	1740 Price Rs.As	1742 Price Rs.As	1744 Price Rs.As	1750 Price Rs.As	1751 Price Rs.As
Photaes fine	28 x $2^3/_4$	4	x	x	x	x	x
" "	28 x $2^1/_2$	x	3.12	3.12	4.8	4.8	4.8
" "	28 x $2^1/_4$	x	2.12	2.12	x	x	x
Garras	72 x $2^1/_4$	x	93p.c.	99p.c.	x	x	x
" fine	72 x $2^1/_4$	x	106p.c.	112p.c.	x	160p.c.	160p.c.
"	36 x $2^1/_4$	x	46.8p.c.	49.8p.c.	x	x	x
" fine	36 x $2^1/_4$	x	53p.c.	56p.c.	x	80p.c.	80p.c.

[Source and note: same as in Table 10.5]

10.3 SILK PRICE

Turning to raw silk, we find a slightly different picture from that in the case of textiles. In the Table below (Table 10.7) we note the price of raw silk for several years from 1733 to 1753 to see the movement of prices of this important export commodity.

The trend of raw silk prices that emerges from Table 10.7 is somewhat erratic and shows wide fluctuations over the period. But what is clear is that the rise in the price of raw silk between 1733 and 1745 is almost negligible and does not support the thesis of a general increase in prices in Bengal from the early 1740s. What is significant is that there was a marked increase in the price of raw silk in 1747 and 1748 from the level of 1733 or 1745. But this seems to have been a temporary phenomenon as from June 1748 the prices began to fall and remained more or

TABLE 10.7

Price of Raw Silk Procured by the English Company 1733-1753

Date	Variety of Silk	Price per seer (Rs.As.)
March 1733	November band	5 : 12
	Gujarat	6 : 6
	Kumarkhali	5 : 12
January 1745	November band	5 : 14
	Gujarat	6 : 7
	Kumarkhali	5 : 11
April 1747	November band	9 : 4
	Gujarat	9 : 13
	Kumarkhali	9 : 1
January 1748	November band	9 : 4
	Gujarat	9 : 13
	Kumarkhali	9 : 1
June 1748	November band	7 : 8
	Gujarat	8 : 1
	Kumarkhali	7 : 5
October 1749	November band	7 : _
	Gujarat	7 : 9
	Kumarkhali	6 : 13
February 1751	November band	8 : _
	Gujarat	8 : 9
	Kumarkhali	7 : 13
March 1752	November band	7 : 14
	Gujarat	8 : 7
	Kumarkhali	x
April 1753	November band	7 : 12
	Gujarat	8 : 5
	Kumarkhali	x

[Source: Fact. Records, Kasimbazar, vol. 5, 7 March 1733; vol. 6, 19 Jan. 1745; vol. 7, 2 June 1748; vol. 10, 22 Feb. 1751; BPC, vol. 19, 22 April 1747; vol. 22, 31 Oct. 1749; vol. 25, 16 March 1752; vol. 26, 18 April 1753; C & B Abstr., vol. 5, 10 Jan. 1748.]

less at the same level except in February 1751 when there was again a slight increase from the level of June 1748. In short, it can be stated that the price rise in silk was not so precipitate as most historians would have us believe. The price trend is to some extent erratic because of the fact, which we have analyzed in detail elsewhere,[22] that silk was one of the most sensitive articles, the production of which, right from the mulberry plantation, depended so much on the whims of nature. Moreover, as we have argued earlier, the demand of the Asian merchants was one of the major factors which determined the price of silk in the market. An important point that is reflected in the above Table 10.7 is that the English Company was not exporting the cheaper Kumarkhali silk from around 1752 and only concentrating more on the comparatively expensive varieties like Gujarat and November band. As such, the unit price of silk is bound to go up from that of the earlier period and so the rise in the unit price after 1752 would not necessarily mean any intrinsic rise in the price of the commodity. From the analysis made here, it can be said that the dominant trend in silk price over the period can hardly be described as a 'marked and sustained' increase in prices.

10.4 PRICES OF FOOD GRAINS

As pointed out earlier, rice is the most important food item, the price of which should be looked into to determine any precise price movement in Bengal during the period under review. But the main difficulty here is the wide variety of rice and its equally wide price variation depending on quality. This is well illustrated in Table 10.8 which indicates the different varieties of rice and their prices.

So it is not a simple case of fine or coarse rice only; when the price of coarse rice can vary so very widely from 4 mds.15 seers to 7 mds. 20 seers per rupee (the difference being about 71%), there is a grave risk in taking the price of rice as an indicator of price movement until and unless one can be absolutely sure of the exact quality of rice when its price is taken into account.

[22] See chapter 8.

TABLE 10.8
Price of Rice, 1729

Variety	Maunds Seer	per Rupee
Fine Rice		
Bansephool		
1st sort	1—10	"
2nd sort	1—23	"
3rd sort	1—35	"
Coarse Rice—Desna	4—15	"
Coarse Rice—Poorbie	4—25	"
Coarse Rice—Munsurah	5—25	"
Coarse Rice—Kurkashallee	7—20	"

[Source: Sixth Report (1782-83), Appendix 15]

Otherwise the result could be extremely erratic and gravely misleading. Yet depending on such data and sometimes even fragmentary at that, recent authorities including the latest on the subject have made such assertions as 'Rice which was sold at 100 to 120 seers for a rupee in 1738, was being sold only thirty seers for a rupee' in the mid-1740s as evidence to show that 'production declined and prices soared' or that by the 1740s 'Bengal's advantages seemed to be disappearing'.[23] Basing his evidence on earlier authorities, the most recent authority affirms that 'between 1738 and 1754 it was thought that the price of rice in Calcutta had risen by three or four times' and reiterates that 'local shortages' led to 'greatly increased food prices'.[24]

Now let us see how far such assertions are borne by strong evidence. Regarding the price of rice in 1738, earlier authorities[25] solely depended on the letter written by the Dhaka factors to

[23] Brijen K. Gupta, *Sirajuddaullah*, p. 33; P.J. Marshall, *East Indian Fortunes*, p. 35.

[24] P.J. Marshall, *Bengal*, p. 73; *East India Fortunes*, p. 35.

[25] K.K. Datta, *Bengal Suba*, p. 463-64; Brijen K. Gupta, *Sirajuddaullah*, p. 33.

Calcutta in 1752 in an answer to the allegation of inferior quality of cloth supplied by the former which we have quoted earlier. Not only that the letter was written in self defence but one has to take into account the fact that the Dhaka factors were writing in 1752 about the prevailing price of rice in 1738. For that they probably depended mostly on their own imagination which again might have been coloured by their desperate attempt to cover up their shortcomings. Moreover, the significant fact that it referred to price of rice only in Dhaka is ignored by our authorities. It is too much to expect that the price of rice would be the same in Calcutta and Dhaka, and the price of rice in the latter place in 1738 could be compared with that in the former place in 1752 or 1754. Again, numerous references in the Company records clearly indicate that the price of rice in Calcutta mostly depended on the supply of the commodity from Bakherganj and Douleah in south-eastern Bengal, without which the city was 'reduced to the greatest necessity and misery' and the price was often manipulated by the city's rice merchants who took advantage of the fluid situation in the growing city.[26]

As a matter of fact, as is indicated in the following Table 10.9, the price of rice in Calcutta in 1738 was 30 seers per 'Madras' rupee at which rate the Fort William Council decided to buy rice for the garrison (coarse, of course, but yet which one even among the coarse varieties?) while in 1744 the rate was 30 seers for 'common sort'. The Council blamed the importers of rice for raising the price to such an 'exorbitant' rate and asked the Calcutta zamindar not to permit the coarse rice to be sold under 1 md. per 'Arcot' rupee.[27] It will also be clear from Table 10.9 that in 1754 fine rice was sold at $32\frac{1}{2}$ seers per rupee while the coarse variety was sold at 1 md. per 'Arcot' rupee. Hence the assertion of our authorities that the price of rice had gone up 'three to four times' between 1738 and 1754 is hardly tenable.

[26] BPC, vol. 26, ff 56vo-57, 19 Feb. 1753; ff. 152-54, 24 May 1753; ff. 336-36vo, 19 Nov. 1753; vol. 27, f.181, 10 June 1754; ff. 244vo-245, 12 Aug. 1754; ff.378-78vo, 5 Dec. 1754.
[27] BPC, vol.16, f.401vo, 7 Jan. 1744.

TABLE 10.9
Prices of Rice in Bengal, 1738—1754

Date	Place	Mds.Seer	per Rupee	Quality
12 June 1738	Calcutta	0—30	'Madras' Rup.	Coarse (?) (for garrison)
2 April 1739	Calcutta	1—30	'Madras' Rup.	'very good sort'
31 May 1743	Dhaka	0—35	Dasmasha "	'fine'
31 May 1743	Dhaka	1—10	Dasmasha "	'ordinary'
7 Jan. 1744	Calcutta	0—30	Arcot "	'common sort'
7 Jan. 1744	Calcutta	1—00	Arcot "	'coarse'
20 Sept. 1751	Calcutta	0—35	Arcot "	'good Nov. sort'
20 Sept. 1751	Calcutta	1—10	Arcot "	'ordinary'
Oct. 1751	Calcutta	1—32	Arcot "	?
2 Jan. 1752	Calcutta	0—35	Arcot "	'good Nov. sort'
2 Jan. 1752	Calcutta	1—10	Arcot "	'ordinary'
Oct. 1752	Calcutta	1—16	Arcot "	?
19 Feb. 1753	Calcutta	0—25	Arcot "	?
10 June 1754	Calcutta	0—32$\frac{1}{2}$	Arcot "	'fine'
10 June 1754	Calcutta	0—35	Arcot "	'middling'
10 June 1754	Calcutta	1—00	Arcot "	'coarse'

[Source & note: BPC, vol. 13, f.262vo, f. 527; vol.16, f.401vo; vol.24, f.323; vol. 25, f.297vo; vol. 26, ff.56vo-57; vol. 27, ff. 224vo-25; Fact. Records, Dacca, vol.2, 31 May 1743. Arcot or Madras rupees were coined by the English in Arcot/Madras and 'Dasmasha' rupees were used in Dhaka.]

While it is obvious from the above Table 10.9 that no clear trend of the price of rice emerges, one has to take into consideration in analyzing the Table that some of the prices shown were during the times of scarcity and famine, and not under normal conditions. In 1738, for example, the price was affected by the severe storm and flood that swept Bengal in

September and October 1737.[28] Again, after the Maratha invasions were over and when monsoon failed, there was famine in 1752 which is said to have resulted in 'worst shortages in 60 years' and the price of rice had reportedly gone up sharply to 25 seers a rupee. At the same time one should note here that the price was reported by Holwell who was prone to exaggeration and also he emphasized the sharp rise because of the large export of rice from Calcutta on the one hand and the delay in the import from Douleah on the other.[29] But Orme's assertion that the price of rice in Murshidabad rose by 6 times its previous level seems to be an obvious exaggeration and can hardly be corroborated by contemporary evidence.[30] That the abnormal price rise in early 1753 was only a temporary phenomenon and prices came down to their normal level in 1754 become quite evident from Table 10.9. As such, the price of rice can hardly be taken as an index of price movement because of the lack of precise data as also the anomaly of the data available to us at this stage.

10.5 MARATHA INVASIONS, EUROPEAN TRADE AND PRICES

Historians including the latest authorities have unduly empha-sized the effects of the Maratha invasions and the impact of the European trade while dealing with the price movement in Bengal.[31] The report of the two English warehousekeepers, Manningham and Frankland, came in handy to substantiate the thesis of price rise in Bengal from the 1740s.[32] As we have argued earlier,[33] the report was self-contradictory, motivated and written

---

[28] S. Bhattacharyya, *East India Company*, pp. 214-15.

[29] BPC, vol.26, ff.56vo-57, 19 Feb. 1753.

[30] Orme, *Historical Fragments*, p. 405. P.J. Marshall, however, depended on Orme and Holwell's description of the effects of the famine in Calcutta (Holwell, *India Tracts*, p. 165) as evidence of the marked rise in food prices, P.J. Marshall, *Bengal*, pp. 18, 73.

[31] K.K. Datta, *Bengal Suba*, pp. 465-68; K.N. Chaudhuri, *Trading World*, pp. 99-108; P.J. Marshall, *Bengal*, pp. 73, 142-44.

[32] Manningham & Frankland's report, BPC, vol. 26, Annex to Consult. 7 June 1753. Both K.N. Chaudhuri (*Trading World*, pp.99,102) and P.J. Marshall (*East Indian Fortunes*, p. 35), depended a lot on this report.

[33] See chapter 5.

with the ulterior objective of changing over from the *dadni* to the *gomasta* system. Hence it should be handled with more caution. Moreover, the very fact that these two Company servants wrote that the 'necessaries of life had been greatly enhanced over *the previous ten or twenty years*' only betrays the casual nature of their assertion. As they wrote in 1753, it could have meant price rise either from about 1733 or 1743, something which is very curious as our authorities assert that the marked and sustained increase in prices took place only in the early 1740s. By implication the price situation was completely different in the early 1730s and the early 1740s. Hence one part of the assertion of the two Englishmen ('since the last 20 yrs') becomes superfluous. If the increase of prices is to be dated from the early 1740s, the report then, no doubt, tallies with the thesis of our authorities but as we have seen in our analysis earlier, that was not the case at all. So there is hardly any justification for relying so much on the report of Manningham and Frankland as evidence of price rise.

Like most of the historians, these two Englishmen, too, have attributed the alleged price increase in Bengal to a condition of real scarcity following the Maratha invasions. There is no denying the fact that the Maratha incursions resulted in serious dislocation in the economy of some areas of Bengal. But the impact of the invasions has been greatly exaggerated. The Marathas caused destruction generally along the lines of their march, leaving the remaining part of the country more or less unaffected. Even in the affected areas, as Richard Becher, a Company official present in Bengal during the period, pointed out, the Marathas were obliged to return at the approach of the rainy season, and the inhabitants were again safe till next January. So they immediately began to work and arranged to raise and sell their crops before next year's impending invasion.[34] That the country was not so much impoverished is proved by the fact that the zamindars paid Alivardi Rs 10 million at one time and Rs 5 million at another besides their annual revenue to enable him to meet the increased military expenditure.[35] The argument that many merchants in Bengal 'were crippled by losses

----

[34] Richard Becher's letter to Governor Verelst, 24 May 1769, quoted in W.K. Firminger, *Fifth Report*, pp. 183-84.
[35] Ibid.

and exactions' following the Maratha invasions and as a result of this both the English and the Dutch Companies increasingly turned to direct dealings with the artisans is hardly tenable. As we have shown earlier,[36] the Dutch Company made such an experiment for a few years only from 1747 to 1749 in view of the 'bankruptcy' of several merchants in a particular *aurung* but reverted to contracts with *dadni* merchants from 1750. The change over in the English Company's investment pattern from *dadni* to *gomasta* system in 1753 was not because of any decline of Bengal merchants but the result of the Fort William Council's attempt to resolve its commercial crisis concerning private trade by cutting out the *dadni* merchants.[37]

Again, historians rely too much on contemporary vernacular literature and Persian chronicles to corroborate the disastrous effects of the Maratha invasions. That these are mostly exaggerated accounts is clear from the very nature of the evidence. For example, the poet Gangaram wrote 'rice, pulses, *dal* of all sorts, oil, ghee, flour, sugar, salt began to be sold at one rupee per seer .... All of them from the lowest to the highest, including the nawab himself, had to subsist on boiled roots of banana trees'.[38] It is simply absurd that rice, oil, ghee (butter oil), sugar, salt were all sold at one rupee per seer. Equally unbelievable is the assertion that even the nawab subsisted on roots of banana trees. Even making allowance for the poetic effusion, the above can hardly be taken as evidence of the impact of the Maratha invasions. The author of *Riyaz* refers to human beings living on banana roots to avert death by starvation. But even if true, this was a description mostly of Burdwan city when its granaries were burnt down and the supply of imported grains was completely cut off by the Marathas for a short while.[39] Another Bengali poet, Bharatchandra, gives an account of Nalini's shopping in Burdwan but the prices she paid for different articles though regarded as 'abnormal' cannot be compared with earlier prices (for lack of precise data) to see if they were really so.[40] The simple fact that the total value of the investments of the major European companies, especially

---

[36] See chapter 5.
[37] For details, see chapter 5.
[38] Gangaram, *Maharastrapurana*, lines 234–42.
[39] *Riyaz*, p. 340.
[40] Bharatchandra quoted in K.K. Datta, *Bengal Suba*, p. 466.

the English and the Dutch, as also the export by Asian merchants was hardly affected during or after the Maratha incursions is sufficient proof that the invasions had really no long-term disastrous effects on the overall economy of Bengal.[41]

The assertion of a recent authority that 'prices were rising with a high level of European purchases financed by imports of silver in the decade or so before the battle of Plassey' (in 1757), though in line with the general assumption that there was an upward movement in prices from the early 1740s (the period referred to coinciding with the commencement of the Maratha invasion) can hardly be tenable.[42] Of the two major European exporters of Bengal goods, the Dutch fell far behind the English from the 1720s. As far as the English were concerned—and they were the most dominant of the European companies in Bengal during this period—there was hardly any remarkable increase in their total exports from Bengal in the 1740s and 1750s as compared with the level in the 1730s. This will be evident from Table 10.10.

TABLE 10.10
Quinquennial Total and Average Annual Value of English
Exports from Bengal, 1727-1755

Years	Total Value (£s.)	Average Annual Value (£s.)
1726/27-1730/31	2,289,323	457,865
1731/32-1735/36	2,046,150	409,230
1740/41-1744/45	2,401,785	480,357
1745/46-1749/50	2,173,524	434,705
1750/51-1754/55	2,033,235	406,648

[Source and note: Computed from K.N. Chaudhuri, *Trading World*, pp. 509-10 with one-year lag. As the real boom in English exports began in 1726/27 when the value of the export amounted to over 0.5 million pounds, the second highest in the first half of the eighteenth century, our computation here began with that year. Again as the increasing purchases of the Europeans and consequent price rise are linked up, presumably from the 1740s, we concentrated here mainly on the period 1740-1755.]

[41] For the value of Dutch and English exports, see chapters 3, 7 and 8, and for Asian exports, chapters 7 and 8.
[42] P.J. Marshall, *Bengal*, pp. 163-64.

It is well beyond doubt from Table 10.10 that the value of the English exports, though fluctuated a little from 1726/27 to 1754/55, the increase or decrease in the average annual value was only marginal. Though there was a trend of decline from the mid-1740s, this was balanced, so far as Bengal's export trade was concerned, by the increase in Dutch exports during this period, something we have shown earlier.[43] In other words, the total European export from Bengal remained more or less stable from the early 1730s to the mid-1750s. That would substantiate our two important assertions that neither did the Maratha invasions have a disastrous effect on the economy nor had the increasing purchases of the European companies pushed up the prices Moreover, it can be pointed out, for the sake of argument, that had there been even an increase in the European exports from Bengal, it would not have necessarily resulted in a spurt in prices. As an authority has argued recently, the overall increase in the prices of the export commodities 'would have constituted a clear signal for reallocating resources to increase the output of these goods'.[44] It is beyond doubt that Bengal was one of the most fertile provinces of Mughal India, and supplied food grains and other provisions not only to several other parts of the country but also to quite a few neighbouring countries. As such it can be argued, as has been done by the said authority, that 'the availability of a food surplus created a margin within which a relative shift from food to commercial crops in response to challenging demand could be affected without generating unduly severe strains'.[45]

Regarding the impact of the influx of bullion as a result of the European trade, as we cannot estimate the total supply of money in the economy, it is not possible to have any idea of the relative significance of the addition to the money supply as a consequence of the import of precious metals by the Europeans. In all probability, not all the silver brought by the Companies was converted into Mughal coins, and as such did not mean an automatic and corresponding increase in money supply. More often than not, the Companies had to sell their silver to the

[43] See chapter 3, Table 3.
[44] Om Prakash, *Dutch Company*, p. 238.
[45] Ibid.

banking house of Jagat Seth which because of its many sources
of income did not always have to coin the silver in the mint.[46]
Moreover, leaving aside the 'Oriental penchant for hoarding'
which is explained as one of the major factors why the import of
precious metals had had no pressure on prices,[47] there is little
doubt that the nawabs of Bengal and the merchant princes
amassed a huge fortune during this period. Even after paying the
revenue to Delhi to the tune Rs 13 million a year from the early
eighteenth century to at least the early 1740s, the nawabs of
Bengal could enrich their treasury to such an extent that after the
battle of Plassey, the British were astounded to find '20 million
of rupees in gold and silver' only in the royal treasury. If we are
to believe the author of *Tarikh-i-Mansuri*, besides the above
amount, there was a hidden treasure in the harem which
amounted to ' no less than 80 million rupees' in gold, silver and
jewels, and which was appropriated by Mir Jafar, Rai Durlabh
and Raja Nabakrishna, Clive's *munshi*.[48]

At the same time, we have seen earlier what an enormous
amount of wealth was accumulated by the merchant princes
namely, the Jagat Seths, Umichand and Khwaja Wazid.[49] Then
there were the fabulously rich zamindars and mansabdars who
achieved their prosperity in the first half of the eighteenth
century. All this will only indicate that quite a substantial part of
the precious metals brought in by the trade did not possibly filter
down to the primary producers and a large chunk of it was
appropriated by the upper section of the society. The main
factor, however, for the absence of any marked price rise in
Bengal was the basic question of demand and supply. Whatever
the level of demand was, the fact that Bengal could easily provide
it without requiring any change in the basic technology only
underlines that the demand was not so huge as compared to the

[46] See chapters 4 and 5.

[47] For example, Earl J. Hamilton, 'American Treasure and the Rise
of Capitalism, 1500-1700', *Economica*, 27, Nov. 1929, 338-57; Rudolph
C. Blitz, 'Mercantilist Policies and the Pattern of World Trade, 1500-
1750', *Journal of Economic History*, 27, March 1967, pp. 39-55, quoted in
Om Prakash, *Dutch Company*, p. 250.

[48] *Tarikh-i-Mansuri*, tr. H. Blochmann, *Journal of the Asiatic Society*,
no. 2, 1867, pp. 95-96.

[49] See chapter 5.

existing capacity of production. This mitigates against the contention of any marked rise in prices. If the supply side could meet the demand easily without having any significant pressure on the structure and organization of the industries (as is evident especially in the textile and silk sectors), the demand which brought in precious metals in consequence need not necessarily have much effect on the price level. All the evidence analyzed so far will confirm this.

11

TRADE, BULLION AND CONQUEST

The British conquest of Bengal after the battle of Plassey, 23 June 1757, was not wholly accidental. Nor is it that the British had no active role in the Plassey conspiracy which resulted in the downfall of the young nawab. Sirajuddaullah and ushered in the domination of the British in Bengal.[1] If not the Court of Directors in London so much, the Company servants and other merchant adventurers closely connected with the British trade in India did from time to time advocate in no uncertain terms the acquisition of territory in India. However, it is fair to note that full-fledged imperialism was perhaps not thought of but certainly there was a conscious and deliberate attempt for establishing a 'dominion' in India though primarily for the ostensible reason of carrying on trade vigorously. But trade here meant not only the corporate trade of the Company but also private trade of the Company servants which really was the latter's primary interest. I shall argue here that the private trade interest of the Company servants ultimately led to the British conquest of Bengal.

Of late, historians are keen on explaining the origin of the Anglo-nawabi conflict (which resulted in the Plassey revolution and the British conquest of Bengal) in terms of a broad

---

[1] For the latest advocacy of the thesis, see P.J. Marshall, *Bengal*, pp. 77, 91; C.A. Bayly, *Indian Society*, p. 50; Rajat Kanta Ray, 'Colonial Penetration and Initial Resistance', *IHR*, vol. XII, Nos. 1-2, July 1985-Jan. 86, pp. 7,8,11,12. I have tried to refute the above thesis in details in 'Sirajuddaullah and the battle of Palashi' in the *History of Bangladesh*, vol. 1, Dhaka, 1992.

generalization — the breakdown of the alliance of military aristocrats, merchant-bankers and zamindars which sustained the nawabi regime from Murshid Quli till Alivardi Khan. Near-contemporaneous Persian chronicles written mostly at the behest or under the patronage of British 'masters' came in handy. A selective use of European sources helped build the general thesis that with the accession of Sirajuddaullah the 'class alliance' broke down and everything began to fall apart. The British had to intervene almost in a fit of 'absent-mindedness' in order to avert the 'crisis' in Bengal's body politic (as also in the Bengali economy).[2] Hence the obvious conclusion is that Plassey should be explained as a consummation of internal crisis arising out of the alienation of the dominant ruling class by the nawab which inevitably brought in the British. The actual role of the British in the conspiracy against the nawab is thus conveniently lost in the maze of 'theorization' and the young nawab remains the villain of the piece. To use the age-old cliché, this is nothing but old wine in new bottle—the ghost of S.C. Hill (1905) is very much alive beneath the facade of the broad generalization.[3]

The above hypothesis is being reinforced very recently by bringing in the issue of the European trade and the consequent influx of bullion which inevitably leads to the pet 'collaboration' thesis. And once it could be proved that the conquest was nothing but collaboration between the British and the Bengali ruling elite (warriors, merchant-bankers and landholders), the role of the British does not become so awkward even in the face of the

[2] In a recent seminar in Calcutta (1989), P.J. Marshall emphasized the economic 'crisis'.

[3] For such broad generalization, see P.J. Marshall, *Bengal*, pp. 56,63; Rajat Kanta Ray, 'Colonial Penetration and Initial Resistance', *IHR*, vol. XII, Nos., 1-2, July 1985—Jan. 1986, pp. 4, 6, 7, 14. It should not be misconstrued that I am against any 'theorization' but my point is while doing so, one should not lose sight of the specific issues involved. Further, a recent study has pointed out (Munshi Mazibor Rahman, 'Nizamat in Bengal: A Study of its Rise, Growth and Decline, 1700-1757', unpublished M. Phil. thesis, J.N.U., 1988) that the new class alliance or 'compact' was more of a personal character to serve vested interest without any institutional basis and hence bound to be short-lived. For Hill's views, see S.C. Hill, *Bengal in 1756-57*, vol. 1, p. lii.

Plassey conspiracy. Such old themes die hard. Though restated in a sophisticated manner in recent works, this is nothing but an elaboration of the hint given by Hill long ago and of the more recent hypothesis of Brijen K. Gupta.[4]

I have an altogether different story to tell, based on all the important available sources. For the convenience of analysis, I shall discuss it under the following heads:

a)   Private Trade and Sub-Imperialism
b)   Trade, Import of Bullion and Plassey
c)   British Attack on French Chandernagore paving the way for Plassey

11.1 PRIVATE TRADE AND SUB-IMPERIALISM

There is no denying the fact that though the specifics of the Anglo-nawabi conflict in 1756-57 are important for a proper understanding of the situation, the 'crisis' could be better understood if it is explained in the context of the delicate relationship between the Fort William Council and the nawab's government. That depended upon the prosperity of the British corporate and private trade in Bengal. Though theoretically the corporate trade of the Company was to be the prime concern of the servants, for all practical purposes their own private trade through which to accumulate a quick fortune and retire to a decent life in Europe was the sole aim of these officials who braved the seas to work in a distant and completely alien land. Hence in all their activities in Bengal, private trade interest was the motive force. This attitude of the Company servants and their activities to enhance their own private interest and in the process, if possible, the British national interest may be termed sub-imperialism which had developed as an *imperium in imperio* within the framework of the trading corporation. Separated as they were from the effective control of London by a sailing time of about six months, the Company servants had little difficulty in

---

[4] Brijen K. Gupta, *Sirajuddaullah*, p.32. For recent emphasis on the role of the European companies and the influx of bullion, see P.J. Marshall, *Bengal*, pp.65,67; C.A. Bayly, *Indian Society*, pp. 49, 50.

pursuing their sub-imperialism. Hence most often decisions were taken locally. The employees of the Company did not hesitate to exploit Company's local resources when their own private trade interest was imperilled, and this is what they did in 1756-1757. Here one should not forget that they were not completely unaware of the inclinations of the authorities in London and knew very well that if their actions resulted in advantages for the Company, those would be approved by the Directors in London.

It might be argued that sub-imperialism was the resultant of the circumstances in which the Company servants were trading in India. But this argument would not hold water if one carefully analyzes the trading pattern of the British—both in the sphere of corporate and private trade. There is little doubt that the Company servants not only often misinterpreted the provisions of the *farman* of 1717 to suit their own purpose, but abused the privileges of duty-free trade to cover illegally their own private trade as also the trade of the Asian merchants, thus depriving the state of its legitimate customs duties.[5]   Naturally, the ruling authorities protested against such violations of the law of the land but the Company servants often made up matters by paying a lump sum whenever things came to a pass. Any critical and impartial study of the interaction between the British traders and native authorities, at least in Bengal where the foundation of the empire was laid in 1757, would not certainly confirm the popular thesis that the nawabs treated the Europeans as milch cows. Of course, no one would try to defend the Bengal nawabs when they were at fault in their dealings with the British or other Europeans. It is true that the European companies were allowed certain privileges for trade under the imperial *farmans*, and also that the Bengal nawabs turned to them as they did to Asian merchants whenever faced with financial difficulties. But it can hardly be said that the nawabs were in the habit of fleecing the Asian merchants; so too the allegation that they treated the European companies as milch cows is unwarranted.[6]

[5] For details, see my article 'Sirajuddaullah, English Company and the Plassey Conspiracy - A Reappraisal,' *IHR*, vol. XIII, nos. 1-2, July 1986 - Jan. 1987, pp. 117-119.

[6] For these *farmans* and the controversy regarding the privileges sanctioned by them, see S. Chaudhury, *Trade and Commercial Organiza-*

The fact of the matter was that the servants of the Company wanted to amass fortunes through illegal private trade and by selling the *dastaks* or official permits exempting goods from customs duties illegally to cover the trade of Asian merchants. It was because of this that the nawabs and their officers caught the British on the wrong foot and tried to extort money from them. The distinction between the Company's trade and private trade of the servants was often blurred. The servants on their part never tried to clarify this to the administration in Bengal as it would have hampered their own interest. The extent of the abuse of *dastaks* impelled a near-contemporary anonymous author of an English manuscript to wonder at the 'shameful prostitution did this trade in Dustuks arrive'. He even asserted that the abuse of *dastaks* was 'too truly a real cause' for the exactions and hence they 'were not extraordinary'.[7] In fact, Sirajuddaullah 'declared he would prove from vouchers in his possession that since the grant of the Firman by Ferroekseer [in 1717], the English had defrauded the Shah in his legal revenue of customs to the amount of a crore and half [15 million rupees] by covering the trade of the Natives with the Company's dustuck'.[8] Yet the Company servants clamoured about the exactions of the native authorities and made this one of the 'excuses' for doing away with the 'peaceful trade' advocated by Sir Thomas Roe. The main reason for this, however, was not so much the concern for the corporate trade of the Company as it was the private trade of the Company officials in India.

It can be reasonably argued that the private trade interest of the Company servants was the motive force behind the British conquest of Bengal. As I have tried to argue earlier,[9] the change over in the Company's investment pattern from *dadni* (advance system) to *gomasta* (paid agents) system in Bengal in 1753 was the

tion, pp. 39-42; S.Bhattacharyya, *East India Company*, pp. 28-32; S. Chaudhury, 'The Myth of the English East India Company's Trading Privileges in Bengal, 1651-1681', *BPP*, vol. 89, 1970, pp. 287-92.

[7] Mss. Eur. D. 283, ff. 15, 25. For detailed note on this manuscript, see my article 'Sirajuddaullah, English Company, etc.', *IHR*, vol. XIII, nos. 1-2, p. 117, f. n.1.

[8] Mss. Eur. D 283, f. 25.

[9] See chapter 5.

result of the Fort William [Calcutta] Council's attempt to resolve its commercial crisis, mainly concerning private trade, by cutting out the *dadni* merchants and appointing *gomastas* who certainly augmented the private trade of the Company servants. The main argument which I shall try to develop here is that it was the private trade interest of the Company's servants which made imperative the British attack on Chandernagore in March 1757, thus paving the way for Plassey. It would be shown that the British private trade was declining in the late 1740s and reached its nadir in the early 1750s. In Bengal's intra-Asiatic trade, the French along with the Hughli merchants now enjoyed the supreme position. The destruction of the French and the Hughli merchants, both trading from Hughli, was essential for the revival of the supremacy of the British private trade which could be perpetuated by the conquest of Bengal. Hence the attack on Hughli and Chandernagore to which we shall come back shortly. The traditional explanation that the destruction of French Chandernagore was necessary to prevent a Franco-Bengali alliance or that it was the result of the outbreak of Anglo-French war in Europe is rather inadequate. It seems that the more important consideration for the British was the destruction of the French private trade which had expanded to an alarming proportion so far as the British were concerned. Its destruction was essential to retrieve the private trade fortunes of the Company servants.

Be that as it may, to revert to the story of the development of sub-imperialism, the clarion call for the change from 'peaceful trade' to 'armed trade' was given by Gerald Aungier who became President at Surat and governor in Bombay in 1669 and recommended a 'severe and vigorous' policy to ensure the stability of the Company's trade in India. He wrote to the Court of Directors in 1677: 'Justice and necessity of your estate now require that in violent distempers, violent cures are only successful; that the times now require you to manage your general commerce with your sword in your hands'.[10] The advice of Aungier fell on the willing ears of the Company which in 1681, under the guidance of Sir Josiah Child as governor, resolved to resort to a 'forward policy' in India. Similarly, Agent Hedges in

[10] OC, 4258, vol. 37, f.8, 22 Jan. 1677.

Bengal and Sir John Child at Surat had repeatedly urged the Company for some years to fortify settlements for the protection of English trade in Bengal and elsewhere.[11]

One of the main objectives of the English East India Company's war with the Mughals in India in the 1680s was to have a fortified settlement in Bengal. The Court of Directors wrote:[12]

> We shall be exceeding glad to hear you have obtained a fortified settlement in Bengal, which if it pleases God to grant us, we would have you cultivate with all the vigour and strength you can; that we may be well fixed and settled in a good posture of defence before the Dutch can form any design to drive us out; which may be a means to prevent any attempts from them as well as to secure our interest if they should attempt to disturb us under any colour or pretence....

More significant and revealing fact in this regard that the war was commercial for establishing English dominion in India (and the beginning of empire) is contained in the despatch of the Court of Directors to its President and Council at Fort St. George on 12 December 1687:[13]

> That which we promise ourselves in a most especial manner from our new President and Council is that they will *establish such a politie of Civil and Military power*, and create and secure such a large revenue to maintain both at that place, as may be *the foundation of a large, well grounded, sure English dominion in India for all time to come.*

Such was the wild dream then cherished for the acquisition of an extensive, secure and strongly-founded British dominion in India which was to be realized only seventy years later. So how could the conquest of Bengal in 1757 be considered unintentional

---

[11] For Hedges' views, see *The Diary of William Hedges*, vol. 1, pp. 133-34.

[12] DB, vol. 91, para. 25, f. 37, 14 Jan. 1686.

[13] Ibid., vol. 91, f. 466, 12 Dec. 1687, emphasis mine.

or accidental?

The war with the Mughals ended in a dismal failure for the British and hence fortified settlement could not be established either in Bengal or anywhere else. But the quest for a fortified settlement in Bengal was successful as a result of an unexpected development towards the close of the seventeenth century. Following the rebellion of Sobha Singh in Bengal in 1696, the subadar out of scarce gave general permission to the Europeans for fortifying themselves and the British were quick to take the opportunity in building fortifications.[14] This was the beginning and the fortifications were strengthened from time to time even in defiance of the nawab's authority. One of the main causes of the conflict between the nawab and the British in 1756-1757 was the question of fortifications.[15]

In order to understand the specifics of the Bengal conflict in 1756-57, we need to probe beyond the question of fortifications and the abuse of *dastaks*. The crisis could be better understood if we look at the delicate relatioship between the Fort William Council and the nawab's government which depended upon the prosperity of British corporate and private trade in Bengal. With the British settlement in Calcutta, the city soon developed as a major centre of intra-Asiatic trade. The period between the mid-1720s and the mid-1730s was the high period of British sea-borne private trade from Calcutta. A number of related factors seems to have enabled the British to dominate the carrying trade. The markets they traded in were relatively stable and they were able to depend upon a pool of private capital and an Asiatic commercial organization based in Calcutta, Bombay and Madras. There was close cooperation among the Company servants in the three Presidencies, and their trading farms and partnerships provided a continuity of organization and expertise so essential for commercial success. Moreover, the British private traders operating on a net margin of 20 per cent per voyage[16] could easily undercut the corporate 'country trade' of the Dutch and the

[14] For details, see S. Chaudhuri, *Trade and Commercial Organization*, pp. 39-41.

[15] See my article, 'Sirajuddaullah, English Company, etc.' *IHR*, vol. XIII, nos. 1-2, pp. 117-122.

[16] R.C. Temple, *Scattergoods and the East India Company*, pp. 128-29.

French who expected a net return of 50 per cent on their ventures.[17] The Company servants also seem to have traded at an advantage in comparison with Asian merchants who paid high customs duties in Asian ports. It was claimed in the 1740s that a ship of the Armenian merchant of Hughli, Khwaja Wazid, sailed under French colours because at Basra it could pay the French rate of 3 per cent while the Asians had to pay 6 per cent.[18]

But the British private trade in Calcutta began to decline from the late 1730s and was faced with a crisis in the 1740s, mainly because of the competition from the French private traders under the energetic commercial management of gover- nor Dupleix at Chandernagore.[19] From about the mid-1730s French corporate trade too recovered from its nadir of the 1720s to a level near that of the British.[20] The French Company's servants who were not officially allowed to participate in the country trade were permitted to do so in 1722.[21] As a result, they were now at par with the English Company servants and emerged as a serious rival to British private traders. The main threat occurred in Bengal through the impetus Dupleix had given to private participation in Asian trade. The primary concern of Dupleix as governor of Chandernagore was commercial, not political.[22] From 1731 to 1742 Dupleix organized at least 90 voyages and the pattern of ships sent out by Dupleix and his associates brings out clearly the predominantly east-west orien- tation of India's Asian trade during this period,[23] as described by Holden Furber.[24]

The emergence of major French competition in the Asiatic trade of Bengal, however, resulted in bitter commercial rivalries between the French and the British. So far as the country trade of Asia is concerned, the French undoubtedly became the main rival of the British in Bengal towards the beginning of 1740. This

[17] A. Dasgupta, *Malabar*, p. 85.

[18] J.D. Nichol, 'The British in India, 1740-63', p. 79.

[19] For Dupleix's activities in Bengal, see I. Ray, 'Dupleix's Trade at Chandernagore', *IHR*, vol. 1, 1974, pp. 279-94.

[20] Virginia M. Thompson, *Dupleix*, p. 73.

[21] I. Ray, 'Dupleix's Trade', *IHR*, vol. 1, 1974, p. 283.

[22] Ibid., p. 281.

[23] For details, see Ibid., 284-87.

[24] Holden Furber, *John Company*, p. 162.

is apparent from the following table of Anglo-French shipping in Bengal:[25]

TABLE 11.1
French and British Ships in Bengal, 1738-42

	French Ships			British Ships		
Year	Total	Company	Private	Total	Company	Private
1738	14	N.A.	N.A.	25	N.A.	N.A.
1739	16	7	9	24	6	18
1740	23	2	21	23	10	13
1741	27	4	23	26	7	19
1742	N.A.	N.A.	18	29	7	22

[Source: Collected and computed from shipping lists in VOC records]

The crisis of the British private trade was so acute in the early 1740s that the Fort William Council accused the French of disrupting the British private trading fortune. In a desperate attempt to rescue the British private trade, the Fort William Council prohibited further commercial intercourse with the main French settlement at Chandernagore. In 1742 the Council took the following resolution:[26]

The French having for some time past been of great disservice to the private trade of this place by the assistance and supply of money and goods that they have had from Calcutta and more particularly to the ports of Judda, Mocha and in the Gulph of Persia and as we have ships bound this year to those places. In order therefore to prevent any ill consequence in future such as we have formerly experienced thereby.

Resolved that no merchants of this place white or black either in the Company's service or otherwise under their protection

[25] Collected and computed from VOC, 2469, ff. 1007-8; 2489, ff. 291-91vo, 293; 2504, ff. 1065-66; 2518, ff. 515, 517; 2556, ff. 575-76.
[26] BPC, vol. 15, f. 237, 7 Oct. 1742.

be permitted to sell or furnish the French with any sortments of goods whatever or to freight goods on any of the French ships bound out of this river....

It was perhaps not an empty boast when Dupleix later wrote of his period as governor of Chandernagore: 'I made the English tremble for they saw their commerce dwindling and their merchants forced to declare themselves bankrupt. I accomplished all this in nine years'.[27]

From about the early 1750s, the British corporate and private trade in Bengal was facing renewed difficulties. The end of the Anglo-French war in 1748 and the peace treaty between the Marathas and Bengal nawab meant the renewal of French and Asian competition in the already competitive market of Bengal. The French pursued their trade in Bengal with renewed vigour, opened a new factory at Dhaka in 1750,[28] and resumed their commercial operations in Hughli, Kasimbazar, Dhaka and Patna.[29] To this was added the competition of the Armenian and other Asian merchants.[30] The tight situation in Bengal's money market aggravated the Company's difficulties with its creditors, notably the Seths, demanding repayment of loans accumulated in the 40s and imposing restrictions on further credit.[31]

The situation in the key area of private trade became critical. There was a sharp decline in the consulage which reflected a definite slide in the British private trade of Calcutta. Robert Orme, who was in Calcutta then, wrote to his friend Mr. Robbins in 1751: 'The consulage in years of extensive trade used to be from 20 to 30 thousand rupees to the best of my memory, it is now scarce 5 or 6 clear.'[32] Two leading members of the Fort William Council, Charles Manningham and William Frankland, commented, in all probability referring to the decline of private trade, when they wrote to Clive, then in Madras, in 1753: '...the situation of trade since you left us has continued so bad.'[33]

[27] Virginia M. Thompson, *Dupleix*, p. 723.
[28] BPC, vol. 23, f. 150vo, 4 Jan. 1750.
[29] Ibid., f. 407vo, 8 Dec. 1750.
[30] Ibid., vol. 24, f. 58, 7 Feb. 1751.
[31] *FWIHC*, vol. 1, p. 472; BPC, vol. 23, f. 303vo, 23 Aug. 1750.
[32] Orme to Mr. Robbins, 10 May 1751, Orme, OV 12, f. 83.
[33] Eur. G. 37, Box 21, 1 Sept. 1753.

TABLE 11.2

British and French Shipping in Bengal, 1751-54

Year	Tot. Ships	Private	Co's	500 tons & above	2-400 tons	100 & Above	Below 100	Total Tonnage	Private Tonnage
1751 (British)	24	21	3	3Co.+ 3Pvt.	8	7	3	7,420	5,020
1754 (French)	27	22	5	5Co. + 6Pvt.	10	6	-	10,450	7,450
1754 (British)	20	8	12	N.A.	N.A.	N.A.	N.A.	N.A.	N.A.

[Source: Collected and computed from the shipping lists in VOC records.]

The competition of the French trade was one of the main causes of this decline in the British private trade from Calcutta. In 1752 Captain Fenwick, a resident of Calcutta, wrote: 'The French it is probable are now in their zenith of trade in Bengal.'[34] The shipping lists in the Dutch archives leave little doubt that in the mid-1750s there was an extremely powerful French fleet in Bengal in direct competition with the British in Calcutta, endangering the supremacy of the British private trade. The above table (11.2) of Anglo-French shipping in Bengal in the mid-1750s will illustrate our point, though due to the gaps in the shipping lists we are not in a position to give a more comprehensive picture.[35]

The Table (11.2) indicates that in the mid-50s, French private trade had a remarkable revival which even surpassed the golden period under Dupleix. In 1754 while the total English fleet that touched Calcutta numbered only 20 (12 Company's and only 8 belonging to private traders), the French fleet numbered 27 of which as many as 22 were engaged in private trade. While the British shipping in 1751 totalled 7,420 tonnes, the shipping capacity of the French fleet in 1754 amounted to 10,450 tonnes, of which the British private shipping comprised 5,020 tonnes, and the French private shipping totalled 7,450 tonnes respectively. This is a definite indication of a remarkable increase in French private trading.

The substantial increase in French private trade, obviously at the cost of the British, scared the Fort William Council. In the early 1750s the Council, in an attempt to arrest the decline in British private trade, took recourse to several measures. The first was the *dastak* reforms of 1750 by which the Council decided that in private trade the Indian and French traders were henceforth to be debarred from using the Company's *dastaks*.[36] In addition, the Council restricted in 1753 the issue of trading passes in order to protect the Company servants' country trade.[37] These passes conferred an exemption of the vessels' cargoes from customs duties at the Indian ports. John Wood, a free merchant of

---

[34] Orme Mss., India VI, f. 111vo.
[35] VOC, 2754, f. 277; 2829, ff. 294-97.
[36] BPC, vol. 23, f. 328, 17 Sept. 1750.
[37] Ibid., vol. 26, ff. 23-24, 13 Jan. 1753.

Calcutta, angrily pointed out that this would effectively create a monopoly in the hands of the Company servants over the private maritime commerce of Calcutta. In October 1755 Roger Drake, the governor, suggested more restrictions.[38] The *dastak* and trading pass reforms were matched by the change over in the Company's investment pattern from *dadni* to *gomasta* system in 1753.[39] Needless to say, the Fort William Council embarked on all these measures in an attempt to rescue their battered private trading fortunes. So it seems quite probable, from what we have analyzed so far, that on the one hand the conquest of Bengal and the destruction of the French at Chandernagore on the other, were essential for augmenting the declining private trade of the Company servants in Bengal.

11.2 TRADE, IMPORT OF BULLION AND CONQUEST

In recent years it has been suggested that the Plassey revolution should be explained in the light of the emergence of Hindu/Jain banking and commercial class connected with the European trade in the first half of the eighteenth century. Though presented in a new garb, here also there is no escape from Hill who hinted at this long back. It was Brijen K. Gupta who fairly recently elaborated that as a result of Indo-European oceanic trade, 'a community of interest has developed between Hindu mercantile class and the European Companies'—the class which became the 'catalytic' agent in the British conquest of Bengal.[40] The latest studies emphasize the role of European trade as the major source of bullion import and fostering close relations between the European companies and the commercial-banking class in Bengal. These authorities even suggest that the interests of the Indian merchants and zamindars 'had become far too closely intertwined with the fate of the Europeans' so that the 'expulsion' of the British from Calcutta 'could not be borne long' by the former and hence the Plassey revolution.[41] In short, the

---

[38] Ibid., vol. 28, f. 263vo, 20 Oct. 1755.

[39] For details, see chapter 5.

[40] Brijen K. Gupta, *Sirajuddaullah*, p. 32.

[41] C.A. Bayly, *Indian Society*, pp. 49-50, P.J. Marshall, *Bengal*, pp. 65, 67.

favourite 'collaboration' thesis, with the emphasis now that the initiative came from the Indian side, conveniently reduces the role of the British in the Plassey conspiracy.[42]

The above implies two significant assumptions, on both of which the latest research casts grave doubts. The first assumption is that by 1757 i.e. on the eve of Plassey, European trade was the most important factor in the commercial life of Bengal. Of course the major works in the field so far (not excluding my small contribution to some extent!) would have us believe in such a thesis.[43] But in a recent paper, Shireen Moosvi has very ably challenged this stating that the situation might have been quite different and the Europeans were not the only importers of bullion, and not possibly even the largest importers at that.[44] From whatever quantitative evidence we could gather from different sources so far, it seems that the volume of trade carried on by the Asian merchants in Bengal was much larger than that of the Europeans even in the late forties and early fifties of the eighteenth century. It can be established that the share of the Asian merchants in the trade of the two major export commodities namely, textiles and silk, was much higher than that of the Europeans.[45] And it need not be emphasized that like the Europeans, the Asians too had to import silver/cash to make their purchases in Bengal as nothing else was accepted. As such, the thesis that the Europeans were the principal agencies through which silver came to Bengal is hardly tenable and so is the thesis of the connection between European trade and the Plassey revolution.

The second assumption appears to be equally doubtful. It could have been said that the interest of the commercial and

---

[42] See for instance, P.J. Marshall, *Bengal*, p. 77 where he states: 'By April it was clear to the British that there was a party of malcontents in Bengal led by the Jagat Seths who were prepared to try to use British power to gain their ends.' Also Rajat Kanta Ray, 'Colonial Penetration and Initial Resistance', *IHR*, vol. XII, nos. 1-2, p.15.

[43] S. Chaudhuri, *Trade and Commercial Organization*; K.N. Chaudhuri, *Trading World*; Om Prakash, *Dutch Company*.

[44] Shireen Moosvi, 'The Silver Influx, Money Supply, Prices and Revenue Extraction in Mughal India', *JESHO*, vol. XXX, 1987, pp. 92-94.

[45] See chapters 7 & 8.

banking class as also that of the zamindars was closely interlocked with the fate of the Europeans only when it could be established that the main source of income, and hence the rise to power of this class was through its connection with European trade. But as we have already pointed out, European trade was not the major factor in the commercial life of Bengal and Asian trade was still more important than the former, the question of their hanging on to the fortunes of the European companies does not arise. This can further be corroborated from the source of accumulation of wealth by this class and hence the power of three merchant princes—the Jagat Seths, Umichand and Khwaja Wazid—who were the Indian ring leaders of the revolution. It can be established from the estimate of the annual income of the house of Jagat Seths, made by Luke Scrafton in 1757, that out of an annual income of Rs 5 million, the share from coinage which was a monopoly of the house, *batta* and loans to European companies could not have been more than Rs 1.5 million at the most.[46] And after what we have said earlier, there is no reason to believe that the income from coinage and *batta* was solely owing to European import of bullion alone. Similarly though Umichand and Khwaja Wazid were more directly connected with European trade, the main source of their income was however monopoly trade in saltpetre and salt. Umichand also attempted at the monopoly of opium and grain trade while Wazid was largely engaged in the Surat, Red Sea and Persian Gulf trade with his own considerable fleet of seafaring vessels. So, in the face of all the evidence it is difficult to maintain that the interest of the merchant princes representing the commercial and banking class in Bengal was intertwined with the fortunes of the European companies.

11.3 BRITISH ATTACK ON CHANDERNAGORE PAVING THE WAY FOR PLASSEY

It was Sirajuddaullah, the last independent nawab of Bengal, who for the first time raised the awkward issues of the abuse of *dastaks* and unauthorized fortifications at a time when the British private trade which flourished earlier to a great extent because of these was in a critical state. So a rupture in the relations between the

[46] See chapter 5.

nawab and the Company became inevitable.[47] In an attempt to resolve the differences with the British amicably, the nawab sent several letters and emissaries to Calcutta. But while on his way to Purnea he heard at Rajmahal about the ill-treatment meted out to Narain Singh, the bearer of the first letter, he swung back and moved against Kasimbazar factory which capitulated quickly. Then he began his march towards Calcutta. The governor of Calcutta, Roger Drake, who was actively engaged in private trade, was reported to have reacted to mediation offers by declaring 'the sooner he [Sirajuddaullah] came [to Calcutta] the better and he [Drake] would make another nawab'.[48] The nawab overran Calcutta and the British were forced to take refuge at Fulta down the Ganges. An appeal for reinforcement had to be sent to Madras and it was carried personally by no other person than Manningham, one of the members of the Fort William Council and one who was actively engaged in private trade. In its instruction of 13 October 1756, the Fort St. George (Madras) Council outlined the objective of the expeditionary force sent to Bengal under Clive and Watson, and recommended 'not mere retaking of Calcutta' and 'ample reparations' but urged to 'effect a junction with any powers in the province of Bengal that might be disatisfied with the violence of the nawab's government or that might have pretensions to the nawabship'.[49] No less significant is the fact that to the above suggestion of bringing about a *coup d' état* in Bengal, the Fort St. George Council added the idea of dispossessing the French of their settlement at Chandernagore:[50] 'We have desired Mr. Watson, if he thinks it practicable, to dispossess the French of Chandernagore....Should you be of this opinion we desire that you will enforce our recommendation.'

The British expeditionary force recaptured Calcutta and on the ostensible ground of avenging the nawab's earlier attack on Calcutta sacked the premier port of Hughli. A close scrutiny of

[47] See my article, 'Sirajuddaullah, English Company etc.', *IHR*, vol. XIII, nos. 1-2, pp. 113-122.

[48] Watts and Collet to the Court of Directors, 17 July 1756, quoted in S.C. Hill, *Bengal in 1756-57*, vol. 1, pp. 116-17.

[49] *Records of Fort St. George, Diary and Consultation Books*, Military Dept., 1756, p. 330; Orme Mss. vol. 170, f. 90.

[50] Fort St. George Select Committee to Select Committee, Fort William, 14 Nov. 1756, Hill, *Bengal in 1756-57*, vol. I, p. 302.

the events, however, makes one suspect that one of the motives behind the sack of Hughli was to crush the intra-Asiatic trade carried on from Hughli mainly by the Asian merchants and French private traders. The British onslaught on Hughli severely jeopardized the trade of the Armenian merchant prince Khwaja Wazid. The attack on Hughli was also partly aimed at fomenting discontent in the nawab's camp, as will be evident from the Fort William Council's letter of 31 January 1757: 'The capture and destruction of Hugli was esteemed so essential to strike a terror into the Subah's troops and encourage any malcontents to declare in our favour.... This we have reason to believe has had the desired effect.'[51] After a skirmish with the nawab's army in which the latter was defeated, the British entered into the treaty of Alinagar with the nawab on 9 February 1757. The swiftness with which the treaty was concluded led the British to believe that the French could be quickly reduced with the nawab's permission, and they employed William Watts and Umichand for the purpose of obtaining the necessary permission from the nawab.

Sirajuddaullah, however, was intent on preventing any conflict among the Europeans in his dominion. His instructions to his deputy Nandakumar who was in charge of Hughli were explicitly clear on this point.[52] But the British managed to bribe Nandakumar through Umichand, thus preventing him from coming to the assistance of the French in the event of a British attack. Determined as they were to drive the French out of Chandernagore ever since the treaty of Alinagar, the British would have attacked Chandernagore immediately, but a few things stood in the way of immediate prosecution of the British design. The reinforcement from Bombay which was daily expected did not yet arrive. So it was risky to attack Chandernagore which might have embroiled the British in a conflict with the nawab also. In that case, with available resources it was impolitic to fight a possible Franco-Bengali alliance. Admiral Watson's hesitation was attributed to the absence of the nawab's permission to attack the French. In such a situation Clive was undecided till

[51] Beng. Letters Reed., vol. 23, f. 405, 31 Jan. 1757.

[52] Watts to Clive, 18 Feb. 1757, Hill, *Bengal in 1756-57*, vol. II, p. 288; Clive to Select Committee, 22 Feb. 1757, Hill, *Bengal in 1756-57*, vol. II, p. 240.

4 March.[53]

But within the following two days the whole complexion changed because of two developments of considerable importance. The first was the arrival of the Bombay troops with the *Cumberland*.[54] The second was a letter from the nawab to Clive stating that he intended to proceed to Patna in the face of a possible attack of Bengal by Ahmad Shah Abdali and inviting Clive to join him with the British army for which the nawab was ready to pay Clive Rs 0.1 million a month.[55] No sooner had these two opportune developments taken place than Clive changed his earlier position and two days later 'no longer waxing eloquent about the world's opinion of English plottings', Clive began his march towards Chandernagore on 8 March. Alarmed, the French wanted to know the intention of the British. Clive replied on 9 March:[56] 'I very sincerely declare to you that at this present time I have no intention to attack your settlement. If I should alter my mind, I shall not fail to advise you of it.'

With the Abdali invasion lurking and yet sincerely trying to prevent any Anglo-French conflict in his dominion, the young nawab wrote a letter to Admiral Watson, the real purpose of which was to appeal to him to accept the earlier French offer of a treaty of neutrality. But the letter was written on his behalf by his secretary whom William Watts managed through a handsome bribe 'to pen this important epistle in a proper style so as to permit the attack immediately and to desptach it without delay'.[57] It has been suggested that this letter removed Watson's scruples regarding the attack on Chandernagore without the nawab's permission.[58] Scrafton, the British resident at Murshidabad, thought that the letter may be well understood as a consent to our attacking Chandernagore though certainly it was not meant as

[53] Brijen K. Gupta, *Sirajuddaullah*, pp. 108-110.

[54] Orme, *Military Transactions*, vol. II, pp. 142-43.

[55] Sirajuddaullah to Clive, 4 March 1757, Hill, *Bengal in 1756-57*, vol. III, pp. 270-71.

[56] Clive to the French Council at Chandernagore, 9 March 1757, Hill, *Bengal in 1756-57*, vol. II, p. 277.

[57] John Campbell, *Memoirs*, pp. 42-43.

[58] Especially by Watts and Ives, the two contemporaries: for details see Brijen K. Gupta, *Sirajuddaullah*, p. 111.

such'.[59] The fact of the matter, however, was that Watson never really bothered much about any permission from the nawab. For, even before he received the letter from the nawab which was alleged to have removed his scruples about attacking Chandernagore, he had sent his men-of-war to cover the advance of Clive's forces by land.[60]

The French would fall soon but not as yet, and not so easily, had it not been for the betrayal of a French renegade and the vacillation of the nawab. On 13 March Clive asked the French chief Renault to surrender the fort and the latter's refusal led to the outbreak of hostilities the same night. The siege of Chandernagore began on 14 March. The nawab, true to his earlier resolution to assist one European power in case of an attack by the other, asked his deputy Nandakumar to defend the French. The deputy who received a fresh bribe from the British wrote to the nawab: 'That as the French were unable to resist the English, he had therefore ordered his troops to Hughli, lest his [the nawab's] victorious colours should be involved in their [the French] disgrace'.[61]

Yet all was not lost. Jean Law, the French representative at the nawab's court in Murshidabad, received the news of the British attack on 15 March. He graphically described in his memoirs the events that followed which reflect the uncertainty and vacillation of the nawab. He was apprehensive of a possible conspiracy in Murshidabad court which was partly responsible for the irresolution on his part to come forward to the aid of the French. At last when the nawab ultimately sent his assistance under the able commanders, Rai Durlabh Ram and Mir Madan, which reached Hughli on 22 March, it was too late—the French chief Renault signed the capitulation on 23 March by which the French were obliged to leave Chandernagore, leaving behind all their fortunes and effects at the virtual disposal of the British.[62] Scrafton was partly right when he pointed out that the French had fallen because the 'Nabob floated between his fears and his

[59] Luke Scrafton, *Reflections*, p. 75.

[60] Clive to Watson, 11 March 1757, Hill, *Bengal in 1756-57*, vol. II, p. 280.

[61] Luke Scrafton, *Reflections*, p. 70.

[62] For detailed account, see Brijen K. Gupta, *Sirajuddaullah*, pp. 112-13.

wishes'—his fears of the Abdali invasion, of the betrayal of his court officials—his wish to help the French, the arrival of Bussy with reinforcements and the ultimate defeat of the British.

The attack on Chandernagore was imperative not only, as traditional explanation has always emphasized, as a consequence of the outbreak of the Anglo-French war and/or for the prevention of a Franco-Bengali alliance. As our foregoing evidence and arguments will bear out, it was to a large extent to retrieve British private trade fortunes which faced a severe crisis from the late 1740s through the mid-1750s, and for which the French and their allies in intra-Asian trade from Bengal—the Hughli merchants under the leadership of Khwaja Wazid—were largely responsible. The imperative of the empire necessitated that the French who might have stood in the way of the British ambition for territorial acquisition in Bengal should be driven out before striking at the local ruler who would be isolated after the fall of the French. The elimination of the French from Bengal would also ensure that the pro-French lobby in the Murshidabad court would be weakened so that there would be very few to support the cause of the nawab. And this was proved right by the betrayal at the last moment by Khwaja Wazid who from the beginning was pro-French, anti-British and a close confidant of the nawab. The French fell, paving the way for the smooth recovery of the British private trading fortunes and the British conquest of Bengal. There is little doubt that the seeds of the Plassey conspiracy were sown by the instructions of the Fort St. George Council which, as we have seen earlier, contained such positive and direct hint as 'to effect a junction with any powers' that might have been 'disgruntled or had pretensions to nawabship'. This actually opened the floodgates of the conspiracy. Had there been even resentment against or dissatisfaction with the nawab's rule, they might have only created the necessary but not the sufficient condition for hatching a conspiracy. As a matter of fact there is ample evidence to show that the British engineered and encouraged the coup against the nawab. It was they who roped in several leading figures of the *darbar* to their side for carrying 'our [British] project [of deposing the nawab] into execution'.[63] And thus followed the British conquest of Bengal.

[63] Orme Mss., India V, f. 1228; O.V. 170, f.265. For details, see my article 'Trade, Bullion and Conquest - Bengal in the mid-18th Century' in *Itinerario*, vol. 15, 1991, no. 2, pp. 27-30.

12

CONCLUSION

In the general scenario of decadence, chaos and instability in
most parts of the erstwhile Mughal empire in the first half of the
eighteenth century, Bengal was a singular exception which
enjoyed a strong and stable government under the nawabs. The
nawabs of Bengal who were independent of the centre at Delhi
for all practical purposes except a nominal recognition of the
suzerainty of the Mughals drew the prominent members of
ruling elite—zamindars, merchant-bankers and military aristocrats, most of whom owed their eminence and rise to power to
the nawabs' personal favour—into a collaborative partnership.
But this partnershp did not represent a broad class alliance—it
was more or less an exigent arrangement on a personal level to
serve the vested interests of the people involved. However the
significant fact is that this led to a stable political order and the
foundation of a strong nizamat. As a result, new outlets were
found in increasing economic activity, in production and maximization of revenue, in the fostering of trade and industry, and
the expansion of the markets. The rich prospects of trade in
Bengal, and the comparative peace and stability in the region in
the first half of the eighteenth century attracted to the province
merchants and traders from different parts of India and Asia as
also from Europe.

Of the Europeans, the Dutch and the English East India
Companies were most active in Bengal trade. The Asiatic trade
of these Companies which began as a bilateral trade between
Europe and the spice islands changed into triangular trade
between Europe, India (for cheap piece-goods) and the spice
islands (where the Indian textiles were exchanged for spices to
be exported to Europe). It eventually became bilateral again,

mainly between Europe and Bengal, with the marked difference that Bengal emerged as the chief partner of the Asiatic trade of the European companies from around the 1680s, and this trend was maintained throughout the first half of the eighteenth century. Though the Dutch were ahead of the English in their export trade from Bengal in the early years of the eighteenth century, the English had established a substantial lead over the Dutch in the 1730s and 1740s. In the 1750s they were nearly equal though the Dutch intra-Asian trade, which was an integral part of the overall trading strategy of the Dutch Company, declined to a considerable extent during this period. The important fact to consider in this context is that the Companies had to import into Bengal bullion and specie which generally formed about 75 to 94 per cent of the total value of their imports to pay for the export commodities from Bengal.

It was this very prosperity of Bengal, not its decline or weakness, which made its conquest so lucrative to the Europeans. The notion that it was the political instability in Bengal prior to Plassey which made the British intervention inevitable can hardly be accepted. Thus the suggestion even in recent studies that the alienation of the dominant ruling class by the new and young nawab Sirajuddaullah (1756-57) broke down the new 'class alliance'and led to the subsequent political crisis resulting in the British conquest is not tenable. The so-called 'class alliance' was in fact an adjustment at a personal level for mutual benefit for exploiting the resources and had no institutional base, and hence quite fragile. Moreover, there was nothing unusual in the political situation in the mid-eighteenth century. With every succession question since the death of Murshid Quli (1728/29), the ruling clique was divided and so it was in 1756-57. Though a dominant group with the active support of the British opposed the succession of Sirajuddaullah, there was another group including merchant princes, zamindars and military aristocrats which supported the young nawab. This was the pattern in 1728/29 as also in 1739/40. So Plassey can hardly be explained as the consummation of internal political crisis in Bengal.

Neither was there an 'economic crisis' in Bengal in the mid-eighteenth century. The advocates of this thesis (though no one speaks of 'economic crisis' as such, there are explicit as well as implicit hints on this point in several recent writings) tried to establish that prior to Plassey, economic conditions deteriorated, trade and industry languished, merchants were impoverished, prices of different commodities sky-rocketed and the exports of the English Company declined. But it has been shown here with quantitative evidence that there was hardly any perceptible decline in the total value of the exports of the European companies. True, the value of the English trade showed a marginal decline in the late 1740s and the early 1750s but this was not because of any serious disruption in the Bengal economy. As a matter of fact, the decrease in the English trade was compensated, as far as Bengal's export trade was concerned, by the increase in the Dutch exports during this period. Again, in this context, what is significant is that the export trade of the Asian merchants from Bengal, especially in raw silk and textiles, was quite substantial even in the mid-eighteenth century.

All this will negate the thesis that trade and industry in Bengal were seriously impaired in the pre-Plassey period. The very fact that the Asian merchants and the European companies exported such a huge amount of silk and textiles from Bengal even in the mid- eighteenth century would only establish that both trade and industry flourished in the pre-Plassey period.

Neither was there any decline of the Bengal merchants in the mid-eighteenth century. The recent assertion that the English and the Dutch Companies increasingly turned to direct dealings with the artisans, as the mercantile community of mid-eighteenth century Bengal was crippled, is untenable. The Dutch made such experiment for three years (1747-49) only and reverted to *dadni* system in 1750. The English change over from *dadni* to *gomasta* system in 1753 was the result of the Fort William Council's attempt to resolve its commercial crisis, in the face of dwindling private trade, by cutting out the *dadni* merchants and replacing them by *gomastas* who would augment the private trade of the Company servants. It is too well-known a fact to be emphasized that the *gomastas* became the main instruments of coercion, and how aided and abetted by them, the Company servants invaded every conceivable branch of Bengal's inland trade in the post-Plassey period.

Again, it has been asserted recently that the import of bullion by the Europeans and their increasing purchases along with the severe damage to the economy caused by the Maratha depredations ultimately pushed up the price level in Bengal in the pre-Plassey period. This theory is discounted here on the basis of a detailed analysis of the prices of important export commodities like textiles and raw silk on the one hand and prices of wage goods like rice on the other. Such an analysis shows clearly that there was hardly any 'marked and sharp' increase in the price of either textiles or raw silk. On the contrary , the prices of the two most important types of *muslins* namely, *khasas* and *mulmuls* which were the main staples in the export list of the Companies, actually show a downward trend in the early 1750s from the level in the 1730s and the early 1740s. Nor was there any appreciable rise in the price of wage goods like rice which can be described as 'marked and sustained'. In other words, there was hardly any 'economic crisis' in mid-eighteenth century Bengal.

At the same time it should be noted, contrary to prevailing theory, that the impact of the European trade bringing in its train influx of bullion has been overestimated so far. Bengal enjoyed a favourable balance of trade even in the sixteenth and seventeenth centuries, and all the traders—whether Asians or Europeans—had to import silver/cash for their purchases in Bengal. Even in the early fifteenth century, a Chinese traveller remarked that 'long-distance merchants in Bengal settled their accounts with *tankas* (silver coins)'.[1] So the inflow of bullion and specie was not a new phenomenon for which the Europeans were mostly responsible. In fact, even in the mid-eighteenth century it was the Asians, not the Europeans, who were the major as also the traditional importers of bullion. However there is no denying the fact that the European trade brought in a large amount of bullion and specie into Bengal but the impact of this on the economy seems to have been only marginal, touching as it did the fringe of the economy. The only plausible explanation for this, it appears, was that a large part of the treasure brought into Bengal was appropriated by the ruling elite and the merchant-middlemen while only a little filtered down to the primary producers.

Nor were the European companies able to effect fundamental changes in the traditional system of commercial organization.

---

[1] W.W.Rockhill, 'Notes on the Relations and Trade of China with the Eastern Archipelago and the Coast of the Indian Ocean during the Fourteenth Century', *Toung Pao*, 16, pt.2 (1915), p. 144, quoted in Richard M. Eaton, *The Rise of Islam*, p. 96.

They had to adjust themselves, more often than not, to the traditional commercial norms and practices in the given areas of their trade. Yet their activities resulted in the introduction of certain important elements in the existing system. The office of the chief merchant, the formation of joint stock of saltpetre merchants in Bihar and the fixing of prices of goods according to samples at the time of contract were in a way novel in the commercial order of the time. But these were not very significant in the overall structure of the pre-modern South Asian commercial organization.

A distinctive feature of the mercantile world of Bengal was the co-existence of small and big merchants of different castes and communities, operating side by side in the various trade marts of the province. The merchant princes namely, the Jagat Seths, Umichand and Khwaja Wazid collectively predominated both the commerce and financial administration of Bengal. The scale of their operations, the extent of their business empires and their ability to undertake extensive and organized commercial ventures would negate the thesis that the 'ordinary entrepreneurial character of the Asian trade was a sum of peddling activities'. The close collaboration between the merchants and the ruling elite in Bengal as also the great influence exerted by the former in the political, administrative and financial affairs of the province is well illustrated by the careers of these merchant princes.

The Bengal merchants in the early eighteenth century were not subservient in any way to the European companies—partnership or interdependence as distinct from a later period of subjugation was the hallmark of the relationship between Asian merchants and European traders. In Bengal, as in other parts of India, trade or business was the concern of individual merchants rather of groups acting in concert. Merchants tended to act as individuals, as members of families, at most one in a group thrown together in the course of business. Impersonal cooperation in the institution of business, as had already developed in Europe by this time, was relatively uncommon. Even cooperation at a personal level was not easy to come by. Any commercial venture was the risk of the individual merchant or a very small group of merchants taking part in it. But it appears that business transactions were not confined only within the same

caste or communal group—these transcended, more often than
not, caste or communal boundaries. It was not unusual to find
a Hindu *bania* of a Muslim merchant or a Muslim associate of a
Hindu or Armenian trader. The merchant community, especially
in the urban areas, though probably organized on caste lines at
the primary level, was a homogeneous group in general, acting
in concert whenever necessary with little regard to caste or
regional affiliations.

So far as the textile industry of Bengal is concerned, it was
characterized by certain distinct features. It was basically a rural
domestic handicraft industry with extraordinary diffusion and
marked by extreme localization and high specialization. Weaving
was often a subsidiary occupation to agriculture. The basic unit
of production was the weaver operating as an independent
artisan with his wife and children assisting him. As the family was
the working unit, the weaver's home was the typical workshop.
The rudimentary character of the technique with emphasis on
simple instruments and a low ratio of fixed to working capital
implied a minimal concentration of labour and capital in
individual units of production. In the pre-colonial period the
weaver-artisan in Bengal appears to have enjoyed considerable
independence. He retained the ownership of his means of
production—his looms—bought his own yarn independently and
at least in theory was the owner of his product. The *dadni* system
at most promoted the control of merchant capital over the
producer and not the process of production itself. It was only
under the Company and its servants in the post-Plassey period
that the weavers became wage workers in terms and conditions
over which they had no control.

As far as the British conquest of Bengal is concerned, it can
hardly be explained by the 'collaboration' thesis. The suggestion
that the European trade bringing in its train influx of bullion and
thus resulting in the intertwining of the interests of merchant-
bankers with the fate of the European companies and finally
leading to the Plassey revolution is a doubtful proposition. There
is no denying the fact that the European trade was quite
significant in the mid-eighteenth century but it was not the most
important factor in the commercial economy of Bengal. Even in
the mid-eighteenth century, the export by the Asian merchants
from Bengal was much higher than that of the European

companies and as such it was the Asians, not the Europeans, who were the major importers of bullion into Bengal, Thus the main source of accumulation of wealth by the merchant princes of Bengal who represented the merchant-banking class was not their link with European trade. So the thesis of the interlocking of interests of the indigenous merchant-banking class with those of the Europeans and hence the collaboration between them can hardly be tenable, and so is the theory of the connection between European trade and Plassey revolution. Of course, it is true that some leading members of the ruling elite joined hands with the British to bring about the revolution of 1757. But the initiative was taken by the British. It was they who roped in several important members of the ruling clique in their 'project' of the revolution. The Indian conspirators did not realize the full implications of the British design and hence paid dearly for their follies in not too distant future when they were completely ruined by the new victors.[2]

The British conquest of Bengal followed not because of any internal crisis, either political or economic, in Bengal. The conquest became necessary for the retrieval of the private trade fortunes of the Company servants. This private trade interest was the motivating force behind the conquest. The golden days of the British private trade began to decline from the late 1730s and it was facing a severe crisis in the late 1740s and the early 1750s because of the substantial increase in the French private trade. So the destrucion of the French, thus nipping in the bud any possibililty of Franco-Bengali alliance against the British and the deposition of the nawab who was threatening to stop illegal private trade and misuse of *dastaks* by the British—both essential for rescuing the battered private trade fortunes of the British—became the main target of the Company servants' sub-imperial-ism. These Company servants were determined to use Company's local resources when their own private trade interest was at stake and knew well that their activities, if those resulted in advantages for the Company, would be approved in London. This was actually what happened in Bengal in 1756-57.

[2] S. Chaudhury, 'Trade, Bullion and Conquest', *Itinerario*, vo. 15, no. 2 (1991), pp. 27-30.

After the conquest, the British became the virtual rulers of Bengal, and this ushered in an unprecedented aggrandizement of British private trade. Not only did the British gradually drive away all the competitors in both intra-Asian and European trade but there was an invasion of almost every branch of the province's inland trade by the British private traders. Under the Company and its servants in the second half of the eighteenth century, the traditional trade of the Asian merchants which was so very significant earlier was now systematically wiped out. The merchant community of Bengal headed by the merchant princes who played such an important role in the commercial and political affairs of Bengal was gradually eliminated and replaced by a new class of compradors who unlike the earlier Bengal merchants were completely subservient to the British.

The ruthless oppression and exploitation by the Company and its servants almost ruined the traditional industries and brought in its train untold misery for the weaver-artisans. In the pre-Plassey period, the weaver-artisan had the freedom to produce any kind of textile and sell it to whomever he wanted to. And though he may not have been very affluent, he had at least a living from the subsistence level to a rather comfortable one. He was not reduced to the position of a wage earner as yet. The Bengali weaver in the pre-colonial period owned his looms, bought his yarn, and could produce and sell his wares with a certain measure of freedom. But in the second half of the century, the Company and its servants monopolized the weaver-artisans who were now asked by the former to produce only certain quantity of a particular type at a given price. The *gomastas* of the Company and its servants ushered in almost a reign of terror, coercing and exploiting the weaver-artisans. The weavers were now registered with a particualr *gomasta* and not permitted to work for any one else. And they were transferred from one *gomasta* to another 'like so many slaves'. As a near-contemporary British observer pointed out, 'their hardship is scarcely to be described'.[3] So it can be reasonably asserted that the weaver-artisans on whom Bengal depended so much for her prosperity had a much more enviable position in the first half of the

[3] Mss. Eur. D. 243, ff. 37-38.

eighteenth century than their counterparts in the second half of the century.

Briefly, Bengal's prosperity which was so very pronounced under the nawabi rule in the first half of the eighteenth century gradually came to an end after Plassey and in the second half of the century there followed an economic impoverishment of the province under the aegis of the Company and its servants. It was not only responsible Company officials like Harry Verelst[4] or William Bolts[5] who pointed out unequivocally to the decline of Bengal in the post-Plassey period but even the near-contemporary historian, Alexander Dow, stated categorically that 'the misfortune of Bengal began with the revolutions and changes which succeeded the death of Surge-ul-Dowla'. Referring to Bengal's prosperity under the nawabi rule, he asserted that Bengal 'at that time was one of the richest, most populous and best cultivated kingdoms in the world'. He further wrote : 'We may date the commencement of decline from the day on which Bengal fell under the dominion of foreigners.'[6] All the evidence, quantitative as well as qualitative, put forward in this volume will clearly bear this out.

[4] H. Verelst to the Court of Directors, 2 April 1769, BPC, Vol. 44, f. 324, para. 6.

[5] William Bolts, *Considerations*, p. 200.

[6] Alexander Dow, *Hindostan*, vol. III, p. Ixxvii.

APPENDICES

Appendix 1

English Company's Contract with *Dadni* Merchants of Calcutta, March 1739 (Source: BPC, Range 1, Vol.13, f. 509)

I do hereby contract with the President and Council at Fort William on behalf of the Honb'le United Company of Merchants of England... for pieces of sundry goods, the particulars as underwritten amounting to ... Current Rupees and are calculated at the medium price of the whole. In consideration whereof I do acknowledge to have received...Rupees in part thereof and is sixty percent on Gurrahs, sixty on the Photaes and Roemalls and fifty percent on all other goods. I do also hereby oblige myself to deliver into the Company's factory the whole quantity of these goods so contracted for before the expiration of the month of December next at furthest and I do agree that the fine goods shall be sorted into five sortments, the middling into four and coarse goods into three sortments and that three pieces shall be drawn out of each sortment and the middle piece of the three so drawn shall be the piece on which the price shall be made for the whole sortment and if the said piece should prove worse than the muster contracted by, then an abatement shall be made thereon in proportion to the said muster and I do further consent and agree that in case the amount of this contract being...Rupees calculated at the medium price as aforesaid should not be delivered into the Company's factory in the particular species contracted for within the month of December according to the tenor thereof then I do allow a premium of ten percent to be paid to the Company on the deficiency that may happen thereupon and it is also agreed that on the arrival of the shipping expected from Europe there shall be another payment made to me of seventeen percent on the Gurrahs, twentyfive percent on the Photaes and Roemalls and thirtyfive percent on the other goods and it is further agreed that when the whole quantity of goods shall be delivered in as aforesaid and the several accounts made up and adjusted then I am to receive whatever balance shall appear due to me thereon. Dated in Fort William this ...day of March 1738/39.

Appendix 2

Resolution of the Merchants' Panchayat, 11 December 1753 (Source : Factory Records, Kasimbazar, Vol. 12, Annex. to Conslts., 21 October 1754)

We the country merchants who transact business for the English at Cassimbazar are come to a common agreement on the following motives: First, we have received dadney for Silk, Silk piece-goods and Gurrahs for the year 1753; also we have accounts with the Company for the year 1752. The gentlemen here are very hard on us in examining and prizing our goods for the Company, as well as in their resolution to charge us the penalty in our accounts for the deficiency in our contracts with the said Company for the year 1752. These motives obliging us to come to an agreement: we do hereby agree never to suffer ourselves to be injured in our accounts with the said year 1752 nor in the examining or prizing of our goods. If the Gentlemen do settle accounts with us and do examine and prize our goods to our satisfaction, in such case we shall submit to them. But if in anger they get any of us imprisoned, we do agree to confine ourselves with the person so imprisoned. And if they happen to turn any of us out of their business, we all do promise to quit their business likewise. If any one amongst us is dismissed the Company's business and the rest continue in it, we do hereby promise to be accountable to any claim which the person dismissed may lay on us, and if any man amongst us do for his own interest come to an agreement with the gentlemen, we leave such man to the punishment of Heaven. We further agree to bring no more goods into the factory from this very day; and if any one among us do violate the agreement, such a one doth hereby submit to pay a penalty, as well to the rest of us merchants as to the country Government. If the gentlemen do settle account with us to our satisfaction, whoever among us appears debtor to the Company, he is to be answerable for his debt without involving others in the payment of it. In the like manner if any one appears a creditor, hs is to demand and receive his due from the Company without calling others to make good the same. But if the gentlemen be inclined to settle accounts to our prejudice,

we do agree to be all of one Mind. On these terms we have signed
to this common agreement. Dated at Cassimbazar, this month of
Aughun the 20th and in the year 1160 or in the month of
December, the 11th day in the year 1753.

Appendix 3A

Quinquennial Total of Various Types of Textiles Exported
by the Dutch Company
1730-1755

Types of Textiles	1730/31- 1734/35	1740/41- 1744/45	1750/51- 1754/55
Cossaes Nadona	—	2200	1100
Atchiabanijs	9500	4700	—
Effene dubbelde Armosijnen	38700	20174	1740
Enkelde geruite Armosijnen	1920	2730	3715
Effene enkelde Armosijnen	—	1442	2421
Allabanijs	8730	2700	1150
Allabalijs	—	—	1554
Allegiassen zijde	5000	5205	690
Allegiassen Tessrse	1980	2470	4623
Bandanoes of Tafta de Foula	28600	29976	36209
Bethilijs Cangam	7760	19181	13375
Atlassen in zoort	860	2490	984
Adentijs d'Balasore of half Cossaes	750	—	100
Baftas	700	9091	67195
Beddelijken	—	—	195
Foelijs of dubbld. geblmd. Armosijnen	585	—	—
Cossaes	72350	110319	103355
Cossaes d'Jangal	—	—	233
Chalbafts	—	—	385
Cherchannijs	600	865	700
Cacatoestoffen	229	374	—
Chiklaes	—	—	970
Dotanijs of Armosijnen met bloemen	700	757	—

(contd.)

(Appendix 3A contd.)

Types of Textiles	1730/31-1734/35	1740/41-1744/45	1750/51-1754/55
Dongrijs	14700	19600	74932
Doriassen Ordin.	6678	19945	24589
Doriassen Chikon	—	—	108
Dasjes d'Dacca	16750	3900	620
Dherijs of dubbld.			
gestrpt. Armosijnen	4000	890	6614
Doriassen superfine	540	345	270
Geblmd. Doriassen of			
Jamdanijs	200	50	—
Diverse Lijwaten	—	—	237
Elatchijs	—	—	75
Fotassen	19800	26100	34822
Ginghams effene	3800	2365	1165
Gingham Taffachelas	7935	11330	2845
Gingham gestrepte	6700	900	—
Gingham geruite	1520	300	—
Gingham geruite			
Sichtermans	896	100	—
Gerassen	92900	82000	156610
Guinees Lijwaat	173600	96571	89451
Gekepert Lijwaat	—	100	—
Hamans d'Handialse	13646	17715	23585
Kharradarijs of Hglse.			
gestrpt. Armosijnen	15695	5570	4388
Keper d'Mohunpur	—	400	1322
Malamollen in zoort	40391	66512	26019
Malamollen geblmd.			
d'Dacca	1008	1050	775
Malamollen d'Santipur	—	—	860
Malamollen d'Haripal	—	—	98
Neusdoken Kismisse	—	6345	10560
Neusdoken Haripalse	—	1913	1278
Neusdoken witte	—	—	1825

(contd.)

(Appendix 3A contd.)

Types of Textiles	1730/31- 1734/35	1740/41- 1744/45	1750/51- 1754/55
Pinascoes	—	—	139
Restassen zijde	1000	1800	1128
Roemalls zijde	2795	4782	6485
Roemalls	116250	168861	139646
Roemalls 1/2 gaarne 1/2 zijde	1000	900	—
Roemalls Sichtermans	—	2663	1035
Seerbands	—	—	1409
Seerhaudconnaes	—	—	2537
Salamporeijs	2800	78120	176796
Sjappa sarrijs of vrouwe kleedjes	200	5576	30321
Sjappalens of gedrukte neusdoeken	—	19920	55747
Sjautars d'Santipur/ Sripur	—	5700	1720
Sirsiken d'Santipur/ Sripur	—	3500	9309
Soosjes	19640	8380	9787
Sologesjes fine	1375	1275	2140
Serbetties	—	2541	3751
Sichtermans Saaij of Saaijen	—	738	3791
Milmils	558	—	145
Tanjebs	1960	26361	9483
Tanjeb Daccasse	6420	1180	1859
Tanjeb d'Daudpur	—	—	11234
Tanjeb gebloemde	—	—	1065
Tepoy d'Olmara	—	200	352
Terendams Daccasse	—	—	750
Terendams d'Santipur	4100	7688	11062
Terendams d'Haripal	—	—	300
Sanen/Zanen	3725	6700	8165
Ruwe of neuwe zeijlkleeden	34380	17600	51492

(contd.)

(Appendix 3A contd.)

Types of Textiles	1730/31- 1734/35	1740/41- 1744/45	1750/51- 1754/55
Lungi	720	412	—
Zeijde stoffen	—	1610	—
Tasser in zoort	—	1650	—
Sjoucoutassen	100	—	—
Cossaes Bourangse	—	—	4700
Gerassen fijn Bourangse	—	—	2000
Nainsooks	—	—	1856
Textiles from Bihar			
Amritijs	17561	33826	38566
Bihar Cossaes	2450	7700	4737
Dherriabadijs	12000	25371	18392
Lakhorijs	1800	7405	15016
Chitsen	4800	—	—
Armosijnen effene dubbld.	—	765	—
Sitarijs	—	—	3517
Tuckerijs	—	—	8715
Grand Total (No. of Pieces)	835357	1021899	1342789

[Source: Compiled and computed from Bengal export invoices in VOC records.]

Appendix 3B

Quinquennial Total of Various Types of Textiles Exported by the English Company, 1730 - 1755

	1730/31 - 1734/35	1740/41 - 1744/45	1750/51 - 1754/55
Ordinary Calicoes			
Atchiabanies	—	3222	400
Baftas	127319	209481	158485
Chilaes	16233	14323	3628
Chints	205588	68177	39738
Coopees	30630	21484	14353
Dosooties	67946	15093	7647
Emerties	49942	100979	27344
Gurrahs	789146	444873	331684
Lackowries	53746	6491	—
Photaes	51936	41825	17950
Total (pieces)	1392486	925948	601229
Average (pieces)	278497	185190	120246
Fine Calicoes			
Chowtars	21027	17965	4719
Dysooksoys	—	6167	6866
Handkerchieves	16545	2532	—
Romalls	532702	629922	355994
Sannoes	43957	24009	6448
Total (pieces)	614231	680595	374027
Average (pieces)	122846	136119	74805
Muslins			
Adaties	18790	39729	23705
Alliabalies	1112	8585	14658
Cossaes	332676	425938	303076
Dooreas	39092	67293	70018
Dimities	—	16443	4394
Humhums	110318	71193	52519
Jamdanies	102	753	329
Mulmuls	74565	153589	146417

(contd.)

(Appendix 3B contd.)

	1730/31 - 1734/35	1740/41 - 1744/45	1750/51 - 1754/55
Muslins			
Nainsooks	946	4747	8045
Shalbafts	2440	820	259
Seerhaudconnaes	1012	1407	7470
Serbetties	9791	34672	13146
Seerbands	12360	13863	6480
Tanjebs	116458	150787	71122
Terrindams	20096	41582	44701
Total (pieces)	739758	1031401	766339
Average (pieces)	147952	206280	153268
Silk piece-goods			
Bandanoes	—	86736	73147
Cuttanies	3717	8215	2998
Jamwars	124	3649	345
Silk Lungees	—	3380	8287
New Silk Romalls	—	3240	10092
Silk Lungee Romalls	25142	303	—
Taffetas	67393	32365	29370
Total (pieces)	96376	137888	124239
Average (pieces)	19275	27578	24848
Mixed piece-goods			
Allibanies	865	1729	669
Cariadaries	5493	36152	15758
Charconnaes	2584	1170	398
Cushtaes	5631	18118	4454
Chuklaes	9613	5214	1077
Elatchies	—	11040	1113
Ginghams	16122	10114	1898
Nillaes	33475	55961	12139
Peniascoes	7724	9543	1104

(contd.)

(Appendix 3B contd.)

	1730/31 - 1734/35	1740/41 - 1744/45	1750/51 - 1754/55
Mixed piece-goods			
Seersuckers	25599	8033	5535
Soosies	72715	77741	26837
Tepoys	1030	3842	1650
Total (pieces)	180851	238657	72632
Average (pieces)	36170	47731	14526
Miscellaneous	2452	11916	13486
Grand Total	3026154	3026405	1951952

(Source : Computed from the detailed data provided by K. N. Chaudhuri)

Appendix 4A

Quinquennial Total of Dutch Textile Exports : Pieces (Categorywise) and Share Percentage 1730 - 1755

Categories	1730/31 - 1734/35		1740/41 - 1744/45		1750/51 - 1754/55	
	Total Pcs.	% Share	Total Pcs.	% Share	Total Pcs.	% Share
Ordn. Calicoes	387566	46.40	407184	39.85	747759	55.69
Fine Calicoes	125235	14.99	203275	19.89	170069	12.66
Muslins	168976	20.23	267906	26.22	238861	17.79
Silk piece-goods	87189	10.44	103023	10.08	150207	11.19
Mixed piece-goods	66391	07.94	40511	03.96	35893	02.67
Grand Total	835357	100	1021899	100	1342789	100
Average	167071		204380		268558	

(Source: Compiled and computed from Bengal export invoices in the VOC records in Algemeen Rijksarchief, Den Haag)

Appendix 4B

Quinquennial Total of English Textile Exports : Pieces (Categorywise) and Share Percentage
1730 - 1755

Categories	1730/31-1734/35		1740/41-1744/45		1750/51-1754/55	
	Total Pcs.	% Share	Total Pcs.	% Share	Toatal Pcs.	% Share
Ordn. Calicoes	1392486	46.02	925948	30.60	601229	30.80
Fine Calicoes	614231	20.30	680595	22.49	374027	19.17
Muslins	739758	24.44	1031401	34.08	766339	39.26
Silk piece-goods	96376	3.18	137888	4.56	124239	6.36
Mixed piece-goods	180851	5.98	328657	7.88	72632	3.72
Miscellaneous	2452	0.08	11916	0.39	13486	0.69
Grand Total	3026154	100	3026405	100	1951952	100
Average	605231		605281		390390	

(Source: Compiled and computed from detailed data provided by K.N.Chaudhuri)

Appendix 5A (1)

Volume of Dutch Silk Exports
1730-1755

Years	Silk Varieties			Total (Dutch) Ponds)
	Tanny	Adapangia	Tanna Banna	
1730/31	59473	22314	—	81787
1731/32	15666	—	—	15666
1732/33	83185	25206	—	108391
1733/34	83489	18287	8706	110482
1734/35	5295	—	13698	18993
1740/41	75755	20246	—	96001
1741/42	51586	10862	—	62448
1742/43	51165	5073	—	56238
1743/44	72090	—	5842	77932
1744/45	15829	—	—	15829
1750/51	58788	15265	4739	79152
1751/52	53314	12597	8829	74740
1752/53	42838	14618	3494	60950
1753/54	35777	20697	4475	60949
1754/55	22338	26328	8753	57419

[Source and note : See Appendix 5A (2)]

Appendix 5A (2)

**Quinquennial Total, Average and Annual Value of
Dutch Silk Exports, 1730-1755**

	1730/31- 1734/35	1740/41- 1744/45	1750/51- 1754/55
Quinquennial Total (Dutch Ponds)	335319	308448	333210
Average (Dutch Ponds)	67064	61689	66642
Average (English lbs.)	73100	67241	72640
Average (Maunds)	975	897	969
Total Price (Rs)	273000	251160	271320

(Source and Note: Bengal export invoices in VOC records in Algemeen
Rijksarchief, Den Haag. Dutch ponds = 1.09 English lb. (avordupois).
In Bengal silk was weighed in maunds and seers, 40 seers making a
maund. One Bengal maund was equivalent to roughly 75 lb. i.e. lb.
avordupois or what was called small English lb. The average price of
silk is taken as Rs 7 which was the price at which the price of silk exported
by Asian merchants was calculated in English records in the late 1740s
and early 1750s.)

Appendix 5B (1)

Volume of English Silk Exports
1730-1755

Years	Volume (great lb.)
1730/31	94450
1731/32	85539
1732/33	171695
1733/34	209166
1734/35	142057
1735/36	118708
1736/37	155932
1737/38	181963
1738/39	127782
1739/40	129619
1740/41	160197
1741/42	104749
1742/43	90044
1743/44	121107
1744/45	119954
1745/46	148045
1746/47	94729
1747/48	800
1748/49	22010
1749/50	34417
1750/51	46000
1751/52	82774
1752/53	70634
1753/54	27199
1754/55	60013

[Source and note : See Appendix 5B (2)]

Appendix 5B (2)

Quinquennial Total, Average and Annual Value of English Silk Exports, 1730-1755

	1730/31- 1734/35	1740/41- 1744/45	1750/51- 1754/55
Quinquennial Total (great lbs.)	702907	596051	286620
Average (great lbs.)	140581	119210	57324
Average (small lbs.)	210872	178815	85986
Average (Maunds)	2812	2384	1146
Total Price (Rs)	787360	667520	320880

[Source & Note : Figures for yearly export taken from K.N. Chaudhuri, *Trading World*, p. 534, with one year lag. 1 great 1b. = 1.5 small 1b. For the rate at which silk price is calculated here, see note in Appendix 5A (2)]

GLOSSARY

abwab	additional imposts
amin	revenue official, collector
anna	a denomination of rupee, 16 annas make a rupee
assamies	workers who extracted and refined saltpetre
aurung	localized centre of manufacturing production
band	a term used to denote periodical harvesting of silk cocoons
banyan	a Hindu trader, often the agent of the Europeans
banjara	a hereditary group of travelling grain traders
batta	discount charged for converting coins
cauri	small white shells current as money, specially in small transactions
chauki	special entry point where goods were taxed
cootie	factory, sheds for assembly of artisans; also branch office
corge	20 pieces
covid	an indigenous measure with considerable regional variations. In Bengal it was about 18 inches
dadni	advance, from dadan which means advance given against order; merchants who contracted for goods against advance were called dadni merchants
dalal	broker; agent who worked on commission

darbar	court of a ruling prince or governor
daroga	an officer of law; an inspector
dastak	permit, generally given for transit of goods
dastur-al-amal	code of procedures
diwan	head of revenue department
farman	letter patent; an imperial decree or order
faujdar	Mughal military under-governor of a district
ganda	a denomination of rupee; 20 gandas = 1 pun; 4 puns = 1 anna
ganj	village market, usually on river banks
gomasta	agent; generally employed by a merchant or zamindar at a certain wage
hat	village market held on certain days a week
hundi	bill of exchange
husb-ul-hukm	literally means 'according to order'. This was usually a letter written by a minister under the emperor's directions and conveying his orders
jagir	assignment of land
jaluha	weaver of Muslim weaving caste
jugi	weaver of Hindu weaving caste
kareegar	apprentice
karkhana	a manufactory or workshop
kashida	embroidery work
khalisha	denoting land whose revenue went directly to the central Mughal treasury
khush khareed	goods bought with ready money
krore	100 lakhs; 10 million
lakh	Indian word for 100,000
masnad	throne
maund	a measure of weight; 40 seers make one maund which is about 74.5 Ib. and equivalent to 68 Dutch ponds
mukim	an appraiser who supervised the weaver's work and examined his yarn
mulbus khas	royal clothing

nakhuda	captain of an Indian ship
nawab	often a title of a subadar or governor
nazim	the title of governor, also called nawab-nazim
nikiri	apprentice
nishan	an order or permit generally issued by the subadar
nizamat	government
paikar	petty dealer, especiaially in silk and textile trade
panchayat	corporate body of merchants, artisans, often caste- based but sometimes cutting across caste or regional barriers
pargana	a territorial or administrative unit in a Mughal suba
parwana	letter patent, permit
pattan/patni	advance; goods bought against advance was called pattan or patni goods
pun	a denomination of rupee; see ganda
qazi	a Muslim judge
rafugar	artisan who separated torn knots of cloth
rahdari	transit duty on land
rupee	silver coin
seer	a measure of weight; 40 seers make one maund
shroff	money changer
sicca	Mughal coin of current year's mintage
suba	province
subadar	governor of suba or province
taqavi	agricultural loan
tankshal	Mughal mint
vakil	a political agent employed in diplomatic negotiations
zamindar	landholder

SELECT BIBLIOGRAPHY

A. MANUSCRIPT SOURCES

1. *India Office Library and Records*

Accountant General's Department:
Commerce Journal
General Ledgers
Bengal General Ledgers and Journal
Bengal Public Consultations
Bengal Letters Received
Bengal Secret and Military Consultations
Bengali Manuscripts, IO 4045, 4046
Board of Revenue, Misc. Proceedings, Range 98, vols. 18, 20, 22
Coast and Bay Abstracts
Despatch Books
European Manuscripts
Factory Records: Calcutta, Dacca, Hughli, Kasimbazar, Patna, Misc.
Home Miscellaneous Series, Vols. 393, 456F.
India Office Tracts
Original Correspondence
Orme Manuscripts

2. *British Museum*
Additional Manuscript 34,123

3. *Edinburgh University*
Mss. 144 (Risala-i-Zira'at)

4. Algemeen Rijksarchief, The Hague
Verenigde Oostindische Compagnie (VOC)
Overgekomen brieven en papieren and Inkomend briefbook, 1720-
1757
VOC, Vols. 1946-2874
Resolutien genomen op de ordinaries en extra-ordinaries vergaderingen
Heeren XVII
VOC, Vols. 117-130
Kamer Zeeland: Copie Missive en Rapporten: Bengalen
VOC, vols. 8774 (1733), 8806 (1754), 9558 (1756)
Hoge Regering van Batavia, 246 (Taillefert's 'Memorie', 17 Nov.
1763)
Collectie Thomas Hope
8403, Tabular Surveys of the Company's Trade, 17-18th
Century
8464, Tabular Surveys concerning the Asian Factories of the
VOC, 18th Century

5. Stadsarchief Antwerpen, Antwerp
General Indische Compagnie (The Ostend Company) 5768
(The 'Memorie' of Alexander Hume).

6. National Archives of India
Home Public
Home Miscellaneous: Letters to Court: Letters from Court

B. PRINTED SOURCES

1. Persian Works

Abul Fazl, Ain-i-Akbari, vol. 1, trans. H. Blochmann, revised by
D.C. Phillot, Calcutta, 1927.
Gholam Hossein Khan, Seir Mutaqherin, vol. II, trans. Haji
Mustafa, Second Reprint, Lahore, 1975.
Gulam Husain Salim, Riyaz-us-Salatin, trans, Maulavi Abdus
Salam, Calcutta, 1904.
Salimullah, Tarikh-i-Bangala, trans. Gladwin, Calcutta, 1788.
Ysuf Ali Khan, Tarikh-i-Bangala-i-Mahabatjangi, trans.
Abdus Subhan, Calcutta, 1982.

2. Works in European Languages

(a) *Published Records*

Datta, K.K. ed., *Fort William-India House Correspondence*, vol. 1 (1748-56), Delhi, 1958.

Firminger, W.K. ed., *The Fifth Report from the Select Committee of the House of Commons of the Affairs of the East India Company*, 1812, 3 vols., Calcutta, 1917-18.

Long, J. *Selections from Unpublished Records of Government for the Years 1748 to 1767 and 1784 to 1805*, Reprint, Calcutta, 1973.

Sinha, H.N. ed., *Fort William - India House Correspondence*, vol. II, (1764-66), Delhi, 1962.

Sinha, N.K. ed., *Fort William-India House Correspondence*, vol. V, (1767-69), Calcutta, 1959.

Temple, R.C. ed., *The Diaries of Streynsham Master*, 2 vols., London, 1911.

Wilson, C.R. ed., *The Early Annals of the English in Bengal*, 3 vols., London, 1895-1917.

Yule, H. ed., *The Diary of William Hedges*, 3 vols., London 1887-89.

(b) *Travellers' Accounts, Pamphlets and other Contemporary Sources*

Barbosa, D. *The Book of Duarte Barbosa*, 2 vols., trans. M.L. Dames, London 1921.

Bernier, F. *Travels in the Mogul Empire, 1656-1668*, ed., A. Constable, Oxford, 1934.

Bolts, W. *Considerations on Indian Affairs*, London, 1772.

Bowrey, Thomas, *A Geographical Account of Countries Round the Bay of Bengal, 1669-1679*, ed., R.C. Temple, Cambridge, 1905.

Cary, J. *A Discourse on the East India Trade*, London, 1696.

Child, Josiah, *Discourse of Trade*, London, 1696
——————*Treatise Concerning the East India Trade*, London, 1681.

Fryer, John, *A New Account of East India and Persia, 1672-81*, ed., W. Crooke, 3 vols., London, 1909-15.

Hamilton, Alexander, *A New Account of the East Indies*, 2 vols., ed., W. Foster, London, 1930.

Martin, François, *Memories de François Martin, 1665-1696*, ed., A. Martineau, Paris, 1931.

Orme, Robert, *Historical Fragments of the Mogul Empire*, London, 1805.

————— *History of the Military Transactions of the British Nation in Indostan*, 3 vols., London, 1803.

Ovington, J. *A Voyage to Surat in the Year 1689*, ed. H.G. Rawlinson, London, 1929.

Pollexfen, H. *Essay on East India Trade*, London, 1697.

Pyrard de Laval, François, *The Voyages of ...*, trans. and ed., Gray, 2 vols., London, 1887-89.

Stavorinus, J.S. *Voyage in the East Indies*, trans., S.H. Wilcoke, 3 vols., London, 1798.

Tavernier, Jean-Baptiste, *Travels in India, 1640-67*, trans. V. Ball, London, 1889.

van Dam, Pieter, *Beschrijvinge van de Oost-Indische Compagnie*, ed., F.W. Stapel & others, 4 books in 7 parts, The Hague, 1927-1954.

Vansittart, H. *A Narrative of the Transactions in Bengal from 1760-1764*, London, 1766.

Verelst, H. *A View of the Rise, Progress and Present State of the English Government in Bengal*, London, 1772.

(C) *Secondary Works*

Aiolfi, Serigo, *Calicoes und Gedrueckes Zeug*, Stuttgart, 1987.

Arasaratnam, S. *Merchants, Companies and Commerce on the Coromandel Coast, 1650-1740*, New Delhi, 1986.

————— 'Handloom Industry in South-Eastern India, 1750-1790', *Indian Economic and Social History Review*, 17, (1980), 257-81.

————— 'The Indian Merchants and their Trading Methods', *Indian Economic and Social History Review*, 3, (1966), 85-95.

Aymard, Maurice, ed. *Dutch Capitalism and World Capitalism*, Cambridge, 1982.

Bayly, C.A. *Imperial Meridian: The British Empire and the World, 1780-1830*, London, 1989.

————— *Indian Society and the Making of the British Empire: New Cambridge History of India*, Cambridge, 1987.

————— 'Putting Together the Eighteenth Century in India: Trade, Money and the 'Pre-Colonial Political Order', Paper presented to the Second Anglo Dutch Conference on Colonial

Comparative History, Leiden Univ., 1981.

Bayly, C.A. and Subrahmanyam, S. 'Portfolio Capitalist and the Political Economy of Early Modern India' *Indian Economic and Social History Review*, 25, 4 (1988), 403-24.

Bence-Jones, M. *Clive of India*, London, 1974.

Bhattacharya, S. *The East India Company and the Economy of Bengal from 1704 to 1740*, London, 1954.

Blitz, Rudolph C. 'Mercantilist Policies and the Pattern of World Trade, 1500-1700', *Journal of Economic History*, 27, (March 1967), 39-55.

Blochman, H. *Contributions to the Geography and History of Bengal*, Reprint, Calcutta, 1962.

Boxer, C.R. *The Dutch Seaborne Empire*, New York, 1965.

Braudel, Fernand, *The Mediterranean and the Mediterranean World in the Age of Phillip* II, tr. by Sián Reynolds, 2 vols., London 1972- 73.

——————, *Civilization and Capitalism, 15th-18th century, II, The Wheels of Commerce*, tr. by Sián Reynolds, New York, 1982.

Brenning, Joseph J. 'The Textile Trade of Seventeenth Century Northern Coromandel: A Study of Pre-Modern Asian Export Industry', Ph. D. dissertation, Univ. of Wisconsin, 1975.

Bruijn, J.R., F.S. Gaastra and I. Schoffer, *Dutch-Asiatic Shipping*, 3 vols., The Hague, 1979-87.

Calkins, P.B. 'The Formation of a Regionally Oriented Ruling Group in Bengal, 1700-1740', *Journal of Asian Studies*, vol. XXIX, no. 4, Aug. 1970, 799-806.

—————— 'The role of Murshidabad as a Regional and Subregional Centre in Bengal', in R.L. Park, ed., *Urban Bengal*, East Lansing, Michigan, 1969.

Chandra, Satish, *The Indian Ocean: Explorations in History, Commerce and Politics*, New Delhi, 1985.

—————— 'Commercial Activities of the Mughal Emperors during the Seventeenth Century', *Bengal Past & Present*, 78 (1959), 92-97.

Chatterjee, Kumkum, 'Trade and Durbar Politics in the Bengal Subah, 1733-1757', *Modern Asian Studies*, 26(1992), 233-73.

Chaudhuri, K.N. *Asia before Europe*, Cambridge, 1990.

—————— *Trade and Civilization in the Indian Ocean: An Economic History from the Rise of Islam to 1750*, Cambridge, 1985.

—————— *The Trading World of Asia and the English East India*

Company, Cambridge, 1978.

————— 'The Structure of the Indian Textile Industry in the Seventeenth and Eighteenth Centuries', *Indian Economic and Social History Review*, II, (June-Sept. 1974), 127-82.

Chaudhury, Sushil, 'International Trade in Bengal Silk and the Comparative Role of Asians and Europeans, circa. 1700-1757', *Modern Asian Studies*, **28**, 4 (1994).

————— 'European Companies and the Bengal Textile Industry in the Eighteenth Century: The Pitfalls of Applying Quantitative Techniques', *Modern Asian Studies*, **27**, 2 (May 1993), 321-340.

————— 'Sirajuddaula and the battle of Palashi', *History of Bangladesh*, vol. 1, Dhaka, 1992, 93-130.

————— 'Trade, Conquest and Bullion: Bengal in the mid-Eighteenth Century', *Itinerario*, vol. 15, no. 2, (1991), 21-32.

————— 'Khwaja Wazid in Bengal Trade and Politics', *Indian Historical Review*, vol. XVI, nos. 1-2, 137-48.

————— 'The Imperatives of Empire—Private Trade, Sub-Imperialism and the British Attack on Chandernagore, March 1757', *Studies in History*, vol. VIII, no. 1, Jan.-June 1992, 1-12.

————— 'General Economic Conditions in Nawabi Bengal, 1690-1757', *History of Bangladesh*, vol. 2, Dhaka, 1992, 30-66.

————— 'European Trading Companies and Bengal's Export Trade, 1690-1757', *History of Bangladesh*, vol. 2, Dhaka, 1992, 183-224.

————— 'Continuity or Change in the Eighteenth Century? Price Trends in Bengal, circa. 1720-1757', *Calcutta Historical Journal*, vol. XV, nos. 1-2, July 1990-June 1991, 1-27.

————— 'Asian Merchants and Companies in Bengal's Export Trade, circa, mid-18th Century', paper presented at the International Conference on 'Merchants, Companies and Trade, Asian and European Scene, 16-18th Century', Maison Des Sciences De L'Homme, Paris, 30 May - 1 June, 1990.

————— 'Sirajuddaullah, the English Company and the British Conquest of Bengal—A Reappraisal', *Indian Historical Review*, Vol. XIII, No. 1-2, July 1986 - Jan. 1987, 111-134.

————— 'Merchants, Companies and Rulers—Bengal in the Eighteenth Century', *Journal of the Economic and Social History of the Orient*, vol. XXXI (Feb. 1988), 74-109.

————————— 'European Companies and Pre-Modern South Asian Commercial System: A Study of Bengal in the Eighteenth Century', *Calcutta Historical Journal*, vol. XI, Nos. 1-2, July 1986 -June 1987, 118-165.

————————— *Trade and Commercial Organization in Bengal, 1650-1720*, Calcutta, 1975.

————————— 'The Rise and Decline of Hughli—A Port in Medieval Bengal', *Bengal Past and Present*, Jan. - June 1967, 33-67.

Chicherov. A.I. *India: Economic Development in the 16th-18th Centuries*, Moscow, 1971.

Colebrooke, H.T. *Remarks on the Husbandry and Commerce of Bengal*, Calcutta, 1804.

Das Gupta, Ashin, *Indian Merchants and the Decline of Surat c. 1700 - 1750*, Wiesbaden, 1979.

————————— 'Trade and Politics in 18th Century India' in D.S. Richards, ed., *Islam and the Trade of Asia*, Oxford, 1970.

————————— *Malabar in Asian Trade, 1740-1800*, Cambridge, 1967.

Das Gupta, Ashin and Pearson, M.N. *India and the Indian Ocean, 1500-1800*, Calcutta, 1987.

Datta, K.K. *Alivardi and His Times*, 2nd edn., Calcutta, 1963.

————————— *Survey of India's Social Life and Economic Conditions in the Eighteenth Century, 1707-1813*, Calcutta, 1961.

————————— *Studies in the History of Bengal Suba, 1740-60*, Calcutta, 1936.

Eaton, Richard M. *The Rise of Islam and the Bengal Frontier, 1204-1760*, Delhi, 1994.

Emmer, P.C. and H.L. Wesseling, eds., *Reappraisals in Overseas History*, Leiden, 1979.

Ferrier, R.W. 'The Armenians and the East India Company in Persia in the Seventeenth and Early Eighteenth Centuries', *Economic History Review*, 2nd series, 26 (1973), 38-62.

Feldbaeck, Ole, 'Cloth Production and Trade in Late Eighteenth Century Bengal', *Bengal Past & Present*, Vol. LXXXVI (July-Dec. 1967), 124-41.

Foster, W. 'Gabriel Boughton and the Trading Privileges in Bengal', *Indian Antiquary*, 40, (1911).

Furber, Holden, *Rival Empires of Trade in the Orient, 1600-1800*, Minneapolis and Oxford, 1976.

————————— 'Asia and West as Partners before 'Empire' and After', *Journal of Asian Studies*, 28, (1969).

—————— *John Company at Work*, Cambridge (Mass.), 1951.

—————— *Bombay Presidency in the mid-Eighteenth Century*, Bombay, 1965.

Gaastra, F.S. 'The Dutch East India Company and its Intra-Asiatic Trade in Precious Metals', in *The Emergence of a World Economy*, papers of the IX International Congress of Economic History, ed., Wolfram Fischer, R. Marvin McInnis and Jurgen Schneider, pt. I, 1500-1800, Wiesbaden, 1986, 97-112.

Geoghegan, J. *Silk in India*, Calcutta, 1872.

Ghoshal, H.R. *Economic Transition in the Bengal Presidency (1793-1833)*, Patna, 1950.

Glamann, K. *Dutch Asiatic Trade, 1620-1740*, Copenhagen, The Hague, 1958.

—————— 'Bengal and the World Trade About 1700', *Bengal Past & Present*, vol. LXXVI, s. no. 142, 1957, 30-39.

Gupta, Brijen K. *Sirajuddaullah and the East India Company, 1756-57*, Leiden, 1962.

Habib, Irfan, 'Merchant Communities in Pre-Colonial India', in James D. Tracy, ed., *The Rise of Merchant Empires : Long Distance Trade in the Early Modern Period, 1350-1750*, Cambridge, 1990, 371-399.

—————— *Atlas of the Mughal Empire*, Delhi, 1983.

—————— 'The Technology and Economy of Mughal India', *Indian Economic and Social History Review*, vol. XVII, no. 1, Jan. - March, 1980, 1-34.

—————— ' Changes in Technology in Mughal India', *Studies in History*, II, 1, 15-39.

—————— 'Notes on Indian Textile Industry in the 17th Century', *Professor S.C. Sarkar Felicitation Volume*, New Delhi, 1976.

—————— 'The System of Bills of Exchange (Hundis) in the Mughal Empire', *Proceedings of the Indian History Congress*, 1972.

—————— ' Potentialities of Capitalistic Development in the Economy of Mughal India', *Journal of Economic History*, 29, (March 1969).

—————— 'Usury in Medieval India', *Comparative Studies in Society and History*, VI, 1964.

—————— *The Agrarian System of Mughal India, (1556-1707)*,

Bombay, 1963.
——————— ' The Currency System of the Mughal Empire (1556-
1707)', *Medieval India Quarterly*, 4 (1961), 1-21.
——————— ' Banking in Mughal India' in *Contributions to Indian
Economic History*, 1, ed., Tapan Raychaudhuri, Calcutta, 1960.
Hamilton, Buchanan, *Dinajpur*.
Hartkamp-Jonxis, R.E., *Sits: Oost-West Relaties in Textiel*, The
Hague, 1987.
Hasan, Aziza, 'The silver currency output of the Mughal Empire
and Prices in India during the sixteenth and seventeenth
centuries', *Indian Economic and Social History Review*, 6, (1969),
85-107.
Hill, S.C. *Bengal in 1756-57*, 3 vols., London, 1905.
——————— *Three Frenchmen in Bengal*, London, 1905.
Hobson-Jobson.
Hossain, Hameeda, *The Company Weavers of Bengal*, Delhi, 1988.
——————— ' The Alienation of Weavers : Impact of the Conflict
between the Revenue and the Commercial Interests of the
East India Company, 1750-1800', *Indian Economic and Social
History Review*, 26, no. 3, July-Sept. 1979, 323-45.
Irwin, J. and Schwartz, P.R. *Studies in Indo-European Textile
History*, Ahmedabad, 1966.
Karim, Abdul, *Murshid Quli Khan and His Times*, Dacca, 1963.
Khan, A.M. *The Transition in Bengal*, 1756-75, Cambridge, 1969.
Krishna, Bal, *Commercial Relations between India and England*,
London, 1924.
Leonard, Karen, 'The "Great Firm" Theory of the Decline of the
Mughal Empire', *Comparative Studies in Society and History*, 13,
1979.
Little, J.H. *The House of Jagat Seths*, Calcutta, 1956.
Marshall, P.J. *Bengal : the British Bridgehead*, Cambridge, 1987.
——————— *East Indian Fortunes*, Oxford, 1976.
——————— 'Private British Investment in Eighteenth Century
Bengal', *Bengal Past and Present*, 86 (1967), 52-67.
Martineau, A. *Dupleix*, Paris, 1931.
Meilink-Roelofz, M.A.P. *Asian Trade and European Influence in the
Indonesian Archipelago between 1500 to about 1630*, The Hague,
1962.
Mitra, D.B. *The Cotton Weavers of Bengal*, Calcutta, 1978.
Mohsin, K.M. *A Bengal District in Transition : Murshidabad*, Dacca,

1973.

Moreland, W.H. *From Akbar to Aurangzeb*, London, 1923.

———— *India at the Death of Akbar*, London, 1923.

Moosvi, Shireen, *The Economy of Mughal Empire, c. 1595*, Delhi, 1987.

Narang, Indira, 'The Ostend Company Records and the "Instructions" of Alexander Hume', *Indian Economic and Social History Review*, 2 (1967), 17-37.

Nichol, J.D. 'The British in India, 1740-63 : A Study in Imperial Expansion into Bengal', Unpublished Ph. D. thesis, University of Cambridge, 1976.

O'Malley, L.S.S. and Chakrabarti, M. *District Gazetteer : Hooghly*, Calcutta, 1912.

Pearson, M.N. *Merchants and Rulers in Gujarat*, Berkeley & Los Angeles, 1976.

Perlin, Frank, 'Proto-Industrialization and Pre-Colonial South Asia', *Past and Present*, 98 (1983), 30-95.

———— 'Pre-Colonial South Asia and Western Penetration in the Seventeenth to Nineteenth Centuries : A Problem of Epistemological Status', *Review*, 4 (1980).

Prakash, Om, 'On Estimating the Employment Implications of European Trade for Eighteenth Century Bengal Textile Industry—A Reply', *Modern Asian Studies*, **27**, 2, 341-356.

———— *The Dutch East India Company and the Economy of Bengal*, Princeton, 1985.

———— ' Asian Trade and European Impact: A Study of the Trade from Bengal, 1630-1720', in Blair B. Kling and M.N. Pearson, eds., *The Age of Partnership: Europeans in Asia before Dominion*, Honolulu, 1979.

———— 'Bullion for Goods', *Indian Economic and Social History Review*, 13 (1976).

Ray, Indrani, 'Dupleix's Private Trade in Chandernagore', *Indian Historical Review*, 1 (1974), 279-94.

———— 'The French Company and the Merchants of Bengal, 1680-1730', *Indian Economic and Social History Review*, 7 (1970).

Ray, Rajat Kanta, 'Colonial Penetration and Initial Resistance: the Mughal Ruling Class, the English East India Company and the Struggle for Bengal', *Indian Historical Review*, 12 (July 1985 - Jan. 1986).

Richards, J.F. *Precious Metals in Late Medieval and Early Modern*

Worlds, Durham, 1983.
———— 'The Seventeenth Century Crisis in South Asia', *Modern Asian Studies*, **24**, 4 (1990).
———— 'Mughal State Finance and the Pre-Modern World Economy', *Comparative Studies in Society and History*, **23** (1981).
Richards, D.S. *Islam and the Trade of Asia*, Oxford, 1970.
Sarkar, J.N. *The History of Aurangzeb*, 5 vols., London, 1924.
Sexe, Elizabeth Lee, 'Fortune's Tangled Web : Trading Networks of English Enterprises in Eastern India, 1657-1717', Unpublished Ph.D. Dissertation, Yale University, 1979.
Seth, M.J. *Armenians in India from the Earlist Times to the Present Day*, Reprint, Calcutta, 1973.
Sinha, N.K. *The Economic History of Bengal*, 3 vols., Calcutta, 1958-65.
Slomann, V. *Bizarre Designs in Silk*, Copenhagen, 1953.
Speed, D.W.H. 'Notes on the Culture of Silk in the East Indies', *Transactions of the Agricultural and Horticultural Society of India*, Vol. III, 1837.
Steensgaard, Niels, 'Asian Trade and World Economy from the 15th to the 18th Centuries' in T.R. de Souza, ed., *Indo-Portuguese History*, New Delhi, 1984.
———— *The Asian Trade Revolution of the Seventeenth Century*, Chicago, 1974.
Taylor, J. *A Sketch of the Topography and Statistics of Dacca*, Calcutta, 1840.
Temple, R.C. *Scattergoods and the East India Company*, London, 1931.
Thomas, P.J. 'The Indian Cotton Industry about 1700 A.D.', *Modern Review*, Feb. 1924.
Thompson, Virgina M. *Dupleix and His Letters, 1742-54*, New York, 1933.
Tracy, J.D. *The Merchant Empires of Europe*, Cambridge, 1990.
———— *The Political Economy of Merchant Empires*, Cambridge, 1991.
van Leur, J.C. *Indonesian Trade and Society*, The Hague, 1955.
van Santen, H.W. *De Verenigde Oost-Indische Compagnie in Gujarat en Hindusthan, 1620-1660*, Leiden, 1982.
Wallerstein, Immanuel, *The Modern World System, II : Mercantilism and the Consolidation of the World Economy, 1600-1750*, New York, London, 1980.

Watson, Bruce I. *Foundation for Empire : English Private Trade in India, 1659-1760*, New Delhi, 1980.

Weber, Max, *General Economic History*, trans., F.H. Knight, New York, 1966.

Wink, André, 'Al-Hind : India and Indonesia in the Islamic World-Economy, c. 700-1800 A.D.', in *Itinerario*, special issue, *The Ancien Régime in India and Indonesia*, 33-72, Leiden : Gravaria, 1988.

INDEX